Legal aspects of midwifery

4th Edition

by

Bridgit Dimond

Quay Books Division, MA Healthcare Ltd, St Jude's Church, Dulwich Road, London SE24 0PB

British Library Cataloguing-in-Publication Data
A catalogue record is available for this book

ISBN-10: 1-85642-504-5
ISBN-13: 978-1-85642-504-9

Edited by Jessica Anderson

Printed by Mimeo, Huntingdon, Cambridgeshire

Contents

Foreword

I am pleased that we now have this updated, concise and eminently readable text to guide midwives through the complexities of the law, as applied to their practice. The law is always close to midwifery and the key is to understand and be aware of it without it stifling the midwife's role and her decision making. As midwives work with their clients, they need to understand the balance between their professional skills and advice and responding to the views and wishes of the women for whom they provide care. This balanced relationship has legal, professional and ethical under-pinnings.

It is a measure of Bridgit's skilful explanations and direct relevance to practice that this text, now in its 4th edition, is well established as a must-have for midwives. A glance at the contents in my well-thumbed first edition shows how, in the intervening period, the balance of application of the law has changed. Child protection and safeguarding is a daily issue for many midwives as is the whole area of freedom of information and access to records. The advent of electronic methods of communication and data storage has not changed the law but has, as is well explained, served to remind midwives of their obligations whatever record format they are using.

I trust that this latest edition will become as much of a support and guide for today's midwives as previous editions have been.

Louise Silverton
Director for Midwifery, Royal College of Midwives

Preface

This is an updated but more concise version of the third edition of this book which was published by Elsevier in 2005. This new edition concentrates on aspects of the law relevant to the student and practitioner of midwifery, leaving those areas relevant to midwifery management to a later volume.

Account has been taken of other books published by Quay Books, including those relating to legal aspects, and reference is made to those publications rather than repeating the information in this work. Note has also been taken of the fact that in the 20 years that have elapsed since I started writing, the world of communications has been revolutionised. Almost without exception, students have immediate access to the internet and can download with ease original documents, reports, memoranda, guidance from professional bodies and a great variety of other forms of information. Increasingly, information from official bodies is published online and not in printed format. Michele Klein (2011) sets out very clearly the advantages to midwives in engaging with this new technology (see also an article by Suzanne Wedlake, 2010, on midwives' perceptions of using e-learning for continuing professional development). There is much to be said for not repeating this information in this book, but rather referring the reader to the relevant websites and providing some advice on accessing the sources. However, there is also merit in ensuring that this is a stand alone book, which, certainly to the practising midwife, will assist in a speedier answer to some of the legal questions she may face in her time-pressured work. The compromise adopted here is to set out the basic legal principles for each of the topics covered and also cite the relevant statutory provisions and detail the appropriate cases. In addition, guidance is provided on the relevant websites, setting down exercises for those wishing to access the appropriate internet information. Perhaps a later edition of the book may put more emphasis on internet access.

It is a challenging time for midwives and other health professionals. It is hoped that this book will help lay the foundations of an understanding of the law and how it impacts upon practice

Klein M (2011) Informed choice: web-based midwifery. *MIDIRS Midwifery Digest* **21**(2): 172–5

Wedlake S (2010) Examining midwives' perceptions of using e-learning for continuing professional development. *MIDIRS Midwifery Digest* **20**(2): 143–50

Acknowledgements

Hundreds of midwives have assisted me over this years in developing a content and style appropriate for a student or practising midwife who wishes to develop an understanding of the relevant law, and I give my thanks to them all.

I would like to give particular thanks to Joy James at the University of Glamorgan who has provided invaluable advice on which areas of the law are of particular significance thus assisting me in producing a more concise book.

As usual I pay tribute to the support which I receive from my family and especially to Bette to whom I am particularly indebted for her help in checking the proofs and preparing the indexes and to whom this book is dedicated.

Dedication

To Bette

Section A

Introduction

In this Section, we explore how laws are formed and the structure of the legal system in the UK.

Chapter 1

The legal system and the accountability of the midwife

What is the law?

"It is against the law" is a powerful statement, and anyone making it should be able to declare the source of the law to which reference is being made. If the statement is accurate then either an Act of Parliament/Statutory Instrument/ directive of the European Union (known as a statute or "legislation") or a decided case would be cited. (See Glossary for further explanations of legal terms.)

Legislation

Legislation consists of both Acts of Parliament (with approval by the Houses of Commons and Lords, and the Queen's signature), and directives and regulations emanating from Parliament or the European Community (EC), which we, as a member state, are required to implement and obey.

Legislation can be primary or secondary. Primary legislation consists of Acts of Parliament, known as statutes, which come into force at a date set either in the initial Act of Parliament or subsequently fixed by order of a Minister (i.e. by Statutory Instrument). The date of enforcement is often later than the date the Act is passed by the two Houses of Parliament and signed by the Crown.

A statute sometimes gives power to a Minister to enact more detailed laws, and this is known as secondary legislation. Some regulations have to be laid before the Houses of Parliament and in certain circumstances have to receive express approval. Statutory Instruments are an example of this secondary legislation.

Legislation, both statute and Statutory Instruments, can be accessed on the legislation website (www.legislation.gov.uk). EC legislation can be accessed on the bailii website (www.bailii.org./). EUR-Lex also provides free access to EU law (eur-lex.europa.eu/en/index.htm).

Increasingly, the devolved assemblies of the UK are enacting their own legislation and this can be accessed on the following websites:

- Wales: www.wales.gov.uk/topics/health
- Scotland: www.scotland.gov.uk/Topics/health
- Northern Ireland: www.northernireland.gov.uk

This book will be predominantly concerned with the law relating to England, but reference to the relevant websites of the devolved legislative assemblies will be given where appropriate.

Decided cases

The other main source of law is the decisions of the courts. This source is known as case law, judge-made law, or the common law. The courts form a hierarchy and the highest court in this country is the Supreme Court of Justice (formerly the House of Lords). If the Supreme Court of Justice sets out a specific rule, then this is binding on all courts in the country, except itself. A principle set out by a senior court is known as a precedent. Judges decide cases that may involve interpretation of Acts of Parliament, or situations where there does not appear to have been any enacted law or relevant case.

Each decision of the courts is reported, so that lawyers and judges can refer to the case, and the principles it established (known as the *ratio decidendi*) can be applied to any matters in dispute. If there is a dispute between a case and a statute, the latter would take priority: judges have to follow an Act of Parliament. Parliament can enact legislation which would overrule a principle established in the courts.

Appeals in cases based on European law can be made to the European Court of Justice in Luxembourg which gives interpretations of European laws. Its decisions are binding on the courts of member states.

Cases can be accessed on line on the British and Irish Legal Information Institute website (www.bailii.org/). If the name of the case is known, a case search can be carried out, otherwise there can be a search by subject matter.

The Human Rights Act 1998

This country was a signatory of the European Convention on Human Rights in 1950 and accepted the articles on human rights. However, the Convention was not incorporated into our law at that time. If a person considered his or her rights had been infringed then he or she had to take the case to Strasbourg, to the European Court of Human Rights, to argue the case there. The Human Rights Act 1998 gave legislative force to most of the articles of the European Convention on Human Rights in the UK. It is considered in *Chapter 2*.

The Act and the articles of the European Convention on Human Rights, set out in Schedule 1 to the Human Rights Act 1998, can be found on the legislation website (www.legislation.gov.uk). The Convention can be accessed on its website (www.echr.coe.int/ECHR/EN).

The articles that are most relevant to the midwife are discussed in *Chapter 2*.

Effect of the European Community

Since the United Kingdom signed the Treaty of Rome in 1972, it has become one of the member states of the European Community. The effect of this is that the UK is now subject to the laws made by the Council of Ministers and the European Commission. In addition, secondary legislation of the European Community in the form of regulations is binding on the member states. Directives of the Community must be incorporated by Act of Parliament into the law of each member state. See, for example, the European Directive 80/155/EEC Article 4, which sets out the definition of the activities of a midwife. This has now been incorporated into Article 42 of EEC directive 2005/36/EC which sets out the pursuit of the professional activities of a midwife and can be seen in *Box 1.1*.

Box 1.1. Professional activities of the midwife
(Article 42 of EEC directive 2005/36/EC)

1. The provisions of this Section shall apply to the activities of midwives as defined by each Member State, without prejudice to Paragraph 2, and pursued under professional titles set out in Annex V, point 5.5.2.
2. The Member States shall ensure that midwives are able to gain access to and pursue at least the following activities:
   (a) Provision of sound family planning information and advice.
   (b) Diagnosis of pregnancies and monitoring normal pregnancies, carrying out the examinations necessary for the monitoring of the development of normal pregnancies.
   (c) Prescribing or advising on the examinations necessary for the earliest possible diagnosis of pregnancies at risk.
   (d) Provision of programmes of parenthood preparation and complete preparation for childbirth including advice on hygiene and nutrition.

Box 1.1/cont

(e) Caring for and assisting the mother during labour and monitoring the condition of the fetus in utero by the appropriate clinical and technical means.

(f) Conducting spontaneous deliveries including, where required, episiotomies and, in urgent cases, breech deliveries.

(g) Recognising the warning signs of abnormality in the mother or infant which necessitate referral to a doctor and assisting the latter where appropriate; taking the necessary emergency measures in the doctor's absence, in particular the manual removal of the placenta, possibly followed by the manual examination of the uterus.

(h) Examining and caring for the newborn infant; taking all initiatives which are necessary in case of need and carrying out where necessary immediate resuscitation.

(i) Caring for and monitoring the progress of the mother in the postnatal period and giving all necessary advice to the mother on infant care to enable her to ensure the optimum progress of the newborn infant.

(j) Carrying out treatment prescribed by doctors.

(k) Drawing up the necessary written reports.

The International Conference of Midwives set out a definition on 15 June 2011 which can be accessed on its website (www.internationalmidwives.org/ Portals/5/2011/Definition). It is due to be reviewed in 2017. The World Heath Organization has also prepared information for Accession countries on the European Union Standards for Nursing and Midwifery. The second edition prepared by Thomas Keighley can be accessed on the internet (www.euro.who. int/_data/assets/pdf_file/0005/10220).

Criminal laws and civil laws

A major distinction in the law of the UK is that between criminal and civil laws.

Criminal laws

These laws, mostly derived from statutes, create offences which can be followed by criminal proceedings in the form of a prosecution. An example of a statutory provision giving rise to criminal proceedings is Article 45 of the Nurses, Midwives and Health Visitors Order, which makes it a criminal offence for a person other than a registered midwife or doctor, or student of either, to attend a woman in childbirth, except in an emergency (see *Chapter 12*).

An example of case law which gives rise to criminal proceedings is the definition of murder which was set out in a case in the 17th century. Most of our criminal laws are enforced by prosecutions brought by the Crown Prosecution Service, which was created in 1985. Other bodies also have powers to prosecute in specific cases, e.g. the Health and Safety Executive, the National Society for the Prevention of Cruelty to Children, and environmental health officers.

There are other criminal laws, such as those created by local authority powers, known as by-laws, which create local offences. There is also a right of an individual to bring a private prosecution, but this can be costly and of uncertain benefit. (See *Chapter 12* for the criminal laws.)

Civil laws

These are laws (both statutory and case law) which enable citizens to claim remedies against other citizens or organisations as a result of a civil wrong. A large group of civil wrongs are known as torts, of which negligence is the main one, but the group also includes action for breach of statutory duty, nuisance and defamation. Actions for breach of contract are not included in the definition of tort (see *Chapter 8*).

An example of a statute that can give rise to civil action is the Congenital Disabilities (Civil Liability) Act 1976, which gives a child who is born alive the right to sue in respect of negligence which led to him or her suffering from a congenital defect (see *Chapter 7*).

An example of a case which applies to civil proceedings is that of *Whitehouse v Jordan,* in which an obstetrician was sued for negligence on the grounds that he had allegedly pulled too long and too hard in a trial of forceps. The House of Lords (the predecessor of the Supreme Court of Justice) held that an error of clinical judgement may or may not be evidence of negligence, and that it had not been established that Dr Jordan failed to follow the reasonable standard of care required in the circumstances, based on the approved standard of practice at the time (see *Chapter 8*).

Some Acts may be actionable as both a criminal offence and a civil wrong. For example, in *Chapter 3*, the action for trespass to the person is discussed. This action can be brought where treatment is given without the consent of the individual and in the absence of other factors that would be a defence to the action (e.g. acting with consent or under the Mental Capacity Act 2005 where the individual lacks the capacity to give consent). A trespass may, however, also be a criminal act of assault, and there could be a prosecution in the criminal courts. It can be seen from this that there is not necessarily a moral difference between a crime and a civil wrong.

The accountability of the midwife

The midwife can be called to account for herself in four different legal settings: the civil and criminal courts, the Nursing and Midwifery Council (NMC) professional conduct hearings, and disciplinary proceedings before an employer (followed possibly by an employment tribunal hearing). Sometimes all four kinds of hearings may take place on the same set of facts, but they may have different outcomes. For example, if a baby has died, the parents may allege that the midwife is to blame. They may bring civil proceedings against the midwife or her employer for its vicarious liability for the negligent actions of the midwife (see *Chapter 8*). The police may investigate the circumstances and the Crown Prosecution Service might decide to bring criminal proceedings against the midwife for manslaughter and/or against the midwife's employer under the Corporate Manslaughter and Corporate Homicide Act 2007 (see *Chapter 12*). In these circumstances the midwife would also face fitness to practise proceedings before the NMC. Finally the midwife's employer would have to consider whether disciplinary proceedings should be brought against the midwife. It might, after reasonable investigation, decide to dismiss the midwife, in which case the midwife might consider making an application for unfair dismissal to an employment tribunal.

The results of these different proceedings may not be the same. The criminal courts might find the midwife not guilty of murder or manslaughter, yet the parents may succeed in their civil action against the employer. The employment tribunal might find that the midwife has been unfairly dismissed (for example the employer may not have followed the appropriate procedures in dismissing the midwife) but the NMC committee may find that the midwife was not fit to practise and she could be struck off the register. Clearly if that were to happen the midwife could no longer be employed as a registered midwife and would lose her job.

In this book, we consider the criminal law (see *Chapter 12*) and the civil law (see *Chapter 8*). Professional conduct proceedings of the NMC are considered in *Statutory supervision of midwives: A resource for midwives and mothers* (Osbourne, 2007). The professional conduct cases involving midwives can be accessed on the NMC website (www.nmc-org.uk). For example, on 6 March 2009 it was reported that a midwife had been struck off following a number of incidents including failure to diagnose a breech presentation, despite having been on supported practice for previous undetected breech. A spokesperson for the NMC stated that

...her actions had the potential to cause very serious patient harm, she had no insight into her failings and no rehabilitative or corrective steps have been taken.

New rules and standards published by the Nursing and Midwifery Council came into force on 1 January 2013. These are more concise than those published previously. They do not repeat legal principles that are found in other NMC guidance such as record keeping and medicines. The Midwives' Rules have legal force, the standards are guidance by the NMC which will be taken into account in any hearing before the NMC. They will be referred to constantly throughout this book and can be downloaded from the NMC website (www. nmc-uk.org). From 14 January 2013 the NMC has introduced a process of voluntary removal from the register by which a registrant who is subject to fitness to practise proceedings and who does not intend to continue practising can apply to be removed from the register.

What about ethics?

Some civil and criminal wrongs may also be ethically wrong. Some may not be considered as ethical issues. For example, failure to register the birth of a baby may not give rise to ethical issues if it has occurred simply from absent-mindedness. It would however be a criminal offence.

In this book we are concerned with the law and therefore there is little discussion of ethical issues. However, the reader is referred to the Further Reading list for sources on ethics in midwifery. Codes of practice and conduct are not in themselves "laws". They do, however, provide guidance for professional practice, and could be used in evidence in civil or professional conduct proceedings to demonstrate that reasonable practice has not been followed. This is discussed further in *Chapter 8.*

Legal personnel

Lawyers in this country are trained as solicitors or barristers. The former, in the past, have had direct dealings with clients and arranged with barristers (known as Counsel) for the paperwork to be drafted and for representation of the client in court. Now, increasingly, solicitors are being trained for advocacy and have rights of presenting a case in court, and barristers may have direct contact with clients.

It is impossible in a work of this size to deal adequately with the complexities of the legal system and the procedures that are followed. The interested reader is therefore referred to the works in the list of Further Reading.

Conclusions

An understanding of the different sources of law and how laws can impact on practice is essential for the midwife. The aim of this book is to introduce the midwife to the basic principles and language of law, indicating where further information can be obtained online, so that gradually knowledge and confidence can develop. Details of websites are given where possible to enable further information to be obtained.

Questions and exercises

1. Look at the Glossary and identify the words and terms with which you are not familiar. Use your internet links to access further information on these terms.
2. Try and arrange a visit to a court of law, and make notes of the procedure which is followed, the language used, the level of formality followed (e.g. in clothes that are worn), and the purpose of the proceedings. What preparations would you need to make if you were required to give evidence?
3. Access the legislation website (www.legislation.gov.uk) and look up Schedule 1 to the Human Rights Act 1999. Consider those Articles in Schedule 1 that would appear to be relevant to the practice of midwifery and the rights of the woman, and discuss with colleagues what action needs to be taken to implement them. (Compare your answer with the Articles discussed in *Chapter 2*.)
4. The husband of a client attacks a midwife by grabbing her arm. She is contemplating bringing proceedings against him. What is the difference between a civil action and a criminal prosecution in this context? (See also *Chapters 8* and *12*.)
5. A client dies following an unsuccessful Caesarean operation. What factors would lead to a prosecution being brought against the staff involved or the hospital management? (See also *Chapter 12*.)

6. A community midwife has not insured her car for use in transporting clients. She takes a pregnant woman to hospital in an emergency situation. What are the likely repercussions? (Consider the insurance issues as well as issues of reasonable professional practice.)
7. In what circumstances would a midwife be entitled to receive compensation from the Criminal Injury Compensation Scheme? (See *Chapter 12.*)

References

Osbourne A, Wallace V, Moorhead C, Jones D (2007) *Statutory supervision of midwives: A resource for midwives and mothers.* Quay Books, Dinton

The Nursing and Midwifery Order 2001. SI 2002 No 253

Whitehouse v Jordan [1981] 1 All ER 267

Section B

Clients' rights

Chapter 2

Woman-centred care

Basic principles

Clients' rights in law derive from statute or the common law (see *Chapter 1*). Some rights set out in international conventions are recognised by statute in this country and thus become enforceable. One such example is the Human Rights Act 1998 which incorporated into UK law most of the Articles of the European Convention on Human Rights. The NHS legislation places a duty on the Secretary of State to provide specified services.

Statutory duty to provide maternity services

Under Section 1 of the Health and Social Care Act 2012 (which replaces Section 1 of the National Health Service Act 2006) it is the Secretary of State's duty to promote a comprehensive health service:

(1) The Secretary of State must continue the promotion in England of a comprehensive health service designed to secure improvement:
    (a) in the physical and mental health of the people of England, and
    (b) in the prevention, diagnosis and treatment of physical and mental illness.

Under Section 3 of the 2006 NHS Act (as amended by the Health and Social Care Act 2012):

(1) The Clinical Commissioning Group (see *Chapter 19*) arrange for the provision of the following to such extent as it considers necessary to meet the reasonable requirements of the persons for whom it has responsibility:
    (a) hospital accommodation,
    (b) other accommodation for the purpose of any service provided under this Act,
    (c) medical, dental, ophthalmic, nursing and ambulance services,
    (d) such other services or facilities for the care of pregnant women, women who are breastfeeding and young children as he considers are appropriate as part of the health service.

This duty is not absolute. It must provide services to such extent as it considers necessary to meet the reasonable requirements of the persons for whom it has responsibility, and in respect of maternity services as it considers are appropriate as part of the health service. However, it is impossible to have a waiting list in maternity care: nature does not wait. Therefore, minimum standards for antenatal, intrapartum and postnatal care must be provided. In other fields of healthcare, court actions against the Secretary of State for the provision of services have usually failed. Thus patients who had been waiting several years for hip replacement operations in the West Midlands failed in their action against the Secretary of State (*R v Secretary of State for Social Services*) and a mother who was concerned at the delay in providing her child with heart surgery lost her case (*R v Central Birmingham Health Authority*). The court held that it was not for the court to substitute its own judgment for that of those responsible for the allocation of resources. It would only interfere if there had been a failure to allocate funds in a way that was reasonable or where there had been breaches of public duties. The same principle was followed by the Court of Appeal in the much-publicised case of Jamie Bowen, a 10-year-old girl who suffered from leukaemia (*R v Cambridge HA ex parte B*).

Human Rights Act 1998

Following the Second World War, this country, together with many other European countries, was a signatory to the European Convention on Human Rights. People who considered that their rights had been infringed could take a case to the European Court of Human Rights which was based in Strasbourg. (This is entirely separate from the European Economic Community which has its European Court of Justice in Luxembourg.) The Human Rights Act 1998 brought most of the Articles of the European Convention into force in the UK.

- It requires all public authorities to implement the Articles of the European Convention on Human Rights.
- It gives a right to anyone who alleges that a public authority (or an organisation exercising functions of a public nature) has failed to respect those rights to bring an action in the courts of this country.
- It enables judges who consider that legislation is incompatible with the Articles of the Convention to refer that legislation back to Parliament.

The Articles are set out in Schedule 1 to the Act and can be found on the legislation website (www.legislation.gov.uk).

The Ministry of Justice published a handbook for public authorities entitled *Human rights: Human lives* in 2011 which is available on its website (www.justice. gov.uk/downloads/human-rights/human-rights-handbook-for-public-authorities. pdf). This handbook provides background information on the Convention and the Act and an explanation for each Article with emphasis on its relevance to the public sector. For each Article it gives a case study and an example of best practice.

Articles 2, 3, 5, 6, 8, 9, 10 and 14 are likely to be of particular concern to midwifery practice.

Article 2

Everyone's right to life shall be protected by law. No one shall be deprived of his life intentionally, save in the execution of a sentence of a court following his conviction of a crime for which this penalty is provided by law.

In one case (*A National Health Service Trust v D*), parents lost their attempt to ensure that a severely handicapped baby, born prematurely, was resuscitated if necessary. The judge ruled that the hospital should provide him with palliative care to ease his suffering, but should not try to revive him as that would cause unnecessary pain. Article 2 rights were not infringed. (The case and other letting die cases are considered in *Chapter 12*.)

Article 2 was also invoked in the case of *Re A(Minors)(Conjoined Twins: Separation)* involving the separation of Siamese twins, in which the Court of Appeal decided that they could be separated even though this would undoubtedly lead to the death of the one who depended upon the heart and the lungs of the other.

The Article may be relied upon where a patient alleges that failure to provide health services is infringing his or her right to life. However, it has to be established that there is an intention to take life and this has proved the stumbling block to those who have argued that letting die in the case of persistent vegetative state patients or severely disabled babies is a breach of Article 2 (*NHS Trust A v M; NHS Trust B v H*) (see *Chapter 12*).

In the case of *Osman v United Kingdom*, the European Court of Human Rights held that the obligation to preserve life was not absolute, especially in the context of operational choices, priorities and resources.

Article 3

No one shall be subjected to torture or to inhuman or degrading treatment or punishment.

While it is hoped that torture does not take place in healthcare, there are examples of degrading and inhuman treatment. Most midwives would probably agree that a case where a pregnant prisoner was handcuffed to the bed during her labour would appear to be a *prima facie* breach of this right (see below). The European Court of Human Rights has ruled that corporal punishment by parents to discipline their children was a breach of Article 3 of the European Convention on Human Rights (*A v The United Kingdom*) (see *Chapter 17*).

In the case of *Z v UK 1999*, the Commission found a violation of Article 3 arising from the failure of the local authority to take action in respect of serious ill-treatment and neglect caused to four siblings by their parents over a period of more than four and a half years. In another case, the failure of police and health services to deal effectively and within the specified time limits of a mentally ill man with learning disabilities who was kept in a police cell was seen as a breach of his Article 3 rights by the European Court of Human Rights even though there was no intention to humiliate him or debase him (*MS v UK*).

Article 3 and women prisoners

It was reported in 1994 that a prisoner who was transferred to Wythenshawe Hospital for the delivery of her child was handcuffed during the confinement (*The Times*, 1994; see also Dimond, 1997). It appeared that she had absconded three times before and therefore staff kept her handcuffed at all times, including during the birth. The incident led to the Director General of the Prison Service issuing an official apology to the mother (*Midwives Chronicle*, 1994) and an undertaking in Parliament that "Handcuffs must be removed in any case if the doctor treating the patient so requests it" (*Midwives Chronicle*, 1994).

In spite of these new guidelines and apologies that a situation of handcuffing a woman during labour would not recur, in 1996 it was reported that Annette Walker was taken from Holloway prison to the Whittington Hospital in handcuffs, where she spent 10 hours in labour chained to a bed, in the presence of a male and a female officer (Walker, 1996). It was later reported that the Home Office, following discussions with the Royal College of Midwives, was dropping the policy of keeping pregnant women in handcuffs during labour and delivery (Travis, 1996). Subsequently, supported by the Association for Improvements in the Maternity Services, Annette Walker sued the prison service and accepted £19000 compensation (Beech, 1998).

In 2003 the European Court of Human Rights held that inadequate medical care by prison authorities towards a prisoner, which caused distress and discomfort but which did not amount to physical or psychological injury, could amount to a breach of Article 3 (*McGlinchey and others v United Kingdom*).

Many individuals and organisations have fought valiantly to ensure that the rules are changed and that pregnant women are not shackled: Sheila Kitzinger and the National Childbirth Trust, Beverley Beech and the Association for Improvements in the Maternity Services, the Maternity Alliance, the Royal College of Midwives, and the Howard League for Penal Reform to name only a few. Their campaigning has ensured that such gross breaches of human rights are brought to public attention and promises secured over improvements. Sheila Kitzinger reviewed the challenges facing those concerned about pregnant women in prison (Kitzinger, 2004). See also Sally Price in the *Midwifery Digest* (2004) and a case study illustrating the work of the Howard League for Penal Reform by Finola Farrant (2004).

A pack has been funded by the Department of Health (through the charity Medact) known as Maternity Access and Advocacy Pack as a pre-clinical information resource to assist women who are in situations of disadvantage, such as asylum seekers, migrants, homeless people, women with mental health problems and those from ethnic minorities. More information about this resource can be found on the RCM website. The Government's Directgov website provides information about mother and baby units in prisons, prisoners' rights, and complaining about a prison (www.direct.gov.uk/en/CrimeJusticeAndTheLaw/).

Questions on women's prisons and prisoners can also be put to the National Offender Management Services by email (womensteam@noms.gsi.gov.uk).

A review of women with particular vulnerabilities in the criminal justice system chaired by Baroness Jean Corston was published in 2007 and can be downloaded from the justice website (www.justice.gov.uk/publications/docs/corston-report).

Article 5

Everyone has the right to liberty and security of person. No one shall be deprived of his or her liberty save in the following cases and in accordance with a procedure prescribed by law.

Many exceptions are then given, including:

(f) The lawful detention of persons for the prevention of the spreading of infectious diseases, or persons of unsound mind, alcoholics or drug addicts or vagrants.

The House of Lords decided in the Bournewood case (*R v Bournewood Community and Mental Health NHS Trust*) that a person who lacked the mental capacity to consent to admission to psychiatric hospital could be detained there in his or her best interests without being detained under the Mental Health Act 1983. However, the European Court of Human Rights subsequently held that the NHS Trust was in breach of Article 5 (*L v United Kingdom*). This decision required a change in UK law, and the Mental Capacity Act 2005 was enacted in 2007. This makes provision for decision-making on behalf of mentally incapacitated adults and replaces common law powers (*Re F [Adult: Court's Jurisdiction]*). (The Act is considered in *Chapter 3*.)

Article 6

Article 6 concerns the right to a fair trial. This right has significant implications since it applies not just to criminal charges but also to the determination of civil rights and obligations.

Article 8

Under Article 8:

- Everyone has the right to respect for private and family life, his home and his correspondence.
- There shall be no interference by a public authority with the exercise of the right except such as is in accordance with the law and is necessary in a democratic society in the interests of national security, public safety or the economic wellbeing of the country, for the prevention of disorder or crime, for the protection of health or morals, or for the protection of the rights and freedoms of others.

This right requires greater sensitivity about patient privacy than has been shown in the past within healthcare. The traditional ward round, where a curtain is seen as a sound-proof barrier but in fact all those on the ward can hear the intimate details of a patient's diagnosis, prognosis and treatment, has had to be reviewed. Many other actions have been taken in order to ensure that this right of the patient is recognised and protected. The Caldicott Guardians, whose role is considered in *Chapter 4*, have the responsibility for ensuring that there is no breach of Article 8.

The respect for family life did not enable a prisoner to obtain artificial insemination (*R v Secretary of State for the Home Department*) and it was held that high security restrictions on child visits were valid and not a breach of Article 8 (*R v Secretary of State for Health*). However, Kirk Dickson, serving a life sentence for murder, whose request for artifical insemination had been turned down won his appeal to the European Convention on Human Rights in 2007 (*Dickson v United Kingdom*). The European Court of Human Rights held that turning down a request was a breach of Article 8 rights and awarded the applicants €5000 in respect of non-pecuniary damage and €21000 for costs and expenses, less the legal aid paid by the Council of Europe. Subsequently it was reported that a request from an inmate to father a child by artifical insemination was granted and five further applications are being considered (Collins, 2011).

A woman in Holloway prison won her appeal against the decision that her baby would be taken away from her at birth. This was held to be a breach of Article 8 of the Human Rights Convention and the United Nations Convention on the Rights of the Child. Article 8 of the European Convention could be interpreted as giving a baby a right to be breastfed if the mother so wished, and of continuing contact with the mother, irrespective of her being in custody. In contrast, the High Court has ruled in two cases (brought by *P* and by *Q*) that the policy of the prison service that children should cease to live with their mothers in prison at 18 months old was lawful and not contrary to Article 8 (*R [P] v Secretary of State for the Home Department; R [Q] v the same. June 2001*). Article 8 gave a right to respect for family life and the qualifications contained in Article 8.2 were in play by reason of the legality, recognised by Article 5, of the prisoner's imprisonment. The Court of Appeal held (*R [P] v Secretary of State for the Home Department; R [Q] v the same. August 2001*) that the prison service was entitled to have a policy that children aged 18 months should cease to stay with their mothers in prison, but such a policy should not be operated rigidly. The reasons for the need for flexibility were firstly the aim of promoting the welfare of the child (which had to be related to the circumstances of the prison) and secondly the interference with the child's family life had to be justified under Article 8.2 of the Human Rights Convention.

In the case of *Re P (A child)(Adoption:Unmarried couples)*, it was held that there was a breach of Article 8 by Northern Ireland Adoption Order which required adopters to be married or single and therefore an infringement of the Article 8 rights of unmarried couples. The case of *B and L v UK*, which held that a statutory prohibition on a father-in-law marrying a daughter-in-law was contrary to Article 8 rights, led to the Marriage Act 1949 (Remedial) Order 2007 changing the law.

A patient at Ashworth High Security Hospital lost his application for judicial review on the grounds that the provisions relating to the discretionary power of Special Hospitals to record and listen to a random 10% of telephone calls infringed his right to respect for privacy under Article 8. The court held that the recording was a justified infringement of Article 8 since it was a proportionate measure and necessary to achieve security for high risk patients (*R [on the application of N] v Ashworth Special Hospital Authority*). In contrast, the interception of private phone calls by an employer were held to be a violation of Article 8 (*Halford v UK*). Alison Halford won her case claiming violation by the Merseyside Police, her employer, since the Interception of Communications Act 1985 only applied to a public telecommunications system.

In the case of *Munjaz v United Kingdom,* the European Court of Human Rights held that there was no breach of Article 5 and 8 when the seclusion policy at Ashworth Hospital departed from the Code of Practice, since the departure was based on cogent reasons and the policy was foreseeable. There was no arbitrary interference with the applicant's human rights.

Article 8 has to be interpreted in relation to Article 10, which recognises a right to freedom of expression. Both Articles 8 and 10 are qualified by specified circumstances in which the right is limited, and the courts will balance one against the other in determining whether there has been a breach of either Article. For example, when the Beckhams sought an injunction to prevent publication of their nanny's account of their home life arguing that their right to a private life should be supported, they lost because they had promoted their image of a harmonious family (*The Times*, 2005).

Other significant Articles

While these Articles have been looked at in detail there are others which have considerable significance for healthcare. Article 14, for example, prohibits discrimination. Article 2 of the First Protocol recognises a right to education, which may be significant for staff who are caring for children with chronic conditions. Parents also have the right to ensure that such education and teaching is in conformity with their own religious and philosophical convictions.

Equality Act 2010

This Act consolidated the law relating to sex, race, disability and other forms of discrimination. It defines nine protected characteristics shown in *Box 2.1*.

Box 2.1. Protected characteristics under the Equality Act 2010

- Age
- Disability
- Gender reassignment
- Marriage and civil partnership
- Pregnancy and maternity care

- Race
- Religion or belief
- Sex
- Sexual orientation

The Act protects those with the key characteristics from direct discrimination, indirect discrimination, harassment and victimisation. The Act prohibits conduct which amounts to direct and indirect discrimination, harassment and victimisation in those providing a service, disposing of or managing premises, work or employment services and education and other areas.

Under Section 17 pregnancy and maternity discrimination in non-work cases are protected characteristics in relation to:

(a) Part 3 (services and public functions).

(b) Part 4 (premises).

(c) Part 6 (education).

(d) Part 7 (associations).

Discrimination can arise if a person (A) discriminates against a woman. If A treats her unfavourably because of a pregnancy of hers, or, in the period of 26 weeks beginning with the day on which she gives birth, A treats her unfavourably because she has given birth (including, in particular, a reference to treating her unfavourably because she is breastfeeding). Giving birth includes giving birth to a stillborn child (i.e. after 24 weeks gestation).

Under Section 18: pregnancy and maternity discrimination in employment, a person (A) discriminates against a woman if, in the protected period in relation to a pregnancy of hers, A treats her unfavourably (a) because of the pregnancy, or (b) because of illness suffered by her as a result of it.

A also discriminates against a woman if he or she treats her unfavourably because she is on compulsory maternity leave, or because she is exercising or seeking to exercise, or has exercised or sought to exercise, the right to ordinary or additional maternity leave.

Public sector equality duty (S.149)

Part 11 (plus Schedules 18 and 19) establish a general duty on public authorities: to have due regard, when carrying out their functions, to the need to eliminate unlawful discrimination, harassment or victimisation; to advance equality of opportunity; and to foster good relations. The Act also contains provisions that enable an employer or service provider or other organisation to take positive action to overcome or minimise a disadvantage arising from people possessing particular protected characteristics.

Further information on the Equality Act and the NHS Equality Delivery System (EDS) can be found on the NHS Employers' website (www.nhsemployers.org).

Standards for maternity care: Government, professional and other guidance

Box 2.2 shows the indicators of success as set out in the Cumberlege Report which was published in 1993 (*The Times*, 1993).

What specific rights might a pregnant woman or mother claim?

The right to a home birth

It is clear that government policy as set out in the Cumberlege Report and in the NHS Plan favoured the right of patient decision-making and maximum involvement of patients in the care they obtain. If, however, a woman were to request that she had a home birth, it appeared that there were considerable pressures against her.

There was early evidence that the average uncomplicated vaginal birth costs 68% less in a home than in a hospital (Andeson and Anderson, 1999). There was also some evidence that, following careful selection for home birth, the risks were lower (Chamberlain et al, 1997). However, there was evidence that bullying to deter women from seeking home births existed (Stephens, 2005), see also the case of Paul Beland (*Practising Midwife*, 2004). It will be noted from the discussion above that the courts in the past have been reluctant to become involved in decisions against the Secretary of State where resource issues arise. If a woman were to bring a court action against a trust to compel provision for a home birth the court may be reluctant to issue an order for specific performance requiring arrangements to be made for her home confinement. This is because there is a general reluctance for the court to order persons to carry out particular activities

---

Box 2.2. Indicators of success

Within five years:
- All women should be entitled to carry their own notes.
- Every woman should know one midwife who ensures continuity of her midwifery care – the named midwife.
- At least 30% of women should have the midwife as the lead professional.
- Every woman should know the lead professional who has a key role in the planning and provision of her care.
- At least 75% of women should know the person who cares for them during their delivery.
- Midwives should have direct access to some beds in all maternity units.
- At least 30% of women delivered in a maternity unit should be admitted under the management of the midwife.
- The total number of antenatal visits for women with uncomplicated pregnancies should have been reviewed in the light of the available evidence and the Royal College of Obstetrics and Gynaecology guidelines.
- All front-line ambulances should have a paramedic able to support the midwife who needs to transfer a woman to hospital in an emergency.
- All women should have access to information about the services available in their locality.

---

when the court cannot itself supervise them. However, payment of compensation may be seen as an alternative for not having a home birth. In theory, there may well be a legal right for the woman to insist upon a home confinement, if she can show that it is in her best interests and that the resource implications benefit the NHS, but in practice it may be very difficult for her to secure this. In Ireland an attempt by four home birth mothers to force the state to recognise the right to home births failed (O'Connor, 2004). A report published in 2011 concluded that, as a whole, home births are as safe as those in medical settings and that on average the costs per birth were highest for planned obstetric unit births and lowest for planned home births (National Perinatal Epidemiology Unit Birthplace 2011). In 2012, researchers at Southampton University reported that overuse of medical intervention techniques during childbirth may be partly to blame for excessive bleeding after birth and that the chances of postpartum haemorrhage are significantly higher for a planned hospital birth than for a planned home birth.

Many organisations have worked strenuously to support the woman's right to have a home birth, if clinical conditions permit. The National Childbirth Trust, the Association for the Improvement in Maternity Services, the Association of Radical Midwives, the Royal College of Midwives, the Association of Community Based Maternity Care and the International Home Birth Movement have all promoted the provision of information to women so that they have clear choices over the place of birth. Twenty years have passed since the publication of *Changing childbirth* (Department of Health, 1993) and there is little evidence that the situation for women has significantly altered. Sheila Kitzinger (2005) has argued strongly that it is a woman's right to have a home birth. The legal and ethical issues are explored by Jones (2003). Liz Stephens (2005) discusses some of the hurdles to providing a woman with a real choice of a home birth and how these could be overcome.

In 2006, the NMC recognised that midwives owe a professional duty of care to attend any woman who chooses to give birth at home (Nursing and Midwifery Council, 2006). In July 2010, in Annexe 2 (entitled Supporting women in their choice for home birth) of the papers provided to the Midwifery Committee of the NMC (M/10/15) it was stated that:

> ...*implicit in the Government policy in all four constituent countries of the UK is the promotion of choice for women in relation to their pregnancy care and place of birth. This includes being offered the choice of planning a birth at home.*

The NMC identified some of the common barriers in accessing a home birth. The paper emphasised the duty of the midwife to act within her competence, the action she should take to support a woman in her choice of a home birth if she is not competent to supervise one, the assessment which should be carried out and resource issues. It concluded that midwives have a duty to respect the choice of a competent woman.

> *The midwives rules and standards and the code therefore protect women and, at the same time, protect midwives by providing a sound framework for their practice.*

The paper can be accessed on the NMC website (www.nmc.uk.org/ Documents/CouncilPapers).

The National Institute for Health and Clinical Excellence (NICE) published its guidance on intrapartum care in September 2007. In paragraph 1.1 on planning place of birth it states that women should be offered the choice of planning birth at home, in a midwife-led unit or in an obstetric unit.

Elizabeth Prochaska, a barrister, explored whether women have a legal right to choose where they give birth and concluded that a case heard in the European Court of Human Rights (*Ternovszky v Hungary ECHR*) supported the use of Article 8 in protecting the right of choosing the circumstances of becoming a parent.

The Court is satisfied that the circumstances of giving birth incontestably form part of one's private life for the purposes of this provision.

The author pointed out that Article 8 is not absolute and a trust could argue limited resources or staffing shortages as a defence, but clear evidence would be required. She herself was able to use the European Court of Human Rights case and Article 8 to compel a London trust to reinstate its original plan to permit a home birth (this had been withdrawn on grounds of staff shortages).

There is no right in law to force a mentally competent woman to go to hospital for the birth (See *Chapter 3*).

The right to a Caesarean section?

Like the right to a home birth, the right to have a Caesarean (in the absence of any clinical conditions justifying it) has also met with considerable controversy.

Almost one in four births is now by Caesarean section and this increase has been partly the result of increasingly defensive practice by obstetricians, but also because of pressure from women. The author has argued that there is no legal right for a patient to demand care when there is no clinical justification (Dimond, 1999). However, a midwife may come across a situation where a consultant, although he or she does not personally see a clinical need for a Caesarean section to take place, is prepared to support the woman's request. In such circumstances the midwife has no alternative other than to provide the woman with all the appropriate care that she would have if the Caesarean was clinically indicated.

In 2011 NICE issued new guidance on Caesarean sections (CG132) (replacing the earlier guidance issued in 2004). This considers the importance of giving women full information to make an informed choice. Paragraph 1.2.9 considers maternal request for Caesarean section. If there are no clinical reasons why a Caesarean section is indicated, and the woman has been referred to appropriate health professionals but still requests a Caesarean section, then paragraph 1.2.9.5 applies:

For women requesting a Caesarean section, if after discussion and offer of support (including perinatal mental health support for women with anxiety about childbirth), a vaginal birth is still not an acceptable option, offer a planned Caesarean section.

Paragraph 1.2.9.6 states:

An obstetrician unwilling to perform a Caesarean section should refer the woman to an obstetrician who will carry out the Caesarean section.

In practice this amounts to the recognition of a woman to have Caesarean section on request even if this is not justified on medical grounds.

The full document can be accessed on the NICE website (www.nice.org.uk) (see *Chapter 8* for the legal significance of NICE guidelines).

Any midwife discussing the possibility of a Caesarean delivery should be mindful of both the NICE guidelines and also the risks involved (Gaskin, 2011). The Health Protection Agency warned that 10% of women suffered from infection after a Caesarean (Smyth, 2012).

The right to breastfeed

The Scottish Parliament passed the Breastfeeding etc. (Scotland) Act 2005 which makes it a criminal offence to deliberately prevent or stop a woman breastfeeding (www.scottish.parliament.uk). It is an offence to deliberately prevent or stop a person in charge of a child from feeding milk to that child in a public place or on licensed premises. An exception to this offence is if the child at the material time, is not lawfully permitted to be in the public place or on the licensed premises otherwise than for the purpose of being fed milk. The Act also places a duty on the Scottish Ministers to make arrangements to such extent as they consider necessary to meet all reasonable requirements for the purpose of supporting and encouraging the breastfeeding of children by their mothers. The Scottish Ministers are given the power to disseminate, by whatever means, information promoting and encouraging breastfeeding.

The Equality Act 2010 gives protection against discrimination on grounds of sex, and under Section 16 this includes a woman who is breastfeeding. A woman cannot therefore be treated unfavourably because she is breastfeeding. Anyone who is providing services, benefits, facilities and premises to the public must not discriminate against, harass or victimise a woman who is breastfeeding. Further explanation of this right can be found on the maternity action website (www. maternityaction.org.uk/) and in their information sheet published in February 2012 entitled *Breastfeeding in public places*, and also in a very interesting article by Melanie Fraser who looks at the general legal issues surrounding the legal right to breastfeed (Fraser, 2010).

Human Rights and the NHS

An Audit Commission report (2003) on human rights in the public sector showed that 73% of NHS trusts were not taking action to adopt a strategy for human rights. Health bodies consistently lag behind other public services in recognising human rights issues and are vulnerable to the risk of challenge because they are failing to protect themselves and will not secure service improvement. The Audit Commission emphasised the importance of developing a human rights culture in each public organisation. It suggested the following steps:

- Learning lessons from case law.
- Raising awareness.
- Developing strategy, policies and procedures to promote human rights.
- Managing complaints effectively using human rights.
- Ensuring contractors comply with human rights legislation.

Further information on the work of the Audit Commission can be found on its website (www.audit-commission.gov.uk).

Midwifery management

The actual configuration of maternity services also continues to be subject to controversy. In September 2012, the Royal College of Obstetrics and Gynaecology published a report, *Maternity services: Future of small units* (following an earlier paper in May 2008) recommending the closure of smaller maternity units so that larger, but fewer, obstetric units could provide 24-hour consultant cover. The implementation of these plans may have implications for midwifery-managed units. It is reported that a pregnant woman is suing to force the reopening of the maternity unit at Berwick Hospital in Northumberland which was closed because of serious safety concerns. Tara Smith was three months pregnant and the closure meant that she was faced with an 80-mile round trip to the nearest hospital with maternity services. The Northumbria Healthcare NHS Foundation Trust said that there had been only 13 births at the unit in the previous year and that midwives were not carrying out sufficient deliveries to practise their skills (Templeton, 2012a). Subsequently, it was announced that the unit would reopen temporarily in April 2013 and that the suspension was entirely for reasons of safety.

The debate over the safety of midwife-managed units was fuelled in November 2012 by a report that a baby died following delivery in a birth centre staffed by midwives. At the inquest, the jury concluded that being born at the midwife-led unit at Ludlow Community Hospital in Shropshire contributed to the infant's death (Templeton, 2012b). The mother had suffered complications in the final month of her pregnancy. Following the verdict, the head of midwifery stated, "We will now be taking the time to reflect on the jury's findings. Assessing the risks of pregnancy and delivery is complex and risks can never be completely removed." (See *Chapter 10* on risk assessment.)

The present shortage of midwives means that changes within the maternity services are not necessarily protective of the rights of the woman or the midwife. An article about using grandmothers as volunteers in maternity units highlights the benefits to both midwives and patients (they nurse newborn babies, help with meals, fill vases of flowers, take messages and ensure women have fresh drinking water). However, Louise Silverton, Director of Midwifery at the Royal College of Midwives, is quoted as saying, "We have to be careful that the NHS should fund a good maternity service and I would hate that any of these roles crept into taking anything on other than these softer personal care issues" (Templeton, 2012c).

In January 2010, at an inquest into the death of a baby at Milton Keynes General Hospital, the coroner highlighted a lack of resources, including a shortage of midwives and beds. The Care Quality Commission stated that it was considering the coroner's findings as part of a follow-up report on the maternity unit.

On 22 January 2013 a report by the Royal College of Midwives presented to Parliament warned that maternity wards were at tipping point as the baby boom has resulted in massive shortages of midwives. It stated that an extra 5000 midwives were needed in England to deal with the highest birth rate since 1971. The report resulted from a survey of heads of midwifery at NHS trusts conducted by the Royal College of Midwives and showed that more than a half had had to close the door to admissions on average seven times during the year, because they could not cope with the numbers. One-to-one care was not always available, in breach of government pledges.

In 2011 the Kings Fund analysis of staffing in maternity services pointed out that in the next 15 years 50% of midwives will be eligible to retire and considered the shift to the use of midwifery support workers.

Conclusions

At the present time there is considerable discussion over whether this country should continue to be a signatory to the European Convention on Human Rights and recognise the jurisdiction of the European Court of Human Rights. Suggestions have been made that the Convention should be replaced by a Bill of Rights. Whatever the outcome, there is likely to be continuing debate over which human rights should be protected, not least within midwifery services. A strong warning about the dangers to midwives who are attempting to protect and respect the rights of women is given by Mavis Kirkham and others in a paper on midwives and human rights (Kirkham et al, 2012).

In December 2012 the Chief Nursing Officer of the Department of Health, Jane Cummings, together with the Director of Nursing at the Department of Health, Viv Bennett, published a three year strategy for nursing (www.dh.gov. uk) to bring back compassion into nursing. She identified six "Cs": care, compassion, competence, communication, courage and commitment, which should be embedded in nursing. These same qualities also apply to midwifery practice. Many are not easily enforced through law, only the most grievous breaches would amount to an infringement of human rights, but they should be integral to any code of professional practice.

Questions and exercises

1. Consider the targets set out in *Box 2.2* in the light of your own practice and determine the extent to which they have been achieved and what steps still need to be taken to implement them.
2. Do you consider that a woman should have a legally enforceable right to receive the kind of care she wants?
3. Analyse the implications of Article 3 of the European Convention on Human Rights for midwifery practice. Are there any aspects of your practice that could be criticised as "inhuman or degrading treatment or punishment"?
4. Further information on human rights, recent cases and the implications for health service practitioners can be found on the websites of the Ministry of Justice, the Nursing and Midwifery Council, the Department of Health, and professional associations such as the Royal College of Midwives. Access some of these sites to develop further your understanding of the rights of the pregnant woman before, during and after birth.

5. Demand for services is infinite; resources to meet those demands are finite. How does this apply to maternity services? What services in your view should be given priority?
6. How do you see the role of the maternity support worker developing?

References

A National Health Service Trust v D. Times Law Report 19 July 2000; [2000] Lloyds Rep Med 411

A v The United Kingdom (100/1997/884/1096) judgement on 23 September 1998

Andeson RE, Anderson DA (1999) The cost effectiveness of home birth. *Journal of Nurse-Midwifery* **44**(1): 30–5

Audit Commission (2003) *Human rights: Improving public service delivery*. Audit Commission, London

B and L v UK [2006] 1 F L R 35

Bale J (2005) Beckham family affairs are fair game for public. *The Times* 25 April: 11

Beech BAL (1998) Shackled prisoner wins compensation. *AIMS Journal* **10**(2): 13

Birthplace in England Collaborative Group (2011) Perinatal and maternal outcomes by planned place of birth for healthy women with low risk pregnancies: The Birthplace in England national prospective cohort study. *British Medical Journal* **343**: d7400

Bulletin of Medical Ethics (1994) News item. Handcuffing pregnant prisoners. *Bulletin of Medical Ethics* **98**: 9

Chamberlain G, Wraight A, Crowley P (eds) (1997) Home births: The report of the 1994 confidential enquiry by the National Birthday Trust Fund. *MIDIRS Midwifery Digest* **March**: 109

Dabrowski R (2012) Higher risk in planned hospital birth. *Midwives* **4 December**

Daily Telegraph (2011) Nick Collins prisoner granted right to father child from jail. *Daily Telegraph* **1 June**

Department of Health (1993) *Changing childbirth: Report of the Expert Maternity Group*. HMSO, London

Dickson v United Kingdom [2007] ECHR 1050

Dillon A (2004) NICE clinical guidance: Supporting implementation. *Focus* **July**: 10–11

Dimond B (1997) Dilemma: The prisoner. *Accident and Emergency Nursing Journal* **5**(4): 219–20

Dimond B (1999) Is there a legal right to choose a Caesarean? *British Journal of*

Midwifery **7**(8): 515–8

Farrant F (2004) An age of innocence? *MIDIRS Midwifery Digest* **14**(3): 298–9

Flint C (2004) Maternity hospitals and suspensions. *British Journal of Midwifery* **12**(9): 558

Fraser M (2010) Law and breastfeeding. *MIDIRS Midwifery Digest* **20**(12): 493–7

Gaskin IM (2011) The risk associated with the relentless rise in caesarean births. *British Journal of Midwifery* **19**(12): 820

Halford v UK (1997) 24 EHRR 523

Jones S (2003) Ethico-legal issues in home birth. *RCM Midwives Journal* **6**(3): 126–8

Kirkham M, Davies S, Edwards N, Murphy Lawless J (2010) Midwives and human rights. *MIDIRS Midwifery Digest* **22**(4): 441–5

Kitzinger S (1999) Birth in prison: The rights of the baby. *Practising Midwife* **2**(1): 16–8

Kitzinger S (2004) Pregnant prisoners. *NHS Magazine* **November**: 10–11

Kitzinger S (2005) Home birth: A social process, not a medical crisis. *Practising Midwife* **8**(4): 26–9

L v United Kingdom (Application No 45508/99) Times Law Report 19 October 2004

Marx H, Wiener J, Davies N (2001) A survey of the influence of patients' choice on the increase in the Caesarean section rate. *Journal of Obstetrics and Gynaecology* **21**(2): 124–7

McGlinchey and others v United Kingdom Lloyd's Rep. Med. [2003] 264

MS v UK [2012] ECHR 804

Munjaz v United Kingdom (Application No 2913/06) ECHR The Times Law Report 9 October 2012

National Institute of Health and Clinical Excellence (2007) *Clinical Guidelines 55. Intrapartum care*. NICE, London

National Perinatal Epidemiology Unit (2011) *Birthplace in England Study*. Available from: www.npeu.ox.ac.uk/birthplace see also www.nhs.uk/news/2011/11November/Pages/hospital-births-home-births-compared.aspx

NHS Trust A v M; NHS Trust B v H [2001] Fam 348

NICE (2011) *Caesarean section CG132*. NICE, London

Nursing and Midwifery Council (2006) *Circular 6/2006*. Available from: www.nmc-uk.org

O'Brien B (2000) Homebirth. *Home Birth Association of Ireland Newsletter* **21**(4): 7–9

O'Connor M (2004) Medical monopoly – a short lived triumph? *Midwifery Matters* **100** Spring: 38–9

Osman v United Kingdom (2000) 29 EHRR 245

Practising Midwife (2004) News item: Midwife sacked for attending homebirth. *Practising Midwife* **7**(8): 8

Price S (2004) Women in prison. *MIDIRS Midwifery Digest* **14**(3): 295–8

R (on the application of N) v Ashworth Special Hospital Authority [2001] EWHC Admin 339; The Times 26 June 2001

R (P) v Secretary of State for the Home Department; R (Q) v the same [2001] 2 FLR 1122

R v Bournewood Community and Mental Health NHS Trust ex parte L [1998] 3 All ER 289

R v Cambridge HA ex parte B [1995] 2 All ER 129

R v Central Birmingham Health Authority ex parte Walker [1987] 3 BMLR 32; The Times 26 November 1987

R v Secretary of State for Health ex parte Lally. Times Law Report 11 October 2000

R v Secretary of State for the Home Department ex parte Mellor. Times Law Report 31 July 2000

R v Secretary of State for Social Services ex parte Hincks and others. 29 June 1979 [1979] 123 Solicitors Journal 436

Re A(Minors)(Conjoined Twins: Separation) [2000] Lloyd's Rep Med 425

Re F (Adult: Court's Jurisdiction) [2000] 2 FLR 512 Court of Appeal; [2000] Lloyds Rep Med 381

Re P (A child)(Adoption:Unmarried couples) 2008 UKHL 38

Royal College of Midwives (2004) *Information paper: Caesarean sections without health indications*. RCM, London

Royal College of Midwives (2005) *Campaign for normal birth*. RCM, London

Royal College of Midwives (2005) *RCM disappointed with Caesarean section figures*. News item 31 March. RCM, London

Royal College of Midwives and National Childbirth Trust (2001) *The rising Caesarean rate: Causes and effects for public health*. Conference Report November 2000; RCM and NCT, London

Royal College of Midwives Journal (2004) News item. *Royal College of Midwives Journal* **7**(2): 54

Smyth C (2012) Infection danger for Caesarean mothers. *The Times* **1 August**

Stephens L (2005) Worrying truth behind home birth figures. *British Journal of Midwifery* **13**(1): 4–5

Templeton S-K (2012a) Women sue over axed baby unit. *The Sunday Times* **4 November**

Templeton S-K (2012b) "My baby's dead, isn't she nurse?" *The Sunday Times* **18 November**

Templeton S-K (2012c) Granny? No, I'm a maternity buddy. *The Sunday Times* **4 November**

Ternovszky v Hungary ECHR application 67545/09 14 December 2010; see also European Court on Human Rights Press Unit 2011 Fact sheet – Reproductive rights: Home Birth

The Guardian (1996) End to chains for pregnant prisoners. *The Guardian* **16 January**

Travis A (1996) Manacles policy loosened. *The Guardian* **16 January**

Walker A (1996) The shame I felt in chains. *The Guardian* **11 January**

Walsh D (2004) Home birth, staffing and acute service. *British Journal of Midwifery* **12**(10): 616

World Health Organization (1985) Appropriate technology for birth. *Lancet* **ii**(8452): 436–7

Z UK (1999) 28 EHRR CD 65

Chapter 3

Consent

Scenario 3.1. Refusal to have Caesarean

A woman in her 38th week of pregnancy is advised that because of her previous obstetric history and the position of the fetus, that she should have a Caesarean section. She is adamant that she would never give consent: she is terrified of injections and is refusing to sign a form agreeing to a Caesarean. The obstetrician is of the view that failure to undertake a Caesarean within the next few hours could lead to the death of the fetus and even that of the woman. What is the law?

The Department of Health's (2001b) reference guide to consent to treatment is a useful source for this situation.

Scenario 3.1. is discussed on p. 51.

Introduction

The right of a mentally competent adult to give or withhold consent to mental and/or physical treatment has long been accepted as a major principle in English law. For the most part this has been part of the common law (judge-made law) but since the Mental Capacity Act 2005 and specific legislation covering human tissue, embryos and fertility, provisions relating to consent are increasingly to be found in statute law. Different rules apply to children and young persons (see *Chapter 6*) and those suffering from a mental disorder (see *Chapter 18*). Further information can be found in the author's textbook on consent (Dimond, 2009). Useful websites include:

- For accessing cases: www.bailii.org.
- Statutes can be found on the bailii site or on the legislation website: www.legislation.gov.uk.
- Department of Health and its reference guide on consent to treatment: www.dh.gov.uk.
- NMC and its guidance on consent: www.nmc-uk.org.
- Royal College of Midwives: www.rcm.org.uk.

Basic principles

Trespass to the person

To carry out treatment against the wishes of a mentally competent adult is a civil wrong, known as a trespass to the person. It is actionable (i.e. a victim could sue) without having to show that she had suffered harm. Even if she had benefited from the treatment, her lack of consent means that it is a civil wrong. In some circumstances the action might even constitute a criminal act. The consent must be freely given, without duress or any other form of compulsion or fraud.

The definition of trespass to the person is shown in *Box 3.1*.

Box 3.1. Trespass to the person

An act of the defendant which directly and intentionally causes either some physical contact with the person or the claimant without the claimant's consent (this is known as a battery) or causes the claimant immediately to apprehend a contact with this person (this is known as an assault).

This means that, even where the midwife has acted out of good will and in the best interests of the mother, if she has failed to obtain consent and in the absence of any of the other defences mentioned below, she could be liable to an action for trespass to the person. In practice, the claimant would sue the midwife's employer who is vicariously liable for the actions of an employee who is acting in the course of employment (see *Chapter 8*), unless of course the midwife was self-employed. The case of *Re B* (see p. 45) illustrates the principle that if a person is mentally competent, then to treat contrary to her wishes is a trespass to her person.

Consent

This is the main defence to an action for trespass to the person, i.e. that the individual who was touched, or feared a touching, gave consent to that action.

What, however, is meant by consent? Are there any factors that could invalidate an apparently valid consent? What capacity is required of the person in order to give a valid consent? Does the law require it to be given in any specific form?

Requirements of a valid consent

Absence of duress or fraud

To be valid as a defence to an action of trespass to the person, the consent which the defendant is relying upon must be given freely and without duress and without fraud, by a mentally competent person. Evidence of compulsion or fraud would invalidate the consent. However, where prisoners claimed that the very nature of their confinement in a prison institution made consent invalid, they failed in their action for trespass to the person (*Freeman v Home Office*). The Court of Appeal stated that they were not incapable in law of giving a valid consent by reason of the fact they were in prison and that refusal might adversely affect prison privileges or even parole.

Relevant to the defendant's action

Clearly the consent must be relevant to the act of the defendant. Consent to a Caesarean would not be a defence to carrying out a hysterectomy, although other defences (lack of mental capacity of the woman) might be relevant. This is an important area for the midwife since it must be clear whether or not the mother has given consent to an intimate examination, and the midwife must protect the mother against any unauthorised intimate examinations (Caswell, 1992). When consent is given, the person should have a general idea as to the purpose of the contact proposed. However, absence of sufficiently detailed information is more likely to be grounds for an action for negligence, for failure on the defendant's part to fulfil the duty of care in informing the patient, and would not invalidate the consent for the purpose of defending an action of trespass. This was explained clearly by the High Court in the case of *Chatterton v Gerson*.

> The claimant ran kennels with her twin sister. When her sister became a nurse, she worked as a universal aunt. In 1973 she went into hospital for treatment of varicose veins and she was advised at that time that a hernia repair operation should be carried out. Unfortunately, afterwards she suffered intractable and chronic pain as the result of the ilio-linguinal nerve being trapped. After various unsuccessful treatments, she was referred to Dr Gerson, a pain specialist, and was given treatment which unfortunately resulted in her right leg becoming completely numb, considerably impairing her mobility. She claimed damages against the defendant, alleging that he had not given her an explanation of the

operations and their implications so that she could make an informed decision about whether to risk them, and that

(a) he had committed a trespass to the person since her consent to the operation was vitiated by the lack of prior explanation, and

(b) he had been negligent in not giving an explanation as he was required to do as part of his duty to treat a patient with the degree of professional skill and care expected of a reasonably skilled medical practitioner.

She failed on both counts: point (a) is considered here; point (b), the allegation that there was negligence in failing to give the requisite information, is discussed on page 52.

In deciding that her action for trespass to the person failed, Judge Bristow said:

In my judgment once the patient is informed in broad terms of the nature of the procedure which is intended, and gives her consent, that consent is real, and the course of action on which to base a claim for failure to go into risks and implications is negligence, not trespass... In this case Miss Chatterton was under no illusion as to the general nature of what an intrathecal injection of phenol solution nerve block would be, and in the case of each injection her consent was not unreal.

Methods of evidencing consent

The agreement of the person that the touching may take place can occur in various ways:

- In writing (this may or may not be on a specially designed consent form).
- By word of mouth.
- By implication.

Written consent

Forms have been issued by the Department of Health (2001a) as part of its Good Practice in Consent implementation guide, replacing those issued by the NHS Management Executive in 1990 and updated in 1992. The Department of Health (2001b) has stated that:

It is good practice to obtain written consent for any significant procedure, such as a surgical operation or when the person participates in a research project or a video recording (even if only minor procedures are involved)

Where special forms are not required, written consent which is not on one of the recommended forms will not be invalid, provided that it clearly indicates the object of the consent and gives the signature of the person consenting. It must be remembered that the form is not the actual consent, but evidence that consent was given.

The forms may incorporate a phrase such as "I also give consent to any other procedure deemed necessary". This would be interpreted in the light of the treatment or procedure for which consent has been given. It would not cover a procedure unrelated to the treatment. For example, if a mother has signed such a statement in relation to a Caesarean, it would not necessarily cover a sterilisation.

In certain circumstances failure by the surgeon to obtain consent to a procedure could be treated as a criminal offence of battery and assault. The legal significance of birth plans is considered below.

Consent by word of mouth

Consent by word of mouth may be just as valid as consent in writing, but in the event of dispute it is very much more difficult for the fact that consent was given to be proved. Unless witnesses were present, it may be a case of the mother's word against that of the midwife. It is therefore recommended that for cases where the procedure is risky or hazardous, and where there could be a controversy as to whether consent was ever given, the midwife should attempt to obtain consent in writing.

Implied consent

The view has been taken that simply coming into hospital or seeing a midwife, automatically implies that the woman agrees to all the treatments and procedures recommended. In the light of the variety of treatments and procedures now available and the emphasis upon the involvement of the mother in decision making, it would be better to confine the term "implied consent" to those circumstances where the mother indicates by her non-verbal behaviour that she agrees that certain treatment can be given. For example, she raises her sleeve for blood pressure readings to be taken or for an injection to be given, she lies on the couch for a physical examination; such actions denote an agreement for the midwife or other professional to proceed.

However, care must be taken that the action carried out is that to which the implied consent refers. This shows the weakness of relying upon the implied consent of the mother, and the problems of misinterpretation. Where any risky procedure is contemplated, written consent (preferably) or consent by word of mouth should be obtained.

Mental Capacity Act 2005

The Mental Capacity Act 2005 makes provision for the determination of the capacity of an adult (over 16 years) to make her own decisions and to provide a framework for decisions to be made on her behalf if the requisite mental capacity is lacking.

The Mental Capacity Act 2005 can be accessed on the legislation or bailii websites. Sections 1–4 set down the principles that apply in the Act (see below), the definition of mental capacity and how the "best interests" of a person can be determined.

The determination of mental capacity

In order to give a valid consent, a person must have the requisite mental capacity as defined in the Mental Capacity Act 2005.

The MCA provides a two-stage test for incapacity.

Stage 1. An impairment of, or a disturbance in the functioning of, the mind or brain

The first stage is to assess whether P is unable to make a decision because of an impairment of, or a disturbance in the functioning of, the mind or brain. It does not matter whether the impairment or disturbance is permanent or temporary. Nor can a lack of capacity be established merely by reference to (a) a person's age or appearance, or (b) a condition of his, or an aspect of his behaviour, which might lead others to make unjustified assumptions about his capacity.

If there is a question over whether a person lacks capacity within the meaning of this Act, it must be decided on the balance of probabilities.

The Act therefore warns against superficial judgements and unjustified assumptions about a person's capacity. An objective assessment must be carried out, even though at first sight it would appear that the person is mentally incapacitated. For example, a tramp may come into the accident and emergency department and refuse to have stitches in his arm. The nurse attending him should not assume because of his dishevelled appearance that he is incapable of giving a valid refusal.

Stage 2. Inability to make decisions

If it is established that a person has an impairment of, or a disturbance in the functioning of, the mind or brain, the next question to be asked is: Does this impairment or disturbance result in an inability to make decisions?

The Act states that a person is unable to make a decision for himself if he is unable

(a) to understand the information relevant to the decision,
(b) to retain that information,
(c) to use or weigh that information as part of the process of making the decision, or
(d) to communicate his decision (whether by talking, using sign language or any other means).

This is very similar to the test of capacity used by Judge Thorpe in the case of *Re C (adult: refusal of medical treatment) Family Division,* involving a chronic schizophrenic in Broadmoor Hospital.

Principles of the Mental Capacity Act 2005

The Act lays down basic principles:

• Every adult must be assumed to have capacity unless it is established that he lacks capacity.
• A person is not to be treated as unable to make a decision unless all practicable steps to help him have been taken without success.
• A person is not to be treated as unable to make a decision merely because he makes an unwise decision.
• An action done, or decision made, under this Act for or on behalf of a person who lacks capacity must be done, or made, in his best interests.
• Before the act is done, or the decision is made, regard must be had to whether the purpose for which it is needed can be effectively achieved in a way that is less restrictive of the person's rights and freedom of action.

Best interests

Anyone who makes decisions on behalf of a person who lacks mental capacity must make those decisions in the best interests of that person. The person making the determination must consider all the relevant circumstances. The decision must not be made merely on the basis of a person's age or appearance or a condition of his, or an aspect of his behaviour, which might lead others to make unjustified assumptions about what might be in his best interests.

The steps that the decision maker must take are then identified as including, in particular, whether the incapacity is temporary or permanent, how the person can be encouraged to participate in the decision making, take into account the person's present and past wishes and feelings, including the beliefs and values that would have been likely to influence his decisions had he the necessary capacity, and other factors the person would have considered. The views of others must be taken into account, if it is practicable and appropriate to consult them. The principles set out above must apply to the decision making process.

Court of Protection

A new Court of Protection with powers to cover welfare and treatment decisions (in the past it has been confined to property and affairs) is able to appoint deputies who have the responsibility of making decisions on behalf of a mentally incapacitated adult. The deputies can be given specific powers in relation to where the person is to live, what contact, if any, he or she is to have with any specified person, and powers in relation to decisions on healthcare and treatment.

The Court of Protection is supported by a new officer known as the Public Guardian, whose functions include establishing and maintaining registers of lasting powers of attorney and of orders appointing deputies, supervising deputies appointed by the court, and directing a Court of Protection Visitor to visit.

Lasting power of attorney

Provision is made for a person (the donor), who has the requisite mental capacity, to draw up a lasting power of attorney to a donee, who can act on behalf of that person, should the donor lose his or her capacity.

Advance directions

Living wills are also given statutory recognition and enable a person when mentally capacitated to refuse treatments in the future if he or she then lacks capacity (see *Chapter 12*).

Codes of Practice

The whole Act is underpinned by the duty of the Secretary of State to prepare Codes of Practice covering most of the statutory provisions. These give detailed guidance for those responsible for acting on behalf of mentally incapacitated persons. They are accessible on the Ministry of Justice website (www.justice.gov.uk).

Case of Re B (Consent to treatment: Capacity)

Miss B suffered a ruptured blood vessel in her neck which damaged her spinal cord. As a consequence she was paralysed from the neck down and was on a ventilator. She was of sound mind and knew that there was no cure for her condition. She asked for the ventilator to be switched off. Her doctors wished her to try out some special rehabilitation to improve the standard of her care and felt that an intensive care ward was not a suitable location for such a decision to be made. They were reluctant to perform such an action as switching off the ventilator without the court's approval. Ms B applied to court for a declaration to be made that the ventilator could be switched off.

The main issue in the case was the mental competence of Miss B. If she were held to be mentally competent, then she could refuse to have life-saving treatment for a good reason, a bad reason or no reason at all. She was interviewed by two psychiatrists who gave evidence to the court that she was mentally competent. The judge, Dame Elizabeth Butler-Sloss, President of the Family Division, therefore held that she was entitled to refuse to be ventilated. She held that B possessed the requisite mental capacity to make decisions regarding her treatment and thus the administration of artificial respiration by the trust against B's wishes amounted to an unlawful trespass. The President of the Family Division found that there had been a trespass to B's person and awarded her a nominal amount as compensation. The judge restated the principles that had been laid down by the Court of Appeal in the case of *St George's Healthcare Trust v S* (see facts of this case below).

- There was a presumption that a patient had the mental capacity to make decisions whether to consent to or refuse medical or surgical treatment offered.
- If mental capacity was not an issue and the patient, having been given the relevant information and offered the available option, chose to refuse that treatment, that decision had to be respected by the doctors. Considerations of what the best interests of the patient would involve were irrelevant.
- Concern or doubts about the patient's mental capacity should be resolved as soon as possible by the doctors within the hospital or other normal medical procedures.
- Meanwhile the patient must be cared for in accordance with the judgement of the doctors as to the patient's best interests.
- It was most important that those considering the issue should not confuse the question of mental capacity with the nature of the decision made by the patient, however grave the consequences. Since the view of the patient might reflect a difference in values rather than an absence of competence, the assessment of capacity should be approached with that in mind and doctors should not allow an emotional reaction to, or strong disagreement with, the patient's decision to cloud their judgement in answering the primary question of capacity.
- Where disagreement still existed about competence, it was of the utmost importance that the patient be fully informed, involved and engaged in the process (which could involve obtaining independent outside help) of resolving the disagreement, since the patient's involvement could be crucial to a good outcome.
- If the hospital was faced with a dilemma that doctors did not know how to resolve, that must be recognised and further steps taken as a matter of priority. Those in charge must not allow a situation of deadlock or drift to occur.
- If there was no disagreement about competence, but the doctors were for any reason unable to carry out the patient's wishes it was their duty to find other doctors who would do so.
- If all appropriate steps to seek independent assistance from medical experts outside the hospital had failed, the hospital should not hesitate to make an application to the High Court or seek the advice of the Official Solicitor.
- The treating clinicians and the hospital should always have in mind that a seriously physically disabled patient who was mentally competent had the same right to personal autonomy and to make decisions as any other person with mental capacity.

It was reported on 29 April 2002 that Miss B had died peacefully in her sleep after the ventilator had been switched off.

This case was decided before the Mental Capacity Act 2005 came into force, but the same principles would apply now: if a person has the capacity to make her own decisions then to provide treatment contrary to her wishes would be unlawful as a trespass to her person.

Refusal of treatment in a Caesarean case

Controversy has arisen over several earlier cases where women in psychiatric hospitals have been forced to have Caesareans. The Court of Appeal in the case of *Re MB* set out the principles that should apply and these were reaffirmed in the following case.

St George's Healthcare NHS Trust v S; R v Collins ex parte S

A woman who was about 36 weeks pregnant was diagnosed as suffering from severe pre-eclampsia, severe oedema and proteinuria. She was advised to have early induction of labour as a life-saving necessity. She refused on the grounds that she would prefer to let nature take its course. She was then examined by an approved social worker and two doctors and was detained in hospital under Section 2 of the Mental Health Act 1983. From there she was transferred to St George's Hospital for obstetric treatment. She was advised by a solicitor that she had the right to refuse treatment. The hospital made an ex parte application to the High Court judge stating that it was a life and death situation and the patient had gone into labour. This latter information was incorrect, and the judge was not informed that the patient had instructed solicitors. The judge made the declaration that S's consent could be dispensed with. S was then given a Caesarean section. She was transferred back to the psychiatric hospital where a doctor decided that she was not suffering from mental disorder and ended the detention under Section 2, following which she took her own discharge.

The case eventually came before the Court of Appeal which emphasised the pregnant woman's right of self-determination, that the Mental Health Act should not have been used when a person was refusing treatment for hypertension, and that an unborn child is not a separate person from its mother.

Lord Justice Judge held that:

[A pregnant woman] is entitled not to be forced to submit to an invasion of her body against her will, whether her own life or that of her unborn child depends on it. Her right is not reduced or diminished merely because her decision to exercise it may appear morally repugnant. The declaration in this case involved the removal of the baby from within the body of her mother under physical compulsion. Unless lawfully justified, this constituted an infringement of the mother's autonomy. Of themselves, the perceived needs of the fetus did not provide the necessary justification.

The same principles would now apply under the Mental Capacity Act 2005. It is only where the woman lacks the mental capacity to make her own decision that a decision could be made on her behalf in her best interests. As we have seen above, defining her best interests would include taking account of her present and past wishes and her beliefs and values, as previously expressed.

Validity of a refusal

Where the patient refuses life-saving treatment, the Court of Appeal has emphasised that the professional has a duty to ensure that the refusal is valid.

Re T (1992)

The patient was a 20-year-old pregnant woman who had been brought up by her mother who was a Jehovah's Witness. She was injured in a road accident and when admitted to hospital told the nurse that she would not wish to have a blood transfusion. At that stage it seemed highly improbable that one would be required. However, her condition deteriorated and she went into labour. She was transferred to the maternity unit and told the midwife that she was a Jehovah's Witness and would not accept a blood transfusion. The midwife got her to put her name on a form which she had not read and of which she probably did not understand the significance. Her condition worsened until it was realised that a blood transfusion was essential. At this stage the father and the cohabitee referred the case to court.

The judge, hearing all the facts, decided that her refusal was not valid and the transfusion should proceed. His decision was upheld shortly afterwards by the

Court of Appeal which, while it stated that the adult mentally competent person has a right to refuse treatment, emphasised that professionals must ensure that a refusal of life-saving treatment is given by a person who is mentally competent and who is not overborne by the views of another or under the influence of drink or drugs. The situation would now be covered by the provisions of the Mental Capacity Act 2005 which sets out the stages and factors that must be taken into account in determining the validity of a refusal of life-sustaining treatment.

Statutory authorisation

Certain Acts of Parliament justify actions that would otherwise be regarded as a trespass to the person. Thus the Mental Health Act 1983 (as amended in 2007) has provisions that enable treatment for mental disorder to be given to a detained patient under specific conditions without the person's consent. The care of those with a mental disorder is considered in *Chapter 18*.

The Police and Criminal Evidence Act 1984 enables a citizen to carry out a lawful arrest in certain circumstances, and if the specified circumstances exist, an action for trespass to the person would not succeed.

Declaration of the court

If there is doubt over the capacity of the woman to give consent, and life-saving action is required, a declaration can be sought from the Court of Protection. The issue before the court would be whether or not the person has the mental capacity to make his or her own decisions. If the person is deemed to lack the appropriate mental capacity (and evidence would have to be given of the incapacity) then there has to be a determination as to what is in the person's best interests. A declaration could be then issued, where appropriate, that treatment could proceed in the person's best interests. In a case heard on 9 January 2013 the Court of Protection held that a person with learning difficulties could decide herself whether to have a termination of pregnancy. The woman suffered from sickle cell disease and was 18 weeks pregnant. While she did not have the mental capacity to participate in the legal proceedings and required the assistance of the Official Solicitor, she was mentally capable of making a decision about the pregnancy (Davies, 2013).

The protective jurisdiction of the family court was used in the case of *Re SA a Local authority and MA and NA*. SA was profoundly deaf and lacked speech and oral communication but was considered to have the mental capacity to give consent to marriage. The family court held that it had the protective jurisdiction to ensure that SA's true wishes were ascertained in relation to any proposal of marriage so that she could exercise her free will.

The statutory requirements relating to the giving of consent include:

- The Abortion Act 1967 requires forms to be completed by the doctors who confirm that the statutory requirements are met (except in an emergency).
- The Mental Health Act 1983 Part IV (as amended by the 2007 Act) covers the giving of treatment for mental disorder. The responsible medical officer has to confirm, in specified circumstances, that the patient is capable of understanding the nature, purpose and likely effects of the treatment and has given consent (see *Chapter 18*).
- The Human Fertilisation and Embryology Act 1990 (as amended) sets out specific requirements on consent, preceded by counselling in relation to the use of gametes and embryos (see *Chapter 14*).

Professional guidance

Guidance has been provided by the Department of Health on consent, which can be accessed on its website (www.dh.gov.uk) and is intended to be updated on a regular basis (Department of Health, 2001b). There are separate guidelines for use by adults, children and young persons, those with learning disabilities, parents and relatives, and carers. The Department of Health identifies 12 key points on consent which are expanded upon in the guide.

The law relating to 16 and 17-year-olds and those under 16 is considered in *Chapter 6*.

Application to midwifery: Midwifery interventions

Firstly, what are the various kinds of treatment and diagnostic procedures over which the woman might wish to exercise choice?

Box 3.2 sets out a few of the decisions which may be made during the course of a pregnancy. The list in *Box 3.2* is not exhaustive but it shows the many decisions which may have to be made during the pregnancy. Most, however, are not of a life-saving necessity, either for the mother or baby, and the mother could refuse most of these procedures without any major health disadvantages. However, to carry out any of these tasks or procedures without consent would, in the absence of lawful justification, be regarded as a trespass to the person.

Box 3.2. Decisions during pregnancy	
Caesarean section*	Water birth
Vitamin K injections	Examination by students
Episiotomies*	Catheterisation
Syntometrine	Fetal blood sampling
Epidurals*	Blood tests*
Anaesthetic*	Suppositories
Admission to obstetric unit*	Forceps*
Tubal ligation	Enemas
Home confinement	Intravenous infusion/treatment*
Seeing the doctor	Intrauterine monitoring*
Fetal monitoring*	Suturing*
Blood transfusion*	Fetal scalp electrodes*
Induction	Vaginal examination
Screening for syphilis and HIV	Rectal examinations
Artificial rupture of membranes*	Removal of jewellery
Anti-D injections	Ultrasound scanning

Procedures that could lead to serious harm to the mother or baby, if the mother refused to give consent for them.

Birth plans

Where a birth plan is agreed between midwife and client, it is important to ensure that the client understands that unexpected complications may make adherence to the birth plan unwise or even dangerous. The client should be assured that while she is mentally competent she has the right to give or withhold consent to any procedure.

Answer to Scenario 3.1: Refusal to have Caesarean

The crucial issue in this situation is: Does the patient have the mental capacity to make her own decisions? The two-stage test introduced by the Mental Capacity Act 2005 should be used. Ideally, a psychologist who could make the decision in an emergency should be brought in. If the assessment concludes that she has the requisite mental capacity, then her refusal to undergo the Caesarean cannot be overruled. On the other hand, if the assessment concludes that she does not have the requisite mental capacity, then the Caesarean operation would be lawful if it were in her best interests following the stages set out in the Mental Capacity Act 2005. In practice, an application would be made to the Court of Protection to determine both the mental capacity and, if that is deemed to be lacking, then what action should be taken in her best interests. (See also *Chapter 12* and advance decisions.)

Negligence in failing to give information

Even if consent has been obtained in general terms, a woman may have an action in negligence if she has not been given the appropriate information relating to risks inherent in any specific procedure. The majority in the House of Lords in the *Sidaway v Bethlem Royal Hospital Governors and Others* case ruled that professionals should follow the Bolam Test in informing a patient about relevant risks, but it recognised a right to withhold information if it would cause unnecessary anxiety or concern – known as therapeutic privilege. The Sidaway case was cited and followed in the case of *Blyth v Bloomsbury Health Authority*. It was also followed in the case of *Pearce v United Bristol Healthcare NHS Trust*. In this case, the Court of Appeal held that the consultant who had advised the mother to wait for natural birth to take place rather than have a Caesarean was not negligent in giving her that information or for the stillbirth.

The House of Lords held that the patient did not have to prove that she would not have had the treatment had she known of the serious risks of harm: it was sufficient if that information would have caused her to reconsider the proposed treatment (*Chester v Afshar*).

In the case of *Chinchen v University Hospital of Wales Healthcare NHS Trust,* where a patient underwent surgery for a revision decompression of his spine, it was held that he had not been given proper advice and he was successful in his action for negligence in failure to inform him of the risks. In the case of *Chatterton v Gerson* discussed above, the claimant failed both in her allegation of trespass to the person and also of breach of the duty to inform her of the significant risks of substantial harm.

Conclusions

The Mental Capacity Act 2005, supplemented by the Codes of Practice, has filled a vacuum in the law which had been temporarily filled by decisions made by judges. The new Court of Protection and the Office of Public Guardian provide a service that can be valuable where midwives are concerned about significant life-saving procedures being undertaken on women who appear to lack the capacity to make their own decisions. Each midwifery unit should have clear procedures for enabling decisions to be lawfully made.

Questions and exercises

1. The mental capacity of a woman to refuse life-saving treatment is central to the question of whether action can be taken in the best interests of the woman and the baby. What arrangements do you have for determining the mental capacity of a mother?
2. Do you consider there are any dangers or advantages in making birth plans legally enforceable?
3. Analyse your practice and, during a week of work, consider the different ways in which you obtain the consent of the mother to treatments proceeding. What proportion of the total number are obtained in writing?
4. A girl of 14 is pregnant and wishes to keep the child, but her mother is pressing for an abortion. What legal principles apply? (See also *Chapter 6*.)
5. A woman of 24 has profound learning disabilities. She is 6 months pregnant. Her doctor is recommending that she should have a Caesarean section and she should be sterilised at the same time. What legal issues arise and how should they be resolved?

References

Blyth v Bloomsbury Health Authority The Times, 11 February 1987; [1993] 4 Med LR 151

Caswell A (1992) Medical rape. *Medical Journal of Australia* **157**(8): 561–2

Chatterton v Gerson [1981] 1 All ER 257

Chester v Afshar The Times Law Report, 19 October 2004 HL; [2004] UKHL 41; [2004] 3 WLR 927

Chinchen v University Hospital of Wales Healthcare NHS Trust, 8 November 2001 (Current Law, 340, April 2002)

Davies C (2013) Woman with learning difficulties can decide own pregnancy fate, court rules. *The Guardian* **10 January**

Department of Health (2001a) *Good practice in consent implementation guide.* (Revised 2009). Department of Health, London

Department of Health (2001b) *Reference guide to consent for examination or treatment.*

(Revised 2009). HMSO, London. Available from: www. doh.govuk/consent

Dimond B (2009) *Legal aspects of consent* (2nd edn). Quay Books, Dinton

Freeman v Home Office [1984] 1 All ER 1036

Pearce v United Bristol Healthcare NHS Trust (1998) 48 BMLR 118 CA

Re B (Consent to treatment: Capacity) The Times Law Report 26 March 2002; [2002] 2 All ER 449.

Re C (adult: refusal of medical treatment) Family Division [1994] 1 All ER 819

Re MB (an adult: medical treatment) [1997] 2 FLR 426

Re SA a Local authority and MA and NA [2005] EWHC 2942

Re T [1992] 4 All ER 649; [1992] 3 WLR 782

Sidaway v Bethlem Royal Hospital Governors and Others [1985] 1 All ER 643

St George's Healthcare NHS Trust v S [1998] 3 All ER 673

St George's Healthcare NHS Trust v S; R v Collins ex parte S [1998] 44 BMLR 160 CA

Chapter 4

Confidentiality, access to records and freedom of information

This chapter discusses the law relating to confidentiality, access to records and the Freedom of Information Act, which enables certain information held by public authorities to be made available to the general public.

Confidentiality

One of the most important rights for patients/clients is that the confidentiality of their personal information should be respected. This is a right recognised both in statute law and by common law (the rulings of judges) and Article 8 of the Human Rights Convention (see *Chapter 2*). (For more detailed work on this topic, see Dimond, 2010.) There are, however, many exceptions to the duty of confidentiality that are recognised in law and by the codes of the professional regulatory organisations. Of the many websites relevant to this area, perhaps the most important are those of the Information Commissioner, the Department of Health and the Nursing and Midwifery Council.

The Information Commissioner (www.ico.gov.uk) is responsible for overseeing the implementation and operation of the data protection legislation and the Freedom of Information Act. Guidance on the Data Protection Act and access to records can be obtained online. In addition the Information Commissioner encourages organisations to sign up to a personal information promise that is intended to help strengthen public trust and confidence, and while it does not provide any additional legal safeguards it shows a public commitment by the organisation to comply with data protection provisions.

The Department of Health published a code of practice on confidentiality in November 2003 which is accessible on the Department of Health website (www. dh.gov.uk/publications/confidentiality).

Subsequently, in 2012 the Department of Health published a strategy relating to information, *The power of information: Putting all of us in control of the health and care information we need.* It is only accessible online on the publications section of the Department of Health website. This strategy envisages a time (2015) when a patient will be able to access her records on line. The Health and

Social Care Information Centre has the responsibility of managing safeguards to protect confidential data.

The Nursing and Midwifery Council's professional code and midwifery rules and practice give guidance to registered practitioners (www.nmc-uk.org).

Confidentiality and exception

Scenario 4.1. Possible child abuse?

Midwife Beryl Rees is concerned that Janet Bridges, who is expecting her second child, is mistreating her first child. Angie, who is 3 years old, appears to be very dirty, frightened and pasty looking. Janet said that she was hoping to have a boy as her partner was very keen to have a son and had fitted out a nursery room, with cot and decorations all in blue. Beryl is reluctant to report this to social services as she is so uncertain about the true situation. What is the law?

Scenario 4.1 is discussed on p. 68.

To answer this question access the websites, in particular the Department of Health Code of Practice on Confidentiality (www.doh.gov.uk/en/Publicationsandstatistics), and look in particular at the definition of public interest. (See, in particular, Annex B and confidentiality decisions, and Paragraphs 30–34 and model B3 for disclosure.)

Basic principles

Sources of the duty of confidentiality

The duty to respect confidentiality arises from a variety of sources that are set out in *Box 4.1*. Should the health professional be in breach of the duty of confidentiality, then the patient could bring an action in the civil courts and have the usual remedies for breach of trust.

Exceptions to the duty of confidentiality

The main exceptions to the duty of confidentiality are shown in *Box 4.2*.

Box 4.1. Sources of the obligation to respect the confidentiality of patient information

(a) Duty set out in the Nursing and Midwifery Council (2008) *Code of professional conduct: Standards for conduct, performance and ethics.*
(b) Duty in the contract of employment.
(c) Duty as part of the duty of care owed to the patient in the law of negligence.
(d) Duty set out in specific statutes, especially the Data Protection Act 1998 and Human Rights Act 1998.
(e) Duty as part of the trust obligation between health professional and patient.

Box 4.2 Exceptions to the duty of confidentiality

(a) Consent of the client.
(b) Information to the supervisor.
(c) Information given to other professionals in the interests of the client.
(d) Order from the court before or during legal proceedings.
(e) Statutory justification, e.g.
  – Notification of registration of births and stillbirths
  – Infectious Disease Regulations
  – Police and Criminal Evidence Act.
(f) Public interest.

Statutes

Data Protection Act 1998

The European Directive on Data Protection was implemented in this country by the Data Protection Act 1998. Under the legislation, members had to establish a set of principles with which users of personal information must comply. The legislation also gives individuals the right to gain access to information held about them and provides for a supervisory authority to oversee and enforce the law. NHS guidance on the Act was provided by a circular published in March 2000 (NHS Executive, 2000) and the NHS Information Authority action plan for the NHS which is available on the website of connecting for health (www.connectingforhealth.nhs.uk/). This aimed at ensuring that the processing of personal data within the organisation was in compliance with the Act. The NHS Information Authority was abolished in the Health and Social Care Act 2012 and replaced by the Health and Social Care Information Centre. Its duties (set out in Sections 252–277 of the 2012 Act) include the duty to publish a Code of Practice on confidential information (Section 263).

In 2001 an Information Commissioner was appointed to fulfil duties under both the Freedom of Information Act 2000 (see below) and the Data Protection Act 1998.

The main provisions of the Data Protection Act are shown in *Box 4.3*.

Terminology

The following are definitions of terms used in the Data Protection Act 1998.

- The "data subject" is "the individual who is the subject of personal data". Under the 1998 provisions, the law applies only to living people and if the information is anonymous, then the person will not be considered to be identifiable, unless it is possible to link together separate items of information in order to identify an individual. If that is possible, the Act would then apply.
- "Processing" under the 1998 Act includes any operation involving personal data including the holding of the information.
- The term "data user" (from the 1984 Act) is replaced by the term "controller" and is the person who determines the purposes for which and the manner in which any personal data are to be processed.
- "Computer bureaux" is replaced by "processor".
- The "Data Protection Registrar", who is the national officer responsible for the oversight of the implementation of the law, is now to be known as the Commissioner.

Data Protection Principles

The 1998 Act slightly amends the Data Protection Principles and the new wording is shown in *Box 4.4*.

Interpretation of these principles is provided in Part 2 of Schedule 1 of the 1998 Act.

Box 4.3 Data Protection Act 1998

Part 1 Preliminary: • Basic interpretative provisions. • Sensitive personal data. • The special purposes. • Data protection principles. • Application of Act. • Commissioner and Tribunal.

Part 2 Rights of data subjects and others: • Rights of access. • Rights to prevent processing likely to cause damage or distress. • Rights to prevent processing for direct marketing. • Rights in relation to automated decision-taking. • Compensation for failure to comply with certain requirements. • Rectification, blocking, erasure and destruction.

Part 3 Notification to the data controller: • Duty to notify. • Register of notifications. • Offences. • Preliminary assessment by Commissioner. • Power to make provision for appointment of data protection supervisors. • Duty of certain data controllers to make certain information available. • Functions of Commissioner in relation to making of notification regulations. • Fees regulations.

Part 4 Exemptions: • National security. • Crime and taxation. • Health, education and social work. • Regulatory activity. • Journalism, literature and art. • Research, history and statistics. • Information available to the public by or under enactment. • Disclosure required by law or made in connection with legal proceedings. • Domestic purposes. • Powers to make further exemptions by order.

Part 5 Enforcement

Part 6 Miscellaneous and general: • Functions of the Commissioner:

- Schedule 1 Data protection principles
- Schedule 2 Conditions for processing any personal data
- Schedule 3 Conditions for processing sensitive personal data
- Schedule 4 Cases where the 8th principle does not apply
- Schedule 5 Data Protection Commissioner and Data Protection Tribunal
- Schedule 6 Appeal proceedings
- Schedule 7 Miscellaneous exemptions
- Schedule 8 Transitional relief
- Schedule 9 Powers of entry and inspection
- Schedule 10 Assistance under Section 53
- Schedule 11 Educational records
- Schedule 12 Accessible public records
- Schedule 13 Modifications of Act having effect pre-24 October 2007

The Act can be accessed on www.legislation.gov.uk or www.bailii.org/

Box 4.4 Data Protection Principles 1998 Schedule 1 Part 1

1. Personal data shall be processed fairly and lawfully and, in particular, shall not be processed unless:
   (a) at least one of the conditions in Schedule 2 is met; and
   (b) in the case of sensitive personal data, at least one of the conditions in Schedule 3 is also met.
2. Personal data shall be obtained only for one or more specified and lawful purposes, and shall not be further processed in any manner incompatible with that purpose or those purposes.
3. Personal data shall be adequate, relevant and not excessive in relation to the purpose or purposes for which they are processed.
4. Personal data shall be accurate and, where necessary, kept up-to-date.
5. Personal data processed for any purpose or purposes shall not be kept for longer that is necessary for that purpose(s).
6. Personal data shall be processed in accordance with the rights of data subjects under this Act.
7. Appropriate technical and organisational measures shall be taken against unauthorised or unlawful processing of personal data and against accidental loss or destruction of, or damage to, personal data.
8. Personal data shall not be transferred to a country or territory outside the European Economic Area unless that country or territory ensures an adequate level of protection for the rights and freedoms of data subjects in relation to the processing of personal data.

Principle 1 refers to Schedule 2 conditions and these include:

- The consent of the data subject.
- The processing is necessary:
  – for the performance of a contract to which the data subject is a party,
  – for taking steps, at the request of the data subject, to enter a contract.
- The processing is necessary for compliance with a legal obligation of the data subject.
- The processing is necessary to protect the vital interests of the data subject.
- The processing is necessary
  – for the administration of justice,
  – for the exercise of functions conferred by any enactment,

- for the exercise of a function of the Crown, Minister or government department, or
- for the exercise of other functions of a public nature.
- The processing is necessary to meet the legitimate interests of the data controller or a third party.

Clearly patient records are covered by several of these conditions, only one of which is needed to legitimise the processing.

Sensitive personal data

Sensitive personal data is defined in Section 2. See *Box 4.5*.

Box 4.5. Section 2 Data Protection Act 1998

Sensitive personal data means personal data consisting of information as to:
- The racial or ethnic origin of the data subject.
- His political opinions.
- His religious beliefs or other beliefs of a similar nature.
- Whether he is a member of a Trade Union.
- His physical or mental health or condition.
- His sexual life.
- The (alleged) commission of any offence by him.
- Any proceedings for any (alleged) offence, disposal of such or sentence.

Records relating to physical or mental health come within the definition of sensitive personal data and Schedule 3, conditions for disclosure of such information, is shown in *Box 4.6*.

Box 4.6 Schedule 3 Conditions for disclosure of sensitive personal data

1   The data subject has given his explicit consent to the processing of personal data.
2   (1) The processing is necessary for the purposes of exercising or performing any right or obligation which is conferred or imposed on the data controller in connection with employment.

Box 4.6/cont

---

(2) The Secretary of State may exclude the application of sub-paragraph I in such cases as may be specified, or specify further conditions for satisfaction.

3 The processing is necessary:
- (a) to protect the vital interests of the data subject or another person, in a case where:
  - i. consent cannot be given by or on behalf of the data subject, or
  - ii. the data controller cannot reasonably be expected to obtain the consent of the data subject, or
- (b) in order to protect the vital interests of another person, in a case where consent by or on behalf of the data subject has been unreasonably withheld.

4 The processing:
- (a) is carried out in the course of its legitimate activities by any body or association which:
  - i. is not established or conducted for profit, and
  - ii. exists for political, philosophical, religious or trade union purposes,
- (b) is carried out with appropriate safeguards for the rights and freedoms of the data subject,
- (c) relates only to individuals who either are members of the body or association or have regular contact with it in connection with its purposes, and
- (d) does not involve disclosure of the personal data to a third party without the consent of the data subject.

5 The information contained in the personal data has been made public as a result of steps deliberately taken by the data subject.

6 The processing:
- (a) is necessary for the purpose of, or in connection with, any legal proceedings (including prospective legal proceedings),
- (b) is necessary for the purpose of obtaining legal advice, or
- (c) is otherwise necessary for the purposes of establishing, exercising or defending legal rights.

7(1) The processing is necessary:
- (a) for the administration of justice,
- (b) for the exercise of any functions conferred on any person by or under an enactment, or
- (c) for the exercise of any functions of the Crown, Minister of the Crown or a government department.

Box 4.6/cont

7(2) The Secretary of State may by order:
- (a) exclude the application of sub-paragraph (1) in such cases as may be specified, or
- (b) provide that, in such cases as may be specified, the condition in sub-paragraph (1) is not to be regarded as satisfied unless such further conditions as may be specified in the order are also satisfied.

8(1) The processing is for medical purposes and is undertaken by:
- (a) a health professional, or
- (b) a person who in the circumstances owes a duty of confidentiality which is equivalent to that which would arise if that person were a health professional.

8(2) In this paragraph, "medical purposes" includes the purposes of preventative medicine, medical diagnosis, medical research, the provision of care and treatment and the management of healthcare services.

9(1) The processing:
- (a) is of sensitive personal data consisting of information as to racial or ethnic origin,
- (b) is necessary for the purpose of identifying or keeping under review the existence or absence of equality of opportunity or treatment between persons of different racial or ethnic origins, with a view to enabling such equality to be promoted or maintained, and
- (c) is carried out with appropriate safeguards for the rights and freedoms of data subjects.

9(2) The Secretary of State may by order specify circumstances in which processing falling within subparagraphs (1)(a) and (b) is, or is not, to be taken for the purposes of sub-paragraph (1)(c) to be carried out with appropriate safeguards for the rights and freedoms of data subjects.

10. The personal data are processed in circumstances specified in an order made by the Secretary of State for the purposes of this paragraph.

Consent

Schedule 2 requires the consent of the data subject or one of the other conditions to be satisfied for processing to be carried on.

Schedule 3 requires the explicit consent of the data subject and the fact that processing is necessary to protect the data subject's vital interests, where consent cannot be given by or on behalf of the data subject, or the data controller cannot be reasonably expected to obtain the consent of the data subject. This latter situation would obviously cover records relating to the mentally incapacitated adult and children. Another condition of Schedule 3 is that the processing is necessary for medical purposes (defined as including the purposes of preventative medicine, medical diagnosis, medical research, the provision of care and treatment and the management of healthcare services) and is undertaken by a health professional or a person who owes a duty of confidentiality that is equivalent to that which would arise if that person were a health professional. Satisfaction of this condition would obviate the need to obtain the explicit consent of every patient, in order for their health records to be processed.

Rights of the data subject

The rights of the individual under the Data Protection Act 1998 are shown in *Box 4.7*

Box 4.7. Rights of the data subject under the 1998 Act

1. Right of subject access (Sections 7–9).
2. Right to prevent processing likely to cause damage or distress (Section 10).
3. Right to prevent processing for the purposes of direct marketing (Section 11).
4. Right in relation to automated decision-taking (Section 12).
5. Right to take action for compensation if the individual suffers damage by any contravention of the Act by the data controller (Section 13).
6. Right to take action to rectify, block, erase or destroy inaccurate data (Section 14).
7. Right to make a request to the Commissioner for an assessment to be made as to whether any provision of the Act has been contravened (Section 42).

Information Commissioner

The Information Commissioner has the responsibility for, promoting good practice and observance of the laws, providing an information service, and encouraging the development of codes of practice. He has considerable powers of enforcement under Parts 3 and 5 of the Act. These include the power to serve enforcement notices and powers of entry and inspection. Information is available from the Commissioner's office (Information Commissioner, Wycliffe House, Water Lane, Wilmslow, Cheshire SK9 5AF. Information line: 0303 123 1113). An explanatory guide to the new legislation was issued in 1998 and has been updated to provide legal guidance on the Act. It is available online (www.dataprotection.gov.uk).

Box 4.8. Offences under the Data Protection Act 1998

1. Offences relating to failure to notify the Commissioner or comply with his requests.
2. Unlawfully obtaining personal data.
3. Unlawful selling of personal data.
4. Forcing a person to compel access.
5. Unlawful disclosure of information by the commissioner/staff or agent.

Offences under the Act are shown in *Box 4.8*.

Exercise

Access the Information Commissioner's Office website and look at the following cases:

- News release 30 April 2012: it is reported that a Welsh board had become the first NHS organisation to be served a monetary penalty (£70 000) following a serious breach of the Data Protection Act.
- News release 21 May 2012: the Central London Community Healthcare NHS Trust was fined £90 000.
- News release 1 June 2012: Brighton and Sussex University Hospitals NHS Trust was fined £325 000.

Look at the details of these cases. What action do you think should be taken to prevent similar breaches occurring? Further information can be found on the monetary penalty notice issued in respect of each case on the Information Commissioner's Office website.

Human rights

The Data Protection Act 1998 must, after 2 October 2000, be read in conjunction with the Human Rights Act 1998, since Article 8 of the European Convention of Human Rights, which is set out in Schedule 1 of the Act, recognises an individual's right to private and family life subject to specific qualifications. The right to respect for private life is to be balanced against Article 10 and the right to freedom of expression (see *Chapter 2*).

Regulations for the control of patient information

Sections 60 and 61 of the Health and Social Care Act 2001 enabled the Secretary of State to draw up regulations – Health Service (Control of Patient Information) Regulations 2002/1438 – for the control of patient information in the interests of improving patient care or in the public interest and to establish a Patient Information Advisory Group. Powers exercised under this Section must, of course, be compatible with the Articles of the European Convention of Human Rights. The Patient Information Advisory Group was replaced by the National Information Governance Board for Health and Social Care under Section 158 of the Health and Social Care Act 2008. The National Information Governance Board for Health and Social Care was an independent statutory body established to promote, improve and monitor information governance in health and adult social care. Under Section 251 of the NHS Act 2006 there are powers to permit the duty of confidentiality to be set aside. It has provided guidance on:

- The access to health records by diagnostic staff (published May 2011).
- NHS Care Record Guarantee (published January 2011).
- Requesting Amendments to Health and Social Care Records (January 2010).
- Social Care Record Guarantee (published October 2009).

Further information and answers to frequently asked questions can be accessed on the website of the Health and Social Care Information Centre which has replaced the National Information Governance Board for Health and Social Care (www.hscic.co.uk). Under Section 280 of the Health and Social Care Act 2012, the National Information Governance Board for Health and Social Care is abolished and absorbed within the Health and Social Care Information Centre (formerly the NHS Information Centre). This provision was brought into force on 1 April 2013 when the Health and Social Care Information Centre was dissolved as a special health authority and created as a new Executive Non-Departmental Public Body (www.ic.nhs.uk). The existing functions of the Health and Social Care Information Centre continued in the new body. The Secretary of State and the NHS Commissioning Board can direct the new Information Centre to carry out informatics functions on their behalf. The annual report 2011/12 of the Information Centre is available on the official documents website (www.official-documents.gov.uk/documents/hc1213/) or from the Information Centre website (www.hscic.co.uk/).

> **Box 4.9. Sections 250–277 of Health and Social Care Act 2012**
>
> Part 9 Health and Adult Social Care Services: Information
>   Section 250 Powers to publish information standards
>   Section 251 Information standards: supplementary
> The Health and Social Care Information Centre
>   Section 253 General duties
>   Section 254–265 Functions: information systems
>   Section 266–267 Functions: quality of health and social care information
>   Section 268–273 Other functions
>   Section 274–277 General and supplementary

The provisions of the 2012 Act relating to information are shown in *Box 4.9.* The Act can be accessed on the legislation website.

Application to midwifery: Disclosure to the supervisor

Midwives are the only professionals who are required by statute to have a supervisor. The relationship between supervisor and midwife should be a close one with the midwife informing the supervisor immediately she is concerned about the care of the mother. If the mother gives confidential information to the midwife, it should be made clear to the mother that the midwife must inform her supervisor of any relevant information likely to affect her practice and the safety of the mother, and advise the mother that this disclosure would be made. Under Rule 9(c) of the Rules and Standards (Nursing and Midwifery Council, 2012) which came into force on 1 January 2013, all supervisors of midwives within its area (are required to) maintain records of their supervisory activities, including any meeting with a midwife; and under Rule 9(d) all practising midwives within its area have 24-hour access to a supervisor of midwives whether that is the midwife's named supervisor or another supervisor of midwives.

The NMC advice clearly envisages the discussion of individual cases between midwife and supervisor, and it would be a defence against any allegation of breach of client confidentiality. The supervisor of midwives would clearly be bound to respect the duty of confidentiality in respect of information that she learnt from the midwife, unless one of the recognised lawful exceptions discussed here existed.

Scenario 4.1. Possible child abuse: Discussion

The midwife Beryl Rees has a duty of confidentiality to the mother and family. However, one of the exceptions to this duty would be if she feared for the welfare of the child. She needs to have further information about the mental and physical state of the older child, but if she has reasonable doubts about the care of the child then she has a legal duty to report her concerns according to the local procedure.

If any reasonable midwife would have acted in that way, then she is protected in law should it eventually be established that the mother is caring for her child appropriately. If on the other hand it is eventually found that Beryl's fears were justified, then the social services may also need to consider the eventual care of the unborn child once born.

Access to records and exceptions

Client access to records and Human Rights Articles

Article 8 of the European Convention gives a right to respect for private life and this has been held to include access to personal records. Thus, in the case of *Gaskin v UK,* the applicant sought documents from his local authority relating to the period of time when he was in care. The court recognised the need to balance the applicant's interest in obtaining information about his childhood against the importance of confidentiality of public records and held that an independent authority should have decided whether access should be granted.

Data Protection Act

The provisions for access to records are now covered by the Data Protection Act 1998, except for access to the records of those who have died, where the Access to Health Records Act 1990 still applies.

Statutory entitlement by the patient to access health records is given by the statutory instrument enacted under Data Protection legislation. Access is also permitted to medical reports obtained for employment or insurance purposes under the Access to Medical Reports Act 1988. The provisions of the Data Protection Act 1998 apply to both computerised and manually-held records.

Right of access to personal data

Section 7 of the Data Protection Act 1998 enables an individual to be informed of data held about him and to access that data. Special provisions exist in relation to health, education and social work.

Health education and social work

Section 30 of the Data Protection Act enables the Secretary of State to draw up specific provisions setting exemptions from the statutory rights of access in relation to health, education and social work records. Statutory Instruments have been enacted setting out details of the restrictions on access to these records: Data Protection (Subject Access Modification)(Health) Order 2000 SI 2000 No 413; Data Protection (Subject Access Modification)(Education) Order 2000 SI 2000 No 414; Data Protection (Subject Access Modification)(Social Work) Order 2000 SI 2000 No 415.

Right to withhold access

Access can be withheld under the Data Protection Act 1998 in the following circumstances:

- Where, in the opinion of the holder of the record, serious harm would be caused to the mental or physical health or condition of the applicant or of any other individual.
- Where the identity of a third person would be made known and this person has not consented to access. (This does not apply where the other person is the health professional caring for the patient.)
- Where the reports are confidential under a statutory provision, such as information supplied in a report or other evidence given to the court by a local authority, Health or Social Services Board, Health and Social Services Trust or probation officer.

The Department of Health established a Health Records and Data Protection Review Group in May 2002 to advise the Government on helping people to gain access to their health records. The minutes of its meetings are available online via the Department of Health website which also provides the answers to frequently asked questions about accessing health records (www.dh.gov.uk).

Patient-held records: Voluntary system

Before any statutory provisions for access were in place many midwives and obstetric units permitted wide access to records, with many mothers being responsible for their antenatal records. The legislation does not replace this system, and open access can be permitted on a much wider basis than is required statutorily.

Many midwifery units are now permitting mothers to hold their own records. Certainly during the antenatal stage, excellent results have been obtained by entrusting the records to the care of the patient. It has been found that patients are less likely to lose the records than a medical records department. *Changing Childbirth* (Department of Health, 1993) set as one of the targets that all clients should hold their records (see *Chapter 2, Box 2.2*). One of the indicators of success identified in *Changing Childbirth* was that within five years all women should be able to carry their own notes. Antenatal records were often the earliest to be disclosed to or even kept by patients, and in general midwives are able to have a more open policy of disclosure to mothers and do not require formal applications to be made under the Data Protection Act 1998 before access will be permitted.

Exercise

You have been involved in a very difficult labour where the woman had requested a Caesarean but her obstetrician had refused. Although a healthy baby was delivered you have heard that the mother has made a complaint and has asked to see all the midwifery and obstetric records relating to the birth. Can she insist on having copies and can any information be withheld and if so on what grounds?

The fact that the woman wishes to make a complaint, or, since she has had a healthy baby, would apparently seem to have no cause for concern, is no justification for refusing her access to her personal records. She should ensure that she complies with the appropriate procedure that the hospital should give her. They may withhold access for one of the statutory reasons set out above, but would have to justify their refusal which could be challenged. The right of the woman to have a Caesarean is considered in *Chapter 2*.

Access to the records of a child

Where the patient is a child, an application for access can be made by a person having parental responsibility for the patient. However, access can be permitted if the holder of the record is satisfied either

- that the patient has consented (this would not be possible in the case of a very young child), or
- that the patient is incapable of understanding the nature of the application and the giving of access would be in his best interests.

In addition, partial access must be refused by the holder to any part of the record which, in the opinion of the holder of the record, would disclose

- information provided by the patient in the expectation that it would not be disclosed to the applicant, or
- information obtained as a result of any examination or investigation to which the patient consented in the expectation that the information would not be so disclosed. (Section 5(3).)

Freedom of information

The Freedom of Information Act 2000 was brought into force over a period of five years. It gives a right to people to obtain information from public authorities. An Information Commissioner (combining both Data Protection and Freedom of Information statutory duties) has been appointed and an Information Tribunal adjudicates on grievances under the Act. Part 2 of the Act lists many areas of information that are exempt from the access provisions. Under Section 40, access to personal information will come under the Data Protection Act 1998. The Act gives a general right of access to information held by public authorities, but this right is subject to significant exceptions. The main exemptions from the duty are set out in Part 2 of the Act.

Some of the exemptions are subject to a public interest test and these include: information intended for future publication, national security, defence, international relations, relations within the UK, the economy, investigations and proceedings conducted by public authorities, law enforcement, audit functions, formulation of government policy, prejudice to effective conduct of public affairs, communication with Her Majesty, etc., and honours, health and safety, environmental information, personal information, legal professional privilege, and commercial interests. The public interest test means that a public authority must consider whether the public interest in withholding the exempt information outweighs the public interest in releasing it.

Other exemptions are absolute. These include: information accessible to the applicant by other means, information supplied by or relating to bodies dealing with security matters, court records, Parliamentary privilege, prejudice to effective conduct of public affairs, and personal information where the applicant is the subject of the information. This means that for information coming under this category a public interest does not apply and the information does not have to be disclosed.

Another exception to disclosure is contained in Section 14 where a request, which is vexatious or where the public authority has already complied with the request, does not have to be complied with.

Exercise

Access the Information Commissioner's website and study some of the cases which have been heard relating to the access of public information under the Freedom of Information Act and the extent to which disclosure is prevented by the Act.

Conclusions

Making the Information Commissioner responsible for the implementation and enforcement of both Data Protection and Freedom of Information legislation has ensured that there is consistency and a vigorous approach to protecting personal confidentiality, but at the same time supporting the public right to access information held by public bodies. The Health and Social Care Act 2012 consolidates provisions in relation to the holding of health and social care information. At the time of writing it remains to be seen how effective the NHS Commissioning Board and the Health and Social Care Information Centre are in protecting the right to confidentiality of the individual patient and at the same time ensuring that health and social care information is used effectively and efficiently across the sector. Recognition of the duty to maintain confidentiality is at the heart of the professional practice of a midwife who must ensure that in these days of social networking she does not blur the distinction between professional duties and personal gossiping.

Questions and exercises

1. What measures do you think could be taken to ensure higher standards of confidentiality in midwifery units?
2. Disclosure in the public interest causes considerable difficulty. In the light of the Nursing and Midwifery Council guidance on confidentiality, draw up a protocol to be followed if disclosure in the public interest appears to be justified.
3. There is no absolute right of access by the patient to her records. In what circumstances, if any, do you consider that the right of the client to access should be withheld?
4. Consider the provisions of the Freedom of Information Act and decide how it could work for the benefit of pregnant women.

References

Department of Health (1993) *Changing childbirth (Cumberlege Report)*. HMSO, London

Department of Health (2012) *The power of information: Putting all of us in control of the health and care information we need*. Available from: www.dh.gov.uk/publications

Dimond B (2010) *Legal aspects of confidentiality* (2nd edn). Quay Books, London

Gaskin v UK (1990) 12 EHRR 36

NHS Executive (2000) *Data Protection Act 1998*. HSC 2000/009

Nursing and Midwifery Council (2008) *Code of professional conduct: Standards for conduct, performance and ethics*. NMC, London

Chapter 5

Complaints

Scenario 5.1. Failing to recognise the wishes of the client

Maggie was expecting her second child and wanted to have a home birth. However, the maternity unit, managed by midwives, was very short of staff and she was advised that it would be safer if she came into the unit. Maggie was very unhappy with that suggestion but seemed to have no alternative but to accept it. Eventually the baby was born safely, but she was left on her own for long periods, her husband was refused admission outside visiting hours and her older child was not permitted to visit. Maggie felt that had she had the home birth she wanted, she would not have had these complaints. She spoke to a midwife, Jean who promised to pass on her complaint. Three weeks later she has had no response.
What action should she take?

Scenario 5.1. is discussed on p. 87.

Introduction

Establishing an effective and efficient system for the handling of complaints relating to health and social care has proved a challenging task. A statutory duty for all hospitals to have a complaints procedure was set up under the Hospital Complaints Procedure Act 1985 and the Secretary of State requested that this duty should be recognised also by NHS community health organisations. The duty was reinforced by the Patient's Charter, which expected all patients to have the opportunity to make known any concerns to the management. However, the deficiencies of the 1985 procedure were clearly set out in the Department of Health's Wilson Report which published a consultation paper in 1994. In 1996 new instructions were issued by the Department of Health on the handling of complaints (NHS Executive, 1996). The NHS Plan (Department of Health, 2000a) also introduced new forms for participation and representation.

The new National Health Service (Complaints) Regulations came into force on 30 July 2004. The Health Service Ombudsman (2005) published a withering attack on the complaints system set up under the 2004 regulations, identifying five key weaknesses including fragmentation of the complaints system within the NHS and between public and private healthcare systems, and inadequate investigation by incompetent staff. The 2004 regulations were replaced in 2009 by new regulations: Local Authority Social Services and National Health Service Complaints (England) Regulations 2009. These can be accessed on the legislation website (www.legislation.gov.uk/).

Arrangements for the handling and consideration of complaints

Each responsible body (defined as a local authority, NHS body, primary care provider and independent provider, i.e. all health and social care providers are covered) must ensure that arrangements are made to handle complaints:

- Complaints must be handled efficiently, properly investigated, and complainants treated with respect and courtesy.
- Complainants must receive, so far as is reasonably practicable, assistance to enable them to understand the procedure or advice on where they may obtain such assistance.
- The complainants must receive a timely and appropriate response; they must be told the outcome of the investigation.
- Action must be taken if necessary in the light of the outcome of the complaint.

Responsibility for complaints arrangements

Each responsible body must designate a person (known as the responsible person) to be responsible for ensuring compliance with the arrangements made under these regulations, and in particular in ensuring that action is taken if necessary in the light of the outcome of a complaint. The responsible person will normally be the chief executive of the organisation.

A person (known as the complaints manager) must also be designated to be responsible for managing the procedure for handling and considering complaints in accordance with the arrangements made under these regulations. The complaints manager may be a person who is not an employee of the responsible body. He/she may also be the same person as the responsible person and may also be a complaints manager designated by another responsible body.

Persons who may make complaints

A complaint may be made by a person who receives or has received the services from a responsible body or a person who is affected, or is likely to be affected, by the action, omission or decision of the responsible body which is the subject of the complaint.

A person may act on behalf of a person who has died, is a child or is unable to make the complaint himself because of physical incapacity or lack of capacity within the meaning of the Mental Capacity Act 2005. Where the complaint is made on behalf of a child, the responsible body must be satisfied that there are reasonable grounds for the complaint being made by the representative instead of the child. Where the complaint relates to a child or person lacking capacity within the meaning of the Mental Capacity Act 2005 and the responsible body is satisfied that the representative is not conducting the complaint in the best interests of the child or mentally incapable person, the complaint must not be (further) considered under the regulations and the representative must be informed in writing.

Duty to handle complaints

Complaints after 1 April 2009 can be made relating to the statutory duties of the local authority or NHS body and where it appears they relate to a second body, then the initial recipient of the complaint can send the complaint to that body.

Complaints about the provision of health services

Where the clinical commissioning group considers the complaint to relate to services by a provider, it can, with the consent of the complainant, ask the provider to handle the complaint. The provider then has the statutory responsibility to handle the complaint.

Complaints not required to be dealt with

Box 5.1 lists the complaints that are excluded from the 2009 regulations.

Box 5.1. Complaints excluded from the 2009 regulations

(a) A complaint by a responsible body.

(b) A complaint by an employee.

(c) An oral complaint that is resolved to the complainant's satisfaction not later than the next working day after the day on which the complaint was made.

Box 5.1/cont

(d) A complaint that is of the same subject matter as a complaint which comes under (c) above.

(e) A complaint previously investigated under these regulations or the 2004 regulations, or the 2006 regulations or a relevant complaints procedure pre 1 April 2009.

(f) A complaint the subject matter of which is being or has been investigated under a Local Commissioner under the Local Government Act 1974 or a Health Service Commissioner under the 1993 Act.

(g) A complaint relating to the alleged failure of a responsible body to comply with a Freedom of Information request.

(h) A complaint relating to a superannuation scheme.

Duty to cooperate

Where a complaint relates to a second body then the first and second body must cooperate for the purpose of coordinating the handling of the complaint and ensuring that the complainant receives a coordinated response to the complaint. The duty to cooperate includes agreeing on coordinating handling, communicating with the complainant, the provision of relevant information, and attending any meeting reasonably required.

Care standards complaints

Where the complaint relates to care standards the local authority must ask for the complainant's consent to send the complaint to a registered person.

Social care provider complaints

The local authority must obtain the consent of the complainant for details of the complaint to be sent to the relevant adult social care provider.

Time limit for making a complaint

A complaint must be made not later than 12 months after (a) the date on which the matter which is the subject of the complaint occurred, or (b) if later, the date on which the matter which is the subject of the complaint came to the notice of the complainant.

This time limit does not apply if the responsible body is satisfied that the complainant had good reasons for not making the complaint within the time limit and, notwithstanding the delay, it is still possible to investigate the complaint effectively and fairly.

Procedure before investigation

A complaint may be made orally, in writing or electronically. An oral complaint may be dealt with immediately to the complainant's satisfaction and will then come under complaints not required to be dealt with (see above). Otherwise the oral complaint must be put in writing by the responsible body with a copy of this written record going to the complainant. A complaint must be acknowledged not later than three working days after the day on which it receives the complaint. The acknowledgement may be made orally or in writing. At the time of acknowledgement the responsible body must offer to discuss with the complainant, at a time to be agreed with the complainant, the manner in which the complaint is to be handled, and the response period, i.e. the period within which the investigation of the complaint is likely to be completed and the response under the Regulations is likely to be sent to the complainant. If the complainant does not accept the offer of a discussion then the responsible body must determine the response period and notify the complainant in writing.

Investigation and response

The responsible body must investigate the complaint in a manner appropriate to resolve it speedily and efficiently, and, during the investigation, keep the complainant informed, as far as is reasonably practicable, as to the progress of the investigation.

As soon as is reasonably practicable after completing the investigation the responsible body must send the complainant in writing a response signed by the responsible person, which includes a report containing an explanation of how the complaint has been considered and the conclusion reached in relation to the complaint and any remedial action which has been or is to be taken. Details of the complainant's right to refer the matter to either the Local Commission or Health Service Commissioner as relevant.

The response must be sent within six months. If not, the responsible body must notify the reason why not and send the response as soon as reasonably practicable after the six-month period.

Form of communications

Any communication may be sent electronically where the complainant has agreed in writing or electronically.

Publicity

Each responsible body is required to make information available to the public as to the arrangements for dealing with complaints and how further information about those arrangements may be obtained.

Monitoring

Each responsible body must maintain a record of each complaint received; the subject matter and outcome of each complaint; and, where the responsible body informed the complainant of the response period or an amendment to that period, whether a report of the outcome of the investigation was sent to the complainant within that period or any amended period.

Annual reports

Each responsible body must prepare an annual report for each year specifying the number of complaints received; the number it decided were well-founded; and the number of complaints that have been referred to the Local Commissioner or Health Service Commissioner. The report must also summarise the subject matter of complaints, any matters of general importance arising out of those complaints or the way they were handled, and any matters where action has been taken to improve services as a consequence of those complaints. The annual report must be made available to any person on request.

The Health and Social Care Information Centre provides an annual report on the written complaints made by or on behalf of patients. NHS trusts have a statutory duty to submit data about the number of written complaints received. (2011–12 was the first year that NHS Foundation Trusts had this duty.) The figures and report can be accessed on the Information Centre website (www.ic.nhs.uk/statistics-and-data-collection). Additional information is available on the Citizens Advice Bureau advice website (www.adviceguide.org.uk/england/healthcare).

The Department of Health (2010) has issued clarification on the 2009 regulations. It states that where a complaint is made to a Patient Advice and

Liaison Service (see below) it must be appropriately recorded and the 2009 regulations apply. Other guidance relates to a situation where "legal action is being taken or where the police are involved. In such situations discussions should take place between the various parties to determine whether progressing the complaint might prejudice subsequent legal or judicial action. If so the complaint will be put on hold and the complainant advised of this fact".

Ways of making a complaint

At present there are many ways in which complaints can be made, as shown in *Box 5.2*.

Box 5.2. Methods of making complaints

- NHS trust or clinical commissioning bodies.
- Local authorities as the commissioners for community social services and residential accommodation or care trusts where these have been established.
- Professional registration bodies in respect of the conduct of individual practitioners.
- Care Quality Commission.
- The Health Service Commissioner as the final stage in the NHS complaints procedure.
- The Local Authority Ombudsman where the complaints relate to local authority services.
- Litigation via solicitors.
- Complaints via the Patient Representation organisations (see below) or Community Health Councils (in Wales).
- Police.
- Members of Parliament, the media, etc.

Each of the organisations/persons listed in *Box 5.2* should ensure that the responsible body has an opportunity to investigate the complaint if this has not yet occurred.

Midwives are increasingly likely to be involved in the hearing of a complaint, either in relation to their own practice or in being asked to give evidence about the practice of colleagues. Complaints may also be made about administrative procedures, property and other topics not directly the concern of the midwife.

The midwife should, difficult though it may be, welcome complaints and regard them as an opportunity to monitor and improve the service to mothers. One of the advantages of the named midwife scheme is that some of the concerns and worries of mothers can be made known to the midwife and therefore addressed at an early stage informally so that they do not eventually become the subject of a formal complaint. However, for this to be so, the midwife must respond positively to the mother, making it easy for her to express her concerns and be vigilant in following up the anxieties. An oral complaint must be satisfactorily resolved before the next working day after the day on which the complaint was made, otherwise it must be dealt with as a formal complaint.

Informal complaints

It is recommended that where concerns are expressed to the midwife, she should keep a brief note of the details shown in *Box 5.3*. Under the 2009 regulations an oral complaint which is resolved to the complainant's satisfaction not later than the next working day after the day on which the complaint was made is excluded from the formal complaints procedure. However, if it is not resolved within that time limit it then comes under the formal procedure. A note should also be made in the mother's records.

Where the midwife has had to refer the issue to a senior manager or other professional, she should follow it up to ensure that action is taken where necessary. Her regular contact with the mother should also ensure that she discovers if the concerns are now allayed.

Box 5.3. Recording informal complaints/concerns

- Date and time.
- Mother/client.
- Brief description of concern.
- Action taken by midwife.

Formal complaints

The midwife should always make it clear to the client that it is always open to the client to make a formal complaint. She must ensure that she knows the procedure and who is the designated Complaints Officer for the unit/hospital.

Where necessary she should offer assistance to the complainant, particularly if the complainant has difficulty in expressing herself in writing. It should be made clear however that there is no requirement for the complaint to be put in writing by the complainant personally, and that someone else could do that on her behalf. Alternatively, it could be dealt with by making an oral complaint, but if not resolved within the time limit, it must then be considered as a formal complaint.

Health Service Commissioner

The Health Service Commissioner, otherwise known as the Health Service Ombudsman, was established in 1973 under the NHS Reorganisation Act 1973. The statutory basis of the Ombudsman's powers is the Health Service Commissioner's Act 1993 (as amended). From the 1st April 1996 the jurisdiction of the Health Service Commissioner was widened to include the investigation of matters concerned with the exercise of clinical judgement and the investigations of complaints about family practitioner services.

The Health Service Commissioner has a duty to prepare a report which is submitted to Parliament, under Section 14(4) of the Health Service Commissioners Act 1993. The Select Committee of the House of Commons has the power to investigate further any complaint reported by the Commissioner, if necessary summoning witnesses to London for questioning. The Commissioner is completely independent of the NHS and the Government and has the jurisdiction to investigate complaints against any part of the NHS about:

- a failure in service, or
- a failure to purchase or provide a service one is entitled to receive, or
- maladministration (administrative affairs).

The Health Service Commissioner has retained its role as the ultimate forum of appeal in relation to complaints within the NHS.

Further information about the Health Service Commissioner can be found on its website (www.ombudsman.org.uk/about-us/our-role/).

NHS Plan

Chapter 10 of the NHS Plan (Department of Health, 2000a) envisaged giving patients more say in their own treatment and more influence over the way the

NHS works. To achieve this, many initiatives were planned, including giving greater information to empower patients; giving greater patient choice; setting up patient advocates and advisers in every hospital; providing redress over cancelled operations; establishing patients' forums and citizens' panels in every area; setting up a new national panel to advise on major reorganisations of hospitals; and providing stronger regulation of professional standards. Most of these initiatives led to the creation of new public bodies, many of which have subsequently been abolished and replaced by other organisations.

Greater information to empower patients has been provided through the publication of patient-friendly versions of National Institute for Health and Clinical Excellence (NICE) guidelines, the establishment of NHS Direct online, digital TV, and NHS Direct Information points in key public places. Better communication between clinicians and doctors has been assisted by letters between clinicians about an individual patient being copied to the patient as of right and by smart cards for patients, allowing easier access to health records. (See *Chapter 9* on electronic patient records.)

Greater patient choice of GP has been facilitated by the provision of more information being provided to patients about GP practices in their area. The Department of Health intention that by 2005 patients would be able to book hospital appointments at times convenient to them has not been achieved universally.

Patient Advocacy and Liaison Service (PALS)

An NHS-wide Patient Advocacy and Liaison Service (PALS) has been set up in every trust. Patient advocates act as independent facilitators to handle patient and family concerns. A patient advocacy team, usually situated in the main reception areas of hospitals, acts as a welcoming point for patients and carers and a clearly identifiable information point. Patient advocates act as an independent facilitator to handle patient and family concerns, with direct access to the chief executive and with the power to negotiate immediate solutions. They work with other organisation such as the Citizens Advice Bureau. Special provision is made in respect of patient and advocacy services for the purposes of the Mental Health Act 1983 Section 134 which concerns the withholding of correspondence. Under Mental Health (Correspondence of Patients, Patient Advocacy and Liaison Service) Regulations of 2003, correspondence with a Patient Advocacy and Liaison Service is exempt from the provisions of Section 134.

Independent Complaints and Advice Service (ICAS)

Under Section 12 of the Health and Social Care Act 2001, the Secretary of State has a responsibility to provide independent advocacy services to assist patients in making complaints against the NHS. The Independent Complaints and Advice Service (www.doh.gov.uk/complaints/) was available nationally from September 2003. A consultation paper, *Involving patients and the public in healthcare,* was issued by the Department of Health in September 2001 (Department of Health, 2001a) for consultation on proposals for greater public representation to replace the Community Health Councils.

The Independent Complaints and Advice Service focuses on helping individuals to pursue complaints about NHS services. It aims to ensure complainants have access to the support they need to articulate their concerns and navigate the complaints system, thereby maximising the chances of their complaint being resolved more quickly and effectively. The Service works alongside the Patient Advocacy and Liaison Service (see above). Information about the Independent Complaints and Advice Service, and the current range of pilot services, is available on the Department of Health website (www.doh.gov. uk/complaints/advocacyservice.htm). A report of the first year of the Service's activity was published by the Department of Health in January 2005.

These organisations replace Community Health Councils which were abolished in England in September 2003.

POhWER is the chosen provider of the Independent Complaints and Advice Service in three regions of England: West Midlands, London and the East of England. It is available online (www.pohwer.net/how_we_can_help/icas).

Other Service providers include SEAP (Support, Empower, Advocate, Promote) for the South East and South West of England (www.seap.org.uk) and the Carers Federation covering the North West, North East, East Midlands and Yorkshire and Humberside region (www.carersfederation.co.uk).

Patient and Public Involvement Forum and Citizens' Panel

Under Section 15 of the NHS Reform and Health Care Professions Act 2002 the Secretary of State had a duty to set up in every trust and primary care trust a body to be known as a Patient and Public Involvement Forum. The members of each Forum were appointed by the Commission for Patient and Public Involvement in Health. The statutory functions were laid down for them in Section 15(3) of the NHS Reform and Health Care Professions Act 2002 and in regulations.

Local Involvement Networks (LINKs) and national and local Healthwatch

Patient and Public Involvement Forums were abolished on 31 March 2008 as was the Commission for Patient and Public Involvement in Health, which had been established to set up and support Patient Forums. The Forums were replaced by Local Involvement Networks (LINKs). These Networks are made up of individuals and community groups working together to improve health and social services. The Networks were replaced in April 2013 by local Healthwatch bodies, with a national organisation Healthwatch England. These are discussed in *Chapter 19*.

Community Health Councils have been abolished in England. The Welsh Assembly decided in favour of the retention of Community Health Councils and details of local Councils can be found online (www.wales.nhs.uk/).

The NHS Confederation of NHS Trusts and health authorities set up NHS Voices in 2012 to provide a blog for NHS leaders. It enables people from all parts of the NHS to share ideas and debate topical issues.

Stronger regulation of professional standards

New quality standards have been introduced into the NHS. A mandatory national scheme for adverse incident reporting, known as the National Patient Safety Agency (now incorporated in the NHS Commissioning Board Special Health Authority) (see *Chapter 10*), was set up and the Chief Medical Officer's proposals for improving standards of doctors, including annual appraisal and clinical audit, have been implemented (Department of Health, 2000b). The National Clinical Assessment Authority was established with the role of reviewing an individual doctor's performance if concerns have arisen (www.ncas.nhs.uk/). On 1 April 2013 the National Clinical Assessment Authority joined the NHS Litigation Authority, leaving its previous hosts, NICE. Eventually it is intended that National Clinical Assessment Authority should be self-funding and independent of central funding. The NHS Tribunal has been abolished and new procedures introduced for the removal or suspension of doctors from practice. New regulatory machinery for registration bodies has been introduced. A Council for the Regulation of Healthcare Professions (now known as the Council for Healthcare Regulatory Excellence) was established under the NHS Reform and Health Care Professions Act 2002 and is responsible for the oversight of the workings of the regulatory bodies such as the Nursing and Midwifery Council and the General Medical Council.

Failures to deal effectively with serious complaints

It is an indictment of the NHS complaints systems that serious allegations of professional misconduct have not been handled promptly and effectively. For example, many complaints about indecent assaults by Clifford Ayling, a registrar in obstetrics and gynaecology, had been made before he was finally sentenced to four years' imprisonment. A report by an independent committee of inquiry recommended significant changes to ensure that sexualised behaviour was recognised and whistleblowers were supported (Department of Health, 2004). A similar inquiry (Ritchie, 2000) into the actions of Rodney Ledward, a gynaecologist who was struck off in 1998, showed many shortcomings in how the NHS dealt with complaints, and emphasised the importance of cultivating a climate of openness. Failures at Mid-Staffs NHS Foundation Trust to respond to grave complaints are discussed in *Chapter 19.*

Scenario 5.1. Failing to recognise the wishes of the client: Discussion

It would appear that Maggie has only made the complaint by word of mouth. However, under the 2009 regulations, if this was not resolved, not later than the next working day after the day on which the complaint was made, then the oral complaint must be put in writing by the responsible body with a copy of this written record going to the complainant. A complaint must be acknowledged not later than three working days after the day on which it was received. Clearly this has not occurred. Maggie must write to the maternity unit, explaining that she made her complaint to the midwife, and setting out the details. She should receive an acknowledgement within three days of the receipt of this letter. If, when she eventually obtains a full reply, she is not satisfied with it, she can apply to the Ombudsman for a further investigation.

The lesson for the midwife is that it cannot be assumed that a criticism voiced by a client is not intended to be treated as a complaint. The midwife should either have resolved the complaint immediately, making a record of the information listed in *Box 5.3*, or, if it was clear that this was not possible, ensured that it was put in writing and the complaints procedure followed.

Conclusions

Major innovations have been introduced into the NHS as a consequence of the Health Act 1999, the NHS Reform and Health Care Professions Act 2002, the

Health and Social Care (Community Health and Standards) Act 2003, the NHS Act 2006, the Health Act 2006 and the Health and Social Care Acts 2008 and 2012. These changes include the new complaints system discussed above. The Bristol Royal Infirmary Inquiry (Department of Health, 2001b), following the deaths of children during heart surgery, recommended that patients must be given the opportunity to pass on views on the service which they have received, and emphasised there is a duty of candour, i.e. a duty to tell a patient if adverse events have occurred, which is owed by all those working in the NHS to patients. It recommended that:

> *...complaints should be dealt with swiftly and thoroughly, keeping the patient (and carer) informed. There should be a strong independent element, not part of the trust's management or board, in any body considering serious complaints which require formal investigation. An independent advocacy service should be established to assist patients (and carers).*

The implementation of the many recommendations contained in the Inquiry Report should have had significant implications for the standards of care of every midwifery patient, including how complaints are handled. The Government published a response to the Kennedy Report which was considered by the author (Dimond, 2002). Yet, in 2011, the Health Service Ombudsman reported on failures in complaints handling and major deficiencies in communications within the NHS. Again, in February 2013, the public inquiry chaired by Robert Francis into the events at Stafford Hospital reported with significant recommendations to change the NHS culture, illustrating failures to learn the lessons from the Bristol Inquiry. The Mid-Staffs report is considered in *Chapter 19*.

Questions and exercises

1. Consider the complaints relating to midwifery services over the past year and discuss the extent to which these could be used to improve the services provided.
2. Consider the complaints procedure drafted by your employer in the light of the new Complaints Regulations and consider how this is implemented in your department.
3. To what extent, if any, do you consider that complaints relating to community services need to be handled differently from those relating to hospital services?

4. How do you ensure that your clients are encouraged to be positively involved in the provision of services and in quality assurance mechanisms?
5. How are women involved in the provision of midwifery services in your organisation?
6. Obtain a copy of the executive summary of the public inquiry into the Mid-Staffs NHS Foundation Trust (www.midstaffspublicinquiry.com). Consider its recommendations in relation to your department and hospital. Are any improvements required? (See also *Chapter 19.*)

References

Department of Health (1994) *Being heard. The report of a Review Committee chaired by Professor Wilson on NHS complaints procedures.* HMSO, London

Department of Health (2000a) *NHS Plan: A plan for investment, a plan for reform.* HMSO, London

Department of Health (2000b) *Supporting doctors, protecting patients.* HMSO, London

Department of Health (2001a) *Involving patients and the public in healthcare.* HMSO, London

Department of Health (2001b) *Learning from Bristol: The report of the public inquiry into children's heart surgery at the Bristol Royal Infirmary 1984–1995 (The Kennedy Report).* Command paper CM 5207. Available from: www.bristol-inquiry.org.uk

Department of Health (2004) *Committee of Inquiry: Independent investigation into how the NHS handled allegations about the conduct of Cliffor Ayling 2004.* Cm 6298. HMSO, London

Department of Health (2005) *Independent Complaints Advocacy Service (ICAS). The first year of ICAS. 1 September 2003–31 August 2004.* HMSO, London

Department of Health (2010) *Clarification of complaints. Regulations 2009.* HMSO, London

Dimond B (2002) After Bristol: Government support and rejection. *British Journal of Midwifery* **10**(3): 169–71

Health Service Ombudsman (2005) *Making things better? A report on reform in the NHS complaints procedure in England.* HMSO, London

Health Service Ombudsman (2011) *Listening and learning: Review of complaints handling 2010–11.* HMSO, London

NHS Executive (1996) *Guidance on the implementation of the NHS complaints procedure. EL(96)19.* Department of Health, London

Ritchie J (2000) *An inquiry into quality and practice within the NHS arising from the actions of Rodney Ledward.* HMSO, London

Chapter 6

Teenage pregnancies

Introduction

Midwives are often confronted with legal issues raised in the care of pregnant teenagers, justifying a chapter on the subject in its own right. This chapter sets out the basic principles and then looks at typical scenarios and also considers the wider cultural issue of sexual health and government strategies. The Department of Health published a guide to commissioning and delivering maternity services for young parents in 2008 and NICE published a model for service provision for pregnant women with complex social factors in 2010. Both documents are available on their respective websites.

Basic principle: Legal position of 16 and 17-year-olds

A young person of 16 or 17 has a statutory right to give consent to treatment under Section 8(1) of the Family Law Reform Act 1969. The definition of treatment under Section 8(2) is comprehensive and covers medical, surgical, and dental treatments and diagnostic and anaesthetic procedures. This would include termination of pregnancy. Under Section 8(3) the right of a parent to give consent on behalf of a young person of 16 or 17 is preserved. However, it would be unwise to rely upon parental consent if the young person was opposed to the treatment offered. If there were a dispute between parents and a young person it would be preferable to seek a declaration of the courts.

For an adult and a young person of 16 or 17 there is a presumption of capacity under the Mental Capacity Act 2005. This can be rebutted if there is evidence to the contrary. The level of capacity must relate to the nature of the decision to be made. The evidence that consent has been given could be shown by the use of Form 2 of the forms recommended by the Department of Health in its *Good practice in consent implementation guide* (Department of Health, 2001a). The youngster, as well as the parents, could sign this form.

Refusal to have treatment by a young person of 16 or 17 years

The fact that young people of 16 or 17 have a statutory right to give consent to treatment does not mean that they cannot be compelled to have treatment, or that their refusal cannot be overruled. The Court of Appeal in the case of *Re W (A Minor)(Medical Treatment: Court's Jurisdiction)* upheld the decision of the High Court judge to order a child of 16 years who was suffering from anorexia nervosa to undergo medical treatment against her will. Clearly overruling a child or young person's refusal is an extremely significant step to take and would only occur in very serious circumstances of a life-saving kind. In the case of a young person of 16 or 17, Form 1 of the forms recommended for use by the Department of Health (2001a) could be completed.

Scenario 6.1. A 16-year-old refusing life-saving treatment

Jane, aged 16 years, has become a member of a religious group which does not believe in surgical intervention. She is pregnant and has made it clear that she will refuse any surgical intervention said to be required. Late on in the pregnancy it is found that the fetus is in a transverse lie and only a Caesarean section will save the life of the child and that of Jane. Jane is adamant that she will not agree to such a procedure.

Scenario 6.1: Discussion

Many factors will influence the answer to Jane's situation. They include:

- an assessment of her competence to refuse treatment,
- her rights under the European Convention (especially Articles 3, 8, 9 and 14),
- the fact that in the UK a fetus does not have a legal personality until it is born, and
- the power of the Court to make an order declaring that action can be taken to overrule the refusal of a young person if that is in that person's best interests.

If Jane is shown to have the requisite capacity to make the decision, then her views should be upheld. Incapacity would be determined by using the tests set in the Mental Capacity Act 2005. If it is established that she lacks the requisite capacity, then action can be taken in her best interests using the stages and factors set out in the 2005 Act (see *Chapter 3*).

Either the Court of Protection or the Family Court could hear the case and determine capacity and best interests. Jane would have the right to be represented.

Basic principle: Legal position of under 16-year-olds

A mentally competent girl under 16 years, who understands the information given to her and appreciates the risks and benefits, can make treatment decisions for herself, without parental involvement. The decisions must be made in her best interests. This is the principle that was established by the House of Lords in the Gillick case (*Gillick v West Norfolk and Wisbech Area Health Authority* and *Re M [A Minor][Medical Treatment]*) from which the term "Gillick competent child" came. An alternative term is "competent according to Lord Fraser's guidelines". Lord Fraser stated that:

> *Provided the patient, whether a boy or a girl, is capable of understanding what is proposed, and of expressing his or her own wishes, I see no good reason for holding that he or she lacks the capacity to express them validly and effectively and to authorise the medical man to make the examination or give the treatment which he advises.*

Refusal by a child or young person under 16 years

The best interests of the child determine the outcome, irrespective of the capacity of the child. In the case of *Re M (A Minor)(Medical Treatment)* a girl of 15 years refused to have a heart transplant, which was essential for her survival. The parents sought an injunction from the court that the transplant operation could proceed and this was granted in the best interests of the child.

Decisions during the pregnancy and labour

If a teenager requires interventions during the pregnancy, who should give consent?

If the teenager is 16 or 17 then she has a statutory right to give consent under Section 8(1) of the Family Law Reform Act 1969 quoted above.

A teenager below 16 years can, if she is Gillick competent, give consent to treatment under the common law principles recognised by the House of Lords in the Gillick case. If, however, she is refusing necessary treatment, then her refusal can be overruled under the principle of *Re W (A minor)(medical treatment)*. This is in contrast to the legal position where a mentally competent adult refuses treatment. The law states that an adult (a person over 18 years) with the requisite mental capacity can refuse to give consent to life-saving treatment for a good reason, a bad reason, or no reason at all (*Re MB*). Parents can give consent where a daughter is refusing life-saving treatment that is in her best interests. However, it is unlikely that health professionals would rely upon parental consent to overrule a refusal by a mentally competent teenager: it would be preferable to seek a declaration from the court. In the case of Glass, the European Court of Human Rights emphasised the importance of a court hearing in a dispute over the appropriate treatment for a child (see *Chapter 12*).

Rights of under-age parents to take decisions on behalf of their children

> #### Scenario 6.2. Who makes the decisions?
>
> Grace is aged 14 years and has a child of 6 months. She has decided that she does not want her daughter to have the triple vaccine. Grace's mother disagrees with her and wants to take her grandchild to have the vaccine. Who has the right to make the decision?

Scenario 6.2: Discussion

If the mother, even though she is under 16 years, is competent to make decisions on behalf of her child, then it is her wishes that will prevail. This is subject to her acting in the best interests of her child. Step-parents and grandparents (and others such as midwives and other health professionals or teachers) who do not have parental responsibilities but have temporary care of the child can make certain decisions in the interests of the child under Section 3(5) of the Children Act 1989. This may well include giving consent to treatment in situations where those with parental responsibilities are unlikely to disagree. However, where there is clear conflict between the wishes of the mother and the grandmother, the wishes of the mother should prevail, provided that the best interests of the baby are served.

Parental responsibilities

Where parents are married, both have decision making powers in relation to the child and these continue unless the child dies or is adopted, even though the parents are divorced or separated. The unmarried father has no parental rights (even though he may be paying child maintenance) unless he has completed the appropriate forms. From December 2003 an unmarried couple have been able to register the birth together in which case they both obtain parental rights (see *Chapter 14*).

Grandparents and their rights and responsibilities

Where a teenager has a child and lacks the capacity to make her own decisions, her parents are asked to make decisions both on behalf of their daughter and also on behalf of their grandchild. Clearly any such decisions must be made in the best interests of both the young person and the child and if it was feared that this was not the case, then action should be taken under the Children Act 1989 to ensure that the best interests of both were being considered. The basic principle at the heart of the Children Act 1989 is that the welfare of the child is the paramount consideration (see *Chapter 17*). Parents have a responsibility under the Children Act 1989 to take action for the welfare of their children. They also have powers at common law, and recognised by the Family Law Reform Act 1969 Section 8(3), to give consent on behalf of their children until they become adults at 18 years (see above).

Termination of pregnancy (see *Chapter 13* for legal principles)

Consent by an under-age girl to abortion

Scenario 6.3. Under-age abortion

Avril, a girl of 14, had agreed to a termination of her pregnancy without the consent or knowledge of her parents. The termination was to be carried out in two stages. She took the required medication for the first stage and then was admitted to hospital for an estimated 12 hours for the termination to take place. At nine o'clock in the evening after she had been in hospital for six hours, she stated that she was now going home. The nurses strongly advised her to stay since she could haemorrhage which could be life threatening. Avril said that her mother was not aware that she was having a termination, that her parents were devout Roman Catholics and would turn her out if they knew about it, and it was essential that she returned home before they found out.

Scenario 6.3: Discussion

It follows from the law stated above that a competent girl of 14 years could make a decision to have a termination of pregnancy. Clearly, any counselling preceding the termination should have included information on how the termination would take place, what the procedure would be and how it would be preferable if the parents were informed. The young person's confidentiality should be respected. However, in Avril's case (*Scenario 6.3*) there are considerable dangers if she leaves hospital, unaccompanied, in the middle of the termination and her parents are ignorant of her condition. Since she is only 14 it is suggested that nursing staff would have a responsibility to ensure that steps are taken in her best interests to prevent serious harm to her, and this may mean informing the parents or ensuring that she is accompanied home.

Mother ignorant of daughter's abortion

In the highly publicised case of *R (On the application of Axon) v Secretary of State* in May 2004, a mother only discovered by chance that her 14-year-old daughter was having an abortion (*Daily Express*, 2004). She failed in her attempt to challenge the law respecting the confidentiality of the Gillick competent child. The court held that the confidentiality of the child could be protected if she was mentally competent.

Parents wishing to prevent termination proceeding

It does not follow that, because parents can give a valid consent for treatment in the best interests of their children, they have the right to forbid a termination of pregnancy taking place. In the case of *Re P (A Minor)*, a girl of 15, who had already given birth to a boy and was in the care of the local authority, became pregnant again. Her parents wished to prevent her having an abortion and refused to give consent. The girl herself wished to have an abortion and the requirements of the Abortion Act 1967 were satisfied. The judge, Mrs Justice Butler-Sloss, using the test that the welfare of the girl was of paramount importance, decided that the termination should proceed (see *Chapter 13*). Parents do not therefore have a right to stop a termination of pregnancy going ahead: as long as the provisions of the Abortion Act 1967 are satisfied and the girl has the mental competence to give a valid consent, the termination can proceed. (For the Republic of Ireland and the Savita Halappanavar case see *Chapter 7.*)

Parents giving consent on behalf of their children

Parents have a responsibility under the Children Act 1989 to take action for the welfare of their children. They also have powers at common law and recognised by the Family Law Reform Act 1969 Section 8(3) to give consent on behalf of their children until they become adults at 18 years. Parents must act in the best interests of their children and failure to care appropriately may become a criminal offence. For example, a Rastafarian couple, who had refused on religious grounds to allow their diabetic daughter who was nine years old to be given insulin, were convicted of manslaughter on 28 October 1993 in Nottingham. The father was given a sentence of imprisonment and the mother a suspended sentence (*The Times*, 2003).

Powers of parents: Overruling of girl who wants to keep child

---

Scenario 6.4. A 14-year-old refusing a termination

Tracey, aged 14 years, has been to the surgery and been diagnosed as 10 weeks pregnant and an antenatal appointment has been made for her. Tracey tells Mavis the midwife that her parents want her to have a termination,. She is totally hostile and wants to have the baby, but she is dependent upon her parents for her home and financial support. She is terrified that she will give in.
What is the law?

Scenario 6.4: Discussion

If Tracey decided to keep the baby, she would of course be dependent upon parental support. If there is evidence that there is a conflict between the young girl, who wishes to keep the baby, and the parents, who wish her to have a termination, the midwife and other health professionals should ensure that the girl's wishes are supported. Social services would be involved in the care and support of the teenager. Where the teenager decides to continue with the pregnancy, many issues arise in relation to the rights of the parents of the teenager (and future grandparents of the baby). If Tracey is Gillick competent then she can give consent both on her own account and also for the care of her child, as long as the decision is in the best interests of the child. However, Tracey is only 14 years old so she is entitled to protection under the Children Act. She will clearly be the responsibility of the social services and it may be that they will provide accommodation for her and her child. However, if her parents are willing to look after her and her baby, there would have to be an agreement between social services, the parents and Tracey as to what is in the best interests of Tracey and her baby.

Confidentiality and keeping information away from the parents

There is no doubt that, on the basis of the Gillick judgment in the House of Lords, the midwife or other health professionals who respected the confidence of the mentally competent girl and failed to tell her parents about a termination taking place would be acting within the law. A test of competence would have been applied to the ability of the girl to decide upon the termination of pregnancy and also to respecting her confidentiality and not informing the parents. If this test of competence is satisfied, then it is lawful for the termination to take place, if the statutory provisions are satisfied (see *Chapter 13*), without informing the parents. However, an exception to the duty of confidentiality recognised by the Courts (*W v Egdell 1989*) and in the Code of Practice of the Nursing and Midwifery Council (2008) is disclosure in the public interest, for example where serious harm to the physical or mental health of the patient or other persons is feared. Notifying the parents about Avril's situation (*Scenario 6.3*) may therefore be a justifiable exception to the duty of confidentiality. Clearly, such a decision must be in the best interests of Avril.

Young persons with learning disabilities

A young person with severe learning disabilities who lacked the capacity to make specific decisions would not be able to use the statutory right to make treatment decisions under Section 8 of the Family Law Reform Act 1969. The presumption of mental capacity would be rebutted under the Mental Capacity Act 2005. Decisions could still be made on the young person's behalf by the parents, in accordance with the Mental Capacity Act 2005. These decisions must be in the best interests of the young person, and an appropriate declaration could be sought from the Court of Protection, which has the power to determine mental capacity and also make decisions relating to personal welfare and financial matters. (However, in a recent case considered in *Chapter 3*, the Court of Protection has held that a mentally disabled woman had the capacity to make decisions about a termination of pregnancy, even though she was not mentally capable in other ways.)

In Scotland, the Adults with Incapacity (Scotland) Act 2000 applies. Where it is recommended that treatment should be carried out in the best interests of a mentally incapacitated adult, Form 4 in the Department of Health's *Good practice in consent. Implementation guide,* could be used as evidence of the fact that the decision was taken in the best interests of the mentally incapacitated adult, and that relatives were advised about the need for such treatment and were aware that the patient was incapable of giving consent him or herself.

Human rights

Under the Human Rights Act 1998 individuals are entitled to have their rights, as set out in the European Convention on Human Rights, to be respected by public authorities. Overriding the wishes of a 16 or 17-year-old could be seen as an infringement of their Article 3, Article 8 or Article 9 rights. These are considered in *Chapter 2*.

The British Medical Association (2011) has published guidance on the rights of the child and young person, which considers both the legal and ethical issues, and human rights dilemmas.

Even where the child and parents both agree that treatment should not be given, as in the case of a Jehovah's Witness's family, the court can order treatment to proceed if it is considered to be in the best interests of the child (case of *Re E [A Minor][Wardship: Medical Treatment]*).

National Service Framework for Children, Young People and Maternity Services

The National Service Framework (NSF) was published in September 2004. It marked the achievement of many working groups considering different aspects of child healthcare. It provided minimum standards for child healthcare across a range of specialities that can be used by health professionals and parents/young people alike. It can be accessed on the Department of Health website (www.dh.gov.uk/publications).

Standard 4 relates to growing up into adulthood and states that all young people should have access to age-appropriate services that are responsive to their specific needs as they grow into adulthood.

The following are subsections under Standard 4.

- Services implement policies and good practice guidelines on consent and confidentiality policies for young people.
- Health promotion for young people is targeted to meet their needs and, in particular, to reduce teenage pregnancy, smoking, substance misuse, sexually transmitted infections and suicide. Young people are actively involved in planning and implementing health promotion services and initiatives.
- Services support young people to achieve their full potential by providing targeted support through coordinated working, for example, Connexions and Youth Services. This includes addressing their social and emotional needs as well as assisting their educational and career development.

- There is improved access to services and advice for young people, in particular, addressing the needs of disabled young people, young people in special circumstances and those who live in rural areas.
- Transition to adult services for young people is planned and coordinated around the needs of each young person to maximise health outcomes, their life chance opportunities and their ability to live independently. This is particularly important for disabled young people or those with long-term or complex conditions.
- Additional support is available for looked after children leaving care and other young people in special circumstances.

Comment on the National Service Framework

Midwives who are involved in the care of young women should find that the Framework is of assistance in attracting resources to implement the stated standards. Strategic planning of the services for teenagers should take account of the Framework and other Department of Health guidance.

Government and other initiatives and teenage pregnancy

In November 2001 the Department of Health (2001b) announced the launch, in 2002, of a national information campaign to promote sexual health as part of its National Strategy for Sexual Health and HIV. An implementation plan for the strategy, published in June 2002 (Department of Health, 2002), set out details of how the interventions proposed would be delivered.

A cross-government unit located within the Department for Education and Skills set up a Teenage Pregnancy Unit to implement the Social Exclusion Unit's report on teenage pregnancy (Social Exclusion Unit, 1999). The Teenage Pregnancy Unit has its own website (www.info.doh.gov.uk/tpu/tpu.nsf/ vwWebHome?OpenView) which contains lists of other useful websites providing advice on sexual health and related issues for teenagers and parents. An overview of the research to support those engaged in implementing the National Teenage Pregnancy Strategy has been provided by the Health Development Agency (2004). The Royal College of Midwives, in conjunction with the Teenage Pregnancy Unit and the Department of Health, launched a guide for maternity services on teenage parents and pregnancies in 2004 which is accessible on the Royal College of Midwives website (www.rcm.org.uk).

An Independent Advisory Group on Sexual Health and HIV was established in 2003 as part of the implementation of the Action Plan for the National Strategy for Sexual Health and HIV. In 2004 this Advisory Group published its response to the Health Select Committee on Sexual Health (Independent Advisory Group on Sexual Health and HIV, 2004). It considered access to services, capacity, commissioning, prioritisation, funding, education, sexual health promotion, and the Patient Voice. It agreed with the Select Committee's conclusions on the six key factors that were the principal causes of the current situation, including failures by local NHS organisations to recognise and deal with this major public health programme, a lack of political pressure and leadership, the absence of a patient voice, and lack of resources and central direction. It believed that sexual health and HIV must be explicitly prioritised at both a local and national level.

The Maternity Alliance produced an updated version of its leaflet, *Money for teenage parents 2004, your benefits and entitlements,* which is available on its website (www.maternityalliance.org.uk). This covered recent changes in benefits which affect young parents, including the Education Maintenance Allowance.

A guide, issued in 2008 by the Department for Education and Department of Health, *Getting maternity services right for pregnant teenagers and young fathers,* gives practical pointers on commissioning and delivery of maternity services for young parents.

In 2010 the Teenage Pregnancy Independent Advisory Group Final Report was published. For 10 years the Teenage Pregnancy Independent Advisory Group had advised ministers and monitored the Teenage Pregnancy Strategy. The report concluded that there had been significant progress in reducing teenage pregnancy but there had also been missed opportunities and disappointments. It set out the positive developments and also the immediate challenges. These included: public spending cuts and the need for cost-effective contraception, improving sexual relationship education, and improving support for young mothers and fathers. The report also made significant recommendations for both national and local initiatives. The report can be downloaded from the Department for Education website (www.education.gov.uk/publications/).

In 2013, *The Times* (Bennett, 2013) reported that teenage pregnancies for 2011 were at their lowest since 1969, possibly showing the effectiveness of the work of the Teenage Pregnancy Independent Advisory Group and reflecting greater access to contraception and the availability of the morning after pill.

Further information on publications can be obtained on the Department for Education website (www.education.gov.uk/childrenandyoung persons).

Sexual offences

The Sexual Offences Act 2003 (see *Chapter 17*) creates offences under Sections 30–33 designed to give protection to persons with a mental disorder that impedes choice. Therefore, even though a young person is over 13 years and does not come under those offences that rule out the consent of a child under 13 as a defence, the young person may still be a victim of a criminal offence. Sections 34–37 create offences in relation to providing inducements to persons with a mental disorder to engage in sexual activity, and Sections 38–43 create offences in relation to care workers and sexual activity with a person with a mental disorder. The Act can be accessed on the legislation website (www.legislation.gov.uk). In 2002, the Home Office issued a paper explaining the purpose of the 2003 Act.

Social services and the police and the child under 13 years

The Social Services Authority has statutory duties under the Children Act 1989 to act in the protection of children. If there is any concern about the welfare of a child and the need to refer a child to court, then social services must be informed. The Sexual Offences Act 2003 creates new offences in relation to sexual contact with under 13-year-olds with the express provision that the consent of a child under 13 years is no defence. This raises major issues of public policy for those providing contraceptives to girls below 13 years. (Refer also to *Chapter 17* on child protection.)

Conclusions

It could be said that there are ambiguities in our present laws: parents who fail to ensure that their under-age child does not attend school could be imprisoned for the truancy of their child, yet those same parents could be kept in ignorance that the child was attending an abortion clinic. Clearly any person counselling a teenager before an abortion would strongly recommend that the girl tells her parents, but if the girl is adamant that she wishes her confidentiality to be respected, and she appears to have the necessary competence, it would be a breach of confidentiality to contact the parents contrary to her wishes. Only if there were serious child protection issues arising or serious harm were feared to the mental or physical health of the girl would a breach of confidentiality be justified. Teenage pregnancies place greater demands upon midwives, for which they require support and training (Shakespeare, 2004). Midwives should also be aware of the possibility of teenagers sharing prescription medication (Daniel et al, 2003).

Midwives should also be concerned that the recommendations in the Final Report of the Teenage Pregnancy Independent Advisory Group are implemented, otherwise there is a danger that some of the progress achieved in the last 10 years will be lost.

Questions and exercises

1. What specific provisions does your unit make for under-age pregnancies? To what extent do you consider them effective and satisfactory?
2. A pregnant girl of 14 years is assigned to you. What additional services would you provide?
3. A girl aged 17 years with learning disabilities is about eight weeks pregnant and her parents wish a termination and sterilisation to take place. What is the law?
4. In what circumstances would the grandparents' views prevail over the wishes of the under-age mother in relation to the child?

References

Bennett R (2013) Teenage pregnancies at new low. *The Times* **27 February**

British Medical Association (2001) *Consent, rights and choices in health care for children and young people.* BMJ Books, London

Daniel KL, Honein MA, Moore CA (2003) Sharing prescription medication among teenage girls: Potential danger to unplanned/undiagnosed pregnancies. *Pediatrics* **111**(2): 1167–70

Department for Education and Department of Health (2008) *Getting maternity services right for pregnant teenagers and young fathers.* HMSO, London

Department for Education, Department of Health and Royal College of Midwives (2008) *Teenage parents: Who cares? A guide to commissioning and delivering maternity services for young persons* (2nd edn). HMSO, London

Department of Health (2001a) *Good practice in consent implementation guide: Consent to examination or treatment.* HMSO, London

Department of Health (2001b) *Press release 2001/0579 29.* HMSO, London

Department of Health (2002) *National strategy for sexual health and HIV implementation action plan.* HMSO, London

Department of Health (2010) *Teenage pregnancy strategy: Beyond 2010.* Department of Health, London

Gillick v West Norfolk and Wisbech Area Health Authority [1986] 1 A.C. 112.

Glass v United Kingdom The Times Law Report 11 March 2004 ECHR; 61827/00 [2004] Lloyd's Rep. Med. 76; [2004] 1 F.L.R. 1019

Health Development Agency (2004) *Teenage pregnancy: An overview of research evidence.* HMSO, London

Home Office (2002) *Protecting the public: Strenghthening protection against sex offenders and reforming the law on sexual offences.* Cmd 5668. HMSO, London

Independent Advisory Group on Sexual Health and HIV (2004) *Response to the Health Select Committee Report on Sexual Health.* Department of Health, London

Nursing and Midwifery Council (2008) T*he code: Standards of conduct, performance and ethics for nurses and midwives.* NMC, London

R (On the application of Axon) v Secretary of State [2006] EWHC 37 admin

Re E (A Minor)(Wardship: Medical Treatment) [1993] 1 FLR 386.

Re M (A Minor)(Medical Treatment) [1999] 2 FLR 1097.

Re MB (An Adult: Medical Treatment) [1997] 2 FLR 426

Re P (A Minor) (1982) 80 LGR 301.

Re W (A Minor)(Medical Treatment: Court's Jurisdiction) [1992] 4 All ER 627

Shakespeare D (2004) Exploring midwives' attitude to teenage pregnancy. *British Journal of Midwifery* **12**(5): 320–326, 329

Social Exclusion Unit (1999) *Report on teenage pregnancy.* HMSO, London

Teenage Pregnancy Independent Advisory Group (2010) *Final report.* Department for Education, London

The Times (1993) News item. *The Times* **29 October**

W v Egdell [1989] 1 All ER 1089

Willey J (2004) School fix abortion for girl, 14. *The Daily Express* **13 May**

Chapter 7

Status and rights of the unborn child

> **Scenario 7.1. Fetal damage**
>
> An amniocentesis needle punctured the brain of a fetus which was subsequently born with severe brain damage. The mother is claiming that had she been told of the harm the fetus had suffered she would have opted for a termination. She is seeking compensation in the name of her child.
>
> *Scenario 7.1. is discussed on p. 112.*

The law protects the unborn child by making it a criminal offence to harm it (subject to exceptions under the Abortion Act 1967 as amended, see *Chapter 13*), but has been reluctant to recognise the unborn child as having the rights of a person, i.e. having a legal personality.

Criminal law

The unborn child is specifically protected in the criminal law by the Infant Life Preservation Act 1929. This statute makes it a criminal offence for any person who, with intent to destroy the life of a child capable of being born alive, by any wilful act, causes a child to die before it has an existence independent of its mother. There is a defence if the act that caused the death of the child was done in good faith for the purposes only of preserving the life of the mother. There is also a defence if the unborn child died during a lawful abortion (see *Chapter 13*).

Under Section 58 of the Offences Against The Person Act 1861, it is illegal for a woman being with child unlawfully to administer to herself any poison or use any instrument unlawfully with intent to procure a miscarriage; it is also unlawful for any other person to attempt to cause a miscarriage by similar means, whether or not the woman is actually pregnant. "Unlawfully" excludes an abortion legally carried out under the Abortion Act 1967 (see *Chapter 13*).

In 2012, Sarah Catt pleaded guilty to administering a poison with intent to procure a miscarriage (Naughton, 2012). She had bought the drug misoprostol online to induce labour and took it when she was more than 38 weeks pregnant. She was arrested after concerns were raised by health professionals and was interviewed several times over the next year. The judge stated that:

...the child in the womb was so near to birth, in my judgment all right thinking people would think this offence more serious than unintentional manslaughter.

She was sentenced to eight years imprisonment.

Section 59 of the Offences Against The Person Act 1861 makes it illegal for anyone to supply a poison or any instrument knowing that it is to be used unlawfully to procure the miscarriage of any woman, whether or not she is with child. Section 60 of the Act makes it an offence to conceal the birth of a child.

These sections are discussed further in *Chapter 13* on abortion.

Legal status of the fetus

The fetus is not regarded as having an independent legal personality. As a result of this principle, actions cannot be brought in its name before its birth. Only after it is born can legal action be brought on its behalf.

Human Rights Act 1998

Article 2 of the European Convention states that:

Everyone's right to life shall be protected by law. No one shall be deprived of his life intentionally, save in the execution of a sentence of a court following his conviction of a crime for which this penalty is provided by law.

The Human Rights Act 1998 (Amendment) Order 2004 abolished the death penalty in all circumstances.

The right to life does not, however, apply to the unborn child, so it could not be argued successfully that termination of a pregnancy is a breach of Article 2. In contrast, in the Republic of Ireland, the Bill of Rights of the Irish Constitution recognises the right to life of the unborn child. At the time of writing an inquiry is being held into a case in Ireland where doctors refused to terminate a pregnancy following a miscarriage, and the mother, Savita Halappanavar, died. The Irish Government has announced that it will legislate for abortion to be lawful when the mother's life is at risk (digitaljournal.com).

Criminal offence in causing the death of a fetus

In the Scottish case of *Hamilton v Fife Health Board* (1992), Lord Prosser held that where a child died in consequence of injuries sustained when he was a fetus as a result of the fault of another person, he was not "a person dying in consequence of personal injuries sustained by him" because at the time when the injuries were sustained he was not a person. This was a decision in interpreting the provisions of the Damages (Scotland) Act 1976. In a case reported in 1992 (*R v Morgan*), a woman who allegedly kicked her neighbour, who was 36 weeks pregnant, in the stomach, killing her unborn baby, was cleared of manslaughter. In the trial of Claudette Morgan the judge told the jury that it could not convict the accused if the child was born dead. For a charge of murder or manslaughter to succeed, the baby would have to be born alive and then die of injuries sustained in the womb.

Box 7.1. Death of baby because of pre-birth injuries (*A-G's Reference*)

In a case in 1994, a violent assault with a knife was carried out on a pregnant woman. She gave birth to a premature child who did not survive. The Court of Appeal held that an intention to cause serious injury to the mother could be transferred to the child once born so that the assailant could be guilty of murder. The House of Lords however rejected the concept of "transferred malice" and held that the accused could not be found guilty of murder of the child once born. At the time of the attack, the fetus did not have a legal personality.

It is not possible to make an unborn child a ward of court (see *Box 7.3* below).

The mother and criminal offences against the child

If the mother smokes or eats or otherwise acts in such a way during the pregnancy that she harms the fetus, is she guilty of a criminal offence?

The answer is probably no, unless her actions can be brought within the Offences against the Persons Act 1861 or the Infant Life Preservation Act 1929. It would probably be difficult for the prosecution to establish the requisite *mens rea* or mental element which these charges require for a prosecution to succeed.

Civil law

Congenital Disabilities (Civil Liability) Act 1976 as amended by the Human Fertilisation and Embryology Act 2008

This Act gives a right of action to the baby who is born disabled as a result of an occurrence before its birth, which affected either parent in having a healthy baby or affected the mother or the child during the pregnancy.

The main features of the Act are shown in *Box 7.2.*

Box 7.2. Main features of the Congenital Disabilities Act

- An action is given to the child, if it is born alive, for harm caused by negligent actions to the father or mother, which resulted in the child being born disabled.
- The mother is not liable to the child, unless she was driving a motor vehicle and is in breach of her duty of care to the unborn child and as a consequence the child is born disabled.
- Liability to the child can be excluded to the same extent and subject to the same restrictions as liability in the parent's own case.
- If the disability arises from an event pre-conception, then the defendant is not liable if both parents knew of the risk of the child being born disabled. However, if the father is the defendant, this does not apply if he knew of the risk but the mother did not.
- The defendant is not liable... if, when responsible in a professional capacity for treating or advising the parent, he took reasonable care having regard to the then received professional opinion applicable to the particular case; but this does not mean that he is answerable only because he departed from received opinion.

Liability of the mother to the child

The mother of the child is only liable under the Act if, when driving a motor vehicle and knowing (or ought reasonably to know) herself to be pregnant, she is negligent, and in consequence of this negligence the child is born with disabilities. The child could then sue in respect of those disabilities. In practice, of course, the child would be suing the insurance company with whom the mother was insured.

Liability of the professional

It can be seen from *Box 7.2* that the professional who takes reasonable care when acting in a professional capacity for treating or advising the parent would not be liable to the child if born disabled. The statute uses the test of the "then received professional opinion to that particular class of case" which is comparable to the Bolam Test discussed in *Chapter 8*. However, as in Bolam itself and Maynard's case (see *Chapter 8*), the fact that a professional departs from the received opinion is not in itself evidence of negligence. Documentation would have to show clearly the reasons why the professional acted in the way she did and the justification for not following the usual practice.

In February 2001, a girl, then aged 8 years, received £2.43 million from Buckinghamshire Health Authority for injuries she sustained when she was stabbed in the head with an amniocentesis needle while a fetus of 16 weeks' gestation. She was born profoundly brain damaged and could barely communicate (*The Times*, 2001).

Exclusions to liability and defences under the Act

It must be emphasised that the child's action under the Congenital Disabilities Act is derivative, i.e. it relies upon a negligent act against the mother or father which results in the child being born disabled. If there would be no liability of the defendant to the parent, then there is no liability to the child. (The exception to this is the mother's duty to the child when driving a car.) The Unfair Contract Terms Act prevents any exclusion of liability for negligence that causes personal injury or death. Voluntary assumption of risk and contributory negligence may however be effective as defences (see *Chapter 8*).

Common law and civil liability to the unborn child

Prior to the commencement of the Congenital Disabilities (Civil Liability) Act 1976, it was possible for a child, if born alive, to bring a case at common law (i.e. judge-made law) in respect of pre-birth negligence or illegal activities. This is shown in the case in *Box 7.3*. It was held that children with disabilities caused by alleged negligent medical treatment before they were born had a cause of action against the health authorities.

However, under Section 4(5) of the Congenital Disabilities (Civil Liability) Act 1976, the common law is replaced by the Act in respect of all births after

---

Box 7.3. B v Islington Health Authority 1991

The facts of this case were that an operation for dilatation and curettage was carried out when the plaintiff was an embryo in her mother's womb. She was born disabled with brain damage and asphyxia after a failed forceps delivery. The birth occurred before the Congenital Disabilities (Civil Liability) Act 1976 was passed and therefore the child had to bring a claim at common law. This claim was recognised. A duty of care was therefore recognised as existing towards an unborn child and this becomes actionable at the suit of the child when born alive.

---

the Act was brought into force on 22 July 1976. The consequence of this is that a child can only sue the mother in respect of pre-birth injuries caused by the mother's negligence, if she were negligent while driving a car, i.e. action can only be brought under the 1976 Act.

No power to make a fetus a ward of court

There is no power for the courts to make the baby a ward of court while still *in utero*. The Court of Appeal has held that there is no jurisdiction to make the unborn child of a mentally disturbed woman a ward of court. It rejected the local authority's application that the court should extend wardship jurisdiction where a viable child was at risk (see *Box 7.4*).

This case was followed in *Bury Metropolitan Borough Council v D* where the local authority applied to court without the knowledge of the mother for a declaration that their plan for an emergency protection order to take the child into

---

Box 7.4. Re F (in utero) 1988

In this case, the mother was aged 36 and had suffered from severe mental disturbance since 1977. Throughout 1982 she had led a nomadic existence, wandering around Europe. She had returned in 1983 and had been settled in a flat in south London. Her only means of support was supplementary benefit. The local authority was concerned about the baby expected towards the end of January. Early in January, the mother disappeared. The local authority instituted wardship proceedings. The Court of Appeal was of the opinion that it did not have the power to institute wardship proceedings in relation to a fetus. It pointed to the difficulties of enforcing such an order against the expectant mother.

---

care as soon as the baby was born should not be made known to the mother and her partner. The mother was in prison having pleaded guilty to attempting to harm an older child. The judge accepted the evidence that there was a real risk of harm to the unborn child were the mother to be made aware of the local authority's plans, and made a declaration that the local authority's proposed course of action was lawful. He recognised the rights of the parents under Article 8 of the Human Rights Convention but followed the ruling of Hale in the cases of *Re O (Supervision Order)* and *Re C and B (Care Order: Future Harm)* where it was held that "proportionality ... is the key, and interference with family life can only be justified by the overriding necessity of the interests of the child."

In the case of *R (on an application of G) v Nottingham CC*, the absence of a court order was a breach of the mother's human rights (see *Chapter 17*).

An action for wrongful life?

What, however, if the child should never have been born, for example, if a sterilisation or abortion operation does not proceed correctly? Does the child have a right of action for wrongful life?

Such a case was *McKay v Essex AHA*. It was held that a child did not have an action because he or she should not have been born. In this case, the mother was wrongly informed that the baby she was carrying was not disabled and therefore she did not have an abortion.

Compensation

Healthy child

In the case of wrongful birth, the mother has a separate right of action from the child. However, where an attempted termination or sterilisation fails as a result of negligence, the mother cannot obtain compensation for a child who is healthy. The House of Lords held that where medical negligence resulted in an unwanted pregnancy and the birth of a healthy child, the parents were not entitled to recover damages for the costs of rearing that child, but the mother was entitled to recover damages for the pain and distress suffered during the pregnancy and in giving birth, and for the financial loss associated with the pregnancy (*McFarlane and Another v Tayside Health Board*).

This ruling also applies where a healthy child is born to a disabled mother. The House of Lords held that a disabled mother (blind) who gave birth to a normal, healthy child after a failed sterilisation operation could not recover by way of damages the extra costs of rearing him which were referable to her disability. However, she was a victim of a legal wrong which it was appropriate to recognise by the award of a conventional sum. This was put at £15 000 to be added to the award for pregnancy and birth (*Rees v Darlington Memorial Hospital NHS Trust*).

Disabled child

In contrast, where the unwanted child, born as a result of negligence in a failed termination or sterilisation, is born disabled then damages are payable. In the case of *FP v Taunton NHS Trust*, liability was accepted by the trust that they had mismanaged FP's antenatal care with inadequate screening which failed to reveal that the baby had a number of congenital disabilities. Had she known of these FP would have had a termination. She claimed compensation for the disabilities. The judge accepted that he was bound by the Court of Appeal decision in *Parkinson v St James and Seacroft University Hospital NHS Trust* (where the Court of Appeal held that the extra expenses associated with bringing up a child with a significant disability could be claimed). He awarded an interim payment of £1.2 million to be allocated in accordance with an agreed schedule to cover the extra costs involved in the care of a disabled child.

A different outcome may arise in private healthcare where the mother is paying for the cost of her care. In such a situation, the mother may be able to rely upon a claim for breach of contract, and not an action for negligence and may obtain compensation for a failed termination or sterilisation which resulted in a healthy baby. (See *Thompson v Sheffield Fertility Clinic* where a mother, following *in vitro* fertilization treatment, believed herself to be expecting twins gave birth to triplets and recovered the cost of bringing up a third child.)

Scenario 7.1. Fetal damage: Discussion

The action on behalf of the infant will succeed, with compensation being awarded if it can be established that there was negligence by the health professional who carried out the procedure. This action would be brought under the Congenital Disabilities Act 1976, and its definition of negligence as being failure to take "reasonable care having regard to the then received professional opinion applicable to the particular case" would be applied. The child would not have a right of action to claim that it should have been terminated. (See *McKay v Essex AHA* above.)

Conclusions

The principle that the unborn child has no legal personality has major implications for the law in this area and there are likely to be constant pressures for change from such groups as the Society for the Protection of Unborn Children (www. spuc.org.uk/) (see *Chapter 13*).

Questions and exercises

1. Do you consider that the unborn child should have clear rights to be protected from an unacceptable lifestyle of the mother?
2. If you were concerned about an unborn baby because the mother was a drug addict, what action would you take?
3. To what extent does the Congenital Disabilities Act give protection to the midwife against litigation being brought in the name of a brain damaged baby?

References

A-G's Reference (No 3 of 1994) [1997] 3 All ER 936

B v Islington Health Authority [1991] 1 All ER 325

Bury Metropolitan Borough Council v D [2009] EWHC 446 Fam

digitaljournal.com/article/339339

FP v Taunton NHS Trust [2009] EWHC 1965

Hamilton v Fife Health Board. Times Law Report January 28 1992

McFarlane and Another v Tayside Health Board [1999] 4 All ER 961 HL; [2000] 2 AC 59

McKay v Essex AHA [1982] 2 All ER 771

Naughton P (2012) Mother given 8 years for aborting full-term baby. *The Times* **18 September**

Parkinson v St James and Seacroft University Hospital NHS Trust [2001] EWCA Civ 530

R (on an application of G) v Nottingham CC 2008 EWHC 400

R v Morgan. The Times, 21 May 1992

Re C and B (Care Order: Future Harm) [2001] 1 FLR 611

Re F (in utero) [1988] 2 All ER 193

Re O (Supervision Order) [2001] EWCA Civ 16

Rees v Darlington Memorial Hospital NHS Trust The Times Law Report, 21 October 2003 HL; [2003] UKHL 52; [2002] 2 All ER 177 CA

The Times (2001) News item. *The Times* **27 February**

Thompson v Sheffield Fertility Clinic (2001) QBD 6th March 2001

Section C

Litigation and accountability

Chapter 8

Negligence

Scenario 8.1. Failure to undertake newborn screening

The maternity department failed to take blood for the usual five screening tests – phenylketonuria, congenital hypothyroidism, sickle cell disease, cystic fibrosis and medium-chain acyl-CoA dehydrogenase deficiency (MCADD) – leaving it to the health visitor to undertake. The health visitor assumed that the screening had been done. By the time the omission was discovered, the baby had already developed the symptoms of phenylketonuria. Who is to blame?

Scenario 8.1. is discussed on p. 141.

Introduction

Maternity claims over the past 10 years have exceeded £3 billion (NHS Litigation Authority, 2012) and every midwife must be aware of the possibility of litigation. An employed midwife, working in the course of her employment, will usually come under the protection of the vicarious liability of her employer (see below) but an independent midwife could be personally sued.

Negligence

An action for negligence is the most frequent civil action brought in order to obtain compensation. It is one of a group of civil wrongs known as "torts". An action would be brought in the county court where less than £50000 was being claimed. Claims above that amount would be brought in the High Court – the Queen's Bench Division (see *Chapter 1*). Information on the courts and the tribunal services can be found online (www.hmctscourtfinder.justice.gov.uk/HMCTS/GetLeaflet).

Other torts that the midwife may come across are set out in *Box 8.1*. Useful websites to access on this topic include:

- Bailii.org./
- National Health Service Litigation Authority (NHSLA) www.nhsla.com/

Box 8.1. Civil actions known as "torts"

- Action for negligence.
- Action for breach of statutory duty.
- Action for trespass to the person, goods or land (this is considered in *Chapter 3* on consent).
- An action for nuisance.
- An action for defamation (which includes libel and slander).

Liability in negligence

To obtain compensation in an action for negligence, the claimant must establish the elements shown in *Box 8.2*.

Box 8.2. Elements in an action for negligence

- The defendant owed a duty of care to the claimant,
- The defendant was in breach of that duty of care, and,
- As a reasonably foreseeable result of that breach,
- Harm recognised by the courts as subject to compensation was caused.

The burden is on the claimant to establish on a balance of probabilities that each of the four elements shown in *Box 8.2* is present.

Duty of care

Usually it is fairly clear if the law would recognise a duty of care as being owed to an individual in the context of healthcare. The midwife clearly has a duty of care towards all her clients. This may include others for whom she is not directly responsible but is asked to care for. It may also, depending upon her contract of employment, require her to return from off duty in a crisis. The duty will certainly involve the need to communicate with the mother, relatives and colleagues. The duty to inform the mother about significant risks is as much part of the duty of care as treatment and midwifery procedures. The duty to inform is considered in *Chapter 3*.

The definition of the duty of care was raised in a House of Lords case in 1932 (*Donoghue v Stevenson*). It was concerned with the question of whether a manufacturer owed a duty of care to the ultimate consumer, regardless of who had paid for the product.

The facts in this case were that the claimant alleged that she had drunk ginger beer which contained the decomposed remains of a snail, and held the manufacturers liable for the harm she suffered. The case went to the House of Lords over the issue of whether the manufacturers owed a duty of care to her. In a majority decision, the House of Lords decided in her favour. This may seem very remote from the duty of care owed by a midwife, but the statement of Lord Justice Atkins is very important in defining duty of care. He said:

> *You must take reasonable care to avoid acts or omissions which you can reasonably foresee would be likely to injure your neighbour. Who then, in law, is my neighbour? The answer seems to be persons who are so closely and directly affected by my act that I ought reasonably to have them in contemplation as being so affected when I am directing my mind to the acts or omissions which are called in question.*

Usually there is no dispute that a duty of care is owed by a midwife to her clients and the babies. However, there can be situations where the existence of a legal duty of care is disputed. For example, it follows from the statement quoted above that the midwife would have a duty of care to ensure that reasonable care was taken of toddlers brought by mothers to clinics: cupboards containing dangerous substances should not be left unlocked and within their reach. However, it also follows that no person has a duty to volunteer help, if a duty of care does not already exist. The law does not require an individual to volunteer help unless there is a pre-existing duty. In terms of fitness to practise, failure of a midwife to offer her services to a person who was not her client would be judged by the Nursing and Midwifery Council according to the perceived professional standards of a registered midwife and the circumstances of the case.

Of what does the duty of care consist?

The duty of care would include not only duties in relation to treatment and care, and in giving information, but also duties relating to the keeping of satisfactory records, duties in relation to management of the situation, of supervision and delegation to other staff, and all actions necessary to ensure that the mother and baby will be reasonably safe. A duty would also be held to exist in relation to colleagues, to ensure that they are reasonably safe. All those elements identified by the European Convention, which are shown in *Box 1.1* in *Chapter 1* as activities of the midwife, would be considered to be part of the duty of care. The World Health Organization (WHO), the International Confederation of Midwives and the International Federation of Gynaecology and Obstetrics published a joint statement in 2004 entitled *Making pregnancy safer: The critical role of the skilled attendant*. It is available on the WHO website (www.who.int/maternal_child_adolescent/documents/).

The Court of Appeal has held that an ambulance service could owe a duty of care to an individual member of the public, once an emergency phone call providing personal details of that person had been accepted by the service (*Kent v Griffiths*). The London Ambulance Service was held liable when the ambulance took 38 minutes to arrive to assist a pregnant woman who was asthmatic. The time of arrival had been falsely recorded. As a result of the delay, the woman suffered respiratory arrest with catastrophic results, including substantial memory impairment, personality change and a miscarriage.

In 2005 the Court of Appeal ruled that council education officers were professionals who owed a duty of care towards a child with special educational needs (*Carty v Croydon London Borough Council*) if it was established that damage was reasonably foreseeable, that the test of proximity was satisfied, and that the situation was one in which it was fair, just and reasonable that the law should impose a duty of care. On the facts of the case, however, the Court of Appeal held that there was no evidence of a breach of that duty of care.

Duty to parents

The House of Lords (in a majority verdict) held that healthcare and other child care professionals did not owe a common law duty of care to parents against whom they had made unfounded allegations of child abuse and who, as a result, suffered psychiatric injury (*D v East Berkshire Community Health NHS Trust and Another; MAK and Another v Dewsbury Healthcare NHS Trust and Another; RK and Another v Oldham NHS Trust and Another*). This was overruled in 2010 in an appeal to the European Court of Human Rights, which held that there were breaches of the European Convention on Human Rights (*MAK and RK v United Kingdom*). The parents who had failed in their applications before the House of Lords (above) succeeded in their claim for compensation (see *Chapter 17*).

The House of Lords held, in the case of *Brooks v Commissioner of Police of the Metropolis and Others,* that the police owed no duty of care to victims or witnesses. It confirmed an earlier decision in a case brought by the mother of one of the Yorkshire Ripper's later victims (*Hill v Chief Constable of West Yorkshire*), that while, ethically, police should treat victims and witnesses properly and with respect, this ethical duty was not converted into a legal duty of care. The prime function of the police was the preservation of the Queen's peace. However, in subsequent cases, there has been a weakening of this principle and a recognition that Article 2 and the right to life of the European Convention may lead to the acceptance of a duty of care by the police in specific circumstances. (See, for example, the case of *Smith v Sussex Police*.)

Standard of care

The claimant (formerly known as the plaintiff, i.e. the person suing for compensation) has to show that the defendant acted in breach of the duty of care. This is the "fault element" that is required under the present laws to obtain compensation. In order to show that there has been a breach, it is first necessary to establish what standard should have been followed and how the defendant's actions differed, if at all, from what it was reasonable to expect.

The courts use a test known as the Bolam Test to determine the standard expected from professionals. The name derives from a case heard in 1957 (*Bolam v Friern Hospital Management Committee*) where a psychiatric patient was given electro-convulsive therapy without any relaxant drugs or restraint. He suffered several fractures and claimed compensation against Friern Hospital Management Committee. Mr Justice McNair, in deciding how to determine the standard which should have been followed, said:

> When you get a situation which involved the use of some special skill or competence, then the test as to whether there has been negligence or not is... the standard of the ordinary skilled man exercising and professing to have that special skill. A man need not possess the highest expert skill; it is well-established that it is sufficient if he exercises the ordinary skill of an ordinary competent man exercising that particular art.

He added later:

> He is not guilty of negligence if he has acted in accordance with a practice accepted as proper by a responsible body of medical men skilled in that particular art.

The Bolam Test has since been applied to a variety of professions including solicitors, architects and surveyors. It relates to the standards that were reasonably expected at the time the alleged negligent act took place. It thus enables the standards applied by the courts to change, and for professionals to be judged against the standards of the time of the alleged negligence acts, not the standards that existed at the time of the court hearing, which may be many years later.

In the actual case of Bolam, the patient lost his claim. However, were the same facts to occur in the 21st century, there would probably be an offer to settle without any attempt to defend the case, since standards are much higher now.

The Bolam Test was applied by the House of Lords in a case involving a brain-damaged baby (*Whitehouse v Jordan 1981*).

The brief facts of this case were as follows:

Stuart Whitehouse was born in January 1970 with severe brain damage. His mother alleged that the brain damage was caused because the doctor pulled too hard and too long with forceps, as a consequence of which the baby was severely disabled. The doctor denied the allegations. The mother won the case in the High Court and £100 000 was awarded.

The doctor appealed, and this was allowed by the Court of Appeal, on the grounds that an error of judgement was not negligence. The mother then appealed to the House of Lords. Among the issues the House of Lords had to decide was the extent to which an error of judgement was or was not negligence. In applying the Bolam Test to the facts, the House of Lords made it clear that there was no absolute rule relating to errors of judgement; they may or may not constitute negligence depending on the circumstances and what would have been the standard of the ordinary skilled man exercising and professing to have that special skill.

If a surgeon failed to measure up to that, in any respect ("clinical judgement" or otherwise) he had been negligent and should be so adjudged.

In applying the Test it found that the obstetrician had not been negligent.

What if there are different opinions over the standard which should be followed?

Mr Justice McNair, in the Bolam case, referred to the fact that there are sometimes differences of opinion and quoted from an earlier case (*Hunter v Hanley*):

In the realm of diagnosis and treatment there is ample scope for genuine difference of opinion, and one man clearly is not negligent merely because his conclusion differs from that of other professional men, nor because he has displayed less skill or knowledge than others would have shown. The true test for establishing negligence in diagnosis or treatment on the part of a doctor is whether he has been proved to be guilty of such failure as no doctor of ordinary skill would be guilty of, if acting with ordinary care.

This principle was followed in the case of *Maynard v West Midlands Regional Health Authority* (see *Box 8.3*).

Box 8.3. *Maynard v West Midlands Regional Health Authority*

Mrs Maynard had been advised to have a biopsy in order to establish whether she was suffering from Hodgkin's disease. It seemed likely that her symptoms were those of tuberculosis, but because of the possibility of the prognosis of recovery from Hodgkin's disease being improved with earlier treatment, it was important to eliminate that possibility as soon as possible. The operation of mediastinoscopy to provide a biopsy was performed and unfortunately caused damage to her left laryngeal nerve. The biopsy was found to be negative and the patient was diagnosed as suffering from tuberculosis. She was then advised that her condition was clearly one of tuberculosis and there was no need for the biopsy to have been performed. She therefore sued the Regional Health Authority and the doctor.

Mrs Maynard lost the case, the House of Lords holding the following:

It was not sufficient to establish negligence for the plaintiff (i.e. claimant) to show that there was a body of competent professional opinion that considered the decision as wrong, if there was also a body of equally competent professional opinion that supported the decision as having been reasonable in the circumstances.

In the *Bolitho v City and Hackney Health Authority* case, the role of experts came into discussion. The House of Lords ruled that experts should be sure that their evidence related to the facts of the case. In this case, the House of Lords stated that:

The court had to be satisfied that the exponents of the body of opinion relied on can demonstrate that such opinion has a logical basis. In particular, in cases involving, as they often do, the weighing of risks against benefits, the judge, before accepting a body of opinion as being responsible, reasonable or respectable, will need to be satisfied that, in forming their views, the experts had directed their minds to the question of comparative risks and benefits and had reached a defensible conclusion on the matter.

The use of the adjectives "responsible, reasonable and respectable" (in the Bolam case) all showed that the court had to be satisfied that the exponents of the body of opinion relied upon could demonstrate that such opinion had a logical basis.

It would seldom be right for a judge to reach the conclusion that views held by a competent medical expert were unreasonable.

The lessons of these cases are clear for midwives.

- First, the midwife must ensure that she understands what are the present standards of care that would be provided by a reasonable midwife in any specific circumstances. This means that she must be aware of the protocols, guidelines and procedures that have been drawn up both nationally and locally.
- Second, she must also have an understanding as to the circumstances in which any reasonable midwife would depart from the agreed protocols because of the particular circumstances of the situation. This means that midwifery will never become simply a book of regulations which must be followed. There will always be a need for professional judgement and discretion to be exercised.
- Third, the midwife should ensure that her records show accurately the particular circumstances that provided the justification for departing from the agreed procedure. Should harm occur to the mother and/or child and the midwife be challenged on what she had done, she would require comprehensive clear records to defend her actions.
- Fourth, she must keep up to date and ensure that her knowledge, skill and experience is constantly updated, since the standards improve and she would be judged against those expected of her at the time, not those that applied several years before.
- Fifth, in any area of development where standards are not certain, she should obtain as much information as possible to ensure that she can care for the mother and baby safely. This is a particular issue with water births.

How do local standards relate to national standards?

The courts are concerned with applying what it is reasonable for a claimant to expect from professionals. Expert witnesses would give evidence for both claimant and defence (there are new rules for expert evidence, see below) on what standards could have been expected. If local standards are lower than what could be expected nationally, they would not suffice. Local standards may however be higher than national standards, where a specialist service is offered. For example, it may be that a trust advertises itself as being able to provide a specific form of childbirth not generally available, and has referrals on that basis. If, in carrying out this special procedure, harm occurs as a result of negligence by a member of staff, it would not be acceptable as a defence for the trust to say that no other hospital could have performed the technique better.

Exercise 1. Analysis of a case

Access the following case on the bailii website and identify the arguments used in deciding that there was no negligence on the part of the defendants.

Arthur Croft (a child) v Heart of England NHS Foundation Trust

You will note that Arthur Croft was born on 15 April 1997. (The case was heard on 16, 17, and 18 May 2012.) What are the implications of this passage of time for those midwives who were called to give evidence? What harm did Arthur suffer during the process of birth? Mr Justice Hinckinbottom heard the case in the High Court.

Points to note

1. Quantum was agreed. This means the parties had agreed the amount of compensation that Arthur would receive, but only if liability (blame) could be proved.
2. Note who gave evidence as witnesses of fact and who gave evidence as expert witnesses.
3. The judge outlines the medical circumstances of shoulder dystocia and the action that should be taken by the professionals present. He also explains what Erb's palsy is and how it can occur.
4. The judge quotes from an earlier case in which the judge cited 80 pieces of

literature on obstetric brachial plexus injuries, what conclusion does he draw from that earlier case and how does he apply it to the case before him?

5. In paragraph 14 he states that the claimant had initially relied upon a doctrine known as "*res ipsa loquitur*". This means "the thing speaks for itself" and can be used by a claimant to give the defendant the task of showing that what happened did not occur as a result of any negligence on its part. (See discussion below.) In this case, Mr Kemp, the barrister (known as counsel) representing the claimant, abandoned reliance upon this evidential doctrine and accepted that the claimant would have to prove negligence.

6. From paragraphs 16 to 23 the judge considers the case history and states in paragraph 22 that the standard to be applied in determining whether there was negligence by the midwife was "well-established, namely that of a reasonably competent midwife carrying out the functions expected of a midwife in the delivery suite of a district general hospital", the principle established in the case of *Bolitho v City and Hackney Heath Authority* (see above).

7. Paragraphs 22 and 23 make it clear that the dispute is over the facts. Did the midwife act in the ways the claimant is alleging, in which case all are agreed that there was negligence, or did she not?

8. From paragraphs 24 to 40 the judge analyses the oral evidence that he has heard, and from 41 to 47 he looks at the medical records and protocols. Note that in paragraph 46 the judge states that the midwife accepted that the notes produced would not have been adequate even in 1997, if the outcome had not been "good" which (she said) in this case it was. (What is the significance of the phrase "not have been adequate even in 1997"?)

9. The judge concludes in paragraph 49 that there was no negligence on the part of the midwife and sets out his reasons for that conclusion in paragraph 51.

10. Note what the judge says about the evidence of Mr and Mrs Croft in paragraph 52.

11. In paragraph 52 he discusses the allegation that a clinician "got onto Mrs Croft" and finds that it did not happen.

12. What view does the judge have of the midwife's evidence and in particular the evidence of midwifery practice (paragraphs 56–59).

13. He then considers the standards of the medical records and the absence of a protocol, holding that this did not assist the claimant's case.

14. The checklist for reviewing the strength of a brachial plexus injury claim is then considered in paragraph 62. How helpful do you consider this to have been to the parties to the case?

15. Note the ultimate paragraph 66, where the judge summarises his conclusion on liability.

General considerations

Most disputed cases will succeed or fail on what facts can be established before the courts. Arthur Croft's case is one example where only liability was in dispute and the judge accepted the midwife's evidence that she followed the reasonable standard of care. Consider any birth with which you have been involved and identify the evidence that you would need to produce to show that you followed the appropriate standard of care. How would you do this in 5 years' time, in 10 years' time or in 20 years' time?

Exercise 2. Establishing the reasonable standard of care

Take any aspect of midwifery treatment and show how the reasonable standard would be determined. What sources would you access? Is there a recognised hierarchy of sources? For example, would you place guidance provided by the Royal College of Obstetricians and Gynaecologists on a higher level than guidance provided by your local NHS trust? Where else would you look for guidance? What do the textbooks say? Have there been new editions and do they differ from the older textbooks?

Has the National Institute for Health and Clinical Excellence (NICE) provided guidelines covering the topic you have chosen? Are there any circumstances where it would not be appropriate to follow NICE guidelines? In December 2012, NICE issued quality standards on antenatal care (QS22). The NICE website also lists other information relating to pregnancy.

Useful websites for guideline/protocol/procedures include the following:

- www.nice.org.uk
- www.nhsla.com/ (look for CNSTMaternityStandards)
- www.nmc-uk.org
- www.rcm.org.uk
- www.rcog.org.uk
- www.who.int/maternal_child_adolescent/documents/

In the case *Jones v NW SHA*, reliance was placed upon guidance on dealing with shoulder dystocia published by the Royal College of Obstetricians and

Gynaecologists. The baby suffered from cerebral palsy, the birth being complicated by shoulder dystocia. On his behalf it was alleged that there was a delay in dealing with the situation which either caused the brain damage or made it worse. It was agreed that his condition was due to the interval between the delivery of his head and body and the fact that the cord was compressed during that time. However, the court held that there was no negligence either in the information given to the mother prior to the birth or in the steps that the obstetricians took in the course of the delivery.

In the case of *Spencer v NHS North West,* the claimant, who was born almost 18 years before the court case, claimed that her cerebral palsy was the result of the midwifery staff failing to suspect on the first night after her birth that she was developing an infection that later resulted in meningitis. As a consequence she suffered irreversible brain damage. The case hinged on whether any reasonable midwife would have detected early signs of an infection. The judge decided that there was no negligence by the midwife, applying the Bolitho Test, and the claimant lost her case. The judge noted that the factual issues in the case were made more difficult by the fact that it was then nearly 18 years since the events in question.

Causation

The claimant must establish that the negligence has caused the harm for which compensation is being sought.

Factual causation

If the baby would have been harmed anyway, then the fact that there has been negligence by the midwife would not, in itself, be sufficient to enable the claimant to obtain compensation. For example, a mother might be able to show that a midwife failed to act appropriately when fetal distress was identified. However, if the child would have been born brain damaged as a result of a congenital defect inherited from its parents, and the midwife's negligence has not caused any additional harm, then no compensation would be payable.

In one decided case (*Barnett v Chelsea HMC*) three night watchmen drank tea which made them vomit. They went to the casualty department of the local hospital. The casualty officer, on being told of the complaints by a nurse, did not see the men, but told them to go home and call in their own doctors. Some hours later, one of them died from arsenic poisoning. The court held that:

- The casualty department officers owed a duty of care in the circumstances.
- The casualty doctor had been negligent in not seeing them, but
- Even if he had, it was improbable that the only effective antidote could have been administered in time to save the deceased, and
- Therefore the defendants were not liable. The patient would have died anyway.

The onus is on the claimant to establish that there is this causal link between the breach of the duty of care and the harm which occurred.

In the case in *Box 8.4*, the claimants failed to establish causation and the House of Lords ordered a new hearing on the issue of causation.

Box 8.4. *Wilsher v Essex Area Health Authority*

A premature baby was being treated with oxygen therapy. A junior doctor mistakenly inserted the catheter to monitor the oxygen intake into a vein rather than an artery. A senior registrar, when asked to check what had been done, failed to notice the error. The baby was given excess oxygen. The parents claimed compensation for the retrolentalfibroplasia that the baby suffered, but failed to prove that it was the excess oxygen that had caused the harm. They therefore failed in their claim. It was agreed that there were several different factors which could have caused the child to become blind, and the negligence was only one of them. It could not be presumed that it was the defendant's negligence that had caused the harm. The House of Lords ordered the case to be reheard on the issue of causation. In the event, the parties settled.

It has also been difficult for claimants to establish causation when suing for compensation for harm which it is claimed has resulted from vaccine damage (*Loveday v Renton and another*). This is discussed further in *Chapter 15*.

In a case where a boy suffering from meningitis was given an overdose of penicillin, the parents claimed compensation for loss of hearing. The House of Lords, however, held that it had not been established that the deafness was caused by the overdose of penicillin, and the parents therefore lost their claim (*Kay v Ayrshire and Arran Health Board*). Factual causation between a brain-damaged baby and negligent care at birth may be difficult to establish, and of crucial importance will be the evidence of early fetal distress.

Causation was not established in the case of *Ball v Wirral HA* where a baby was placed in an incubator in a special care baby unit suffering from respiratory distress syndrome. It was argued on the baby's behalf that he should have been transferred to a hospital with ventilation facilities sooner than he was, before his condition became acute, and that had this been done the baby would not have suffered brain damage. The judge held that the standard of care was not below the standard to be expected as reasonable in 1977 and the staff were justified in waiting before requesting the transfer. However, had they been wrong in that and there had been a breach of the duty of care, then it was not this breach that caused the brain injuries. There was no evidence that ventilation reduced the incidence of intra-ventricular haemorrhage. In fact the most significant cause of death in ventilated babies was intra-ventricular haemorrhage. Therefore transferring the baby earlier would not have prevented his haemorrhage from occurring.

A baby who had a stroke at birth failed in her claim for compensation (*Dowson v Sunderland Hospitals NHS Trust*). On her behalf it was contended that signs of fetal distress should have been noted much earlier from the cardiotocograph, that oxytocin was administered for too long, and that the resultant hypoxia had led to her stroke. The defendants conceded that the Caesarean should have been carried out earlier, but contended that the risk of a stroke did not come within its duty of care and that causation had not been proved. The High Court judge ruled that the management of the labour was mishandled and fell below the required standard of care. However, the claimant had not proved that it had led to her stroke. None of the medical research evidence submitted came close to showing that neonatal stroke was likely to result from hypoxia. Without establishing such a likelihood, the claimant could not prove that one or more of the events in labour which would not have occurred but for the negligence, actually caused the stroke and the necessary causal link had not been made.

In a case in 2007 (*Richards v Swansea NHS Trust*), it was held that, but for a 10-minute delay beyond the acceptable standard for carrying out an emergency Caesarean, the baby would not have suffered cerebral palsy, and £8 million was awarded.

An intervening cause, which breaks the chain of causation, may also prevent causation being established and therefore result in the claimant failing in her claim.

Loss of a chance

The House of Lords (in a majority decision) ruled in January 2005 (*Gregg v Scott*) that where a doctor negligently failed to refer for investigation a patient with possible symptoms of cancer, with the result that there was a nine month delay in treatment for the condition, the patient, whose chances of survival during that delayed period had fallen from 42% to 25%, could not recover damages for that loss of chance. The delay had not deprived that patient of the prospect of a cure because, on a balance of probability, he could probably not have been cured anyway, and loss of a chance was not in itself a recoverable head of damage for clinical negligence.

Harm

To obtain compensation for negligence it must be established that harm has resulted from the negligent act. Harm includes personal injury and death, and loss and damage of property. Some of the forms of harm recognised by the courts as subject to compensation are shown in *Box 8.5*.

Box 8.5. Harm recognised as subject to compensation in the civil courts

- Personal injury, pain and suffering.
- Death.
- Loss of the ability to have children.
- Loss of the opportunity to have an abortion.
- Having a child after being sterilised.
- Post-traumatic stress syndrome or nervous shock.
- Loss or damage of property.

Establishing the facts: The thing speaks for itself (Res ipsa loquitur)

The claimant (formerly known as the plaintiff), i.e. the person bringing the action, normally has the burden of proving that there was negligence by the defendant which caused harm to her. The standard of proof in the civil courts where an action for compensation would take place is "on a balance of probabilities". This contrasts with the standard of proof in a criminal case, which is "beyond reasonable doubt".

However, where certain circumstances arise, it is possible for the claimant to argue that "the thing speaks for itself" and the defendant has the task of showing that he was not negligent. This is known as a *"res ipsa loquitur"* situation. The circumstances that have to be shown by the claimant are:

- The events were under the control of the defendant.

- Something has occurred which would not normally occur if all reasonable care were taken.
- The defendant has not offered any explanation which shows he was not negligent.

A typical example of a *res ipsa loquitur* situation would be where a swab is left in a patient after surgery, or where the wrong limb is amputated. If the above elements can be shown by the claimant then he has made out a *prima facie* case that there is evidence of negligence by the defendants. The burden of proof, however, remains with the claimant to satisfy this on a balance of probabilities. (*Ratcliffe v Plymouth and Torbay HA, Exeter and Devon HA*).

An example of the application of the doctrine of *res ipsa loquitur* from obstetrics is given in *Box 8.6*.

Box 8.6. Brown v Merton, Sutton and Wandsworth AHA (Teaching)

In the course of preparation for giving birth, the claimant underwent epidural anaesthesia in a hospital. She developed severe pain when receiving the second dose of epidural and, as a result, developed quadriplegia.

She brought an action against the defendants who admitted that they were responsible for the management of the hospital; that the claimant was, at all material times, a patient at that hospital; and that the anaesthetic was administered by their servants or agents, for whose acts they were, in law, vicariously responsible. They denied that they had been negligent and specifically denied that the claimant was able to rely upon the doctrine of *res ipsa loquitur*.

At a preliminary hearing on the number of experts permitted, the Court of Appeal held that the pleadings (the documents that pass between the parties in the run-up to the hearing) showed that the defendants now admitted that the treatment was wholly under the management of the defendants and that this type of accident does not happen in the ordinary course of epidural anaesthesia when proper care is used. That is an admission of liability on the pleadings. There was therefore no issue as to liability, only as to damages.

The Court of Appeal therefore amended the order by deleting any reference to the doctors who were to give evidence on the treatment, and limited it purely to the condition and prognosis of the claimant. In total, the sum of £398629 was awarded. (It must be remembered that this was 1982 and considerably more would be awarded today.)

Vicarious liability

It would be usual in the case of an employed midwife for her employer to be sued in the event of her being negligent. For obvious reasons, the employer is more likely to be able to pay the compensation due as a consequence of any harm caused by her negligence. This applies even though the employer has not been negligent in any way. In order to ensure that an innocent victim obtains compensation for injuries caused by an employee, public policy dictates that the doctrine of vicarious liability applies. Under the doctrine of vicarious liability, the employer is responsible for compensation payable for the harm. For vicarious liability to be established, the elements shown in *Box 8.7* must be shown.

Box 8.7. Elements in vicarious liability

- There must be negligence, i.e. a duty of care which has been breached and, as a reasonably foreseeable consequence, has caused harm, or some other failure by the employee.
- The negligent act or omission or failure must have been by an employee.
- The negligent employee must have been acting in the course of employment.

A midwife who is employed by an agency may be regarded as the employee of the NHS trust that has taken her on so that the latter would become vicariously liable for her negligence. "In course of employment" may include acts prohibited by the employer. In one leading case a petrol tanker driver struck a match to light a cigarette and threw it on the floor while transferring petrol from his lorry to the tank, causing an explosion. It was held that this was within the scope of his employment and his employers were held liable for the harm (*Century Insurance Co Ltd v Northern Ireland Road Transport Board*). That was in 1942, but in a more recent case, the House of Lords (now the Supreme Court of Justice) held that the employers of a warden at a school boarding house were liable for the harm caused by the warden's sexual abuse of boys in his care: His actions were so closely connected with his employment that it was fair and just to hold the employers vicariously liable (*Lister and Others v Helsey Hall Ltd*). This principle was followed in a more recent case when the Supreme Court held that the Institute of the Brothers of the Christian Schools was vicariously liable for sexual and physical abuse of the claimants. The Institute was an unincorporated association and its close relationship with the brothers enabled the latter to be placed in trusted teaching positions, including that of headmaster (*The Catholic Child Welfare Society and others v various claimants and Institute of the Brothers of the Christian Schools and others*).

Employer's right of indemnity

While the doctrine of vicarious liability enables the victim of negligence to obtain compensation, it does not necessarily deprive the employer of his rights against the negligent employee. If an employee has been negligent then she is in breach of her contract of employment, which requires her to take all reasonable care and skill. This breach gives the employer a right to be indemnified against the negligent employee. The House of Lords confirmed this principle in the case of *Lister v Romford Ice and Cold Storage Co Ltd*.

In the health service, hospital doctors and dentists, even though employees, accepted that they were personally liable for their negligent acts and were covered by membership of the medical defence unions. However, in 1990, health authorities agreed to pay the compensation resulting from the negligence of employed doctors and dentists (HM Government, 1990).

Indemnity and the midwife: Guidance from the Nursing and Midwifery Council (NMC)

Following a consultation, the NMC decided to introduce a new clause relating to indemnity into its 2004 Code of professional conduct. In the 2008 edition of the Code, this clause has been replaced by a paragraph giving information about indemnity insurance. The Code can be found on the NMC website (www.nmc-uk. org). The NMC recommends that registered practitioners should have indemnity insurance. Indemnity insurance for all registered health professionals becomes a condition of their registration in October 2013 as a result of an EU directive on the application of patients' rights in cross-border healthcare (EU Directive, 2011). The Department of Health is carrying out a consultation on indemnity arrangements which ends on 17 May 2013.

Delegation and supervision

Where a registered midwife delegates an activity to a maternity support worker, it is her responsibility to ensure that the delegation is appropriate (for example, she should not delegate activities that can only be carried out by a registered midwife

– see *Chapter 12*). She must ensure that the assistant has the requisite training and competence and that she gives her an appropriate level of supervision. If she delegates appropriately, she would not then be accountable for any negligence by the assistant, but the assistant would be liable on her own account. The employer would be vicariously liable. Griffin et al (2012) consider the impact of maternity support workers, concluding that they had a positive impact on services including freeing up the time of midwives, increasing breastfeeding rates, and reducing length of stay and hospital admissions.

Defences

The main defences to an action for negligence are set out in *Box 8.8*.

Box 8.8. Defences

- Dispute over facts.
- One of elements of negligence is not present, eg. no duty, no breach, no causation, no harm.
- Limitation of time.
- Contributory negligence.
- Exclusion of liability.
- Voluntary assumption of risk.

Dispute over the facts

The case of Arthur Croft considered above is an example where there was agreement over the standard of care that was required, but a dispute as to whether the midwife had or had not followed that standard. Where the case is heard many years after the events took place it might not be clear who can prove in the court what exactly happened all those years ago and there is heavy reliance upon documentation.

One of the elements of negligence is missing

If it can be shown that there was no duty, or the standard of care was correctly followed, or there was negligence but this failed to cause the harm (i.e. no causation), or the harm suffered was not recognised as subject to compensation, then the claimant's action will fail.

Limitation of time

The time limits within which an action for various torts must be commenced are set out in the Limitation Act 1980. This can be accessed on the bailii website. An action for compensation for harm arising from negligence must be brought within three years of the negligent act. If it was not known at that time that harm had occurred then the action must be brought within three years of that knowledge being acquired. Section 14 defines knowledge as awareness of the following facts by the claimant:

(1) Subject to Subsection (1A) below, in Sections 11 and 12 of this Act references to a person's date of knowledge are references to the date on which he first had knowledge of the following facts:
   (a) that the injury in question was significant; and
   (b) that the injury was attributable in whole or in part to the act or omission which is alleged to constitute negligence, nuisance or breach of duty; and
   (c) the identity of the defendant; and
   (d) if it is alleged that the act or omission was that of a person other than the defendant, the identity of that person and the additional facts supporting the bringing of an action against the defendant; and knowledge that any acts or omissions did or did not, as a matter of law, involve negligence, nuisance or breach of duty is irrelevant.

In the case of *Whiston v London Strategic HA* the claimant was 34 years at the date of the hearing and claimed damages in respect of cerebral palsy incurred through hypoxia around the time of his birth. The court heard the preliminary point as to whether the claim was out of time. The claim was first presented in 2006 and the defendants claimed he was out of time. From the evidence, the judge concluded that he did not have actual knowledge that the hypoxia could be attributed to an act or omission of the medical staff attending his mother and/or carrying out the forceps delivery. Nor could it be concluded that he had constructive knowledge. The case could proceed to the substantive hearing. However, the judge stated that were he wrong about the defendants' knowledge, he would not consider it correct to exercise judicial discretion under Section 33 (see below).

Under a disability

Where a claimant is under a disability and therefore unable to bring an action, the time limit does not apply until the disability ends or the claimant dies. (See

Section 28 of the Limitation Act.) This provision is especially important for midwives in two respects. A child is considered to be under a disability until he or she is aged 18 years, so no time limit applies until then. In addition, a person who has suffered brain damage at birth and is unable to take action on his or her account when he or she becomes 18 is considered to be under a disability for his or her entire life, so there is no time limit on bringing an action until he or she dies. The implications for record keeping are obvious and can be seen in the case of *Bull and Wakeham v Devon Area Health Authority,* where almost 30 years elapsed between the birth and the court hearing.

Judge's discretion

Under Section 32A the judge has a discretion to exclude the time limit if it would be equitable to the claimant. A list of factors which the judge must take into account are set out in Section 32A(2). In the *Bull v Wakeham* case, the judge refused to exercise this discretion in relation to the claim by the mother – her action was held to be statute-barred. However, there was no time limit against the child bringing an action in his own right since he was under a disability. His claim was heard and upheld.

Contributory negligence

If the claimant has in some way contributed to the harm which he or she has suffered then there is the following statutory provision to reduce the compensation payable.

Law Reform (Contributory Negligence) Act 1945. Section 1(1)

Where any person suffers damage as the result partly of the fault of any other person or persons, a claim in respect to that damage shall not be defeated by reasons of the fault of the person suffering the damage, but the damages recoverable in respect thereof shall be reduced to such extent as the court thinks just and equitable having regard to the claimant's share in the responsibility for the damage.

In determining contributory negligence, the court would take into account the extent to which it would have been reasonable to expect the claimant to have taken care of herself. Less care would be looked for in a child than in an adult.

In the case of *Beverley Pidgeon v Doncaster Health Authority,* the claimant had been given a cervical smear test in 1988 which was mistakenly reported as negative. Between 1988 and 1997 she had numerous urgings from both the GP and the Family Health Service Authority to have further smear tests, which she refused. In 1997 a smear was taken and she was found to have cervical carcinoma at stage 2A or 2B. She underwent treatment which included a resection of her bowel. It was agreed that if the result had been noted and acted upon in 1988 the abnormal cells could have been removed by less invasive surgery. She sued for the negligence of the defendants and the court held that she was two-thirds responsible and so was therefore entitled to only one third of the compensation payable.

Exclusion of liability

A defendant may have attempted to exclude or limit his or her liability for his negligence, but as a result of the Unfair Contract Terms Act 1977 this would only be effective where damage is caused to property, not where the harm is personal injury or death. Even if the damage is to property, the exclusion must be reasonable.

The significance for the midwife is that if a mother wishes to have a particular form of delivery which is considered hazardous, the midwife could not say, "Well, provided I am excluded from liability, I will deliver you in the manner you wish." It has been suggested, for example with water births, that the mother should be able to choose that form of birth, but agree that the midwife should not be liable for any harm that occurs. If the midwife is negligent, the 1977 Act prevents her from excluding herself from liability for personal injury or death. This also applies to the independent midwife.

In contrast, liability for loss or damage to property may be excluded, provided that it is reasonable to do so. The requirement of reasonableness is satisfied if it would be fair and reasonable to allow reliance upon the term, having regard to all the circumstances obtaining when the liability arose or (but for the notice) would have arisen. It is for the person claiming that the term satisfies the requirement of reasonableness to show that it does.

Voluntary assumption of risk

Another defence on which a defendant may sometimes rely is that, even though duty, breach, causation and harm can be shown, the claimant voluntarily agreed to waive the right to bring an action for negligence. This is known as *"volente non fit injuria"*, i.e. "to the willing, there is no wrong".

It has been suggested that where a mother wants to have a water birth, which might be contrary to the policy of the hospital, she could, by signing a document, state that she voluntarily took on the risks involved and would not hold the midwives in any way responsible should harm occur to her or the baby. In this way, the midwife could enable the mother to have the confinement she wanted, without the risks of being sued for compensation. If the mother voluntarily assumes the risk of being injured through negligence, and the unborn child is harmed by that negligence and is subsequently born alive, if an action were to be brought in the name of the child under the Congenital Disabilities Act this could be used as a defence.

There are, however, several dangers for the midwife in relying upon this defence to cover for her failure to provide a reasonable standard of care.

- In the first place, it is only effective as a defence against the risks of which the claimant is made aware. Were other risks to occur, the mother could argue that she had not voluntarily agreed to waive a right to sue in respect of the harm caused by negligence.
- Second, if there is evidence that the mother was placed in a situation where she really had no real choice, it is unlikely that the defence would succeed.
- Third, even if the defence were effective in defeating a claim of negligence, the midwife might still be accountable to the Nursing and Midwifery Council for evidence of lack of fitness to practise and to her employer for breach of the contract of employment.

The Road Traffic Act prevents a driver requiring a passenger to travel at his own risk. Thus, if a midwife offered a pregnant woman a lift on the understanding that she travelled at her own risk, this would be illegal, and would not be a valid defence for the midwife to bring were the mother to sue her.

Employers have in the past claimed that employees who worked in particularly dangerous conditions voluntarily assumed the risk of being injured. The courts are, however, extremely reluctant to allow such a defence to prevail. Thus, a midwife whose back was injured as the result of the employer's failure to take care of her health and safety and to use hoists and to provide appropriate training, should not be defeated in her claim for compensation on the grounds that she knew that the practice of midwifery caused back injuries.

The NHS Litigation Authority

The NHS Litigation Authority, a special health authority, was set up in 1995 to oversee the Clinical Negligence Scheme for Trusts in the handling of claims. The Litigation Authority uses an approved list of solicitors to handle litigation. It is subject to an annual performance review. A key function for the NHS Litigation Authority is to contribute to the incentives for reducing the number of negligent or preventable incidents. It aims to achieve this through an extensive risk management programme. It has designed a set of risk management standards for each type of healthcare organisation, incorporating organisational, clinical, and health and safety risks. They cover: NHS Litigation Authority Acute, Primary Care Trust and Independent Sector Standards; NHS Litigation Authority Mental Health and Learning Disability Standards, and NHS Litigation Authority Ambulance Standards. The Litigation Authority oversees the work of the Clinical Negligence Scheme for Trusts which has devised a set of standards for maternity services. These are updated annually and available on the NHS Litigation Authority website (www.nhsla.com/.../CNT/maternitystandards/). The Litigation Authority has a key role to play in encouraging the implementation of NICE guidance and has prepared a joint paper with NICE on litigation which is available on its website.

The Clinical Negligence Scheme for Trusts was established in 1996 (National Health Service [Clinical Negligence Scheme] Regulations XI 1996) to administer a scheme where trusts and other NHS bodies take part in a voluntary scheme whereby compensation is met from a pooling system. The payment into the pool depends on an assessment of the risk (by the Clinical Negligence Scheme for Trusts) presented by that particular trust, and amounts over a specified minimum will be met from the pool. Clinical risk facilitator and midwife, Catherine Doherty, published advice on managing risk in maternity services and achieving accreditation of the Clinical Negligence Scheme for Trusts in the December 2010 issue of *Midwives magazine*). Her advice was prompted by an NHS trust in 2010 being fined £100000 after its failure to manage the risk of drug errors which led to the death of a new mother, when a midwife mistakenly administered an epidural anaesthetic rather than a saline solution via an intravenous drip. (The substances had been mixed up as they were in similar packaging, in the same cupboard.) The trial concluded that avoiding any one of a number of errors would probably have averted the woman's death. (The case is reported by the Health and Safety Executive and is accessible on its website.)

A report published by the NHS Litigation Authority (2012) of an analysis of maternity claims over the 10-year period ending in 2010 concluded that the most effective way to reduce the financial and human cost of maternity claims is to continue to improve the management of risks associated with maternity care, focusing on preventing incidents involving the management of women in labour, including the interpretation of cardiotocograph traces. The report should be essential reading for all midwifery managers and practising midwives. Maternity Clinical Risk Management Standards prepared by the Clinical Negligence Scheme for Trusts and updated in 2011 are available from the NHS Litigation Authority website (www.nhsla.com).

Discussion of the stages of civil actions and the role of witnesses of fact and expert witnesses is considered in *Chapter 9*.

NICE standards and guidance are available on the NICE website (www.nice.org.uk) and midwives should be aware of their importance to their practice. They may become part of the Bolam Test of reasonable professional practice, and justification may be required in relation to a particular client's needs if they have not been followed. NICE guidelines on hypertension in pregnancy were published in 2010.

The value and feasibility of introducing a care pathway for critical care in childbirth is considered by Janet Cotton (2011) who concluded that further studies are required to evaluate the impact of critical care prior to their widespread development and implementation.

Scenario 8.1. Failure to undertake newborn screening: Discussion

The parents of the baby should have little difficulty in establishing that there has been a failure in the duty of care, both by the hospital staff and by the community staff. They would be advised to sue, in the name of the child, both employers for their vicarious liability for the negligence of their staff. They should be able to obtain, through the preliminary proceedings, access to the protocols and procedures for newborn screening. They may find assistance from the newborn screening website (newbornbloodspot.screening.nhs.uk/).

Conclusions

This chapter has set out the basic principles of liability in civil actions for negligence, has considered the context of litigation, has indicated the duty placed in law upon the midwife, and has considered the legal requirement that she practises a reasonable standard of care. The growth in the number of legal actions brought in respect of childbirth incidents and the size of the compensation paid out shows that there can be no complacency in relation to the possibility of litigation. The National Patient Safety Agency report showed that 70% of the total value of maternity claims related to three main causes: mistakes in cardiotocograph interpretation, mistakes in the management of labour, and cases where the baby suffered from cerebral palsy (NHS Litigation Authority, 2012). Significant changes to the legal aid system and no win, no fee schemes may result in calls for no fault liability to be introduced in personal injuries claims. In Scotland a report concluded that no fault liability could be simpler than the existing processes (McLean, 2011). The recommendations of the review group were put out for consultation in August 2012 (www.scotland.gov.uk/Publications).

Questions and exercises

1. List the duties that you think a midwife would be expected to undertake in relation to the mother, her children, colleagues and others.
2. The harm suffered by a claimant must have been caused by the negligence of the defendant (or its servants). What is meant by this? Consider examples from midwifery practice of situations where there could be harm but no causation.
3. Take any incident at work which could have led to an action for compensation and consider the extent to which each of the required elements was established.
4. What evidence would you consider was relevant if you were the defendant in a negligence case arising from the birth of a brain damaged baby?
5. To what extent do you consider that an employer should be able to determine the policies to be followed by professional staff?
6. Examine the publications of NICE and the Clinical Negligence Scheme for Trusts on maternity standards and consider the extent to which these are reflected in your own practice.

References

Arthur Croft (a child) v Heart of England NHS Foundation Trust [2012] EWHC 1470
Ball v Wirral HA [2003] Lloyd's Rep. Med. 165
Barnett v Chelsea HMC [1968] 1 All ER 1068

Beverley Pidgeon v Doncaster Health Authority [2002] Lloyd's Rep. Med. 130

Bolam v Friern Hospital Management Committee [1957] 1 WLR 582

Bolitho v City and Hackney Health Authority [1998] AC 232

Brooks v Commissioner of Police of the Metropolis and Others The Times Law Report 26 April, 2005 HL

Brown v Merton, Sutton and Wandsworth Area Health Authority (Teaching) [1982] 1 All ER 650.

Bull and Wakeham v Devon Health Authority [1989] CA 2 February 1989 Transcript; [1993] 4 Med LR 117 CA

Carty v Croydon London Borough Council The Times 3 February 2005 CA

Century Insurance Co Ltd v Northern Ireland Road Transport Board [1942] AC 509

Cotton J (2010) MIDIRS. *Midwifery Digest* **21**(2): 198–201

D v East Berkshire Community Health NHS Trust and Another; MAK and Another v Dewsbury Healthcare NHS Trust and Another; RK and Another v Oldham NHS Trust and Another The Times Law Report 22 April 2005 HL

D v East Berkshire Community Health NHS Trust; MAK v Dewsbury Healthcare NHS Trust; RK v Oldham NHS Trust [2005] 2 AC 373

Doherty C (2010) Learning to lessen risk. *Midwiver Magazine* **December***:* 36–7

Donoghue v Stevenson [1932] AC 562

Dowson v Sunderland Hospitals NHS Trust [2004] Lloyd's Rep. Med. 177

EU Directive (2011) *Directive 2011/24/EU on the application of patients' rights in cross-border healthcare.* European Commission, Brussels

Gregg v Scott The Times Law Report 28 January 2005 HL

Griffin R, Richardson M, Morris-Thompson T (2012) An evaluation of the impact of maternity support workers. *British Journal of Midwifery* **20**(12): 12–18

Hill v Chief Constable of West Yorkshire [1989] AC 53 HL

HM Government (1990) *Health Service Circular* (89)34. HM Government, London. Available from: http://circulars.gov.ie

Hunter v Hanley [1955] SLT 213

Jones v NW SHA [2010] EWHC 178

Kay v Ayrshire and Arran Health Board [1987] 2 All ER 417

Kent v Griffiths (No 3) [2001] QB 36

Lister and Others v Helsey Hall Ltd. [2001] UKHL 22; [2001] 2 WLR 1311

Lister v Romford Ice and Cold Storage Co Ltd. [1957] 1 All ER 125

Loveday v Renton and another. The Times 31 March 1988

MAK and RK v United Kingdom Application Nos 45901/05 and 40146/06 The Times Law Report 19 April 2010 ECHR

Maynard v West Midlands Regional Health Authority [1985] 1 All ER 871

McLean S (2011) *No Fault Compensation Review Group.* Scottish Government, Edinburgh

NHS Litigation Authority (2012) *Ten years of maternity claims.* NHSLA, London

NICE (2010) *Hypertension in pregnancy. CG 107.* NICE, London

Nursing and Midwifery Council (2004) *Code of professional conduct: Standards for conduct, performance and ethics.* NMC, London

Nursing and Midwifery Council (2008) *The code: Standards of conduct, performance and ethics for nurses and midwives.* NMC, London

Ratcliffe v Plymouth and Torbay HA, Exeter and Devon HA [1998] Lloyd's Rep Med 162 CA

Richards v Swansea NHS Trust [2007] EWHC 487

Smith v Sussex Police [2008] EWCA civ 39

Spencer v NHS North West [2012] EWHC 2142

The Catholic Child Welfare Society and others v various claimants and Institute of the Brothers of the Christian Schools and others [2012] UKSC 56

Whiston v London Strategic HA [2009] EWHC 956 QB

Whitehouse v Jordan [1981] 1 All ER 267

WHO, ICM and FIGO (2004) *Making pregnancy safer: The critical role of the skilled attendant* 2004/9241591692. WHO, Geneva

Wilsher v Essex Area Health Authority HL [1988] 1 All ER 871

Chapter 9

Record keeping, statements and report writing

This chapter considers the duty of keeping clear comprehensive records, making statements, compiling reports and giving evidence in court.

Duty of care and record keeping

Keeping clear comprehensive records is part of the duty of care owed to the client. Midwives have specific statutory duties under the Midwives Rules (Nursing and Midwifery Council, 2012) in relation to the keeping and transfer of records, including those relating to her contact with the midwifery supervisor. The Nursing and Midwifery Council (NMC) has also provided standards for the Local Supervisory Authority (see *Box 9.1*)

Box 9.1. NMC: Local Supervisory Authority standards on Rule 6

1. A local supervising authority must publish local guidelines for the transfer of midwifery records from self-employed midwives which should include:
   1.1 When the records are to be transferred.
   1.2 To whom the records are to be transferred.
   1.3 Methods to ensure the safe transit of records.
   1.4 Documentation to record such a transfer.

The NMC quotes from the Department of Health (2006) in suggesting that all records relating to the care of the woman or baby must be kept for 25 years. This would include work diaries if they contain clinical information. Although the NMC suggests a 25-year retention period, as does the Department of Health in its guidance on the storage of records (NHS Executive, 1999), if there is any sign that the child is brain damaged or suffers from a mental disability, those records should be kept until after the death of that person, since there is no time limit on bringing an action for compensation as long as the complainant who has a mental disability is alive (see *Chapter 8*).

Guidelines for records and record keeping

The NMC published in 2009 updated guidance on record keeping (due to be reviewed at the present time). It emphasises that the principles of good record keeping are well established and should reflect the core values of individuality and partnership working. The NMC (2009a) guidance states that:

> *Good record keeping is an integral part of nursing and midwifery practice and is essential to the provision of safe and effective care. It is not an optional extra to be fitted in if circumstances allow.*

The NMC document sets out the principles of good record keeping in Paragraphs 1 to 16 and these are shown in *Box 9.2*.

The Guidance also covers confidentiality, access disclosure, information systems and personal professional knowledge and skills. It also has a useful list of additional sources of information. It can be accessed on the NMC website (www. nmc-org.uk).

In 2012 an independent midwife successfully appealed against being struck off since she had not deliberately falsified her records – she had altered and added to her notes in an attempt to bolster her position (*Duthie v NMC*). The judge held that the NMC panel was wrong to assume that this made the evidence of the parents more credible. The case is discussed by Symon (2012). Additional advice on record keeping is given in the Royal College of Midwives booklet on litigation (Mason and Edwards, 1993) which, although written in 1993, is still relevant. This points out the need to ensure that all timings should be recorded consistently, preferably from the same clock; the need to record warnings of risks given to the mother and refusal by the mother to consent to recommended treatment or procedures; a note that abnormalities on the trace have been observed; and the procedure that should be followed if an error has been made in the records.

Additional guidance on record keeping is provided by the NHS Executive (1992). See also a two-part article by Mark Solon on facing a fitness to practise hearing: the first covering keeping good records (Solon, 2011a) and the second on appearing at a hearing (Solon, 2011b).

Contemporaneous records

Records should be written up as soon as possible after the events described and in any event not more than 24 hours later. Courts require records to be

Box 9.2. NMC principles of good record keeping

1. Handwriting should be legible.
2. All entries to records should be signed. In the case of written records, the person's name and job title should be printed alongside the first entry.
3. In line with local policy, you should put the date and time on all records. This should be in real time and chronological order and be as close to the actual time as possible
4. Your records should be accurate and recorded in such a way that the meaning is clear.
5. Records should be factual and not include unnecessary abbreviations, jargon, meaningless phrases or irrelevant speculation.
6. You should use your professional judgement to decide what is relevant and what should be recorded.
7. You should record details of any assessments and reviews undertaken and provide clear evidence of the arrangements you have made for future and ongoing care. This should also include details of information given about care and treatment.
8. Records should identify any risks or problems that have arisen and show the action taken to deal with them.
9. You have a duty to communicate fully and effectively with your colleagues, ensuring that they have all the information they need about the people in your care.
10. You must not alter or destroy any records without being authorised to do so.
11. In the unlikely event that you need to alter your own or another healthcare professional's records, you must give your name and job title, and sign and date the original documentation. You should make sure that the alterations you make, and the original record, are clear and auditable.
12. Where appropriate, the person in your care, or their carer, should be involved in the record keeping process.
13. The language that you use should be easily understood by the people in your care.
14. Records should be readable when photocopied or scanned.
15. You should not use coded expressions of sarcasm or humorous abbreviations to describe the people in your care.
16. You should not falsify records.

contemporaneous if they are to be used in evidence. One of the greatest problems in midwifery is the fact that if a midwife is under pressure during a delivery (and in hospital she may be responsible for providing care to more than one woman simultaneously) it is impossible for her to record events at the same time that the delivery takes place. She therefore relies upon being able to write up the delivery at a later stage. Sometimes midwives are known to use scraps of paper or even their arms or aprons for recording information which they later transfer into the proper record, destroying or washing out the original. This is not a recommended practice. It is preferable for the information to be recorded on the document which will be retained in the woman's record. Mistakes can occur when transferring the information from one document to another. Midwives should ensure that even while working under pressure, they keep as complete a contemporaneous account of the events as possible.

Alterations to records

If changes are necessary because inaccurate information has been entered, e.g. the wrong woman's name, then Tippex or correction fluid should not be used, rather a line should be placed through the wrong entry and the correct entry made, signed and dated clearly. Midwives may be under pressure to amend their records to accord with the doctor's account of the events. They should not under any circumstances allow their records to be altered.

Abbreviations

In its advice the NMC makes it clear that abbreviations should not be used. This is the ideal situation, but in practice the midwife makes considerable use of abbreviations and other signs and hieroglyphics to save time. It is essential that no misunderstandings should arise over the intended meaning, and there are advantages in an agreed list of abbreviations being approved by the trust, and enforced through disciplinary action if anyone uses abbreviations or signs not on the list, or uses one on the list for a different meaning (Dimond, 1998).

Storage and destruction of records

Advice is given in the NMC Midwives Rules and Standards (2012) about keeping the records for at least 25 years in the case of children. In addition, records relating to brain-damaged babies should be kept until three years after their death.

There will be local policies on destruction of records that relate to storage or microfilm facilities, but there should be senior midwifery involvement in policies relating to the destruction of midwifery records.

Ownership of records

NHS records are owned by the Secretary of State, but the actual management and responsibility for them are delegated to individual health organisations. The records are not owned by those who complete them. GPs are required under their terms of service to complete the records and return them to the NHS Clinical Commissioning Groups (in Wales, Local Health Boards) when a patient dies or leaves that practice. In contrast, the records of the independent midwife are owned by her, but under the Rules, on ceasing practice, she is obliged to keep them in a safe place or transfer them to the Local Supervising Authority.

Litigation

While the first objective of record keeping is the protection of the mother, inevitably in the event of a complaint or claim, the records become central to the evidence available. The fact that awards of compensation in birth injuries are among the highest, and that there is a greater likelihood of litigation in obstetrics and midwifery than other specialties, may put the records kept by midwives under greater scrutiny by the courts than those kept by any other professional group. In the event of a complaint or litigation, the records of other groups could also be used to complement the midwife's documentation. For example, in an emergency, if an ambulance has been sent for, the ambulance service will have full details of the time the call was made; they may also have tapes of any conversations; they may check drugs with the midwife and this would also be recorded. The midwife should not, however, rely on these records for completing her own notes of the case. This would be regarded as second-hand evidence. The ambulance records should be independent of those of the midwife.

Use of records in litigation

In any legal conflict, one of the biggest areas for dispute is over the facts of what occurred. While records are not in themselves proof of the truth of what occurred (records can be changed, or written incorrectly), they are used in conjunction with the evidence of the writer of the records so that the court can determine the weight that can be attached to them. The more distant in the past that the events occurred, the more dependent the witnesses will be on the documentation that was kept at the time. This is so whether the court proceedings are related to a claim for compensation being heard in the civil courts, a prosecution in the criminal courts, an inquest before the coroner, fitness to practice proceedings, or disciplinary proceedings brought by the employer against the employee. The outcome in many personal injury cases depends upon what can be proved in court, and where there are disputes of fact the records become extremely significant. In one case, *LW Midlands SHA*, where brain damage occurred as a result of cord occlusion, the records showed that the midwives had decided to call the obstetrician and it was the delay in his attending and not any negligence by the midwife that caused the harm. In the case of *Reynolds v Tyneside HA* the records showed that the staff followed hospital policy but the court concluded that the policy was incorrect and negligence was established.

An example of the importance of documentation is the case of *Bull and Wakeham v Devon Health Authority,* which was heard 17 years after the birth of twins.

The NHS Litigation Authority report (2012) analysing 10 years of maternity claims showed that for all settled maternity claims the average time from the incident date to the date when the claim was resolved by the NHS Litigation Authority was 4.32 years. For claims with damages above £1 million, the average time was 8.57 years, reflecting the complex nature of the higher value cases.

Cardiotocograph readings

Cardiotocograph readings were not taken in the *Bull and Wakeham* case, but now intrapartum fetal well-being can be assessed by electronic means or by intermittent auscultation with a Pinard's stethoscope.

The recommendation of the NMC that initials should either not be used or that a local index record of signatures should be kept is important. One of the most difficult tasks in midwifery litigation (which could be seen in the *Bull and Wakeham* case) is to identify the members of staff who were involved in the alleged negligent incident and to track down their current whereabouts.

Another issue in midwifery is the possibility of discrepancy between the records of the midwife and those of the obstetricians. This may sometimes reveal a conflict of evidence. For example, the midwife might have called a doctor to see the mother. Subsequently, the doctor might deny that any such request has been made. In order to prevent such a dispute, the midwife might ask the doctor to sign in the record or on the cardiotocograph the fact that he has seen the mother. The midwife should not regard such a signature as relieving her of all responsibility if harm occurs. She is still accountable for her professional duty of care to the mother and child.

Legal status of records

The question is often asked as to when a record becomes a legal document. The answer is simple: whenever it is relevant in a court of law and is required in evidence. In this sense there is no limit to the nature of records that could be ordered to be produced in court. Even scraps of paper, which a midwife might use to remind herself of significant events in the delivery, could be ordered to be produced in court if they are still available. X-rays, pathology test results, cardiotocographs, and fetal monitoring traces could all be produced in court.

However, records are not evidence of the truth of what is written upon them. Normally the writer of contemporaneous records would be called to give evidence of the circumstances that led to the record being made, and could be cross-examined upon them so that the court could determine the weight that should be attached to their credibility.

In midwifery cases, it may be many years before a court action is commenced. A child can bring a court action at any time before the end of three years of attaining his majority (i.e. 18 years + 3 years). A person under a disability which prevents him or her suing personally is under no time limit. Death initiates a time limit of three years.

Audit

Regular audit of record keeping standards is required to ensure that there is compliance with the Midwives Rules, Standards and Guidance. Regular review and advice by the supervisor of midwives of record keeping standards could ensure that a high standard of record keeping is established and maintained. In addition, midwives might be able to establish small internal groups of colleagues who can, at regular intervals, examine a set of records and monitor their standard, identifying any improvements that should be made. External auditors of record keeping standards may also be brought into the organisation to assist in establishing and maintaining standards. The King's Fund in London provides such a service. In addition, the Clinical Negligence Scheme for Trusts monitors record keeping standards for its members. (See *Chapter 8* on the role of the Clinical

Negligence Scheme for Trusts and the NHS Litigation Authority.) The NMC, in its guidance on records and record keeping (2009), states in Paragraph 34:

> By auditing records and acting on the results, you can assess the standard of the record keeping and communications. This will allow you to identify any areas where improvements might be made.

The Audit Commission (1995), in its report on hospital records, considered that patients were being put at risk because their medical records are not kept carefully and are sometimes lost. Failure to find records led to consultations being cancelled and to operations being postponed. It recommended that hospitals set up one main records library with good security.

The NHS Litigation Authority and the Clinical Negligence Scheme for Trusts

The Clinical Negligence Scheme for Trusts requires those trusts that belong to the scheme to maintain specified standards in relation to a range of topics, including record keeping. Hospital record keeping is one of the core standards. The standards set by the NHS Litigation Authority include in their criteria, principles relating to documentation. For example, criterion 8 for the governance standard relates to health records management. This states that chief executives and senior managers of all NHS organisations are personally accountable for records management within their organisation. These standards, updated in April 2010, can be seen on the NHS Litigation Authority website (www.nhsla.com/home.htm).

These standards can be used as the basis for a regular internal audit of documentation, even by those units that are not members of the Clinical Negligence Scheme for Trusts pool, to ensure that a reasonable standard is being maintained.

Each standard is accompanied by its reference source and additional guidance.

Electronic health records

The then Secretary of State for Health, Frank Dobson, announced on 24 September 1998 that there would be £1 billion investment to put all medical files on computer (Henderson, 1998). The initiative was to take place over seven years enabling records to be available for access on a 24-hour basis across the country and also permitting patients access in their own home. Three years later the Department of Health (2001) stated that by March 2005, every person in the country would have their own electronic patient record. The electronic health record was defined by the Department of Health as holding summarised key data about patients, such as name, address, NHS number, registered GP and contact details, previous treatments, ongoing conditions, current medication, allergies, and the date of any next appointments. The timetable for the electronic health record envisaged that five million people would have their own lifelong electronic patient record by 2003, rising to around 25 million by 2004 and then everyone by March 2005. Those were the hopes but the target was not reached. Regulations to permit electronic transmission of prescriptions were passed in 2001 (The Prescription Only Medicines [Human Use][Electronic Communications] Order). The present Government is aiming to achieve a paperless NHS by 2018. However, the initiative is no longer for large national IT contracts but for a bottom up approach with the St Helen's and Knowsley initiative being held up as a model. There, three NHS trusts and 88 GP practices have achieved a paperless system.

Julie Tindale and Nicholas Hardiker (2012), in a series on the use of technology in childbirth, review the use of electronic maternity records. They discuss the need for the competent midwife to be prepared for change and consider some of the advantages and dangers.

While the use of electronic records may avoid some of the problems resulting from illegible records, other difficulties can arise, as is seen in the case of Ms Simpkin. In August 1998 it was reported (Johnstone, 1998) that a student suffering from meningitis may have died as a result of her name being wrongly spelt on a computer. The omission of the letter "P" in her surname, Simpkin, meant that her records could not be accessed, and an inquiry found that she might have lived if vital results of blood tests, entered into the computerised records under the wrong name, had been seen by staff.

Department of Health strategy on information

In 2012, the Department of Health published a strategy relating to information entitled, *The power of information: Putting all of us in control of the health and care information we need.* It is only accessible online on the publications site of the Department of Health website.

A case study in paragraph 5.18 describes the use by Portsmouth midwives of a digital pen that midwives used to write up case notes. This has halved their paperwork. The pen works just like a normal pen on the paper record, which the mum-to-be keeps, but the pen also reads and automatically uploads the data on the form onto the hospital patient record system.

Woman-held records

In midwifery, it is increasingly the practice that women retain their own records during their antenatal care, bringing them to the clinics for their appointments. While this practice is in general very successful there are certain concerns: what if the mother destroys the records and then sues the trust for compensation? Can the midwife leave out information, e.g. previous pregnancy or abortion, if the woman so wishes? What if the records are lost? Ann Holmes and colleagues (2005) reviewed a pilot project for client-held records in Glasgow Maternity Hospital and concluded that the new system was valued by women and appeared to have improved communication between women and staff.

Destruction of records by mother

In a claim for compensation, the burden is on the claimant to show on a balance of probabilities that the defendant or its employees failed to follow a reasonable standard of care, which caused harm to the claimant. The fact that the claimant has lost the records which were in her custody would therefore work against her case.

Omission of information from the records

It would be contrary to professional practice for a midwife to omit essential information from a woman's obstetric history. Leaving out details of an earlier pregnancy could influence clinical decisions about the care of a mother. For example, if it were thought that the mother was a primagravida, dealing with her Rhesus negative state would be different than if it were known that this was a second or later pregnancy. In July 1998, a GP who allowed a patient to destroy part of her records was found guilty of serious professional misconduct by the General Medical Council (Forster, 1998). He had allowed the patient, who was involved in an acrimonious property dispute with her children, to remove a letter in which she was described as "bad tempered", and another document referring to her drinking. Where a woman wishes to have information deleted, or not kept on her record, because of fears that her partner may discover information of which he was ignorant, then she should be offered the opportunity to have her records kept in the hospital. Alternatively, there should be a note on her records that information kept at the hospital should be consulted before any decisions are taken. Under Data Protection provisions, patients can apply to access their records (subject to specified exclusions). This is considered in *Chapter 4*.

Statement making

Witnesses can refer to any contemporaneous records and statements in giving evidence and therefore, since it takes many years for some court hearings to take place, it is vital that comprehensive clear records have been kept and statements made. Before preparing a statement, a health professional should have advice from a senior colleague and, if possible, a lawyer. The elements shown in *Box 9.3* should be contained in a statement.

Box 9.3. Elements to include in a statement

- Date and time of the incident.
- Full name of statement maker, position, grade and location.
- Full names of any persons involved, e.g. patient, visitor, other staff.
- Date and time the statement was made.
- A full and detailed description of the events that occurred.
- Signature.
- Any supporting statement or document attached.

The statement writer should ensure that the statement is:

- Accurate
- Factual
- Concise
- Relevant
- Clear
- Legible (it will usually be typed) and
- Signed.

The statement maker should read it through, checking its overall impact and whether all relevant facts are included. A copy should be kept. Advice should be sought on its clarity and comprehensiveness, and it should not be signed unless the maker is satisfied that it records an accurate, clear account of what took place.

Report writing

Midwives may be required to prepare reports on a variety of topics, as managers, supervisors or individual midwives. In addition, senior midwives may be invited to provide reports as an expert witness.

Expert witnesses will normally be asked to prepare a report by a solicitor representing one of the parties to the case. This report is vital since, if it is unfavourable to the party seeking it, the outcome may be that the case is settled or even withdrawn.

Box 9.4 illustrates some of the principles which should be followed in report writing.

Box 9.4. Principles to be followed in report writing

- Identify the purpose of the report, likely readership and the kind of language that can be used, and therefore the appropriate style to be used.
- Identify the main areas to be included.
- Decide the order to be followed: sometimes chronological order is appropriate, at other times subject order may be preferable.
- Sign and date it, but only after reading it through and being 100% satisfied with it.
- Identify the different kinds of information used in the report and state the source of the material, e.g. hearsay evidence, factual evidence observed or heard by the author of the report, evidence of opinion of another person, statements by others, similar fact evidence.
- Avoid the mistakes shown in *Box 9.5*.

For most purposes the style likely to be of greatest use is one of simplicity, with short sentences, clear paragraphing and sub-paragraphing, and avoidance of jargon and meaningless clichés. The report should begin with a statement as to its purpose, the person(s) to whom it is addressed, and the name and status of the writer. If it is confidential, this should be highlighted at the beginning. Other documents that are relevant should be carefully referenced.

Giving evidence in court: Witness of fact

As a witness of fact, the midwife may be required to give direct evidence over a matter with which she has been involved. If she is asked to give evidence, an employed midwife would be assisted by senior midwifery management and the solicitors to the trust. In giving evidence she should ensure that she keeps to the facts and does not offer an opinion. She may need guidance and training in how to respond to cross-examination. It is vital that she does not give facts that are outside her knowledge.

Box 9.5. Common mistakes in report writing

- Lack of clarity.
- Failure to follow a logical order.
- Inconsistency.
- Ambiguities.
- Lack of signature and/or date.
- Lack of dates within the report.
- Wrong names included.
- Confusing account.
- Mix of evidence and sources.
- Inaccuracies.
- Opinion without facts.
- Failure to cite facts to support statements.
- Too complex a style for reader.
- Use of inappropriate jargon.
- Use of misleading abbreviations.
- Failure to give conclusions or to base conclusions on the evidence.
- Failure to ask someone else to read.

The following are key points for witness of fact.

Preparation

- Ensure that the records are available, identify significant entries with post-it notes, but do not mark or staple or pin anything to the records. Read them through so that you are familiar with them.
- Try to obtain assistance from a lawyer or senior manager in preparation for the court hearing, so that you are prepared for giving evidence in chief and answering questions under cross-examination.
- Try to visit the court in advance to familiarise yourself with its location, car parking, toilets, catering facilities, etc.

At the court before the hearing

- Be prepared for a long wait, and take work to do or something to occupy yourself.

- Dress appropriately and comfortably, but not too casually.
- Try to relax.

Giving evidence

- Keep calm.
- Give answers clearly and without exaggeration.
- Tell the truth.
- Do not feel that you are there to represent only one side; you must answer the questions honestly, even though it might put the side cross-examining you in a good light.
- Take time over your answers, and do not make up replies if you are unable to answer the question raised.
- Do not answer back or allow yourself to be flustered during the cross-examination.
- If you do not understand any legal jargon that is used, ask for an explanation.
- Keep to the facts and do not express an opinion.
- Ask for time to refer to the records if this is necessary.

Giving evidence in court: Expert witness

An expert witness is invited to give evidence of opinion on any issue that is subject to dispute. This could include the standards of care that would have been expected according to the Bolam Test (see *Chapter 8*), or the opinion may relate to what caused the harm suffered by the mother or baby. Expert opinion may also be brought in if there is a dispute over the assessment of compensation. In the case of *Sutcliffe v Aintree Hospitals NHS Trust*, the Court of Appeal refused to overturn a decision by the trial judge who, relying upon the evidence of an expert witness, held that the only explanation for the contamination of the spinal anaesthetic (which caused chronic adhesive arachnoiditis) was breach of the duty of care by one or other of the clinicians who administered the spinal anaesthetic block.

Where an expert has prepared a report for a solicitor in anticipation or in the course of litigation, that report and any correspondence connected with it, are protected by legal professional privilege (see *Chapter 4*) and it cannot be ordered to be disclosed in court or the expert compelled to appear by the other side. However, once the report is disclosed to the court, it loses its professional privilege (which continues to attach to any correspondence between the parties that has not been disclosed). As a result of the changes in civil procedure following the Woolf Reforms (Woolf, 1996), where an expert's report is used in evidence, all amendments and changes to that report must also be disclosed. The expert has a duty to the court. The court held in *Autospin (Oil Seals) Ltd v Beehive Spinning (A firm)*, that the expert witness had a responsibility to approach the task of giving evidence seriously and an expert should not be surprised if the court expressed strong disapproval if that was not done. In another case, the Court of Appeal upheld the principle that the expert's duty was to the court rather than to the party who had instructed him. The new Civil Procedure Rules set out explicitly the duty of the expert to the court (they can be accessed at www.justice.gov.uk/courts/procedure-rules/civil/rules/).

Rule 35.3 states:

(1) It is the duty of experts to help the court on the matters within their expertise.

(2) This duty overrides any obligation to the person from whom experts have received instructions or by whom they are paid.

Under the Rules, the court has the power to restrict expert evidence (35.4) and there is a general requirement for expert evidence to be given in a written report (35.5). The Woolf Reforms recommended that experts should be agreed between the parties prior to any hearing, in order that the time and costs of the case could be reduced. Under Rule 35.7, the court has the power to direct that evidence is to be given by a single joint expert. This is not always possible in some of the large compensation claims in obstetrics and midwifery, when several different witnesses may be called as experts in different areas of practice.

In the case of *Wardlaw v Dr Farrar* the Court of Appeal considered an application from the claimant that fresh evidence should be admitted by way of some additional pages from a standard medical textbook, part of which only had been before the County Court judge. The Court of Appeal dismissed the appeal holding that such evidence could have been adduced before trial and the standard directions on the exchange of medical expert literature should have been made. It was not prepared to interfere with the decision of the trial judge who was clearly impressed by the expert evidence given on behalf of the defendant. In contrast, the Court of Appeal in *ES (by her mother and litigation friend DS) v Chesterfield and North Derbyshire Royal NHS Trust*, allowed an appeal by a claimant who had requested permission to use two obstetric experts to support a claim that an obstetric registrar had been negligent in the management of her birth. The Court of Appeal held that some exceptional circumstances justified more experts: here the defence would be calling three consultants in obstetrics to respond to the claimant's single expert and under the Civil Procedure Rules it was important to ensure that the parties were on an equal footing.

Civil proceedings

Prior to any hearing in court, a considerable number of documents will be exchanged between the parties in conflict. These are designed to identify the issues in dispute, to ensure that both sides have access to all relevant documentation and that the court hearing is as short as possible commensurate with justice being done. Under the Woolf Reforms, changes were made to civil proceedings to simplify and speed up the process. Further changes for personal injury claims in relation to legal aid funding, no win, no fee systems of payment and civil justice were implemented from April 2012. These increase the small claims limit from £1000 to £5000 where costs are not recoverable, the standard fixed fee category rises from £10000 to £25000 with reduced fees payable, and the success fee payable to solicitors will have to be paid out of compensation, and is not recoverable from the defendant. This may see the end of the no win, no fee system and may make the funding of personal injury claims more problematic.

Conclusions

There is perhaps insufficient sharing between colleagues of the lessons learnt from litigation, even when the defendant professionals and Health Authorities/ NHS trusts win the case. Regular training in record keeping is essential for all professionals, particularly in midwifery where the peaks and troughs of activity are not predictable and when, in the pressure of the delivery, record keeping may be given a low priority. In addition, midwives should have training and assistance in making statements, writing reports and giving evidence in court.

The NHS Litigation Authority, in its report in 2012, stated that maternity claims represent the highest value and second highest number of clinical negligence claims reported to the Authority. It concluded that the most effective way to reduce the financial and human cost of maternity claims is to continue to improve the management of risks associated with maternity care, focusing on preventing incidents involving the management of women in labour, including the interpretation of cardiotocograph traces. The report can be accessed on the internet (www.nhsla.com/safety/Documents/). Clearly, maintaining high standards of record keeping is an essential part of the risk management process.

Questions and exercises

1. Discuss a strategy for keeping records while under pressure of work. Your strategy could include the use of agreed abbreviations, pre-printed forms and other devices that would be safe to adopt in speeding up record keeping.
2. With a colleague, look critically at the records kept over a two-week period. In what ways could the standard be improved?
3. Imagine that, in 15 years' time, you are being cross-examined on the care that you have provided in a particular case. Consider to what extent the records would be satisfactory as evidence in such circumstances.
4. Prepare a checklist for a report to be used in a child abuse case conference.
5. You have been asked to appear in court next week. Identify your worst fears about this request and devise ways of overcoming them.

References

Audit Commission (1995) *Setting the records straight: A study of hospital medical records.* HMSO, London

Autospin (Oil Seals) Ltd v Beehive Spinning (A firm) Times Law Report 9 August 1995

Bull and Wakeham v Devon Health Authority. Court of Appeal [1989] CA 2 February 1989 Transcript; [1993] 4 Med LR 117 CA

CJL v West Midlands SHA [2009] EWHC 259

Department of Health (2001) *Patients to gain access to new at-a-glance Electronic Health Records.* HMSO, London

Department of Health (2006) *NHS code of practice on records management.* HMSO, London

Department of Health (2012) *The power of information: Putting all of us in control of the health and care information we need.* HMSO, London

Dimond B (1998) Abbreviations, record keeping and the midwife. *Practising Midwife* 1(9): 10–11

Duthie v NMC 2012 EWHC 3021 Admin

ES (by her mother and litigation friend DS) v Chesterfield and North Derbyshire Royal NHS Trust [2003] EWCA Civ 1284; Lloyd's Rep. Med [2004] 90

Forster P (1998) GP allowed patient to tamper with records. *The Times* **7 July**

Henderson M (1998) £1bn scheme will put all medical files on computer. *The Times* **25 September**

Holmes A, Cheyne H, Ginley M, Mathers A (2005) Trialling and implementing a client-held record system. *British Journal of Midwifery* 13(2): 112–7

Johnstone H (1998) Spelling mistake may have cost student her life. *The Times* **28**

August

Lord Woolf (1996) *Final report: Access to justice*. HMSO, London

Mason D, Edwards P (1993) *Litigation: A risk management guide for midwives*. Royal College of Midwives in conjunction with Capsticks solicitors, London

NHS Executive (1999) *For the record. Health Service Circular 1999/053*. Department of Health, London

NHS Litigation Authority (2012) *Ten years of maternity claims*. NHSLA, London

NHS Training Directorate (1992) *Keeping the record straight*. Department of Health, London

NHS Training Directorate (1994) *Just for the record: A guide to record keeping for healthcare professionals*. Department of Health, London

Nursing and Midwifery Council (2009a) *Guidance on record keeping*. NMC, London

Nursing and Midwifery Council (2009b) *Record keeping. Guidance for nurses and midwives*. NMC, London

Nursing and Midwifery Council (2012) *Midwives rules and standards*. NMC, London

Peter Wardlaw v Dr Stephen Farrar Lloyd's Rep Med [2004] 98

Reynolds v Tyneside HA [2002] Lloyds Rep Med 459

Solon M (2011a) Where's your evidence? Keeping good records. *Practising Midwife* **14**(4): 24–5

Solon M (2011b) Keep calm and carry on: Appearing at a hearing. *Practising Midwife* **14**(7): 26–7

Stevens v Gullis The Times 6 October 1999

Sutcliffe v Aintree Hospitals NHS Trust [2008] EWCA Civ 179

Symon A (2012) People sometimes lie for reasons other than guilt. *British Journal of Midwifery* **12**: 905–6

The Prescription Only Medicines (Human Use)(Electronic Communications) Order 2001 SI 2001 No 2889

Tindale J, Hardiker N (2012) Electronic maternity records. *Practising Midwife* **15**(4): 38–41

Wardlaw v Farrar [2004] Lloyds Rep Med 98

Chapter 10

Health and safety

This chapter on health and safety is included in the section on accountability since liability for incidents relating to health and safety can lead to hearings in the four main forums that could determine the accountability of the midwife:

- To the public through the criminal law.
- To the patient/client through the civil law.
- To her employer through the contract of employment.
- To her profession through the Nursing and Midwifery Council (NMC) fitness to practice proceedings

This chapter will only attempt a brief introduction to health and safety law with particular reference to midwifery practice and the reader is referred to the more extensive coverage in a book within this series (Dimond, 2010).

The Health and Safety Executive (HSE) website (www.hsedirect.com) provides an online information service giving instant access to all the latest health and safety legislation, Approved Codes of Practice and HSE guidance, among much more.

The Royal College of Midwives (RCM, 2010) provides a health and safety at work resource book which covers the legal framework, duties of employer and risk assessment and safety policies. Appendix C provides very useful checklists for safety inspections. It can be accessed on the RCM website (www.rcm.org.uk/EasysiteWeb/getresource.axd).

Box 10.1 shows the areas of law that relate to health and safety.

Box 10.1. Health and safety laws

- Employer's duty under the contract of employment
- Employee's duty under the contract of employment
- Health and Safety at Work Act 1974 and subsequent Regulations
- Occupier's Liability Acts 1957 and 1984
- Consumer Protection Act 1987
- Medical Devices Regulations 2002 SI 2002 No 618
- Control of Substances Hazardous to Health 2002 SI 2002/2677
- Reporting of Injuries, Diseases and Dangerous Occurrences Regulations (RIDDOR) 1995 SI 1995/3163 (as amended)

Not all of the areas of law shown in *Box 10.1* are covered in detail here since the purpose of this chapter is to give the midwife a general understanding of the broad principles that apply so that she can build upon this knowledge with her own research and reading. The HSE provides information on all these topics and can be accessed at its website (www.hse.gov.uk). The obligations placed by the Acts of Parliament and the common law create similar fields of accountability to those discussed in *Chapter 1*. These are shown in *Box 10.2*.

Box 10.2. Accountability in relation to health and safety

Criminal laws
- Health and Safety at Work Act 1974 and Regulations
- Offices Shops and Railway Premises Act 1963
- Factories Act 1961
- Food Safety Act 1990 and other legislation
- Environmental Protection Act 1990
- Regulations shown in *Box 10.6*

Civil action
- Breach of statutory duty
- Action for negligence
- Occupier's Liability Act 1957
- Occupier's Liability Act 1984
- Consumer Protection Act 1987

Employer and contract of employment
- Laws of contract
- Statutory protection provided by the Employment Protection Legislation
- Rules relating to Employment Tribunals

Professional Registration and Codes
- Nursing and Midwifery Council (Midwives) Rules Order of Council 2004 Statutory Instrument 2004/1764 updated 2012 and in force 2013
- Code of Professional Conduct: Standards for conduct, performance and ethics (Nursing and Midwifery Council, 2008)

Criminal laws

The Health and Safety at Work Act 1974 is enforced through the criminal courts by the Health and Safety Inspectorate which has the power to prosecute for offences under the Act and the Regulations and which also has powers of inspection and can issue enforcement or prohibition notices. The Health and Safety Executive website gives information on criminal prosecutions for health and safety offences. For example, it reported in 2009 that a primary care trust was fined £10000 after a patient fell from a window (Health and Safety Executive, 2009).

The basic duty on the employer is set out in *Box 10.3*.

Box 10.3. Duty under the Health and Safety at Work Act 1974

- Section 2(1): It shall be the duty of every employer to ensure, so far as is reasonably practicable, the health, safety and welfare at work of all his employees.
- Section 2(2) of the 1974 Act gives examples of the various duties which must be carried out but these do not detract from the width and comprehensiveness of the general duty.

The Act also places a specific responsibility upon the employee. This is shown in *Box 10.4*.

Box 10.4. Statutory duty of the employee under Section 7 of the Health and Safety at Work Act 1974

- To take reasonable care for the health and safety of himself and of others who may be affected by his acts or omissions at work.
- As regards any duty imposed on his employer or any other person, to cooperate with him so far as is reasonable to enable that duty to be performed or complied with.

It is also a criminal offence for an employee to interfere with health and safety measures. See *Box 10.5*.

Box 10.5. Section 8 Health and Safety at Work Act 1974

- No person shall intentionally or recklessly interfere with or misuse anything provided in the interest of health, safety or welfare in pursuance of any relevant statutory provisions.

New Regulations came into force on 1 January 1993 as a result of European Directives. These, together with other Regulations, are shown in *Box 10.6*. Many have subsequently been updated.

Box 10.6. Health and Safety Regulations

- Management of Health And Safety at Work Regulations 1992 (SI 1992 2051) (revised 1999 SI 1999 No 3242)
- Provision and Use of Work Equipment Regulations 1992 (SI 1992 2932) (revised 1998 SI 1998/2306)
- Manual Handling Operations Regulations 1992 (SI 1992 2793)
- Workplace (Health, Safety and Welfare) Regulations 1992 (SI 1992 3004) (amended by SI 1999/2024)
- Personal Protective Equipment at Work Regulations 1992 (SI 1992 2966) (amended by SI 1999/3232)
- Health and Safety (Display Screen Equipment) Regulations 1992 (SI 1992 2792)
- Health and Safety First Aid Regulations 1981 (SI 917)
- Health and Safety (Safety Signs and Signals) Regulations 1996 (SI 341)
- Fire Precautions (Workplace) Regulations 1997 (SI 1840)
- Hazardous Waste (England and Wales) 2005 (SI 894)

These Regulations can be accessed online (www.legislation.gov.uk/uksi/) followed by the year and SI number.

The Health and Safety Commission (2000) has provided an approved Code of Practice and Guidance along with the 1999 Regulations on the Management of Health and Safety. The legal status of this Code is explained in the introduction:

> *This Code has been approved by the Health and Safety Commission, with the consent of the Secretary of State... If you are prosecuted for breach of health and safety law, and it is proved that you did not follow the relevant provisions of the Code, you will need to show that you have complied with the law in some other way or a court will find you at fault. This document also includes other, more general guidance not having this special status...*

New and expectant mothers

The 1999 Regulations introduce provisions for the protection of new and expectant mothers and young persons. A "new and expectant mother" is defined

166

as an employee who is pregnant, who has given birth within the previous six months, or who is breastfeeding. Under Regulation 16, employers have a specific duty to carry out an assessment of risk which arises by reason of their condition and if the risk cannot be avoided, then to alter her working conditions or hours of work and if this would not remove the risk, then the employer should suspend the employee as long as is necessary to avoid such a risk.

Regulation 17 states that where a new or expectant mother works at night, and there is a certificate from a registered medical practitioner or registered midwife that she should not work for any period identified in the certificate, then the employer shall suspend her from work as long as it is necessary for her health or safety. The onus is on the woman to notify the employer in writing that she is pregnant (and to provide a certificate of that fact), has given birth within the previous six months or is breastfeeding. The suspension would be on full pay.

Risk assessment

The law

Regulation 3 requires:

> *Every employer shall make a suitable and sufficient assessment of*
> *(a) the risks to the health and safety of his employee to which they are exposed whilst they are at work; and*
> *(b) the risks to the health and safety of persons not in his employment arising out of or in connection with the conduct by him of his undertaking,*
> *for the purpose of identifying the measures he needs to take to comply with the requirements and prohibitions imposed upon him by or under the relevant statutory provisions.*

The duty also applies to independent midwives: Regulation 3 Paragraph (2) requires every self-employed person to make a suitable and sufficient assessment of (a) the risks to his own health and safety to which he is exposed while he is at work; and (b) the risks to the health and safety of persons not in his employment arising out of or in connection with the conduct by him or his undertaking, for the purposes of identifying the measures he needs to take to comply with the requirements and prohibitions imposed upon him by or under the relevant statutory provisions.

There is a duty under Regulation 3(3) to review the assessment when there is reason to suspect that it is no longer valid or there has been significant change in the matters to which it relates.

Regulation 3(4) requires an employer to make an assessment before employing a young person (a person below 18 years).

The Approved Code of Practice and Guidance

The Approved Code of Practice emphasises that risk assessment must be a systematic general examination of the effect of the employer's undertaking, its work activities and the condition of the premises. There should be a record of the significant findings of that risk assessment.

The definition of risk includes both the likelihood that harm will occur and its severity. The aim of risk assessment is to help the employer or self-employed person to determine what measures should be taken to comply with the statutory obligations laid down under the Health and Safety at Work Act 1974 and its Regulations.

Suitable and sufficient is defined in the Approved Code of Practice as:

- Identifying the risks arising out of work.
- Enabling the employer or the self-employed person to take reasonable steps to help themselves identify risks.
- Being appropriate to the nature of the work and having an identified period for which it is likely to be valid.

How is the risk assessment to be carried out?

The Approved Code of Practice states that there are no fixed rules about how a risk assessment should be carried out, and it will depend upon the nature of the work and the types of hazards and risks. The Code sets out some general principles that should be followed and these are summarised in *Box 10.7*.

The HSE published guidance in 2006 on the five steps to risk assessment. The guidance is available on its website.

Recording

The record should represent an effective statement of hazards and risks which then leads management to take the relevant actions to protect health and safety. It should be in writing unless in computerised form and should be easily retrievable.

Box 10.7 Requirements of valid risk assessment

- Ensure that all relevant risks or hazards are addressed.
- Ensure all aspects of the work activity are reviewed.
- Take account of non-routine operations.
- Take account of the management of incidents.
- Be systematic.
- Take account of the way in which work is organised.
- Take account of risks to the public.
- Take account of the need to cover fire risks.

It should include:

- A record of the preventive and protective measures in place to control risks.
- What further action, if any, needs to be taken to reduce risk sufficiently.
- Proof that a suitable and sufficient assessment has been made.

Preventive and protective measures

Schedule 1 of the Regulations specifies the general principles of prevention required by the EEC and in Regulation 4. These include:

- Avoiding risks.
- Evaluating the risks that cannot be avoided.
- Combating the risks at source.
- Adapting the work to the individual.
- Adapting to technical progress.
- Replacing the dangerous by the non-dangerous or the less dangerous.
- Developing a coherent overall prevention policy.
- Giving collective protective measures priority over individual protective measures.
- Giving appropriate instructions to employees.

How do these Regulations relate to the role of the midwife?

For the most part, the midwife would share common health and safety hazards with other hospital or community-based employees, and thus models of risk assessment and management which applied to midwifery would also apply to other health professionals. Hazards relating to the safety of equipment, cross-infection risks, safe working practices or violence at work would all apply to midwives, who should be involved in the assessment of risk. The midwife could also apply these same principles of risk assessment to the care of the woman and baby, identifying any particular circumstances that could cause harm and ensuring that reasonable action is taken to prevent such an occurrence.

Reference should also be made to the work in clinical risk management of the Clinical Negligence Scheme for Trusts discussed in *Chapter 8*. In 2010 Catherine Doherty gave advice on managing risk in maternity services and achieving accreditation for the Clinical Negligence Scheme for Trusts. The advice is available online (www.rcm.org.uk).

The midwife and violence

Many health professionals, including community midwives, work in fear of violence from strangers in the street as well as abuse from relatives of clients and even clients themselves. If this is a real fear in a particular locality then an assessment should be carried out.

- Is it possible to remove the risk altogether? If the answer to this is yes, but only by stopping all home confinements and community visits by midwives, then it could be said not to be a realistic possibility.
- What preventive action or protective measures can be taken? The answer to this might include the provision of two-way radios, personal alarms or, in very dangerous areas or on visits to clients who present a threat, midwives going in pairs or accompanied by another person, who may be a police officer.
- Are attacks due to the view that midwives carry drugs? Could this be prevented by necessary medication being obtained by the patients on prescription and kept at the home, so that midwives do not have to carry them?
- Review the situation to ascertain if the nature of the risk has changed (e.g. the district is more violent than it was formerly assessed to be), and the extent of the success of the measures taken to prevent harm to midwives.
- Are any further measures necessary?

This type of analysis will not relate only to community midwives – it could be part of a wider assessment of all community health professionals into which the community midwife could have an input. Clearly the risk assessment is dependent upon having accurate feedback from employees and others about incidents and threatening situations.

Guidance is published by the Health and Safety Commission (1997). This gives practical advice for reducing the risk of violence in a variety of settings and emphasises the importance of commitment from the highest levels of management. An appendix includes a checklist for home visiting. The RCM has also provided advice on safety in maternity units (RCM, 2000) and for midwives working in the community (RCM, 1996).

There is a 24-hour national domestic violence freephone helpline (0808 2000 247) run in partnership between Women's Aid and Refuge.

An article by Steen and Keeling (2012) provides a useful table of indicators which can alert a midwife to the possibility of potential or actual abuse and suggests how questions could be asked sensitively.

In exceptional circumstances police could be brought into antenatal clinics or onto the wards.

Research carried out by the NHS Business Services Authority concluded that physical violence against NHS employees cost the NHS £60.5 million during 2007/8 (NHS Counter Fraud Service, 2010). Of this total, £29 million was attributable to staff leaving the NHS. The report is available on the website of the NHS Business Services Authority (www.nhsbsa.nhs.uk).

The Criminal Justice and Immigration Act 2008 created a new criminal offence of causing a nuisance or disturbance on NHS hospital premises and refusing to leave.

In July 2010 a research study, *Violence against frontline NHS staff* (available from: www.nhsbsa.nhs.uk), was published. The research was undertaken by Ipsos MORI Social Research Institute on behalf of the NHS Security Management Service which is part of the NHS Business Services Authority. It emphasised the importance of the awareness and attendance at Conflict Resolution Training.

A pack on zero tolerance in relation to violence at work was provided by the NHS and is now available from the NHS Security Management Service. It also has further information on preventing violence (www.nhsbsa.nhs.uk/SecurityManagement).

In June 2004 the Court ordered the banning of Norman Hutchins from every hospital and doctor's surgery in England and Wales (Lister, 2004). The South West London and St George's Mental Health NHS Trust was fined £28 000 and ordered to pay £14 000 prosecution costs for systematic failures which led to a nurse being battered to death by a patient at Springfield Hospital (*The Times*, 2005).

The NHS Security Management Service launched a poster campaign to explain how staff can protect themselves against violence in the NHS. The Health and Safety Executive has issued guidance for employers on tackling violence which can be accessed on its website (www.hse.gov.uk).

Domestic violence against pregnant women

Concern is growing at the numbers of pregnant women who are subjected to domestic violence (Hunt and Martin, 2001). Midwives may be told of the violence in confidence. However, reporting such information may be a justifiable exception to the duty of confidentiality, since it would be in the public interest (see *Chapter 4*) to ensure that a woman, particularly one lacking mental capacity, with learning disabilities, and with children at risk, received protection. The Home Office published a consultation paper in June 2003 on ways to prevent and follow up domestic violence. It looked at three areas: prevention, protection, and justice and support for victims. The Home Office document, *Tackling domestic violence; the role of the health professional* (2004), lists the signs to look out for. The Department of Health (2010a) published, *Responding to violence against women and children – the role of the NHS: Report from sexual violence against women subgroup*, and in the same year, *Improving services for women and child victims of violence: Department of Health action plan*. These are available on the Department of Health website.

The Domestic Violence, Crime and Victims Act 2004 Part 1 covers the following topics:

- Breach of non-molestation order to be a criminal offence.
- Additional considerations if parties are cohabitants or former cohabitants.
- Cohabitants in Part 4 of 1996 Act to include same-sex couples.
- Extension of Part 4 of 1996 Act to non-cohabiting couples.
- Causing or allowing the death of a child or vulnerable adult to be an offence.
- Establishment and conduct of domestic homicide reviews.

Under Part 2 of the Act, common assault becomes an arrestable offence for the purposes of the Police and Criminal Evidence Act 1984, thereby increasing the powers of the police and citizens in relation to such an offence.

The provisions under Part 3 of the Act relating to victims should also benefit those suffering from domestic violence. A Victim's Code of Practice was issued by the Secretary of State under Section 32 of the 2004 Act to cover the services to be provided to a victim of criminal conduct. It can be accessed on the Justice website (www.justice.gov.uk/downloads/victims-and-witnesses). Failure to comply with the Code, while not an offence in itself, could be used in evidence in civil and criminal proceedings.

The 2004 Act was amended by the Domestic Violence, Crime and Victims (Amendment) Act 2012 to include causing serious physical harm. In November 2012 the Protection from Harassment Act was amended by the Protection of Freedoms Act 2012 to create new offences, making stalking a criminal offence. One is the criminal offence of stalking; the other is stalking involving fear of violence or serious alarm or distress. There are also additional related police search powers.

Midwives can play a significant role in the detection and support of women who are exposed to domestic violence (Dimond, 2003; Johnstone, 2003). Midwives should have access to a local policy on domestic violence and good links with any local organisation aimed at protecting partners and children against such violence. They should be aware of research such as that by June Keeling (2012) who considered the impact of violence against women on infant feeding. She found that violence may negatively affect a woman's perception of her baby and may lead to a dislike for a specific part of her body and her choice of infant feeding. Research published in Hunt (2011) found that most pregnant women backed routine domestic violence questioning. Participants in the study who had experienced domestic violence said that they would not have had the courage to bring the subject up if the midwives had not. A report published by the Department of Health in March 2010 (Department of Health, 2010a), written by the Task Force on Health Aspects of Violence Against Women and Children and chaired by Professor George Alberti, sets out a series of recommendations stressing the need for increased awareness, training and education for NHS staff. Melanie Walker, chief executive of Newham Primary Care Trust, is chairing an implementation group (the report can be accessed on www.dh.gov.uk.vawc). In the week of International Women's Day in 2011 the Home Office published an action plan to address and raise awareness of violent crimes against women and girls focusing on identification, intervention and prevention. The plan can be obtained from the Home Office website (www. homeoffice.gov.uk/crime/violence-against-women-girls/).

Risk assessment and midwife-managed units

Other assessments of risk could apply to midwifery activity. For example, it may be that the NHS trust is considering setting up a midwife-managed unit. In the planning of this unit it would be necessary to assess which mothers should not be admitted to such a unit but should be delivered with the facilities of a district general hospital. Such an assessment would require the identification of which tests were required during the antenatal stages to identify contraindications. An analysis would then be necessary of those risks in childbirth which could occur and the measures necessary either to prevent them occurring or to reduce their seriousness. Should the unit have storage facilities for blood? What additional procedures should the midwife receive training in, in case certain risks materialised (e.g. resuscitation of the newborn)? Working parties could plan procedures for coping with emergencies and the necessary cooperation with paramedic ambulance staff, obstetricians and staff in the operation theatres of nearby general hospitals (Dimond, 1994a, b). Reference could also be made to the Royal College of Midwives' Stewards Briefings and newsletters for health and safety representatives. See also the discussion of risk management in relation to the Clinical Negligence Scheme for Trusts considered in *Chapter 8*.

Conclusions on risk assessment and management

The emphasis in the guidance from the Health and Safety Executive is on the assessment of significant risks. There is a realism therefore about the regulations, which may have been lacking in health and safety audits carried out in the past. Midwives are central to the assessment process, since they have first-hand knowledge of the dangers that they face.

Manual handling regulations

Back injuries have been recognised as a major reason for sickness and staff retiring early on grounds of ill health. The Royal College of Midwives (1999) has provided guidance on manual handling and in its resource handbook (Royal College of Midwives, 2010) for health and safety representatives. (See also Royal College of Midwives guidance to workplace representatives online: www.rcm.org.uk.) The Royal College of Midwives resource book states that 11 million working days are lost due to musculo-skeletal disorders, including work-related back pain. The overall cost to industry is £5 billion per annum. Of all the workplace accidents reported to the Health and Safety Executive each year, 33% are associated with manual handling. Within the health services the proportion is considerably higher, accounting for over 50% of accidents reported, over 60% of which involve patient handling.

Regulations have been enacted under the Health and Safety Act 1974 and are published with guidance by the Health and Safety Executive (1992). The guidelines are not themselves the law and the booklet advises that the guidelines set out in Appendix 1 "should not be regarded as precise recommendations. They should be applied with caution. Where doubt remains, a more detailed assessment should be made."

A Working Group set up by the Health and Safety Commission (1992) has produced a booklet of guidance on manual handling of loads in the health services. This document is described as "an authoritative document which will be used by health and safety inspectors in describing reliable and fully acceptable methods of achieving health and safety in the workplace". Part of this health services-specific guidance material relates to staff working in the community.

Content of the regulations

The duty under the manual handling regulations can be summed up as follows:

- If possible, avoid the hazardous manual handling.
- Make a suitable and sufficient assessment of any hazardous manual handling which cannot be avoided.
- Reduce the risk of injury from this handling so far as is reasonably practicable.
- Provide information about the load and centre of weight.
- Review the assessment.

The Royal College of Midwives has identified the following areas as particularly relevant to midwives:

- Helping clients to breastfeed.
- Delivery, particularly in water births and alternative positions.
- Clients with epidurals.
- Clients who have had lower segment Caesarean sections.
- Baby bathing.
- Transfer between ward or theatre.
- Disabled mothers.
- Lifting of equipment, in hospital, home or car.

The assessment should take into account the mother's choice of place of confinement. It may be, for example, that following an assessment, the mother is advised that the accommodation is unsuitable to ensure the health and safety of the mother and baby and also of the midwife during the confinement.

Agency and bank midwives and independent midwives

The duty that is owed by the employer is owed not only to employees but also to temporary staff such as agency or bank midwives who are called in to assist. All such employees are entitled to be included in the risk assessment process, since, as has been seen, the assessment must take into account the individual characteristics of each employee.

Midwives who are unusually small in height or not so strong as an average person might require special provisions in relation to manual handling. Independent midwives are not employees and as self-employed persons would be responsible for carrying out the assessments and taking the necessary precautions for themselves and any staff whom they employ. Where they work alongside employed midwives in maternity delivery units, they should ensure that the NHS trust takes into account hazards to their health and safety, and that the agreement that they have with the NHS trust reflects this duty.

What action can be taken if the employer ignores these Regulations?

The Regulations are part of the health and safety provisions which form part of the criminal law. Infringement of the Regulations can lead to prosecution by the Health and Safety Inspectorate. The Inspectorate has the power to issue enforcement or prohibition notices against any corporate body or individual.

What remedies exist for compensation?

Section 47 of the Health and Safety at Work Act 1974 prevents breach of a duty under Sections 2–8 of the Act being used as the basis for a claim in the civil courts. Breach of the Regulations can, however, be the basis of a civil claim for compensation unless the Regulations provide to the contrary. Even where what is alleged is a breach of the basic duties, a midwife who suffered harm as a result of the failure of the employer to take reasonable steps to safeguard her health and safety, could sue in the civil courts on the basis of the employer's duty of care to her at common law.

Employer's duty at common law and manual handling

The statutory duty to ensure the Act is implemented is paralleled by a duty at common law placed upon the employer to take reasonable steps to ensure the employee's health and safety. Contracts of employment should state clearly the duty upon the employer to take reasonable care of the employee's safety and also the employee's duty to cooperate with the employer in carrying out health and safety duties under the Act and at common law.

Training

Training is essential to ensure that staff have the understanding to carry out the assessments and to advise on lifting and the use of appropriate equipment. Regular monitoring should take place to ensure that the training is effective and the policies for ensuring the safety of midwives are being implemented.

Record keeping

The guidance emphasises the importance of recording significant findings of the assessment and that the record should be kept, readily accessible, as long as it remains relevant. In addition, the Royal College of Midwives has emphasised the importance of the health authority (or NHS trust) keeping adequate statistics. It recommends that the following are kept:

- Numbers and incident rate of injuries.
- Type of injuries.
- Handling methods involved.
- Numbers of staff involved.
- Age and training of the injured parties.
- Location and time of the accident.
- The cause of the accident.
- The related costs, e.g. time lost.

There is a statutory duty under Health and Safety Regulations for certain accidents to be notified to the appropriate authority, usually the Health and Safety Inspectorate.

In keeping records of accidents at work, the principles set out in the guidance by the Nursing and Midwifery Council (2004) should be followed.

It is in the interest of every practising midwife to ensure that the regulations on manual handling are implemented comprehensively. It should be the aim of every midwife to ensure that the level of injuries is reduced. She, her employer, her colleagues and her clients stand to gain.

Lifting Operations and Lifting Equipment Regulations 1998 (LOLER 1998)

These Regulations came into force for all lifting equipment on 5 December 1998, as a result of the lifting provisions of the Amending Directive to the Use of Work Equipment Directive (AUWED 95/63/EC). They are to be read in conjunction with the Provision and Use of Work Equipment Regulations 1998 (PUWER). LOLER is supported by the *Safe use of lifting equipment: Approved code of practice* which can be accessed on the Health and Safety Executive website (www.hse.gov.uk/work-equipment-machinery/loler/htm).

Further information on these Regulations can be found in another book in this series (Dimond, 2010).

In August 2003 the Health and Safety Executive published a manual handling assessment chart (MAC) and also set up a website (www.hse.gov.uk/msd/mac) which can be used by employers, employees, safety representatives and others to obtain information about musculoskeletal disorders, case studies, guidance and research on such disorders.

Manual handling and human rights

In a manual handling case in East Sussex (*A and B v East Sussex County Council*) two severely disabled women claimed that they had a human right not to be manually handled. The outcome of the case was that the judge required East Sussex to carry out the necessary assessments for each activity for A and B, taking into account the considerations and factors that he had set out. The clients did not have an absolute right not to be hoisted, nor did the employees have an absolute right to insist on no manual handling. A risk assessment taking all factors into account had to be carried out.

Only reasonable precautions need be taken to prevent risk of injury from manual handling.

The Court of Appeal (*King v Sussex Ambulance NHS Trust*) found against an ambulance man who had been injured while carrying a heavy man in a chairlift down stairs. It held that the employers were not in breach of the directive or Regulations on manual handling. There was nothing to suggest that calling the fire brigade would have been appropriate in the case. The ambulance service owed the same duty of care to its employees as did any other employer. However, the question of what was reasonable for it to do might have to be judged in the light of its duties to the public and the resources available to it when performing those duties.

Medical Devices Regulations 2002

The Medical Devices Regulations 2002 can be accessed on the Goverment website (www.legislation.gov.uk/uksi/2002/618).

Further information is available from the Medicines and Healthcare Products Regulatory Agency (MRHA) website (www.mhra.gov.uk/Howweregulate/Devices/index). The MRHA provides guidance on the implementation of the Regulations. It is essential that midwives know not only how to access the warnings sent out by the MRHA in relation to dangerous products, but also how to ensure that they themselves are conversant with the procedure for notifying the Agency when they have become aware of defects in products that they use.

Reporting of Injuries, Diseases and Dangerous Occurrences Regulations 1995 (RIDDOR 95)

Regulations were introduced in 1985 to govern the reporting of injuries, diseases and dangerous occurrences. They were replaced by new Regulations which came into force on 1 April 1996. There is now one set of Regulations in place of the four sets under the 1985 Regulations. The list of reportable diseases has been updated, as has the list of dangerous occurrences.

From 12 April 2012 reports must be made after seven (instead of three) days of incapacitation (not including the day of the accident). Incapacitation means that the worker is absent or unable to do work that they would be reasonably expected to do as part of their normal work.

Reports can be made in the following ways:

- By phone: 0845 300 9923.
- By Fax: 0845 300 9924.
- On the website: www.riddor.gov.uk.
- By email: riddor@natbrit.com.
- By post: Incident Contact Centre, Caerphilly Business Park, Caerphilly CF83 3GG.

National Patient Safety Agency

This Agency was set up in following the Department of Health's publication in 2001 of *Building a safer NHS for patients*. It can be accessed on the internet (www.npsa.nhs/uk). On 1 June 2012 its key functions and expertise for patient safety were transferred to the NHS Commissioning Board Special Health Authority when the National Patient Safety Agency itself was abolished by Section 281 of the Health and Social Care Act 2012. The patient safety website continues to offer key information, guidance, tools and alerts (www.patientsafetyfirst.nhs.uk).

Control of Substances Hazardous to Health (COSHH)

All health workers have responsibilities under the Regulations relating to the Control of Substances Hazardous to Health. The Regulations were first introduced in 1988 but have subsequently been updated; the current Regulations date from 2002.

Where the Regulations have not been followed, there can be a prosecution in the criminal courts against the offender. In addition, any person who has been injured as a result of a failure to ensure reasonable care was taken by the employer would have a right of civil action to claim compensation. The Health and Safety Executive (2002) has issued guidance on the implementation of the new Regulations providing both a "COSHH in a hurry publication" as well as more detailed guidance on preventing or controlling exposure to hazardous substances at work. The Health and Safety Executive guidance covers the current legal base; legal developments; key message; the hazardous substances covered by COSHH; the COSHH requirements; assessing risk; preventing or controlling exposure; ensuring that control measures are used and maintained; monitoring exposure; health surveillance; planning for accidents, incidents and emergencies; and ensuring that employees are properly informed, trained and supervised.

Further information, including the eight-step COSHH assessment, can be accessed on the Health and Safety Executive website and in Dimond (2010).

Swansea NHS Trust was held liable when a nurse suffered from latex exposure. She was awarded £345 000 (*Dugmore v Swansea NHS Trust*). The Court of Appeal held that there was a breach of Regulation 7(1) of the COSHH Regulations.

Civil law: Breach of statutory duty

The injured person can bring a civil claim for breach of the statutory duty in certain cases. However, breach of the general duties under the Health and

Safety at Work Act 1974 does not give rise to a civil action of breach of statutory duty, but breach of the Regulations may give rise to such an action (see above).

Action for negligence

The person injured is more likely to bring a claim under the law of negligence (see *Chapter 8*) by establishing that a duty of care which is owed has been breached and that, as a reasonably foreseeable consequence, harm has been caused. Where an employee has been injured by alleged failures of the employer, the employee can sue for breach of contract of an implied term in the contract of employment (see below).

Occupier's Liability Acts 1957 and 1984

These Acts are enforceable in the civil courts where harm has occurred to a visitor (1957 Act) or to a trespasser (1984 Act). Under the 1957 Act, the duty of care owed by the occupier (of whom there may be several) is what is reasonable in the circumstances to ensure that the visitor will be safe for the purposes for which he is permitted to be on the premises. Extra care is required of the occupier when a child is the visitor.

Consumer Protection Act 1987

This Act enables a claim to be brought where harm has occurred as a result of a defect in a product. It is a form of strict liability in that negligence by the supplier or manufacturer does not have to be established. The claimant will however have to show that there was a defect. The supplier can rely upon a defence, colloquially known as "state of the art", i.e. that the state of scientific and technical knowledge at the time the goods were supplied was not such that the producer of products of that kind might be expected to have discovered the defect.

The Consumer Protection Act 1987 is significant for the midwife in that she should ensure that she keeps records of the supplier of any goods (both equipment and drugs) that she provides for the client. If she is unable to cite the name and address of the supplier, she, or her employer, may become the supplier of the goods for the purposes of the Consumer Protection Act 1987 and therefore have to defend an action alleging that there was a defect in the goods which caused harm. Harm includes both personal injury and death, and loss or damage of property.

In one case (*A and others v National Blood Authority and another*) it was held that patients who had contracted hepatitis C from blood and blood products used in blood transfusions were able to bring a claim under the Consumer Protection Act 1987. The Blood Safety and Quality Regulations introduce new safety and quality requirements on human blood collection and storage, thereby implementing an EC Directive (2002/98).

Employer and contract of employment

Under the contract of employment, both employer and employee have duties in relation to health and safety. It is the employer's duty to take reasonable care for the health and safety of the employee. It is the employee's duty to obey reasonable orders (which could include instructions in relation to health and safety) and to act with reasonable care and skill. These duties are enforced on the employer's part by disciplinary procedures and ultimately dismissal, and on the employee's part by an action for breach of contract or an allegation of constructive dismissal which, if the employee has the requisite length of continuous service, may result in a hearing before an employment tribunal.

Under the contract of employment, the employee must obey the express terms on the contract of employment. In addition there are implied terms binding on the employee and employer.

The employee:

- Must obey the reasonable instructions of the employer.
- Must act with all reasonable care and skill in the performance of his duties.
- Must respect confidential information obtained during the course of employment.

The employer must take all reasonable care for the employee's safety in:

- Employing competent staff.
- Ensuring a safe system of work.
- Providing safe plant, premises and equipment.

Failure on the employer's part could lead to an action for constructive dismissal, breach of contract or an action for negligence if harm occurs.

Stress

An example of the employer's duty under the contract to take reasonable care of the employee's health and safety is the legal situation relating to stress. The following facts would have to be proved by the employee:

- The employee is under considerable pressure which is causing unacceptable stress.
- The employer is aware of that fact.
- There is reasonable action that the employer could take but has failed to take.
- As a reasonably foreseeable result of the employer's failure, the employee has suffered severe mental illness.

The earliest case where an employee succeeded in obtaining compensation for stress resulting from the failure of his employers to provide necessary support in a stressful work situation was that of *Walker v Northumberland County Council.*

The House of Lords overruled a Court of Appeal decision in the case involving Barber, head of a maths department, holding that there had been negligence by the employer in failing take necessary action (*Barber v Somerset County Council*). The case can be accessed on the bailii website.

The House of Lords quoted the principle established in an earlier case (*Stokes v Guest 1968*):

> *The overall test is still the conduct of the reasonable and prudent employer taking positive thought for the safety of his workers in the light of what he knows or ought to know.*

Stress and the midwife

There is evidence that a high proportion of midwives consider that they are stressed in their work. In one study, 78% of midwives in a labour ward reported having insufficient time to perform their duties, causing high degrees of stress (Mackin and Sinclair, 1999). The same authors concluded in another article that poor communications between doctors and midwives also caused stress (Mackin and Sinclair, 1998). Work in a neonatal unit can be particularly stressful, especially in dealing with dying babies (Raeside, 2000).

If a midwife considers that she is suffering from unacceptable stress, then she must ensure that she makes senior management aware of this so that reasonable action can be taken to support her. Conversely, a midwife manager should ensure that she identifies when midwives would appear to be under stress and that reasonable action is taken to support them and this is documented. Simply referring a midwife for counselling would not in itself be sufficient to discharge the employer's duty of care to the employee.

Bullying

The duty owed by the employer to the employee to take reasonable care of the health and safety of the employee would also include the duty to protect the employee against bullying. In one case, £100 000 was accepted in an out-of-court settlement by a teacher who alleged that he had been bullied by the head teacher and other staff when he was teaching in a school in Pembrokeshire (Fletcher, 1998). The Andrea Adams Trust (2000), a support organisation that helps health service employees, has provided a fact sheet on workplace bullying. Bullying may be associated with racial or other harassment. For example, in 2004 a black nurse was awarded £20 000 because she was prevented from looking after a white baby (Purves, 2004). The employment tribunal held that her employers, the Southampton University Hospitals NHS Trust, was effectively silent and complicit in the racist demands made by the woman.

The Royal College of Nursing (2012) has issued a fact sheet on advice for its members facing bullying and harassment in the workplace. The Royal College of Midwives (2011) has also provided advice on bullying and harassment at work, giving guidance on how employees should be protected and the duties of the employer. Mavis Kirkham's (2007) paper on the necessity of supporting midwives who are bullied was republished in 2011 and is available on the Royal College of Midwives website.

An extremely useful paper on bullying in the workplace provides a protocol for managers to use appropriate strategies to diminish the intensity of bullying and harassment within their unit (Hollins-Martin and Martin, 2010).

Cross-infection

The problems, dangers and duties that arise from cross-infection are considered in *Chapter 16*.

Protection of employee with health and safety concerns

Changes to the law have boosted the protection of the employee in the event of disputes over health and safety matters. The law provides a right not to suffer detriment in health and safety cases so that an employee who is concerned about a health and safety danger can, if the appropriate procedure is followed, be protected from any victimisation such as dismissal. The criteria for judging the appropriateness of the employee's actions are:

> *...all the circumstances including, in particular, his knowledge, and the facilities and advice available to him at the time.*

There is also provision for the protection of health and safety representatives carrying out their duties. The continuous service requirement of two years (increased from one year from 6 April 2012) does not apply to an application for unfair dismissal in a health and safety or whistleblowing case.

Whistleblowing

The Public Interest Disclosure Act 1998 has extended this provision to protect the whistleblower from victimisation. In 2010, the Department of Health (2010b) published a paper for consultation entitled *NHS Constitution and whistleblowing*. Information on whistleblowing can be found on the Public Concern at Work website (www.pcaw.org.uk). Public Concern at Work is a charity that provides advice and guidance on whistleblowing and runs a telephone helpline (020 7404 6609). It monitors the operation of the Public Interest Disclosure Act 1998. It was concerned at the decision in the Fecitt case (see below) and has asked the Government to consider closing the gap in the legal protection for whistleblowers.

In the *Fecitt and others v NHS Manchester (Public Concern at Work intervening)* case, the Court of Appeal held that the employers could not be held liable for the way employees treated the three whistleblowers who had been victimised by other members of staff. The case is considered by Richard Griffith (2012).

The Royal College of Midwives has an updated notice of unsafe conditions for practice form which can be used by midwives to raise concerns. See also Nursing and Midwifery Council (2010) guidance from its Focus Group.

The failure of the NHS to respond appropriately to whistleblowers was one of the main concerns of the report of the Mid-Staffs NHS Foundation Trust which is considered in *Chapter 19*.

Professional accountability before the NMC

The Midwives Rules (NMC, 2012) contain several provisions in relation to health and safety, and the rules, standards and guidance issued by the NMC are enforceable through the Fitness to Practise proceedings of the NMC. They can be downloaded from the NMC website.

Conclusion

While the areas of accountability and liability have been considered separately, it is of course possible that there could be criminal proceedings, civil proceedings, disciplinary proceedings and fitness to practise proceedings resulting from the same health and safety incident, especially where someone has died. Most NHS organisations employ health and safety officers who provide training, guidance and information for employees and can be contacted for updates on health and safety publications. However, it remains the personal and professional responsibility of the individual midwife to ensure that health and safety laws are implemented and that this implementation is monitored regularly. A survey by the Health Foundation, an independent charity, found that health and safety was not considered to be a top priority by NHS chief executives (Health Foundation, 2004). A lack of commitment from senior management will make the task of the individual midwife in implementing health and safety laws and good practice extremely challenging. The Government has embarked on a campaign to cut red tape and simplify laws relating to health and safety (see hse.gov.uk/news/red-tape-challenge/). Legal issues relating to cross-infection are considered in *Chapter 16*.

Questions and exercises

1. Following the risk assessment regulations, identify the risks in your practice and consider the action that should be taken to prevent them or reduce them.
2. Your trust wishes to protect clients against the possibility of babies being abducted. Carry out a risk assessment on your unit and decide what action it would be reasonably practicable to take.
3. Look carefully at your working practices over a week and identify any dangers to you in relation to manual handling. What changes, if any, should be made?

4. A colleague asks you for advice because she has been injured by the relative of a client and wants to obtain compensation. What form of legal action may she have?
5. You are aware that a senior midwife has a reputation for bullying junior staff. What action would you take if you were (a) a student midwife, (b) a junior midwife.
6. Select one health and safety topic relevant to your practice (e.g. manual handling, stress, bullying) and access the websites of the Health and Safety Executive, the Medicines and Healthcare Products Regulatory Agency, the NMC, the RCM, the NHS and the National Patient Safety Agency to research their guidance on your chosen topic.

References

A and B v East Sussex County Council (The Disability Rights Commission an interested party) [2003] EWHC 167 (Admin)

A and others v National Blood Authority and another Times Law Report 4 April 2001; Lloyd's Law Rep Med [2001] 187

Andrea Adams Trust (2000) *Factsheet on workplace bullying.* Andrea Adams Trust, Brighton

Barber v Somerset County Council 2004 Times Law Report 5 April 2004 HL; [2002] EWCA Cuv 76; [2002] 2 All ER 1

Blood Safety and Quality Regulations 2005 SI 2005 No 50

Department of Health (2001) *Building a safer NHS for patients.* HMSO, London

Department of Health (2010a) *Interim Government response to the report of the Taskforce on the Health Aspects of Violence Against Women.* Department of Health, London

Department of Health (2010b) *NHS Constitution and whistleblowing.* HMSO, London

Dimond B (1994a) Risk management and the midwife. *Modern Midwife* **4**(4) 36–67

Dimond B (1994b) Midwife managed units. *Modern Midwife* **4**(6): 31–3

Dimond B (2003) Domestic violence and the midwife: Can you report it? *British Journal of Midwifery* **11**(8): 557–61

Dimond B (2004) *Legal aspects of health and safety.* Quay Publications, Dinton, Wiltshire

Dimond B (2010) *Legal aspects of health and safety* (2nd edn). Quay Publications, Dinton, Wiltshire

Dugmore v Swansea NHS Trust [2002] EWCA 1689

EC Directive 2002/98 [2003] OJL33/30

European Union Directive 93/42/EEC

Fecitt and others v NHS Manchester (Public Concern at Work intervening) [2011] EWCA Civ 1190 CA

Fletcher V (1998) Teacher 'bullied by staff' wins £100,000. *The Times* **17 July**

Griffith R (2010) Protection and support for midwives who report poor practice threatened. *British Journal of Midwifery* **20**(2): 144–5

Health and Safety Commission (1992) *Guidance on manual handling of loads in the health services.* HMSO, London

Health and Safety Commission (1997) *Violence and aggression to staff in health services.* HSE Books, London

Health and Safety Commission (2000) *Management of health and safety at work: Approved code of practice and guidance.* HMSO, London

Health and Safety Executive (1992) *Manual handling: Guidance on regulations.* HMSO, London

Health and Safety Executive (2002) *Preventing or controlling exposure to hazardous substances at work.* Available from: www.hse.gov.uk/hthdir/noframes/coshh/coshh9a. htm)

Health and Safety Executive (2009) *Press release HSE/E/31.* Health and Safety Executive, London

Health Foundation (2004) *Healthcare Leaders Panel Survey 1. Patient safety report and table of results.* Health Foundation London and YouGov, London

Hollins-Martin CJ, Martin C (2010) Bully for you: Harassment and bullying in the workplace. *British Journal of Midwifery* **18**(1): 25–31

Home Office (2003) *Safety and justice: The Government's proposals on domestic violence.* Available from: http://www.domesticviolence.gov.uk

Home Office (2004) *Tackling domestic violence; the role of the health professional.* HMSO, London

Hunt L (2011) Most pregnant mothers back routine domestic violence questioning. *Midwives* **21 July**

Hunt SC, Martin AM (2001) *Pregnant women: Violent men: What midwives need to know.* Elsevier, London

Johnstone J (2003) Domestic violence – midwives can make a difference *MIDIRS Midwifery Digest* **13**(3): 311–5

Keeling J (2012) Exploring women's experience of domestic violence: Injury impact and infant feeding. *British Journal Midwifery* **20**(12): 843–8

Keen M, Keeling J (2012) Stop! Silent screams. *Practising Midwife* **15**(2): 28–30

King v Sussex Ambulance NHS Trust [2002] EWCA 953; Current law August 2002 408

Kirkham M (2007) Traumatised midwives. *Association for Improvement in Maternity Services (AIMS) Journal* **19**: 1

Lifting Operations and Lifting Equipment Regulations (LOLER) 1998, SI1998/2307

Lister S (2004) Court to ban fetishist from health units. *The Times* 2 June

Mackin P, Sinclair M (1998) Labour ward midwives' perceptions of stress. *Journal of Advanced Nursing* **27**: 986–91

Mackin P, Sinclair M (1999) Midwives' experience of stress on the labour ward. *British Journal of Midwifery* **7**(5): 323–6

NHS Security Management Service (2010) *Cost of violence against NHS Staff 2007/8.* NHS Counter Fraud Service, London

Nursing and Midwifery Council (2004) *Guidelines for records and record keeping.* NMC, London

Nursing and Midwifery Council (2008) *Code of professional conduct: Standards for conduct, performance and ethics.* NMC, London

Nursing and Midwifery Council (2010) *Raising and escalating concerns.* NMC, London

Provision and Use of Work Equipment Regulations (PUWER) 1992, SI 1992/2932, revised 1998, SI 1998/2306

Purves R (2004) Racist abuse ruined my life. *Nursing Times* **100**(32): 24–5

Raeside L (2000) Caring for dying babies: Perceptions of neonatal nurses. *Journal of Neonatal Nursing* **6**(3): 93–9

Royal College of Midwives (1996) *Safety for midwives working in the community.* RCM, London

Royal College of Midwives (1999) *Handle with care: A midwife's guide to preventing back injury* (2nd edn). RCM, London

Royal College of Midwives (2000) *Safety in maternity units.* RCM, London

Royal College of Midwives (2010) *Health and safety.* RCM, London

Royal College of Midwives (2011) *Bullying and harassment at work.* RCM, London

Stokes v Guest, Keen and Nettlefold (Bolts and Nuts) Ltd [1968] 1 WLR 1776,

The Times (2005) News item. *The Times* **6 May**

Walker v Northumberland County Council. Times Law Report 24 November 1994 QBD

Chapter 11

Medication

Scenario 11.1. Restrictions on the midwife

Rachel, an experienced midwife, was briefing Karen who was expecting her first child. During their chat, Rachel discovered that Karen was hostile to any orthodox medicines but was a strong believer in alternative therapies, including homeopathy, herbalism and reflexology. She told Rachel that she did not want to have any interventions during her labour other than complementary and alternative therapies. Rachel feels that her professional skills will be undermined by such demands. What is the legal position?

Scenario 11.1. is discussed on p. 209.

Introduction

The midwife has extended powers in relation to the prescribing and administration of medicines compared with the nurse/health visitor practitioner. These powers have been further expanded as midwives are one of the designated practitioners with additional powers of prescribing under changes to the statutory provisions for prescribing.

Amendments have been made by Section 63 of the Health and Social Care Act 2001 to the Medicines Act 1968, now consolidated in the 2012 Regulations. These Regulations expand the health practitioners who are able to prescribe as a result of the recommendations of the Final Crown Report (Department of Health, 1999) (see below). This chapter looks briefly at the specific powers of the midwife in relation to the statutory provisions dealing with medicines and the legal issues which arise. A more detailed analysis can be obtained from Dimond (2011).

The Nursing and Midwifery Council (NMC) has laid down standards for medicine management (new standards were introduced in 2007 and updated in 2010 with paragraph numbers). The new Midwives Rules were implemented in 2013 (see below). All practising midwives should have an up-to-date copy of the *British National Formulary* (BNF) and the *BNF for Children* which are published jointly by the British Medical Association and the Royal Pharmaceutical Society of Great Britain. Updates on the most recent edition of the BNF can be obtained from its website (www.bnf.org.uk). At the front of the BNF there is a very useful introductory section which gives guidance on prescribing for different categories of drugs and different groups of patients. In addition, a directory is published annually by the Proprietary Association of Great Britain on over-the-counter medicinal products (the OTC Directory). Reference should also be made to the Appendix on Further Reading.

The statutory framework

The two main Acts of Parliament controlling the administration and use of medicines were the Medicines Act 1968 and the Misuse of Drugs Act 1971. The former has now been largely amended and its provisions substantially re-enacted in the Human Medicines Regulations 2012 which came into force on 14 August 2012. The regulations result from an initiative of the Medicines and Healthcare Products Regulatory Agency (MHRA) to consolidate and review UK medicines legislation after wide consultation. The Regulations simplify medicines legislation while maintaining strong and effective safeguards for public health, replacing sections of the Medicines Act 1968 and about 200 Statutory Instruments. Part 12 of the Regulations relates to prescription only medicines and their exemptions. The Statutory Instrument can be accessed online (legislation. gov.uk/uksi/2012/1916).

The 1968 Act (now significantly amended by the 2012 Regulations) set up an administrative and licensing system to control the sale and supply of medicines to the public and retail pharmacies, and the packing and labelling of medicinal products. It classified medicines in the categories shown in *Box 11.1*.

Box 11.1. Classification of medicines under the Medicines Act 1968 and the Human Medicines Regulations 2012

- *Pharmacy only products.* These can only be sold or supplied retail by someone conducting a retail pharmacy when the product must be sold at a registered pharmacy by, or under the supervision of, a registered pharmacist (See Part 2 of Schedule 1 of the 2012 Regulations).
- *General sales list.* These are medicinal products that may be sold other than from a retail pharmacy so long as the provisions of Regulation 221 and Schedule 15 of the 2012 Regulations are complied with. The licensing authority must have authorised its use as a general sales product.
- *Prescription only list.* The medicines are only available on a practitioner's prescription. Part 1 of Schedule 1 of the Regulations lists the prescription only products.

The Misuse of Drugs Act 1971

This Act and subsequent Regulations makes provision for the classification of controlled drugs and their possession, supply and manufacture.

The Act makes it a criminal offence to carry on the manufacture, supply and possession of controlled drugs contrary to the Regulations. Controlled drugs are divided into three categories:

- Class A, includes, among others: cocaine, diamorphine, morphine, opium, pethidine and class B substances when prepared for injection.
- Class B, includes, among others: oral amphetamines, barbiturates, cannabis, codeine.
- Class C, includes, among others: most benzodiazepines, meprobamate.

The Misuse of Drugs Regulations 2001

The Misuse of Drugs Regulations 2001 divides controlled drugs into five Schedules, each specifying the requirements governing activities such as import, export, production, supply, possession, prescribing and record keeping. These schedules are shown in *Box 11.2.*

Box 11.2. Schedules under the Misuse of Drugs Regulations 2001

- Schedule 1, e.g. cannabis, lysergide: Possession and supply prohibited except in accordance with Home Office authority given in a licence. They cannot be used for medicinal purposes and their production and possession is limited to research or other specified purposes. Rules cover the documentation, keeping of records, preservation of records, supply on prescription, marking of containers and procedure for destruction.
- Schedule 2, e.g. diamorphine, morphine, pethidine, glutethimide, amphetamine: These drugs are subject to full controlled drug requirements relating to prescriptions, safe custody, the need to keep registers. These drugs may only be administered to a patient by a doctor or dentist or any person acting in accordance with the directions of a doctor or dentist.
- Schedule 3, e.g. barbiturates, diethylpropion, mazindol: Subject to similar controls as Schedule 2, such as the special prescription requirements, but they may be

Box 11.2/cont

> manufactured by persons authorised in writing by the Secretary of State. There
> is a difference in the classes of person who may possess and supply them,
> entries in the register of Controlled Drugs need not be made in respect of
> these drugs, but invoice or similar records must be kept for at least two years.
> - Schedule 4: Part 1 includes lorazepam and diazepam and Part 2 which are
>   subject to less control. In particular, controlled drug prescription requirements
>   do *not* apply and they are *not* subject to safe custody requirements.
> - Schedule 5 preparations which, because of their strength, are exempt from most
>   controlled drug requirements, other than retention of invoices for two years.

Midwives and supply of medicines

By Statutory Instrument (1997) the midwife can supply:

- All medicines that are not prescription only medicines (POM).
- Medicines under a Patient Group Direction covering her.
- Prescription only medicines for which she is exempt from the statutory
  restrictions.

Under the 2012 Regulations, Schedule 17, Part 1, Paragraph 4 states that a
registered midwife is exempt (from restrictions on sale and supply of prescription
only medicines) in relation to:

- Diclofenac
- Hydrocortisone acetate
- Miconazole
- Nystatin
- Phytomenadione.

Under Schedule 17, Part 3, Paragraph 2, a registered midwife and student
midwife are exempt (from restrictions on the administration of prescription only
medicines) in respect of the following drugs:

- Adrenaline
- Anti-D immunoglobulin
- Carboprost
- Cyclizine lactate

- Diamorphine
- Ergometrine maleate
- Gelofusine
- Lignocaine
- Lignocaine hydrochloride
- Morphine
- Naloxone hydrochloride
- Oxytocin, natural and synthetic
- Pethidine hydrochloride
- Phytomenadione
- Promazine hydrochloride
- Sodium chloride.

Lignocaine, lignocaine hydrochloride and promazine hydrocloride may only be administered by a midwife while attending a woman in childbirth.

The Statutory Instrument can be accessed on the legislation website (www. legislation.gov.uk/uksi/2012/1916) (Schedule 17 Part 3). Further information is available on the website of the Medicines and Healthcare Products Regulatory Agency (www.mhra.gov.uk). Student midwives were added to the list of persons authorised to administer medicines under the above exemptions by the Medicines for Human Use (Miscellaneous Amendments) Order. They must be acting under direct supervision of a registered midwife. They are not allowed to administer diamorphine, morphine or pethidine hydrochloride.

Midwife and controlled drugs

A registered midwife who has notified the local supervising authority of her intention to practise may, as far as is necessary for the practice of her profession or employment as a midwife, possess and administer any controlled drug which the Medicines Act 1968 permits her to administer (Regulation 11 of the Misuse of Drugs Regulations 2001). Supplies may only be made to her or possessed by her, on the authority of a midwife's supply order. This supply order must specify the name and occupation of the midwife, the purpose for which it is required and the total quantity to be obtained. The supply order must be signed:

- By a doctor who is authorised by the local supervising authority for the region or area in which the controlled drug was, or is to be obtained, or

- By the supervisor of midwives appointed by the local supervising authority for that area.

The Regulation defines a midwife's supply order as:

...an order in writing specifying the name and occupation of the midwife obtaining the drug, the purpose for which it is required and the total quantity to be obtained.

Section 10 Standard 26 of the Nursing and Midwifery Council Standards for Medicines Management cover controlled drugs (NMC, 2007). Paragraphs 46–56 are concerned with controlled drugs and the midwife. They can be accessed on the NMC website.

Diamorphine, morphine pethidine and pentazocine may be possessed by a registered midwife in her own right so far as is necessary for the practice of her profession under the Misuse of Drugs Regulations 2001 relating to controlled drugs. The Statutory Instrument is available from the legislation website (www.legislation.gov.uk).

Disposal of unwanted stocks of controlled drugs

A midwife may surrender any stocks of controlled drugs in her possession which she no longer requires to the doctor as identified above (Regulation 11) or any doctor, or pharmacist (Regulation 6).

Documentation of controlled drugs

The midwife must keep a Controlled Drug book in which she must record the following:

- The date.
- The name and address of the person from whom the drug was obtained.
- The amount obtained.
- The form in which it was obtained.

When the midwife receives the controlled drug from the pharmacist, she must sign the pharmacist's Controlled Drugs register and the pharmacist must keep the midwife's supply order for two years.

Non-prescription only medicines

The NMC (2003a) emphasised that midwives can supply and administer all non-prescription only medicines and general sales list medicines in the course of their professional practice. The NMC was concerned that the supply and administration of some non-prescription medicines such as nitrous oxide and oxygen have been wrongly written into Patient Group Directions. In its guidance for employers and registered midwives it emphasises that, under Statutory Instrument 1980 Number 1924, a registered midwife can supply and administer all non-prescription only medicines, including pharmacy and general sale list medicines. A student midwife, during the course of her programme of education, can administer those medicines under the guidance of a practising midwife, for which the registered midwife remains accountable. The NMC feared that including medicines unnecessarily in Patient Group Directions would have implications for student midwives gaining experience in the administration of nitrous oxide and oxygen to women in the course of their education.

The Midwives Rules

Under Part 3 (Obligations and scope of practice) of the Midwives Rules (NMC, 2012b) rule 5 on midwives scope of practice is as follows:

> *A practising midwife who is responsible for providing care or advice to a woman or care to a baby during childbirth must do so in accordance with standards established and reviewed by the Council in accordance with Article 21(1)(a) of the Order.*

The guidance in paragraph 5 on this rule applies to the administration of medicines and is set out in *Box 11.3*.

Box 11.3. Rule 5 Paragraph 5

• You must only supply and administer those medicines for which you have received training as to use, dosage and methods of administration and for which you are exempt (with a reference to the Misuse of Drugs Regulations 2001 and the Human Medicines Regulations 2012).

Records

Rule 7 of the Midwives Rules requires the midwife to keep records but does not specifically mention those in relation to medicines. Record keeping is considered in *Chapter 9*.

Prescription only and other medicines used by midwives

Registered midwives may supply and administer, on their own initiative, any of the substances specified in medicines legislation under the midwives' exemptions, provided in the course of their professional midwifery practice. They may do so without the need for a prescription or patient-specific written direction from a medical practitioner. If a medicine is not included in the midwives' exemptions then a Patient Group Direction or a prescription, or a patient-specific written declaration will be required.

Nurse/midwife prescribing

Following the first Crown Report (Department of Health, 1989), the provisions of the Medicinal Products: Prescription by Nurses Act 1992 introducing nurse prescribing came into force in October 1994 when pilot schemes for prescribing by community nurses and health visitors commenced. Nurses and health visitors who have recorded their prescribing qualification on the NMC Register could prescribe against the Nurse Prescriber's Formulary. Subsequently, a further Crown Report (Department of Health, 1998) recommended the recognition of Patient Group Directions (group protocols) whereby registered nurses, midwives and other registered health practitioners could prescribe in accordance with a protocol containing the information specified in the Prescription only Medicines (Human Use) Amendment Order 2000 Regulations. These provide for Patient Group Directions to be drawn up to make provision for the sale or supply of a prescription only medicine in hospitals in accordance with the written direction of a doctor or dentist. To be lawful, the Patient Group Direction must cover the particulars that are set out in Part 1 of Schedule 16 of the Statutory Instrument (2012) and shown in *Box 11.4*.

Part 4 of Schedule 16 to the 2012 Regulations sets out the classes of individuals by whom supplies can be made under a Patient Group Direction. There are 15 health service professionals including registered nurses and registered midwives. As a consequence of the abolition of primary care trusts on 31 March 2013, new regulations were passed to enable clinical commissioning

---

Box 11.4. Particulars for Patient Group Direction

- The period during which the Direction shall have effect.
- The description or class of prescription only medicines to which the Direction relates.
- The clinical situations which medicinal products of that description or class may be used to treat or manage in any form.
- Whether there are any restrictions on the quantity of medicine which may be sold or supplied on any one occasion, and if so, what restrictions.
- The clinical criteria under which a person is to be eligible for treatment.
- Whether any class of person is excluded from treatment under the Direction, and if so, what class of person.
- Whether there are circumstances in which further advice should be sought from a doctor or dentist and, if so, what circumstances.
- The pharmaceutical form or forms in which prescription only medicines of that description or class are to be administered.
- The strength, or maximum strength, at which prescription only medicines of that description or class are to be administered.
- The applicable dosage or maximum dosage.
- The route of administration.
- The frequency of administration.
- Any minimum or maximum period of administration applicable to medicinal products of that description or class.
- Whether there are any relevant warnings to note, and if so, what warnings.
- Whether there is any follow up action to be taken in any circumstances, and if so, what action and in what circumstances.
- Arrangements for referral for medical advice.
- Details of the records to be kept of the supply or the administration of medicines under the Direction.

---

groups and local authorities to authorise Patient Group Directions and to enable those approved by primary care trusts to continue lawfully to supply medicines under Patient Group Directions.

As noted in the NMC guidance (NMC 2003a) above, Patient Group Directions are only required for drugs that cannot otherwise be prescribed and administered by midwives. Patient Group Directions are not necessary for medicines included in the midwifery exemption legislation and for non-prescription and general sales medicines.

Independent and supplementary prescribers

One of the most significant recommendations of the final report of the Crown Review (Department of Health, 1999) was that the legal authority in the UK to prescribe should be extended beyond currently authorised prescribers and two types of prescribers should be recognised: the independent prescriber and the dependent prescriber (now known as the supplementary prescriber).

Under the 2012 Regulations "a nurse independent prescriber" means a person who (a) is a registered nurse or registered midwife, and (b) is noted in the professional register as qualified to order drugs, medicines and appliances as a nurse independent prescriber or a nurse independent/supplementary prescriber.

A "supplementary prescriber" means a person who is noted in the relevant register as qualified to order drugs, medicines and appliances as a supplementary prescriber (or, in the case of a registered nurse or registered midwife, as a nurse independent/supplementary prescriber) and is (a) a pharmacist, (b) a registered midwife, (c) a registered nurse, (d) a chiropodist, podiatrist, physiotherapist or radiographer, or (e) a registered optometrist.

Paragraph 215 of the 2012 Human Medicine Regulations cover the prescribing and administration of medicines by supplementary prescribers and is shown in *Box 11.5*.

Box 11.5. Prescribing and administration of medicines by supplementary prescribers

Regulation 215
(1) A supplementary prescriber ("S") may not give a prescription for a prescription only medicine unless S meets conditions A and C.
(2) A supplementary prescriber ("S") may not
  (a) parenterally administer a prescription only medicine; or
  (b) give directions for the parenteral administration of a prescription only medicine,
  unless S meets conditions B and C.
(3) Condition A is that S is acting in accordance with the terms of a clinical management plan (see *Box 11.6*) that
  (a) relates to the patient to whom the product is prescribed;
  (b) has effect when the prescription is given; and
  (c) includes the particulars specified in Schedule 14.

Box 11.5. cont/

---

(4) Condition B is that S is acting in accordance with the terms of a clinical management plan that
 (a) relates to the patient to whom the product is, or is to be, administered;
 (b) has effect when the product is administered or (as the case may be) the direction is given; and
 (c) includes the particulars specified in Schedule 14.

(5) Condition C is that S has access to health records that
 (a) are the health records of the patient to whom the plan relates; and
 (b) are used by any doctor or dentist who is a party to the plan.

(6) This Regulation is subject to Regulation 216.

(7) In this Regulation "clinical management plan" means a written plan (which may be amended from time to time) relating to the treatment of an individual patient agreed by
 (a) the patient to whom the plan relates,
 (b) the doctor or dentist who is a party to the plan, and
 (c) any supplementary prescriber who is to prescribe, give directions for administration or administer under the plan.

"Health record" has the meaning given by Section 68(2) of the Data Protection Act 1998(a).

Exceptions to Regulation 215

(1) Regulation 215 does not apply if
 (a) S is a community practitioner nurse prescriber, and
 (b) the prescription only medicine prescribed or administered, or in respect of which S gives directions for administration, is specified in Schedule 13.

(2) Regulation 215(2) does not apply if S is acting in accordance with the directions of another person who is an appropriate practitioner (other than a supplementary prescriber or an EEA health professional).

Schedule 14 to the 2012 Regulations sets out particulars of the clinical management plan. These are shown in *Box 11.6*.

NMC standards on extended independent nurse prescribing and supplementary prescribing

In 2006 the NMC published *Standards of proficiency for nurse and midwife prescribers* replacing the earlier 2002 guidance. The Standards cover the education and training provision to prepare nurses and midwives to prescribe,

---

**Box 11.6. Requirements for a clinical management plan
Schedule 14 to the 2012 Regulations**

A clinical management plan must contain the following particulars:

(a) the name of the patient to whom the plan relates;

(b) the illnesses or conditions which may be treated by the supplementary prescriber;

(c) the date on which the plan is to take effect and when it is to be reviewed by the doctor or dentist who is a party to the plan;

(d) reference to the class or description of medicinal product which may be prescribed or administered under the plan;

(e) any restrictions or limitations as to the strength or dose of any product which may be prescribed or administered under the plan, and any period of administration or use of any medicinal product which may be prescribed or administered under the plan;

(f) relevant warnings about the known sensitivities of the patient to, or known difficulties of the patient with, particular medicinal products;

(g) the arrangements for notification of

(i) suspected or known adverse reactions to any medicinal product which may be prescribed or administered under the plan, and

(ii) suspected or known adverse reactions to any other medicinal product taken at the same time as any medicinal product prescribed or administered under the plan; and

(h) the circumstances in which the supplementary prescriber should refer to, or seek the advice of, the doctor or dentist who is a party to the plan.

---

standards for prescribing practice, and additional guidance. An annexe also covers the principal areas, knowledge, skills and competencies required to underpin the practice of prescribing.

Prescribing in pregnancy

The NMC published a position statement (June 2012a) entitled *Prescribing in pregnancy: The role of independent and supplementary nurse prescribers*. All independent and supplementary prescribers are required to follow the standards for medicines management, standards of proficiency for nurse and midwife prescribers and the NMC (2008) Code.

Independent and supplementary prescribers must be able to recognise when the complexity of clinical decisions requires specialist knowledge and expertise, and consult or refer accordingly. A member of the midwifery or obstetric team is available 24 hours a day by contacting local maternity units.

A record of any treatment prescribed should be made in the woman's hand held notes and the woman's GP and named midwife should also be informed of any treatment prescribed.

In response to a study on the use of over-the-counter medicines by pregnant women, the *British National Formulary* (BNF, 2004) issued advice on medication use during pregnancy. The BNF guidance emphasises that women need to take special care about their entire lifestyle during pregnancy: this means taking care with eating, drinking and exercising, and taking medicines. Women should consult their doctor or pharmacist before embarking on any treatment with medicines or herbal remedies during pregnancy. The BNF advises that medicines should be avoided during pregnancy as far as possible. Drugs which have been extensively used in pregnancy and appear to be usually safe should be prescribed in preference to new or untried drugs, and the smallest effective dose should be used. The BNF advises caution and not overstating the potential for harm.

Prescribing and breastfeeding

Similar precautions about medications taken by the pregnant woman should also be taken by the breastfeeding mother. The BNF (2004) has published a Breastfeeding Network Newsletter which considers an overview of the safety of antibiotics during breastfeeding. A study from The Netherlands provides an insight into drug use during breastfeeding (Schirm et al, 2004).

Routine antenatal anti-D prophylaxis for RhD-negative women

A position statement issued by the United Kingdom Central Council for Nursing, Midwifery and Health Visiting on 11 February 1999 was withdrawn by the NMC in March 2003 (NMC, 2003b). It followed guidance from the National Institute for Health and Clinical Excellence (NICE, 2002). NICE has recommended that pregnant rhesus-negative women should be routinely offered anti-D prophylaxis as preventative treatment (to haemolytic disease in the newborn), unless they already have antibodies to the D antigen in their blood. NICE also recommended that healthcare professionals should explain the options available to rhesus-negative mothers, so they can make an informed choice about treatment.

Controlled drugs: The fourth Shipman Report

Following the conviction of Harold Shipman for murdering 15 patients, an Inquiry was established under the chairmanship of Dame Janet Smith. The fourth report (2004) from the Inquiry was concerned with the regulation of controlled drugs and made recommendations in relation to the setting up of an integrated and multidisciplinary inspectorate of controlled drugs; restrictions on the prescribing of controlled drugs; and the tightening up of the handling and safekeeping of controlled drugs.

As a consequence of these recommendations, the 2006 Health Act provided for an accountable officer to be appointed in each healthcare area responsible for the safe use and management of controlled drugs. The Misuse of Drugs (Safe Custody) Amendment Regulations 2007 enabled the accountable officer to nominate persons to witness the destruction of controlled drugs, extended the powers of operating department practitioners in relation to controlled drugs, rescheduled midazolam from Schedule 4 to 3, and changed the format of the Controlled Drugs Register.

Management of errors or incidents in the administration of medicines

Standard 24 of Standards for Medicines Management of the NMC relates to the management of adverse events (errors or incidents) in the administration of medicines. The NMC in its guidance on the Standard states that:

> *Such incidents require sensitive management and a comprehensive assessment of all the circumstances before a professional and managerial decision is reached on the appropriate way to proceed. If a practising midwife makes or identifies a drug error or incident, she should also inform her supervisor of midwives as soon as possible after the event.*

Drug addicts

What action does a midwife take if she discovers that one of the mothers referred to her is a drug addict? In the past, particulars of persons addicted to specific drugs had to be notified to the Chief Medical Officer or Home Office by the doctor within seven days of his considering or having reasonable grounds to believe the addiction under the Misuse of Drugs (Notification of and Supply to Addicts) Regulations 1973. However, this requirement was revoked by the Misuse of Drugs (Supply to Addicts) Regulations 1997. Doctors are now expected to report on a standard form a case of drug misuse to their local Drug Misuse Database. Guidance on notification is provided in the BNF.

If a midwife suspects that one of her clients is addicted she should ensure that a medical practitioner is informed, who would send the requisite details to the Drug Misuse Database. Apart from the criminal offences relating to the possession and supply of illegal drugs and the Offences Against the Person Act, there are no laws in this country that enable action to be taken against a mother to prevent the fetus being harmed by drugs (unless she is taking them with the intent to cause a miscarriage, see *Chapters 7* and *13*). Nor can the fetus be made a ward of court before it is born, as the case *Re F (in utero)* 1988 illustrates. (The case is discussed in *Chapter 7, Box 7.4*.) However, the midwife would have responsibilities to ensure that appropriate care is taken of a vulnerable adult. It may be that the mother refuses all assistance offered by the midwife. If there are concerns that the mother lacks the mental capacity to make her own decisions, then action can be taken in her best interests (see *Chapter 3*). Close contact with social services will be essential to ensure that action is taken in the best interests of the child once born. A report by the Audit Commission in February 2002 recommended fundamental reforms of the drug treatment services in England and Wales since, at that time, they provided little value for the £234 million spent on helping addicts and misusers.

The National Treatment Agency for Substance Misuse (www.nta.nhs.uk) was set up as a special health authority in 2001 to improve the availability, capacity and effectiveness of drug treatment in England, to allocate central funding, and provide support and guidance to local areas. A Drug Strategy white paper published in December 2010 and the white paper, *Healthy Lives, Healthy People* published in November 2010 (HM Government, 2010a, b), envisaged a locally-led, recovery-oriented system under which most drugs and alcohol services would be commissioned by local authorities through Directors of Public Health supported by Health and Wellbeing Boards. The National Treatment Agency was abolished as part of these developments and its functions transferred to the new national service, Public Health England, set up in April 2013 (see *Chapter 16*).

NICE (see below) published a quality standard for drug use disorders in November 2012 which is available on the NICE website (www.nice.org.uk/quality-standard-for-drug-use-disorders-qs23/).

The NHS Choices website (www.nhs.uk/Livewell/drugs) offers advice for drug users and professionals. A free information phone line named Frank (0800 776600) provides information about drugs and the different options available for help and support. The confidential helpline is open 24 hours a day, every day. It also runs a website (www.talktofrank.com/). In Scotland, Know the Score offers information and advice about drugs (www.knowthescore.info or 0800 5875879); in Wales, Dan is a free and bilingual helpline (www.dan247.org.uk or 0808 808 2234); and in Northern Ireland visit www.nidirect.gov.uk/getting-help-with-drug-or-acohol-problems.

Liability and medicinal products

There are unfortunately many cases where litigation arises as a result of breaches of the duty of care in relation to the prescribing or administration of medicinal products.

In examples of contested cases, £119 302 was ordered to be paid to a man who had suffered permanent brain damage because of a badly written prescription (*Prendergast v Sam & Dee and others*). The doctor had written a prescription for Amoxil, but this was read by the pharmacist as Daonil. The doctor was held 25% liable and the employers of the pharmacist 75% liable.

In another case (*Dwyer v Roderick and others*), the doctor prescribed Migril but failed to heed the manufacturer's warnings and instead of limiting the dose to not more that 12 tablets in the course of one week and not more than one every four hours, prescribed 60 tablets to be taken at two tablets every four hours. The pharmacist did not spot the error. The patient's condition deteriorated and the mistake was not noticed by another doctor in the practice who visited the patient. In the High Court, compensation of £100000 was agreed, 45% payable by the prescribing doctor, 40% by the pharmacist and the remaining 15% by the second doctor who visited. On appeal the second doctor was found not liable and his 15% contribution was accepted by the pharmacist.

In one case, bad handwriting on a prescription for a top-up epidural resulted in a junior doctor administering 30mg instead of 3mg of epidural diamorphine in 10ml of saline to a woman following a hysterectomy operation (Kennedy, 1996). A woman aged 53 years had entered the Princess Grace private hospital in London for a routine hysterectomy. As a result of the drug administration error (it was also only the second time the junior doctor had added drugs to an epidural) and the fact that the junior doctor had not been trained to use the resuscitation equipment, the patient died a few days later.

Other examples of errors in medication and prescribing are described in the journal of the Medical Defence Union and reports are to be found regularly in newspapers and professional journals. The Royal Pharmaceutical Society (2004) has published leaflets on legal and ethical issues in medicines which include a leaflet on dealing with dispensing errors.

At the heart of the issue of negligence is the question of whether the accepted standard of the reasonable professional has been followed. This is known as the Bolam Test (*Bolam v Friern Hospital Management Committee*) and is discussed in *Chapter 8*.

The Consumer Protection Act 1987 can be used by those who have suffered harm as a result of a defect in medication, without having to establish that there was negligence on the part of the manufacturers or suppliers. (The Act is considered briefly in *Chapter 10*.)

In a French case, which may have significant implications for patients in the UK, Didier Jambart won €200000 against GlaxoSmithKline on the grounds that the drug Requip prescribed for his Parkinson's disease turned him into a sex and gambling addict. He had tried to commit suicide on several occasions.

National Institute for Health and Clinical Excellence (NICE)

One of the main functions of NICE is to consider research relating to medicinal products and to identify effective products. Its recommendations are not binding upon the NHS, but in practice any health authority or NHS trust which ignored its guidelines that a specific medication was effective, would probably face an action for judicial review if it prevented the medication from being made available on the NHS within its own catchment area. The NICE guidelines may well become absorbed into any definition of what is reasonable professional practice according to the Bolam Test (see *Chapter 8*), thus creating a presumption that they are followed. Midwives should ensure that they receive information about NICE publications and guidelines and also, if possible, have an input into the thinking behind NICE's publications.

Clinical trials

Specific guidance about a midwife's participation in clinical trials is no longer contained in the Midwives Rules and Standards but the earlier guidance would still be valid that a practising midwife may only participate in clinical trials if there is a protocol approved by a relevant ethics committee. As a result of an EC Directive (2001) strict rules relating to the conduct of clinical trials on medicinal products have been implemented.

Complementary therapies

Women are the most frequent users of complementary and alternative medicines, such products are used in pregnancy for the relief of nausea and vomiting, anxiety, stress, depression, backache, labour induction, headaches and other conditions. Data on the extent of use by pregnant women are very uncertain but Bishop and colleagues' study (2012) found that over 25% of women used complementary and alternative medicine during pregnancy. The midwife should be aware of the possibility that a client is using complementary and alternative therapies and medication and take the appropriate action.

The NMC has provided guidance on the use of complementary and alternative therapies. In its Code of Practice (NMC, 2008) under the heading "You must provide a high standard of practice and care at all times", it states that:

> You must ensure that the use of complementary or alternative therapies is safe and in the best interests of those in your care.

In its Standards of Proficiency for Nurse and Midwife Prescribers (NMC, 2006), Paragraph 3.5 on complementary medicinal products requires the following of its registered practitioners:

> Nurses and midwives need to be familiar with a range of complementary medicinal products that their patients or clients may be using, or may wish to be used, in their treatment. These include homeopathic remedies, herbal remedies, aromatherapy oils, flower essences and the broad area of vitamin and mineral supplements.

Nurses should not prescribe any complementary medicinal products unless they have undertaken appropriate recognised training to do so. Where a nurse or midwife considers that complementary medicinal products could be a substitute for, or a complement to, conventional medication, then patients or clients should be referred to appropriately qualified practitioners to receive such treatment.

Standard 23 of its standards for medicines management (NMC, 2010) states:

Registrants must have successfully undertaken training and be competent to practise the administration of complementary and alternative therapies.

Failure to comply with these standards could lead to professional conduct proceedings. Midwives should ensure that they question a woman on whether she is taking any medication, including complementary therapies.

Scenario 11.1. Restrictions on the midwife: Discussion

As seen in *Chapter 3*, the refusal of a competent woman to accept any recommended treatment is absolute. Only if there are doubts concerning her mental capacity could consideration be given to treatments in her best interests. As long as Karen retains her mental capacity she is able to refuse any orthodox medicines and treatment which would normally be recommended at that point in labour. Even if, during prolonged labour, she were to lose her mental capacity to make decisions, the definition of what was in her best interests would have to take her previous expressed wishes and feelings into account. It is essential that Rachel explains this to Karen so that she is fully aware of the legal situation, pointing out that since for Karen this is her first child, she does not know what she may be facing. Of course as long as Karen retains her mental capacity, she can change her mind about what is acceptable treatment.

Conclusion

Changes in prescribing powers are supporting a radical development in the traditional demarcation boundaries of health professional activities. There are now great opportunities for professional development. However, any such widening of the scope of professional practice must ensure that midwives work within their competence and they obtain the training and necessary practice under supervision (It remains illegal for any health professional other than a midwife or doctor to attend a woman in childbirth, see *Chapter 12*). Errors and negligent practice will be followed by litigation, disciplinary and fitness to practise proceedings and, in situations where there has been gross negligence, criminal prosecution. Midwives should be aware in their concerns with the medicines management of their women of the possibility of low levels of functional health literacy, which can impact upon the women's adherence to medicine regimens. Simple techniques can be used to assist in communication (Bowskill and Garner, 2012).

Questions and exercises

1. Prepare a policy in relation to the supply and administration of controlled drugs in the community.
2. In what ways would you consider that the powers of the midwife could be enhanced by the changes in prescribing legislation?
3. A client is a drug addict. What action do you take?
4. Access the websites for the Royal Pharmaceutical Society (www.rpharms. com/) or the Medicines and Health Care Products Regulatory Agency (www.mhra.gov.uk/) and research their guidance on the administration of medicines and their reports on harm that has resulted from negligence in the administration of medicines.
5. Complementary and alternative therapies have been growing in popularity. What are the implications of this trend for the midwife? Refer to NMC guidance on complementary therapies.

References

Audit Commission (2002) *Acute hospital portfolio: Medicines Management.* Available from: www.auditcommission

Bishop JL, Northstone K, Green JR, Thompson EA (2011) The use of complementary and alternative medicine in pregnancy: Data from the Avon Longitudinal Study of Parents and Children. *Complementary Therapies in Medicine* **19**(6): 303–10

BNF Breastfeeding Network (2004) *Newsletter No 24.* BNF **February**: 9–10

Bolam v Friern Hospital Management Committee QBD [1957] 2 ALL ER 118

Bowskill D, Garner L (20112) Medicines non-adherence: Adult literacy and implications for practice. *British Journal of Nursing* **21**(19): 1156–9

British National Formulary Extra (2004) *News item.* **6 October.** Available from: www. bnf.uk

Department of Health (1989) *Report on nurse prescribing and supply. Advisory Group chaired by Dr June Crown.* HMSO, London

Department of Health (1998) *Review of prescribing, supply and administration of medicines: A report on the supply and administration of medicines under Group Protocols.* HMSO, London

Department of Health (1999) *Final report on the prescribing, supply and administration of medicines. Chaired by Dr June Crown.* HMSO, London

Dimond B (2011) *Legal aspects of medicines* (2nd edn). Quay Books, Dinton, Wiltshire

Dwyer v Roderick and others The Times 12 November 1983

EC Directive 2001/20/EC On the implementation of good clinical practice in the conduct of clinical trials on medicinal products for human use.

HM Government (2010a) *Drug strategy 2010: Building demand, restricting supply, building recovery.* HMSO, London

HM Government (2010b) *Healthy people, healthy lives.* HMSO, London

Human Medicines Regulations 2012 SI 2012/1916

Kennedy D (1996) Hospital blamed in report on overdose death. *The Times* **3 July**

Medicines (Pharmacy and General Sale Exemption) Order 1980 Article 4 Statutory instrument 1980 No 1924

Medicines for Human Use (Miscellaneous Amendments) Order 2011/1327 incorporated into the Human Medicines Regulations 2012 SI2012/1916

Misuse of Drug Regulations 2001 SI 2001/3998

Misuse of Drugs (safe custody) Amendment Regulations 2007 SI 2154

Misuse of Drugs Regulations SI 2001 No 3998 amending and re-enacting the Misuse of Drugs Regulations SI 1985 2066

National Institute for Clinical Excellence (2002) *Guidance for rhesus negative women during pregnancy.* Available from: www.nice.org.uk

Nursing and Midwifery Council (2002) *Circular 25/2002. Extended independent nurse prescribing and supplementary prescribing.* NMC, London

Nursing and Midwifery Council (2003a) *Circular 8/2003.* NMC, London

Nursing and Midwifery Council (2003b) *Routine antenatal anti-D prophylaxis for RhD-negative women. Circular 5/2003.* NMC, London

Nursing and Midwifery Council (2006) S*tandards of proficiency for nurse and midwife prescribers.* NMC, London

Nursing and Midwifery Council (2007) *Standards for medicines management.* (Updated 2010). NMC, London

Nursing and Midwifery Council (2008) *Code of Professional Conduct: standards for conduct, performance and ethics.* Available from: www.nmc-uk.org/

Nursing and Midwifery Council (2010) *Standards for medicines management.* NMC, London

Nursing and Midwifery Council (2012a) *Prescribing in pregnancy: The role of independent and supplementary nurse prescribers.* NMC, London

Nursing and Midwifery Council (2012b) *Midwives rules and standards.* NMC, London

Prendergast v Sam & Dee and others. Independent 17 March 1988.

Prescription only Medicines (Human Use) Amendment Order 2000 SI 2000 No 1917 incorporated into the Human Medicines Regulations 2012 SI2012/1916

Re F (in utero) [1988] 2 All ER 193

Royal Pharmaceutical Society of Great Britain (2004) *Law and ethics facts sheet. Dealing with dispensing errors.* Available from: www.rpsgb.org.uk

Schirm E, Schwagermann MP, Toi H et al (2004) Drug use during breastfeeding. A survey from The Netherlands. *European Journal of Clinical Nutrition* **58**(2): 386–90

Shipman Inquiry (2004) *Fourth report. The regulation of controlled drugs in the community.* Available from: www.the-shipman-inquiry.org.uk/reports.asp

Statutory Instrument 1997 No 1830 consolidated in SI 2012 No 1916

Section D

Statutory provisions

Chapter 12

Criminal law and confinements

Scenario 12.1. Death of baby

After 36 weeks gestation and following a protracted labour the baby was born, lived for a few hours and then died. The midwife manager said that a stillbirth should be registered. A junior midwife disagreed. What is the legal situation and what are the legal consequences?

Scenario 12.2. is discussed on p. 235.

This chapter considers the accountability of the midwife in the criminal courts and looks at the following topics:

- Coroner's jurisdiction
- Murder
- Manslaughter
- The case of *R v Cox* and Dr Bodkin Adams
- Infanticide
- Suicide and assisted suicide
- Letting die
- Other crimes
- Attendance by unqualified persons at childbirth
- Female Genital Mutilation Act 2003
- Forced Marriage (Civil Protection) Act 2007
- Corporate Manslaughter and Homicide Act 2007
- Criminal proceedings
- Criminal injury compensation.

In *Chapter 1* it was explained that criminal offences may be statutory (e.g. theft) or derived from the common law (e.g. murder). In order to establish that the accused is guilty of the offence with which he or she is charged, the prosecution must prove beyond reasonable doubt that both the actual physical requirements of the offence (i.e. the *actus reus*) and the required mental element (*mens rea*) are present. When a client (mother or baby) dies in the course of being cared for by health professionals, the death could be classified as natural, accidental, voluntary manslaughter, involuntary manslaughter or murder.

Coroner's jurisdiction

The death, unless it has resulted from natural causes and can therefore be certified by the doctor caring for the patient, would be reported to the coroner, who then has the responsibility for deciding whether to request a post-mortem and whether or not an inquest should be held. The coroner will also decide whether or not a jury should be summoned to decide upon the cause of death. The purpose of the inquest is to decide:

• The identity of the deceased.
• How, where and when the deceased came by his death.
• The particulars required by the Registration Acts to be registered concerning his death.

The finding of any person guilty of criminal or civil liability is specifically prohibited by the Coroners and Justice Act 2009 Section 10(2).

Following an unexpected death, there would probably be an inquest carried out by the coroner. If criminal offences are suspected, the coroner has the power to adjourn the hearing. The Director of Public Prosecutions may also ask the coroner to adjourn the hearing. Following the coroner's hearing, the papers in the case may be placed before the Crown Prosecution Service (CPS). The CPS has the right to decide if proceedings should be brought in the criminal courts against the defendant. If, following the death of a mother or baby, a midwife is asked to provide a statement and give evidence at an inquest, she should seek assistance from senior management or the solicitor to the trust (see *Chapter 9*). She may also find the advice of a coroner and solicitor involved in health professional legal training of assistance (Solon, 2012).

Major reforms to the coroner's jurisdiction and appointments were recommended by the report following the inquiry into the Shipman murders (2003). A Chief Coroner has now been appointed.

Murder

In order to secure a conviction of murder, the prosecution has to prove beyond all reasonable doubt that the defendant must either have intended to cause death or intended to cause grievous bodily harm. Unless a situation comparable to that of the Beverely Allitt case or the Shipman case exists, which is extremely rare, it would be very unusual to be able to prove the intent necessary to convict a health professional of the murder of a patient. Following a conviction for murder, a judge at the present time has no discretion over sentencing but must sentence the convicted person to life imprisonment, i.e. a life sentence is mandatory. The judge can indicate the minimum time that must be served. Sentencing principles were contained in the Criminal Justice Act 2003.

Involuntary manslaughter

This may arise where death results from the gross negligence of a health professional, where there is no intention to kill or to cause grievous harm. There will not be a charge of murder. In such cases there may be a prosecution for involuntary manslaughter or there may be no prosecution at all. It depends upon the circumstances. If, for example, there is gross recklessness leading to the death, then there may be a prosecution for manslaughter. The following cases illustrate different situations.

- In 1991 two junior doctors were each given a nine-month suspended prison sentence for the manslaughter of a 16-year-old boy with leukaemia. He died after being wrongly injected in the spine with a cytotoxic drug which should have been administered intravenously. The conviction for manslaughter was quashed by the Court of Appeal on the grounds that the jury should have been directed by the judge to decide whether the defendants were guilty of "gross negligence" and not "recklessness'" and whether there were any mitigating circumstances such as the lack of supervision from more experienced staff (*R v Prentice; R v Adomako; R v Holloway*).
- In contrast, in the case of Dr Adomako, the person charged, was, during the latter part of an operation, the anaesthetist in charge of the patient, who was undergoing an eye operation. He failed to note that the endotracheal tube had become disconnected and did not make the appropriate checks. Dr Adomako accepted at his trial that he had been negligent. The issue was whether his conduct was criminal. He was convicted of involuntary manslaughter but appealed against his conviction. He lost his appeal in the Court of Appeal and then appealed to the House of Lords (*R v Adomako House of Lords*). The House of Lords clarified the legal situation setting out the stages that should be followed in determining whether the accused was

guilty of criminal negligence. The House of Lords held that the Court of Appeal had applied the correct test and his appeal was dismissed.

- A husband was charged with manslaughter because he had failed to call medical assistance for his wife following a home birth when the baby was stillborn. The wife refused to allow him to call for help and she died. The judge directed the jury that, because the wife was mentally competent and had refused assistance, the husband's duty of care to seek assistance was removed. He could not therefore be guilty of manslaughter (*R v Smith*).

Parents and duty of care

A Rastafarian couple who had refused on religious grounds to allow their diabetic daughter who was nine years old to be given insulin were convicted of manslaughter on 28 October 1993 in Nottingham. The father was given a sentence of imprisonment and the mother a suspended sentence. They believed in using homeopathic medicine. In contrast, in 2001 parents (Gregoriadis and Peek) who had fed their baby daughter a fruit-only diet pleaded guilty of cruelty to a child, when she died of a chest infection brought on by malnutrition. A manslaughter charge was left on the file.

The case of R v Dr Nigel Cox

Dr Nigel Cox was convicted when he prescribed potassium chloride to a terminally ill patient, and was sentenced to a year's imprisonment which was suspended for a year. He also had to appear before disciplinary proceedings of the Regional Health Authority, his employers and before the General Medical Council. The fact that the patient was terminally ill was no justification for the attempt to kill.

The case of R v Adams (Bodkin)

In contrast to the case of Dr Cox, Dr Bodkin Adams was acquitted following a trial where it was alleged that he had caused the death of Mrs Morell, a resident in a nursing home in Eastbourne, by giving her excessive morphine. The trial judge instructed the jury that a doctor had no right to end the life of a dying patient but if the treatment to provide comfort was the right and proper treatment, the fact that incidentally it shortened life did not give any grounds for convicting him of murder.

Dr Adams was acquitted.

Voluntary manslaughter

This term is used to cover the situation where the defendant has caused the death of a person with intent, but owing to special circumstances a charge or conviction of murder is not appropriate. The term covers:

- Death as a result of the loss of self-control (caused by a qualifying trigger) of the accused. (This replaces the earlier defence of provocation which was repealed by the Coroners and Justice Act 2009.)
- Death as a result of diminished responsibility of the accused.
- Killing as a result of a suicide pact.

Criminal law and the midwife

If a midwife has been responsible for an action of gross negligence which has led to the death of the mother or baby, she may well face criminal proceedings, in addition to professional conduct proceedings by the Nursing and Midwifery Council (NMC) and disciplinary proceedings by the employer (see *Chapter 1*). Civil proceedings for compensation by the relatives of the victim may also take place (see *Chapter 8*). The criminal procedure that would be followed is considered below.

The midwife might also be involved in a criminal case because of the alleged criminal conduct of a colleague and may be asked to provide a statement and give evidence in court (see *Chapter 9*).

Infanticide

Under Section 1(1) of the Infanticide Act 1938 a woman can be found guilty of an offence if she causes the death of a baby under 12 months, but if it is found that the balance of her mind was disturbed by reason of her not having fully recovered from the effect of giving birth or by reason of the effect of lactation, then instead of murder, she can be found guilty of manslaughter. Changes were made to the definition by the Coroners and Justice Act 2009 but the recommendation of the Butler Report (Home Office, 1975) that the offence should be abolished was not implemented.

Suicide and assisting in the suicide of another

While suicide has not been a criminal offence since 1961, it remains a criminal offence to aid or abet another person in committing suicide. Attempts to change the law have failed: Diane Pretty lost her appeal to the House of Lords – *R (on the application of Pretty) v DPP Secretary of State for the Home Department intervening* – and also lost her application to the European Court of Human Rights in Strasbourg (*Pretty v UK ECHR*) which held that the Suicide Act 1961 was not incompatible with the European Convention on Human Rights. Debbie Purdy, who wished her husband to take her abroad to achieve an end to her suffering, failed in her attempt to obtain an advance permission for her partner to assist her death. Her case led to the House of Lords – *R (Purdy) v Director of Public Prosecutions* – demanding that clearer guidance be provided by the Director of Public Prosecutions on when there would be prosecutions under the Act.

Letting die

The law does not require heroic efforts to be made to keep a grossly disabled child alive. To let nature take its course may be within the law. An application to the Court should be made when there is a dispute over the legality of letting die.

Re B (a minor)(wardship; medical treatment) 1981

A child was born suffering from Down's syndrome and an intestinal blockage. She required an operation to relieve the obstruction if she was to live more than a few days. If the operation were performed, the child might die within a few months, but it was probable that her life expectancy would be 20 to 30 years. Her parents, having decided that it would be kinder to allow her to die rather than live as a physically and mentally handicapped person, refused to consent to the operation. The local authority made the child a ward of court and, when a surgeon decided that the wishes of the parents should be respected, they sought an order authorising the operation to be performed by other named surgeons. The judge decided that the parents' wishes should be respected and refused to make the order. The local authority appealed to the Court of Appeal which allowed the appeal. It stated that the question for the court was whether it was in the best interests of the child that she should have the operation and not whether the parents' wishes should be respected.

Re C (a minor)(wardship; medical treatment) 1989

In a contrasting case, a baby was born suffering from congenital hydrocephalus and had been made a ward of court for reasons unconnected with her medical condition. The local authority sought the court's determination as to the appropriate manner in which she should be treated, should she contract a serious infection, or her existing feeding regimens become unviable. A specialist paediatrician assessed C's condition as severely and irreversibly brain-damaged, the prognosis of which was hopeless. He recommended that the objective of any treatment should therefore be to ease suffering rather than prolong life. While not specifying the adoption or discontinuance of any particular procedures, he further advised consultation with C's carers as to the appropriate method of achieving that objective. The judge accepted this report and approved the recommendations as being in her best interests. The Court of Appeal upheld the judge's decision with a slight amendment of the order, Paragraph 4 of which read:

> The hospital to continue to treat the minor within the parameters of the opinion expressed by [the specialist paediatrician] in his report of 13.4.1989 which report is not to be disclosed to any person other than the health authority.

This case raised many issues:

- What is meant by the best interests of the child?
- What is the role of the doctor?
- What is the role of the registered midwife/nurse?
- What rights do the parents have?
- What is the role of the courts?

The best interests of the child are determined by what the professionals, following the Bolam Test, would consider appropriate in the light of the specific circumstances of that individual child. It is clear that heroic surgery and medical intervention will not necessarily always be in the best interests of the child, and the court is unwilling to direct specialists over what should be done, preferring to leave the actual decisions to clinical judgement. (See below the case of *Re J* 1992.)

The doctor has a duty to make a clinical assessment, following the reasonable standard of care.

The role of the midwife/neonatal nurse is to ensure that she provides all the relevant information to the doctor and takes a full part in the multi-disciplinary discussions relating to the future of the baby. She is likely to have greater contact with the parents and should ensure that they have support and if necessary counselling to cope with the decisions that are made.

The parents do not have the right to insist that treatment ends for the child, or even that treatment is commenced. Their participation in the clinical decisions which are made is, however, essential and the midwife/neonatal nurse will have an important role to play in this.

There has recently been a spate of referrals of decisions relating to neonates to the court which has the role of determining what action is appropriate in the best interests of the child.

Re J (a minor)(wardship; medical treatment) 1990

The baby was a ward of court. In contrast with the case of *Re C*, the baby was not at the point of death. However, the prognosis was not good and although he was expected to survive a few years he was likely to be blind, deaf, unable to speak and have serious spastic quadriplegia. The judge made an order that he should be treated with antibiotics if he developed a chest infection, but if he were to stop breathing he should not receive artificial ventilation. The official solicitor on behalf of the child appealed against the order on the grounds that unless the situation was one of terminal illness, or it was certain that the child's life would be intolerable, the court was not justified in approving the withholding of life-saving treatment. The court held that the court can never sanction positive steps to terminate the life of a person. However, the court could direct that treatment, without which death would ensue, need not be given to prolong life, even though he was neither on the point of death nor dying. The court had to undertake a balancing exercise in assessing the course to be adopted in the best interests of the child, looked at from his point of view and giving the fullest possible weight to his desire, if he were in a position to make a sound judgement to survive, and taking into account the pain and suffering and quality of life that he would experience if life was prolonged, and the pain and suffering involved in the proposed treatment.

Can the court order doctors to treat?

Re J (1992)

J was born in January 1991 and suffered an accidental fall when he was a month old, with the result that he was profoundly handicapped both mentally and physically. He was severely microcephalic, his brain not having grown sufficiently following the injury. He also had severe cerebral palsy, cortical blindness and severe epilepsy. He was, in general, fed by a nasogastric tube. Medical opinion was unanimous that J was unlikely to develop much beyond his present functioning, that that level might deteriorate and that his expectation of life, although uncertain, would be short. The paediatrician's report stated that given J's condition it would not be medically appropriate to intervene with intensive procedures such as artificial ventilation if he were to suffer a life-threatening event. The baby was in the care of foster parents with whom the local authority shared responsibility. The local authority applied to the court under Section 100 of the Children Act 1989 to determine whether ventilation should be given to the child. The Court of Appeal thus held that where a paediatrician caring for a severely handicapped baby considered that mechanical ventilation procedures would not be appropriate, the court would not grant an injunction requiring such treatment to take place.

The effect of the court's decision was to set aside the judge's ruling that ventilation should be given, and so leave the health authority and its medical staff free, subject to consent not being withdrawn, to treat J in accordance with their best clinical judgement. That did not mean that in no circumstances should J be subjected to mechanical ventilation. Thus the Court of Appeal affirmed the freedom of doctors to decide for themselves what is the best treatment and showed its reluctance to interfere in medical practice.

Re Charlotte

The Portsmouth NHS Trust sought permission to decline to give invasive medical treatment to prolong the life of a profoundly disabled baby. Charlotte was born at 26 weeks gestation, weighing about one pound. She had chronic respiratory and kidney problems and brain damage that had left her blind, deaf and incapable of voluntary movement or response. She was capable of experiencing pain.

The dispute was over what should be done should she deteriorate and require artificial ventilation. The unanimous medical advice was that to give such treatment would not be in her best interests. However, her parents' view was that such treatment should at least be instituted and that the treatment could best be prepared for by the carrying out of an elective tracheotomy. They believed that it was their duty to maintain life as they did not believe that C was yet ready to die. The court granted the application that any further aggressive treatment, even if necessary to prolong life, was not in C's best interests. The doctors still had a duty of care to C. The order only authorised the doctors not to send C for artificial ventilation or similar aggressive treatment. The court asked the doctors to give further consideration to an elective tracheotomy on the basis of its possible contribution to her palliative care.

Subsequently, when she appeared to be making good progress, the parents asked the court to review its decision. The judge decided on 21 April 2005 that the decision should stand but it was subject to review (*Wyatt v Portsmouth NHS Trust*).

R v Arthur

Even where the parents wish a grossly handicapped baby to die, any professional who intentionally speeded up the process of death could be guilty of causing the death of the child. In the case of *R v Arthur,* a paediatrician was prosecuted for attempting to cause the death of a grossly handicapped baby who was suffering from Down's syndrome and who had other disabilities, when he prescribed dihydrocodeine and nursing care only. The judge stated that:

> There is no special law in this country that places doctors in a separate category and gives them extra protection over the rest of us... Neither in law is there any special power, facility or license to kill children who are handicapped or seriously disadvantaged in an irreversible way.

Dr Arthur was acquitted.

Letting die

Airedale NHS Trust v Bland (1993)

The House of Lords had to decide if it was lawful to permit artificial feeding to be discontinued in the case of a patient in a persistent vegetative state. The patient was a victim of the football stadium crush at Hillsborough and it was established that although he could breathe and digest food independently, he could not see, hear, taste, smell or communicate in any way and it appeared that there was no hope of recovery or improvement. The House of Lords decided that it would be in the best interests of the patient to discontinue the nasogastric feed and he was later reported as having died. The House of Lords recommended that if any similar decisions were required to be made in the future, there should be application before the courts.

Other cases of persistent vegetative state

In two cases it was argued on behalf of women in a persistent vegetative state that it was contrary to their right to life under Article 2 of the European Convention of Human Rights for artificial feeding to be discontinued. The President of the Family Division, Dame Elizabeth Butler-Sloss held that the withdrawal of life-sustaining medical treatment was not contrary to Article 2 of the Human Rights Convention and the right to life where the patient was in a persistent vegetative state (Gibb, 2000) (*NHS Trust A v Mrs M and NHS Trust B v Mrs H Family Division*).

Letting die and human rights

In a case in 2000 it was argued that letting a baby die was contrary to Article 3 of the European Convention on Human Rights (see *Chapter 2*). The court, however, held that it was not contrary to the human rights of a severely handicapped baby to allow him to die (*A National Health Service Trust v D*). Where parents disagree with the medical decision that it is in the interests of a grossly handicapped child to let him die, the case should be referred to the court.

Dispute over treatment

Where parents dispute projected treatment for a child, the paramount consideration is the welfare of the child. Judge Bodey overruled a mother's refusal to consent to radiotherapy treatment for her 7-year-old boy, Neon Roberts, holding that the belief of doctors that Neon would die within months without the treatment was paramount (*The Guardian*, 2012).

In the case of David Glass (*R v Portsmouth Hospitals NHS Trust ex parte Glass*), a boy of 13 who was severely disabled with only a limited life span, there was a dispute between clinical staff and the relatives over the treatment to be given, which resulted in prosecution of the relatives who were convicted of assault. Ms Glass sought a declaration as to the course doctors in the hospital should take. The judge refused the mother's application for judicial review and she appealed to the Court of Appeal (*R v Portsmouth Hospitals NHS Trust ex parte Glass*). The Court of Appeal refused to give an advance order over what should be decided at a future time, but stated that in the event of a dispute between parents and doctors there should be an application to court to determine what was in the best interests of the child. Ms Glass applied to the European Court of Human Rights (*Glass v United*

Kingdom) and won her appeal. The European Court of Human Rights came to the unanimous conclusion that the decision of the authorities to over-ride Ms Glass's objection to the proposed treatment in the absence of authorisation by a court resulted in a breach of Article 8. The European Court of Human Rights awarded Ms Glass €10 000 for non-pecuniary damage and €15 000 for costs and expenses.

The implications of the Glass case are that in the exceptional cases where there are disputes between parents and clinicians over the proposed treatment that cannot be resolved, it is essential that there should be an application to the court, thereby protecting the rights of the child, the parents and the practitioners.

Guidance on letting die

The Royal College of Paediatrics and Child Health (2004) has published guidelines on when it is appropriate to withhold or withdraw medical treatment. The guidelines distinguish between the following clinical situations:

- The brain dead child.
- The permanent vegetative state.
- The "no chance" situation.
- The "no purpose" situation.
- The "unbearable" situation.

In all these situations, the possibility of withholding or withdrawal of curative medical treatment might be considered. The guidance emphasises the importance of the fundamental principles of the duty of care and partnership of care, and the respect for the rights of the child as set out in the United Nations Convention on the Rights of the Child (United Nations, 1989). The guidelines of the Royal College of Paediatrics and Child Health can be accessed on its website (www. rcpch.ac.uk). They represent its interpretation of the law, but are not the law itself. Further advice has been published by the British Medical Association (BMA, 2000). Reference could also be made to Chapter 6 in the BMA's book on consent and the rights of children and young people (BMA, 1995).

The second edition of the Royal College of Paediatrics and Child Health guidance was considered in the case of *K (a child)(withdrawal of treatment)*, where medical evidence suggested that the baby of 5½ months suffering from congenital myotonica dystrophy came within the third and fourth categories of the Royal College guidance, i.e no chance and no purpose. Determining the best interests of the child included an evaluation of the medical, emotional and all other welfare issues. The judge cited the words of Dame Elizabeth Butler-Sloss in the case of *Re L(a minor)*:

> The task therefore is for me to weigh up that which is sometimes called the "benefits and dis-benefits" but which I would prefer to call the advantages of giving or not giving potential treatments, and to balance them in order to decide the best interests of L with regard to his future treatment.

In the light of all the evidence the judge concluded that:

> ...it would not only be a mercy but it is in her best interests, to cease to provide total parenteral nutrition, while she is clinically stable, so that she may die in peace and over a comparatively short space of time, relieved by the palliative treatment contemplated.

The full case can be accessed on the bailii website.

Living wills/advance refusal or directive

A mentally competent person can decide in advance that at a subsequent time (when he or she does not have the requisite mental capacity to make decisions) he or she would not wish to have treatment. The Mental Capacity Act 2005, which came into force in April 2007, set down statutory provision for living wills or advance decisions (see below). Prior to 2007, living wills, also known as advance refusals, or advance directions, had been recognised at common law (i.e. judge-made law, or case law). This was stated by the House of Lords in the Tony Bland case (*Airedale NHS Trust v Bland House of Lords*) (see above).

An advance directive overruled

In the case of *The NHS Trust v T*, the High Court upheld an interim declaration authorising the trust to treat the patient by way of a blood transfusion in order to save or preserve her life or to avoid imminent risk of serious injury to her health. The patient was self-harming and had signed an advance directive refusing blood transfusion. She did not want to continue to live and believed that her blood was evil, and that a transfusion would result in contamination by her evil blood. An emergency situation had arisen because she had lost so much blood. The psychiatrist held that she was mentally disordered and did not have the capacity to refuse blood transfusions. At an earlier court hearing, an order was granted permitting blood to be given to her in an emergency. The NHS Trust subsequently sought a declaration over future treatment to be given to her, including further transfusions.

In another case (*HE v A Hospital NHS Trust*) a father applied to court for a blood transfusion to be given to his daughter. The daughter had been a Muslim until the parents separated at which point she became a Jehovah's Witness. The daughter signed an advance medical directive refusing a blood transfusion and stating that the directive could only be revoked in writing. The daughter suffered from a congenital heart condition, fell seriously ill, was hospitalised and needed a transfusion. The mother stated that the treatment should not proceed because the advance directive was in force. The father said that his daughter would have, if not unconscious, revoked the directive since she was now engaged to a Muslim man. The court held that the proposed treatment could be provided.

Mental Capacity Act 2005 and advance decisions

The above two cases must now be reviewed in the light of the Mental Capacity Act. Sections 24, 25 and 26 of the Mental Capacity Act 2005 make provision for advance decisions. Section 24 defines and recognises the validity of an advance decision, which may be valid even though expressed in layman's terms. A withdrawal or subsequent alteration to an advance decision need not be in writing.

Under Section 25, an advance decision does not affect the liability which a person may incur for carrying out or continuing a treatment in relation to the patient unless it is valid and applicable to the treatment. An advance decision is not valid:

- If the patient has withdrawn it, when he had the capacity to do so.
- Has, under a lasting power of attorney, created after the advance decision was made, conferred authority to give or refuse consent to the treatment covered by the advance decision, or
- Done anything else inconsistent with the advance decision.

An advance decision is not applicable to the treatment in question if the treatment is not specified in the advance decision or if any circumstances specified in the advance decision are absent or if there are reasonable grounds for believing that circumstances exist which the patient did not anticipate at the time the advance decision was created, and which would have affected his/her decision.

Life-sustaining treatment and advance decisions

An advance decision is not applicable to life-sustaining treatment unless:

- The patient has stated that it is to apply to that treatment even if his or her life is at risk.
- The statement is in writing.
- The statement is signed by the patient or by a person on behalf of him or her.
- The signature is made or acknowledged by the patient in the presence of a witness and the witness signs it or acknowledges his signature in the patient's presence.

The legal effect of a valid relevant advance decision is that the decision has effect as if it had been made when the question of whether the treatment should or should not be given arises. A person does not incur liability for carrying out or continuing treatment unless, at the time, he/she is satisfied that a valid, applicable advance decision exists. A person is not liable for withholding or withdrawing treatment, if he/she reasonably believed that a valid, applicable advance decision exists. The court can make a declaration on the validity and applicability of an advance decision and action can be taken to provide life-sustaining treatment or doing any act he/she reasonably believes to be necessary to prevent a serious deterioration in the patient's condition, while seeking a declaration from the court. This last point would cause considerable problems if there was uncertainty as to the validity or applicability of an advance decision drawn up by a Jehovah's Witness refusing blood, since, while waiting for the court declaration on its validity or applicability, the only way of preventing a serious deterioration in the patient may be to give blood. If the court were then to declare the advance decision to be valid, the patient would already have been given the very treatment he or she was refusing.

Assisted Dying Bill

An Assisted Dying Bill, which would have legalised euthanasia in the UK, failed to complete all stages before the 2005 dissolution of Parliament. A House of Lords report on the Assisted Dying Bill was published in 2005. It is available on the internet (www.parliament.uk/briefing-papers/sn04857.pdf). A fresh attempt to introduce an Assisted Dying Bill was announced in January 2013 by Lord Falconer. This would legalise assisted suicide when a patient is certified as terminally ill and expected to live less than a year. It was tabled in the House of Lords in the summer of 2013.

Application to midwifery

If a pregnant woman draws up an advance decision refusing specified treatment during her labour or post-natal care, this would be binding upon professional staff if it is clear that she was mentally competent at the time it was drawn up and, at the time the specified treatment is being considered, she lacks the mental capacity to make her own decisions. (The effect of an advance decision only comes into being when the maker no longer has the mental capacity to make decisions.) If the advance decision relates to life-sustaining treatment then the provisions of the Mental Capacity Act set out above must be satisfied for the instruction to be valid. Where there is concern about the validity of the instruction or the mental capacity of the woman, an application should be made to the Court of Protection.

R (on the application of Burke) v General Medical Council and Disability Rights Commission and the Official Solicitor to the Supreme Court

A patient suffering from cerebellar ataxia, a progressive degenerative condition, who was of full capacity, challenged the General Medical Council guidelines on withholding and withdrawing life-prolonging treatments. He argued that their guidelines were contrary to the Articles of the European Convention on Human Rights. He applied for judicial review and sought clarification as to the circumstances in which artificial nutrition and hydration would be withdrawn. He did not want artificial nutrition and hydration to be withdrawn until he died of natural causes. He succeeded in the High Court which required the General Medical Council to rewrite its guidelines. However, the Court of Appeal overruled this decision in the *R (on the application of Burke) v General Medical Council and Orths* case. The case can be accessed on the bailii website (www.bailii.org/ew/cases/EWCA/Civ/2005/1003.html).

Not-for-resuscitation decisions

Where a patient has the requisite mental capacity or has made a valid advance decision and had refused resuscitation, then the not-for-resuscitation instruction should be followed. Where the patient lacks mental capacity and there is no advance decision, then the provisions of the Mental Capacity Act 2005 apply and action should be taken in the best interests of the patient.

The court considered the validity of a do-not-resuscitate instruction in the case of a seriously disabled boy, *Re R (adult: medical treatment)*, with malformation of the brain and cerebral palsy who had developed severe epilepsy, was blind, incontinent, and had other major disabilities, who at the time of the hearing was 23 years old. The court held that in the light of the medical evidence the overriding principle was that the boy's life was so afflicted as to be intolerable and that it was not in the best interests of the boy to be subjected to cardiopulmonary resuscitation in the event of his suffering a cardiac arrest. This view was supported by the boy's parents. The court held that the do-not-resuscitate instruction was justifiable since cardiopulmonary resuscitation was unlikely to be successful.

In 2001, the British Medical Association, the Resuscitation Council (UK) and the Royal College of Nursing issued a joint statement. It emphasised the importance of each health organisation having a resuscitation policy according to the principles set out in the guidance. Revised guidelines were issued by the Resuscitation Council UK in October 2010 and are only available in electronic form from its website (www.resus.org.uk/). Chapters 9, 10 and 11 of the guidelines cover paediatric basic life support, paediatric advanced life support and newborn life support.

Other crimes

The chances of the midwife being involved in criminal proceedings for murder or manslaughter are extremely rare. However, she does face the possibility of other criminal charges, particularly in relation to property, motor offences or health and safety offences, which are prosecuted in the criminal courts.

Community midwives, in particular, are vulnerable to the allegation that they have been guilty of theft of property in a person's house, particularly where they visit on their own. There should be a clear protocol against the receipt of any gifts to the midwife from clients, to protect the midwife against false accusations.

In addition the community midwife, in driving a car, will have to make arrangements for it to be appropriately insured and that driving it at work has been agreed in advance with the insurers. The nature of the work would have to be specified, including whether or not she uses the car to drive clients and equipment. She would be responsible for any breach of the Road Traffic Acts on her own account.

If it is known that the defendant is a registered midwife, any conviction for a criminal offence would automatically be reported to the Nursing and Midwifery Council. The midwife would not have any right to sue the police for breach of confidentiality (*Woolgar v Chief Constable of Sussex Police and another*).

Other offences are discussed in the context of specific chapters, e.g. abortion (*Chapter 13*), offences against the person (*Chapters 7* and *13*) and offences under the Human Fertilisation and Embryology Act (*Chapter 14*). Breaches of the Health and Safety at Work Act and the Regulations can result in criminal prosecutions, and these are discussed in *Chapter 10*.

Attendance by unqualified persons at childbirth

Under Article 45 of the Nursing and Midwifery Order 2001 it is a criminal offence for a person, other than a midwife or doctor, to attend at a confinement except in an emergency.

(1) A person other than a registered midwife or a registered medical practitioner shall not attend a woman in childbirth.
(2) This paragraph does not apply:
   (a) where the attention is given in a case of sudden or urgent necessity, or
   (b) in the case of a person who, while undergoing training with a view to becoming a medical practitioner or becoming a midwife, attends a woman in childbirth as part of a course of practical instruction in midwifery recognised by the Nursing and Midwifery Council or by the General Medical Council.
(3) A person who contravenes paragraph (1) shall be liable on summary conviction to a fine not exceeding level 5 on the standard scale.

There have been prosecutions under the predecessor to this Article.

Female Genital Mutilation Act 2003

Under the Prohibition of Female Circumcision Act 1985 female circumcision was a criminal offence. There was, however, evidence that some girls from ethnic minorities were being returned home to be circumcised. This led to the 1985 Act being replaced by the Female Genital Mutilation Act 2003 which strengthens the law against female genital mutilation. The full text of the 2003 Act can be accessed on the legislation website (www.legislation.gov.uk).

Midwives may come across information that female circumcision is being carried out illegally in this country or of girls being sent abroad for the procedure. Disclosure of this information to the appropriate authorities would be justified in the public interest and therefore an exception to the duty of confidentiality (see *Chapter 4*). In November 2012, the Director of the Crown Prosecution Service published an action plan to ensure that there were prosecutions of those involved in the practice (*The Guardian*, 2012b). As yet there has never been a prosecution in the UK.

Forced Marriage (Civil Protection) Act 2007

The Act introduced civil remedies to protect individuals at risk of being forced into marriage or to help remove them from a forced marriage situation. The House of Commons Home Affairs Committee reviewed the legislation and its impact in a report in 2011. It can be accessed on the parliamentary publications website (www.publications.parliament.uk/pa/cm201012.cmselect/cmhaff/880/880.pdf).

Corporate Manslaughter and Corporate Homicide Act 2007

The Law Commission (1996) recommended that there should be a new law of corporate manslaughter introduced so that senior managers within an organisation can be held criminally liable when persons die as a result of gross negligence by their organisation. The Corporate Manslaughter and Corporate Homicide Act 2007 was the result of these recommendations. Further information on the implications of the Act for health and safety can be found on the Health and Safety Executive website (www.hse.gov.uk/corpmanslaughter/index.htm).

Midwifery shortages and the Corporate Manslaughter and Corporate Homicide Act 2007

In April 2012 it was reported (Laurance, 2012) that more than 100 mothers had died in childbirth in London in the previous 5 years. The President of the RCM pointed to an extreme shortage of midwives across the capital. If such deaths were the result of criminal negligence, then midwives might find themselves involved in criminal proceedings. In November 2012 (Rhoda, 2012), in response to a report that a baby had died following multiple errors at St James Hospital in Leeds, a spokesman for the RCM said:

Our calculation is that England is short of 5000 full-time equivalent midwives and that Wales is short of over 150.

The coroner stated at the inquest

...if a review had been undertaken at 9.00am it is likely that Ms Ibbitson would have undergone an instrumental delivery and Betsy Wright would have been delivered, and it is likely that she would not have suffered fatal injuries, and she would have survived.

Where there are significant organisational failures leading to death, prosecutions could be brought under the Corporate Manslaughter and Corporate Homicide Act 2007.

The Centre for Maternal and Child Enquiries (CMACE) published its final report covering 2006–2008 in 2011. Its work is being taken over by the National Perinatal Epidemiology Unit in Oxford, which will publish an annual report and which will also look at near misses and not just deaths.

Criminal proceedings

For serious crimes known as "indictable only offences", criminal proceedings would commence with a short hearing before the magistrates court. If the case is to go to the crown court for a trial by jury, a date will be fixed for a plea and case management hearing. For less serious crimes, known as summary offences, (which can only be heard before the magistrates) or offences that are triable either way (i.e. they can be heard by magistrates or in the crown court), the magistrates act as both judge and jury in hearing the case. If they consider that the accused is guilty, then the magistrates sentence the accused. There is power to refer to the crown court for sentencing if the magistrates consider the accused should receive a stiffer sentence than they have power to give.

In a crown court hearing, where the accused enters a "not guilty" plea, the jury is sworn in and the case would begin with an opening speech by the prosecution lawyer. The witnesses for the prosecution give evidence in turn: initially evidence in chief (when they are questioned by the prosecution and leading questions cannot be asked); then they can be cross-examined by the defence, and then re-examined by the prosecution. After the end of the prosecution case, the judge could order the jury to bring forward a "not guilty" verdict if s/he is satisfied that there is insufficient evidence from the prosecution to justify a conviction.

Otherwise, the case proceeds with the evidence of the defence. At present the accused does not have to give evidence, but the prosecution can comment on that fact. After the witnesses for the defence have given evidence, there are closing speeches from the prosecution and defence and the judge then sums up for the jury, directing the jury on the law which applies, the evidence which they have heard and the responsibility upon them. If the jury brings forward a "guilty" verdict or verdicts, the judge then sentences the accused, but may delay this stage in order to have evidence of the accused's social and financial background and hear a plea in mitigation by the defence lawyer.

Criminal injury compensation

A scheme to compensate those who have suffered personal injuries as the result of criminal action has been in existence since 1964. The 2012 scheme excludes some injuries originally recognised as the subject of compensation, and payments for other injuries are reduced. Information is available from the Criminal Injuries Compensation Authority headquarters in Glasgow or from its website (www. justice.gov.uk/victims-and-witnesses). The details of the 2012 scheme and a guide to it can be downloaded from this website.

Claims are processed by the Criminal Injury Compensation Authority and claims officers and adjudicators on a panel determine whether a claim can be met.

Payments are made according to a tariff set out in Annexe E of the Scheme. Claims below £2500 are excluded from the new scheme. (Previously, the minimum payment was £1000.) Information relating to the Criminal Injuries Compensation Authority should be available to all NHS staff who should ensure that, if they are injured at work as a result of a crime, a check is made on their eligibility to receive compensation. It is important that any assaults on staff are reported to the police since information on this would be required by the Authority.

Scenario 12.1. Death of baby: Discussion

Even if the gestation was less than 24 weeks, the fact that the baby was breathing after the birth means that the birth must be registered as a live birth and then also as a death. If the gestation was 24 weeks or longer and the baby clearly was dead at birth then the baby must be registered as a stillbirth. If the gestation was less than 24 weeks and the baby failed to breathe then no registration would be necessary. The parents should be given the same support whether the baby is classified as a stillbirth or as a miscarriage, irrespective of the legal differences between the two situations. The failure of the midwife manager to understand the difference is a matter of great concern and further training is indicated.

Conclusions

While prosecution of midwives for work-related offences are rare, they may find that in the care of disabled persons and babies, the attendance at childbirth of unqualified persons who are not in training, and in health and safety concerns, the criminal law can impact upon their professional practice. Much can be learnt of the operation of the criminal law from a visit to the local magistrates or crown court and such a prior visit is strongly recommended should the midwife be called upon to give evidence in criminal proceedings.

Questions and exercises

1. The husband of a client attacks a midwife by grabbing her arm. She is contemplating bringing proceedings against him. What is the difference between a civil action and a criminal prosecution in this context? (See also *Chapters 1* and *8*.)
2. A client dies following an unsuccessful Caesarean operation. What factors would lead to a prosecution being brought against the staff involved?
3. A community midwife has not insured her car for use in transporting clients. She takes a pregnant woman to hospital in an emergency situation. What are the likely repercussions? (Consider the insurance issues as well as issues of reasonable professional practice.)
4. In what circumstances would a midwife be entitled to receive compensation from the Criminal Injury Compensation Scheme?
5. In which circumstances do you consider that it should be lawful to let a baby die?
6. Do you consider that a lack of resources could be a justifiable reason for letting a baby die?
7. An abortion of a fetus suffering from congenital disabilities results in a live birth. Is there a duty to keep that baby alive? What is the law? (Refer also to *Chapters 7* and *13*.)
8. A woman wishes to draw up an advanced refusal of clinical interventions during her pregnancy and labour. What should such a statement contain to be lawfully valid? (See also *Chapter 3*.)

9. Women who have been injured while pregnant have been kept on life support systems in order that the baby can survive. Do you consider that this practice raises any legal issues?

References

A National Health Service Trust v D. Times Law Report 19 July 2000; [2000] Lloyds Rep Med 411

Airedale NHS Trust v Bland [1993] 1 All ER 821 HL

Assisted Dying for the Terminally Ill Bill (HL) Report, Select Committee Session 2004-5 HL Paper 86-1.

Boseley S (2012b) CPS to crack down on female genital mutilation. *The Guardian* **23 November**

British Medical Association (1995) *Advance statements about medical treatment: Code of practice.* BMA, London

British Medical Association (2000) *Withholding and withdrawing life-prolonging medical treatment* (2nd edn). BMJ Books, London

British Medical Association, Resuscitation Council (UK) and the Royal College of Nursing (2001) *Decisions relating to cardiopulmonary resuscitation: A joint statement from the BMA, Resuscitation Council (UK) and the RCN.* BMA, London

Buchanan R (2012) Maternity care crisis and errors that put babies lives in danger. *The Times* **24 November**

Charter D, Kennedy D (2000) Doctors put on alert for girl butchery. *The Times* **21 August**

Director of Public Prosecutions (2010) *Policy for prosecutors in respect of cases of encouraging or assisting suicide.* DPP, London

General Medical Council (2010) *Guidelines on withholding and withdrawing life-prolonging treatments: Good practice in decision-making.* GMC, London

Gibb F (2000) Rights Act does not bar mercy killing. *The Times* **26 October**

Glass v United Kingdom The Times Law Report 11 March 2004 ECHR; Lloyd's Rep Med [2004] 76

Gregoriadis L, Peek L (2001) Baby starved to death on fruit diet. *The Times* **14 July**

HE v A Hospital NHS Trust [2003] EWHC 1017 [2003] 2 FLR 408

Home Office (1975) *Report of the Committee on Mentally Abnormal Offenders (Butler Report) Cmnd 6244.* HMSO, London

House of Commons (2011) *Home Affairs Committee Forced Marriage. 8th Report of Session 2010–12.* House of Commons, London

K (a child)(withdrawl of treatment) [2006] EWHC 1007 Fam

Laurance J (2012) Doubling of maternal death rate blamed on shortage of midwives. *The*

Independent **30 April**

Law Commission (1996) *Report No 237. Legislating the criminal code: Involuntary manslaughter.* Stationery Office, London

Momoh C (2004) Attitudes to female genital mutilation. *British Journal of Midwifery* **12**(10): 631–5

NHS Trust A v Mrs M and NHS Trust B v Mrs H Family Division [2001] Lloyd's Rep Med 27 Fam

NHS Trust v Ms T [2004] Lloyds Rep Med 433

Pretty v UK ECHR Current Law 380 June 2002 2346/02 [2002] 2 FLR 45

R (on the application of Burke) v General Medical Council and Disability Rights Commission and the Official Solicitor to the Supreme Court [2004] EWHC 1879; [2004] Lloyd's Rep Med 451

R (on the application of Burke) v General Medical Council and Others [2005] EWCA Civ 1003

R (on the application of Pretty) v DPP Secretary of State for the Home Department intervening Times Law Report 5 December 2001 [2001] UKHL 61; [2001] 3 WLR 1598

R (Purdy) v Director of Public Prosecutions The Times Law Report 31 July 2009 HL

R v Adams (Bodkin) 1957 Crim. L.R. 365; Bedford S. 1961. The Best We Can Do. Harmondsworth: Penguin Books

R v Adomako House of Lords Times Law Report July 4 1994; [1994] 2 All ER 79

R v Arthur. The Times 6 November 1981

R v Cox [1993] 2 All ER 19; The Times 22 September 1992; [1992] 12 BMLR 38

R v Portsmouth Hospitals NHS Trust ex p. Glass [1999] 2 FLR 905; [1999] Lloyds Law Report Medical 367

R v Portsmouth Hospitals NHS Trust ex parte Glass [1999] 50 BMLR 269

R v Prentice; R v Adomako; R v Holloway [1993] 4 All ER 935

R v Smith 1979 Crim LR 251

Re B (a minor)(wardship; medical treatment) [1981] 1 WLR 1421

Re C (a minor)(wardship; medical treatment) [1989] 2 All ER 782

Re J (a minor)(wardship; medical treatment) [1990] 3 All ER 930

Re J Times Law Report June 12 1992

Re L (a minor) [2005] 1 FLR 491

Re R (adult: medical treatment) [1996] 31 BMLR 127

Resuscitation Council (2010) *UK Resuscitation Guidelines.* Resuscitation Council, London

Royal College of Paediatrics and Child Health (2004) *Withholding or withdrawing life saving treatment in children* (2nd edn). RCPCH, London

Shipman Inquiry (2003) *Third report. Death and cremation certification*. Available from: www.the-shipman-inquiry.org.uk/reports.asp

SI 2002 No. 253 (re-enacting Section 16 of the Nurses, Midwives and Health Visitors Act 1997)

Solon S (2012) The coroner's inquest. *Practising Midwife* **15**(6): 22–3

The NHS Trust v Ms T. Lloyd's Rep. Med. [2004] 433

The Times (2005) News item. *The Times* **4 May**: 4

United Nations (1989) *Convention on the Rights of the Child*. United Nations, London

Walker P (2012) Neon Roberts to have radiotherapy against mother's wishes. *The Guardian* **22 December**

Woolgar v Chief Constable of Sussex Police and another [1999] 3 All ER 604 CA

Wyatt v Portsmouth NHS Trust [2005] EWHC 2293

Chapter 13

Termination of pregnancy

Introduction

In 2011 the total number of abortions for women resident in England and Wales was 189 931, 0.2% more than in 2010 and 7.7% more than in 2001. The rate for women aged between 15 and 44 was 17.5 per 1000. The under-16 abortion rate was 3.4 per 1000 women. The NHS funded 96% of the abortions with over half taking place in the independent sector under NHS contract. Of all abortions, 91% were carried out at under 13 weeks gestation, and 78% were under 10 weeks. Medical abortions accounted for 47% of the total. In all, 2307 abortions were carried out under Ground E (risk that the child would be born handicapped) (Department of Health, 2012).

Abortion and the criminal law

The Abortion Act 1967, as amended by the Human Fertilisation and Embryology Act 1990 (see *Box 13.1*), provides a statutory defence to certain offences under the Offences Against The Person Act 1861 and the Infant Life Preservation Act 1929. To bring about the death of a fetus, either intentionally or as a result of gross negligence, is unlawful under Sections 58 and 59 of the Offences Against The Person Act 1861, unless the Abortion Act applies. The Infant Life Preservation Act 1929 makes it a criminal offence to destroy the life of a child capable of being born alive (see below). However the Abortion Act 1967 Section 5(1) makes it clear that:

> ...no offence under the Infant Life (Preservation) Act shall be committed by a registered medical practitioner who terminates a pregnancy in accordance with the provisions of this Act.

For further discussion on the rights of the fetus see *Chapter 7*.

To avail oneself of the defence under the Abortion Act 1967 it must be shown that the requirements set out in Section 1 were present (see *Box 13.1*). It would be a question of fact and evidence as to whether this situation existed.

The Human Fertilisation and Embryology Act 1990 added a further amendment to the Abortion Act 1967 Section 5(2) to cover the situation where

---

Box 13.1. Abortion Act 1967 (as amended by the Human Fertilisation and Embryology Act 1990)

1(1)   Subject to the provisions of this section, a person shall not be guilty of an offence under the law relating to abortion when a pregnancy is terminated by a registered medical practitioner, if two registered medical practitioners are of the opinion formed in good faith:

(a) that the pregnancy has not exceeded its 24th week and that the continuance of the pregnancy would involve risk, greater than if the pregnancy were terminated, of injury to the physical or mental health of the pregnant woman or any existing children of her family; or

(b) that the termination is necessary to prevent grave permanent injury to the physical or mental health of the pregnant woman; or

(c) that the continuance of the pregnancy would involve risk to the life of the pregnant woman, greater than if the pregnancy were terminated; or

(d) that there is substantial risk that if the child were born it would suffer from such physical or mental abnormalities as to be seriously handicapped.

1(2)   In determining whether the continuance of a pregnancy would involve such risk of injury to health as is mentioned in Paragraph (a) or (b) of Subsection (1) of this Section, account may be taken of the pregnant woman's actual or reasonably foreseeable environment.

1(3)   Except as provided by Subsection (4) of this Section, any treatment for the termination of pregnancy must be carried out in a hospital vested in the Secretary of State for the purposes of his functions under the National Health Service Act 2006 or the NHS (Scotland) Act 1976 or in a hospital vested in a Primary Care Trust or an NHS Trust or NHS Foundation Trust or in a place approved for the purposes of this Section by the Secretary of State.

1(3)A The power under Subsection (3) of this Section to approve a place includes power, in relation to treatment consisting primarily in the use of such medicines as may be specified in the approval and carried out in such manner as may be so specified, to approve a class of places.

1(4)   Subsection (3) of this Section, and so much of Subsection (1) as relates to the opinion of two registered medical practitioners, shall not apply to the termination of a pregnancy by a registered medical practitioner in a case where he is of the opinion, formed in good faith, that the termination is immediately necessary to save the life or to prevent grave permanent injury to the physical or mental health of the pregnant woman.

---

one or more fetus(es) in a multiple pregnancy is terminated. The termination may be justified either to protect the health or life of the mother or where there is a substantial risk that if the child were born it would suffer from such physical or mental abnormalities as to be seriously handicapped, i.e. Section 1(1)(d).

Such physical or mental abnormalities as to be seriously handicapped

There is no definition in the Act of the meaning of seriously handicapped and the issue was raised when a woman curate challenged the fact that a fetus with a cleft palate had been aborted. Joanna Jepson, a curate at St Michael's Church Chester, was herself born with a congenital jaw defect and has a brother with Down's syndrome, but claimed that, following surgery, her life has not been unbearable as a consequence of that defect and therefore it should not be grounds for a termination of pregnancy (Gledhill, 2004). She brought a legal action in December 2003 and won the right of judicial review from the High Court to challenge the failure of West Mercia Police to investigate the late abortion. There was subsequently a decision not to prosecute. Had the case gone ahead, the court would have had to define "seriously handicapped" for the purposes of Paragraph 1(1)(d) of the Abortion Act (as amended) 1967. Concern about abortions for minor defects has recently been raised following the release of figures from Eurocat, a European network of registers for congenital anomalies, which shows a discrepancy between their figures and those published by the Department of Health (Marsh, 2013). Section 1.7 of the NICE (2008) guidelines on antenatal care covers screening for fetal abnormalities, one aim of the screening being to allow reproductive choice (termination of pregnancy).

Emergency situation

In an emergency situation, Section 1(4) applies, where a registered medical practitioner is of the opinion, formed in good faith, that the termination is immediately necessary to save the life or to prevent grave permanent injury to the physical or mental health of the pregnant woman (see *Box 13.1*). Where an emergency situation as defined in this Section exists, the termination would not have to take place in an NHS hospital or one approved for the purposes of the Act by the Secretary of State, see Sections 1(3) and 1(4). Section 1(4) could also cover the situation where a surgeon, who had no reasonable cause to believe that a woman was pregnant, had no option but to continue with an operation even though this might result in a termination of pregnancy, if the life of the mother was to be saved.

Capable of being born alive and the Infant Life Preservation Act 1929

Prior to the amendments to the Abortion Act 1967 (which came into force on 1 April 1991) it was an offence to terminate a pregnancy where the fetus was capable of being born alive. In the case of *C v S* it was argued by the father, who was trying to stop the termination taking place, that a doctor who attempted to terminate a pregnancy of 18 weeks would be committing an offence under the Infant Life Preservation Act 1929, since the fetus was capable of being born alive. The Court of Appeal held that there was no evidence that the fetus was capable of breathing and so was not a child capable of being born alive. The termination would not therefore be an offence under the 1929 Act. In a case in 1991 (*Rance v Mid-Downs HA*) a claim was made against the Health Authority by a woman who had a baby with spina bifida, on the grounds that the defect could have been found on a scan and therefore she could have had a termination. The claim was lost because the defendants claimed that at 26 weeks the fetus was capable of being born alive and therefore termination would have been an offence under the 1929 Act. The law has now been changed.

The amendments to the Abortion Act 1967 (effected by the Human Fertilisation and Embryology Act) make it clear that:

> ...no offence under the Infant Life (Preservation) Act shall be committed by a registered medical practitioner who terminates a pregnancy in accordance with the provisions of this Act.
>
> Section 5(1) Abortion Act 1967 as amended

Viability of the fetus and the capacity to be born alive are not now concerns in the lawful termination of a pregnancy. The legal limit for a lawful termination became a public issue prior to the general election of 2005, and in 2012 it was again being suggested that the 24 week limit should be lowered to 20 weeks. Much of the discussion appeared to ignore the fact that under the present law, Sections 1(1)(b), (c) and (d) did not require any time limit. The Health Secretary announced on 22 March 2005 that he expected time to be made for an Abortion Bill after the election (*The Times*, 2005). This never took place and new legislation is not planned at the time of writing.

Abortion resulting in a live birth

As can be seen from *Box 13.1*, there can be an abortion after 24 weeks where the conditions set out in Section 1(1)(b), (c) and (d) are present. Section 5(1) enables an abortion to be carried out at a later stage of pregnancy even though the child is capable of being born alive, providing that the conditions set out in Section 1 are met. However if, following a lawful abortion, the child were to be born alive, there is no right to kill the child. If the child were to be considerably disabled with a very poor prognosis, there is no duty to keep the child alive against all the odds (see *Chapter 12*). However, where the child is capable of surviving with a reasonable quality of life, there would be a duty of care to ensure that every reasonable means were taken to do so.

There are now very few abortions which take place after 24 weeks gestation. As shown above, 91% of abortions were carried out at under 13 weeks gestation.

Termination by a registered medical practitioner

The Act requires a termination of pregnancy to be carried out by a registered medical practitioner. The Royal College of Nursing (RCN) challenged the lawfulness of the use of prostaglandins to terminate a pregnancy, since the patient was cared for by nursing staff and therefore the termination was not being carried out by a registered medical practitioner. In a majority decision, the House of Lords (*Royal College of Nursing of the UK v Department of Health and Social Security*) held that when prostaglandins are used to terminate a pregnancy, the termination is lawful provided that it is under the control of a registered medical practitioner. Lord Diplock stated the position as follows:

> ...the doctor need not do everything with his own hands; the Subsection's requirements were satisfied when the treatment was one prescribed by a registered medical practitioner carried out in accordance with his directions and of which he remained in charge throughout.

Midwives might sometimes be asked to take part in prostaglandin abortions but they would be entitled to rely upon the right of conscientious refusal (see below).

Provisions relating to notification

The Secretary of State in respect of England and Wales, and the Secretary of State in respect of Scotland, is empowered to make regulations relating to the notification of terminations, failure to comply with which is a criminal offence. The Abortion Regulations 1991 cover:

- The Certificate of Opinion.
- The Notice of Termination of Pregnancy and information relating to the termination.
- Restrictions on disclosure of information.

Changes were made to the abortion notification form HSA4 in April 2002. These changes redesigned the form:

- To allow for scanning in of the document and optical character reading of its contents.
- To encourage the use of patient identification numbers and postcodes rather than full names and addresses so as to improve confidentiality.
- To collect self-reported ethnicity data where known, and to collect data on whether or not chlamydia screening was offered.

Amendments to the Regulations in 2008 take account of the appointment of an independent Statistics Board and notification to the National Statistician.

Conscientious objection to abortions

A statutory defence is given by the law to a person who refuses to take part in abortions under Section 4 of the Abortion Act. Section 4(1) of the Abortion Act 1967 permits conscientious objection to participation in treatment and is set out in *Box 13.2*.

Midwifery is about preparation for, and care during and after, birth. It is not surprising therefore that some midwives should consider that they have no part to play in the termination of pregnancy. However, methods of termination such as the use of prostaglandins rely on the discharge of the fetus through the birth canal as in normal labour. Midwives may therefore sometimes be asked to assist or even take responsibility for the abortion under the supervision of the registered medical practitioner.

Box 13.2. Section 4 Abortion Act 1967

4(1) Subject to Subsection (2) of this section, no person shall be under any duty, whether by contract or by any statutory or other legal requirement, to participate in any treatment authorised by this Act to which he has a conscientious objection; provided that in any legal proceedings the burden of proof of conscientious objection shall rest on the person claiming to rely on it.

4(2) Nothing in Subsection (1) of this Section shall affect any duty to participate in treatment which is necessary to save the life or to prevent grave permanent injury to the physical or mental health of a pregnant woman.

A conscientious objection provision similar to Section 4 of the Abortion Act is provided by Section 38 of the Human Fertilisation and Embryology Act 1990 in relation to activities covered by that Act (see *Chapter 14*).

Meaning and evidence of conscientious objection

It can be seen from *Box 13.2* that the burden would be on the midwife to prove that she had a conscientious objection. How does she do that? What is the meaning of conscientious objection? There is no statutory definition. Subsection 4(3) provides that, in Scotland, it is sufficient for a person to make a statement on oath, that she has a conscientious objection to participating in any treatment under the Act and that is then sufficient evidence to discharge the burden of proof. That subsection does not apply however in England and Wales.

It would clearly have to be a settled view based perhaps on religious grounds or some other evidence of a belief against abortion. There has been no judicial decision on the definition of the objection but there has on the extent of the defence.

Extent of the defence of conscientious objection

In the case of *Janaway v Salford AHA*, Mrs Janaway was a devout Roman Catholic who was a secretary employed by Salford Health Authority. She refused to type abortion referral letters and was dismissed. She applied to the Industrial Tribunal claiming the dismissal was unfair in that she was protected from having to participate in such activities by reason of her conscientious objection and the defence under Section 4(1) of the Abortion Act 1967. The House of Lords held that she was fairly dismissed since the protection of Section 4(1) did not extend to typing letters. "Participate" actually meant taking part in treatment designed to terminate a pregnancy.

This means that while the midwife would be protected by Section 4(1) in her refusal to take part in the abortion treatment, she could not refuse to give advice to clients about abortion facilities, amniocentesis and other information which may lead to an abortion taking place.

This clearly places the midwife who has a conscientious objection to abortion in a difficult position. If, during antenatal care, for example, a mother became aware of a possible genetic abnormality in her child and the appropriate advice would be to inform her about the possibility and the need for an amniocentesis, a midwife would have a duty of care to ensure that the mother received this information, which might result in an abortion taking place, even though the midwife conscientiously objected to abortions for whatever reason.

The implications are two fold:

- Either the midwife refuses to give the advice, in which case she faces the possibility of being disciplined and even dismissed. The midwife's refusal may also be contrary to the human rights of the woman as set out in the European Convention of Human Rights and enacted in the Human Rights Act 1998 (see *Chapter 2*); or
- The midwife gives the client the information, against her own principles and beliefs.

A possible compromise solution is for another midwife to take over the responsibility for the antenatal care at that stage, but this would be contrary to the philosophy of the Cumberlege Report, *Changing childbirth* (Department of Health, 1993), and the philosophy of continuity of care. In addition, it is recognised by the European Community Midwives Direction (Article 42 of EEC directive 2005/36/EC) that, included within the activities of a midwife (shown in *Box 1.1* in *Chapter 1*), Member states must ensure midwives are at least entitled to take up and pursue the provision of sound family planning information and advice.

This activity might include advice on contraception, including the post-coital pill, and the midwife could not claim protection from carrying out that task. It must not of course be assumed that because the midwife had a strongly held personal view against abortion, she would not be capable of giving impartial sound comprehensive advice. Unpublished research has shown that there was no difference in the uptake of serum screening for risk estimation of Down's syndrome of women in the second trimester, between patients counselled by midwives who held a conscientious objection to abortions and those counselled by midwives who did not object to abortions, provided that there was adherence to a protocol (Jones and Dawson, 1992).

Glasgow case

Two midwives in Glasgow appealed against a court decision that they had to supervise abortions regardless of their conscientious objection. The judge in the Scottish Court of Session (*Doogan and Anor Re Judicial Review*) told the midwives, Mary Doogan and Connie Wood, both labour ward sisters, that the conscience clause in the Abortion Act would exempt them from hands-on involvement in abortions but, as senior midwives, they had to accept management instructions to oversee abortions performed by other midwives on the labour ward. Their costs are being underwritten by the Society for the Protection of Unborn Children (www.spuc.org.uk/). Their appeal (*Doogan and another v NHS Greater Glasgow and Clyde Health Board*) succeeded on the ground that the right of conscientious objection is given because it is recognised that the process of abortion is felt by many people to be morally repugnant. It is consistent (with this reasoning) that the right should extend to any involvement in the process of treatment.

Conscientious objections and an emergency situation

The right to refuse to participate given by Section 4(1) does not apply in the circumstances set out in Section 4(2), which are shown in *Box 13.3*.

Box 13.3. Section 4(2) Abortion Act 1967

Nothing in Subsection (1) of this Section shall affect any duty to participate in treatment which is necessary to save the life or to prevent grave permanent injury to the physical or mental health of a pregnant woman.

Where life is at stake or the possibility of grave permanent injury is present, the duty of care to the mother takes precedence over any conscientious objection held by the midwife.

An earlier version of the NMC Code of professional conduct (NMC, 2004) included a clause relating to conscientious objection but the clause has not been included in the updated Code published in 2008. The midwife who has religious grounds against a termination of pregnancy should make her views known to her managers. Two rights have to be balanced: the right of the mother to secure appropriate advice relating to termination of pregnancy and the right of the midwife to practise within her beliefs. Sensitive management should ensure that both these rights are respected. Section 4(1) provides a compromise, but inevitably it will not always satisfy both sides.

Should the midwife be asked for advice about procuring an abortion, she should make sure that the questioner is referred to the correct authority and should be very careful about giving any advice which could assist a person in carrying out an unlawful termination of pregnancy. To do so would be a criminal offence under the Offences Against The Person Act 1861.

Human rights and abortion

Since a fetus is not recognised as having a legal personality, it does not acquire legal rights until it is born (*Chapter 7,* and the Congenital Disabilities Act). This means that probably no action can be taken on behalf of a fetus which is aborted under the Human Rights Act 1998 and Article 2 and the right to life, although the Strasbourg court has not ruled on the issue (*Paton v UK*). (In the case of *Paton v BPAS* the European Commission on Human Rights ruled that the father had no right to be consulted – his Article 8 rights were subject, under Paragraph 2, to the rights of another person, i.e. the mother). The legal situation is different in Ireland where the Irish Bill of Rights recognises the right to life of the unborn child. The human rights of the mother may become engaged if it is alleged that a woman was unjustly refused an abortion and her Article 3 or 8 or 14 rights were therefore violated. (See case of *an NHS Trust v D* on page 253.)

Post-coital pill and the intrauterine device

There has been some controversy over whether the above forms of family planning are properly regarded as contraception or abortion. They both aim at preventing the fertilised egg being implanted in the womb. In the case of *R v Price,* a doctor was charged and convicted under Section 58 of the Offences Against The Person Act 1861 after fitting a woman with an intrauterine device. His conviction was quashed in the Court of Appeal. Subsequently, the Attorney General ruled that prevention of conception was not an attempt to cause a miscarriage (House of Commons, 1983).

In a more recent case (Gibb, 2001), an anti-abortion group won an application to the High Court to proceed with a case to stop the supply of over-the-counter sales of the morning-after pill to women over 16 years. The drug Levonelle-2 had formerly only been available on prescription, but in January 2001 its classification was changed to enable it to be sold by pharmacists. An attempt to reverse its classification on the grounds that the revised classification permitted the commission of a criminal offence failed and Levonelle One Step is now available at most pharmacies to those over 16 years as an emergency contraceptive.

Securing a miscarriage through the use of menstrual extraction either mechanically or by induction through a drug such as mifepristone would have to be performed in compliance with the requirements of the Abortion Act 1967. Section 1(3) of the Abortion Act 1967 was amended by the Human Fertilisation and Embryology Act 1990 to give the Secretary of State power to approve centres where such treatment may be carried out (Section 1[3A]) (see *Box 13.1*).

In *Chapter 7*, the case of Sarah Catt is discussed. She pleaded guilty to administering a poison with intent to procure a miscarriage, an offence under the Offences against the Person Act 1861 (Naughton, 2012).

Opposition to abortions

In the case *C v S* discussed on p. 248, the father was not married to the mother. In an earlier case a husband, Mr Paton, tried to prevent his wife obtaining a termination (*Paton v Trustees of the British Pregnancy Advisory Service*). He failed on the grounds that, provided the requirements of the Abortion Act 1967 were satisfied, the termination was lawful and the husband had no *locus standi* to bring an action to prevent a lawful termination proceeding.

Mr Paton then took the case to the European Commission of Human Rights in Strasbourg (*Paton v United Kingdom*) claiming that, as a result of Article 8 of the European Convention of Human Rights, which gave a right to respect for family life (see *Chapter 2*), he had a right to stop the termination going ahead. He lost on the grounds that the Commissioner held the rights of the mother were protected under Paragraph 2 of Article 8.

In a Scottish case in 1997, a father separated from his wife attempted to prevent an abortion taking place in the name of the child (*Kelly v Kelly*). The court held that there was in law no justification for recognising the rights of the unborn child against the mother's right to lawfully terminate the pregnancy. The legal status of the unborn child is considered in *Chapter 7*. In cases where the mother is refusing a Caesarean section which is vital to the survival of the fetus, the Court of Appeal has refused to accept the view that the unborn child has rights which are enforceable against the mother (*St George's Healthcare NHS trust v S; R v Collins ex parte S*) (see *Chapter 7*).

In the case *Re P (a minor)*, parents opposed the abortion wanted by their daughter and offered to bring up the child. The judge decided that the abortion was in the best interests of the girl. For further discussion of this case see *Chapter 6*.

In May 2004, considerable media coverage was given to a situation where a mother discovered by chance that her daughter of 14 years was having an abortion – *R (On the application of Axon) v Secretary of State*. The mother failed in her court action. (The case is discussed at greater length in *Chapter 6*.)

Approved place

Section 1(3) (see above) requires the termination to take place in an NHS establishment or a place approved for the purposes of this Section by the Minister or the Secretary of State (except in an emergency situation). Under the Care Standards Act 2000, Regulations were drawn up for the registration and inspection of independent hospitals and clinics (The Private and Voluntary Health [England] Regulations 2001). Independent hospitals, including those which provide terminations, now come under the aegis of the Care Quality Commission. The Care Quality Commission regulations were published in 2009 and are available on the legislation website.

Regulation 20 relates to termination of pregnancies and covers:

- The requirement to have two certificates before a termination is carried out and a fee is demanded.
- Provisions for termination after 20 weeks gestation.
- No termination after 24 weeks.
- A register of service users must be kept for at least 3 years.
- A record must be kept of the total number of terminations undertaken.
- Notice in writing must be sent to the Chief Medical Officer of the Department of Health.
- The Care Quality Commission must be notified of death associated with the termination within a year of the termination.
- The registered person must prepare and implement appropriate procedures to ensure that the fetal tissue is treated with respect.

Right to secure a termination

There appears to be considerable variation across the country in the availability of NHS facilities for termination of pregnancy. An audit carried out by the Royal College of Obstetricians and Gynaecologists (RCOG) in 2001 found that 34% of abortion services failed to meet minimum targets for acceptable waiting periods. The RCOG guidelines suggest that a woman seeking a termination should see a gynaecologist within five days and that the procedure should take place within a week. The conclusion of the report was that some parts of the country appear to be providing a good service, although not always within the NHS (Templeton, 2001). The organisation Abortion Rights campaigns for the right of a woman to obtain an abortion and reacted strongly against the support of the Secretary of State for Health, Jeremy Hunt, for a reduction in the lawful time limit from 24 to 12 weeks (www.abortionrights.org.uk). Other websites of concerned organisations include Marie Stopes International (www.mariestopes. org.uk/Womens_services/Abortion), BUPA (www.bupa.co.uk/individuals/health-information/directory/abortion) and the RCOG (www.rcog.org.uk/termination-pregnancy-fetal abnormality). The RCOG published a report of a working party on termination of pregnancy for fetal abnormality in 2010. It is intended to assist doctors and other health professionals to support women and their families when a fetal abnormality is diagnosed and to help women to decide, within the constraints of the law, whether or not to have the pregnancy terminated. Its recommendations include ensuring that all women should be provided with information about the purpose and potential outcomes of antenatal screening to detect fetal abnormalities and that they should have an opportunity to discuss their options before the test is performed. There should be a robust management pathway in place to ensure that appropriate information and support are available. The full report can be accessed on the RCOG website (www.rcog.org.uk).

Termination and mental incapacity

In the following case the court had to decide whether to issue a declaration that a termination could be lawfully carried out.

An NHS trust v D

An NHS trust sought guidance on when it was necessary to obtain a court declaration prior to terminating the pregnancy of a mentally incapacitated person suffering from severe schizophrenia. The court gave a declaration that it was lawful to terminate D's pregnancy following evidence of her incapacity and to the effect that termination was in her best interests. The Trust and Official Solicitor then sought more general guidance at a second hearing in relation to Article 8 of the European Convention on Human Rights. The court set out the following guidance:

- An application to the court was not necessary where issues of capacity and best interests were beyond doubt.
- An application should be made promptly when there was any doubt as to either issue.
- Applications should ordinarily be made where:
  i.   there was a realistic prospect of the patient regaining capacity during or shortly after the pregnancy,
  ii. there was a disagreement between medical professionals as to the patient's best interests or the patient or her family or the father expressed views inconsistent with termination,
  iii. the procedures under the Abortion Act 1967 had not been followed, or
  iv. there was some other exceptional circumstance, such as the pregnancy being the patient's last chance to bear a child.

A termination in accordance with the Abortion Act 1967 in the best interests of an incapacitated patient was a legitimate and proportionate interference with rights protected by Article 8(1) and 8(2)

The situation would now be covered by the provisions of the Mental Capacity Act 2005 which enables decisions to be made on behalf of an adult who lacks the mental capacity to make her own decisions. The Court of Protection has the jurisdiction to determine both the lack of mental capacity and also what actions could be taken in the best interests of that person (see *Chapter 3*). The law relating to termination of pregnancy and teenagers is considered in *Chapter 6*.

Disposal of products of abortion following termination

Department of Health guidance was issued on the disposal following pregnancy loss before 24 weeks gestation (Department of Health, 2004). Stillbirths and neonatal deaths do not come under this guidance. Any woman or couple can make their own arrangements for disposal if they so wish. Fetal tissue can be buried, cremated or incinerated by an NHS trust provided the consent has been obtained from the woman or couple. Further guidance on this has been issued by the Department of Health (2003). The Codes of Practice on Consent and on Disposal of Human Tissue issued by the Human Tissue Authority now cover the situation.

Paragraph 157 of the Code of Practice on Consent (Human Tissue Authority, 2009) states that the law does not distinguish between fetal tissue and other tissue from the living (this does not include stillbirths born after 24 weeks gestation). Fetal tissue is regarded as the mother's tissue and is subject to the same consent requirements under the Human Tissue Act as all other tissue from the living.

Guidance on the disposal of fetal tissue is contained in the Code of Practice 5 on Disposal of Human Tissue which is available on the website of the Human Tissue Authority (www.hta.gov.uk/legislationpoliciesandcodesofpractice/code5disposal.cfm).

Paragraphs 91–123 cover disposal following pregnancy loss, where fetal tissue means pregnancy loss before 24 weeks gestation. Fetuses and fetal tissue should be stored separately in secure containers in a safe place. Containers should be made from opaque materials and be fit for transporting the tissue (Paragraph 102).

The Code emphasises the importance of communication with the mother and states that the wishes of those who do not want to know about the disposal of fetal tissue should be respected. If a woman or couple decide to arrange disposal themselves they are free to do so.

Disposal of stillbirths and neonatal deaths come under the law which requires the stillbirth or birth and death to be registered and then disposed of by burial or cremation. This also applies to terminations after 24 weeks gestation. See also guidance from the Stillbirth and Neonatal Death Society (SANDS) (www.uk-sands.org/).

Guidance has been issued by the Royal College of Nursing (2001). The independent sector is required to comply with these arrangements as part of its registration rules and NHS trusts may wish to discuss issues relating to the disposal of fetal tissue with the independent sector clinic carrying out abortions on their behalf. NHS trust policies should be developed and can take into account gestational age and the nature of the fetal tissue.

Organ removal, retention and storage

An Inquiry was held into organ removal, retention and storage at Alder Hey Hospital (Department of Health, 2001). Following the report, the government set up a Retained Organ Commission under the chairmanship of Professor Margaret Brazier and made recommendations on improving standards in relation to obtaining the informed consent of parents to the removal and use of organs and other body parts and tissue. These recommendations should improve practice in relation to consent for the disposal or use of aborted fetuses. Many of the recommendations have been given statutory force in the Human Tissue Act 2004.

Confidentiality of abortion

Information relating to an abortion must be reported on the specific forms to the Department of Health. Otherwise the usual rules of confidentiality apply, subject to exceptions where disclosure is justified (see *Chapter 4*). The Axon case (see above) where a girl of 14 whose mother did not know that she was having an abortion is considered in *Chapter 6*.

The question of confidentiality arose in a criminal case over the disclosure of documents relating to abortions (*Morrow and others v Director of Public Prosecutions High Court of Justice*). The defendants jointly organised and participated in a protest outside a clinic run by the British Pregnancy Advice Service at which abortions were regularly performed. The protesters prevented patients and staff from leaving the clinic and failed to comply with police requests to leave the scene. Twenty-six people were arrested and charged under Section 5(1)(a) of the Public Order Act 1986 which makes it:

> *...an offence to use threatening, abusive, or insulting words or behaviour... within the hearing or sight of a person likely to be caused harassment, alarm or distress thereby.*

They were convicted and in their appeal claimed, among other points, that the Crown Court had erred in setting aside a witness summons served on an officer of the British Pregnancy Advice Centre, which would have required him to produce all records relating to abortions that had taken place or were to have taken place at the clinic on the day of the protest. They also claimed that they believed illegal abortions were about to be performed at the clinic on the day of the protest and therefore they were protected by the Criminal Law Act 1967 in that they were using such force as is reasonable in the prevention of a crime. Neither of these grounds of appeal succeeded.

The Court of Appeal referred to the specific provisions of the Abortion Act 1967 and the 1968 Regulations, which ensured the maintenance of a high degree of confidentiality in respect of documents relating to abortions carried out under the Act. The documents were not relevant to the defence raised by the defendants.

The 1991 Regulations, although they came into effect after the case, continued to emphasise the confidentiality of the records. Nor did the defendants come within the protection of the Criminal Law Act 1967, since their actions were aggressive and prevented other people from exercising their legal rights and did not distinguish between legal and illegal abortions.

In contrast, members of an anti-abortion group Abort67 were found not guilty at Brighton Magistrates Court of public order offences of displaying material that is "threatening, abusive or insulting" outside the British Pregnancy Advisory Service clinic in Brighton. Written judgment was provided on 18 September 2012.

The Care Quality Commission published a report on 12 July 2012 on inspections carried out on abortion clinics. It reported that 14 of the 259 clinics were found to have been "pre-signing" abortion certification paperwork. Pro-abortion supporters considered that the inspections were politically motivated and resulted in £1 million of diverted resources from 500 scheduled Care Quality Commission inspections that were cancelled. The Commission's report can be found on its website (www.cqc.org.uk/media/findings-termination). The Care Quality Commission lists the 14 NHS trusts concerned and notes that it did not find any evidence that any woman had poor outcomes of care at any of the specified locations.

Failed abortion

In April 2005 a mother sued Tayside University Hospitals NHS Trust, seeking compensation and damages for the financial burden of raising her daughter, following an abortion that removed only one pregnancy, leaving her with one fetus (Lister, 2005). She lost her case, the Sheriff holding that there was no evidence that the medical centre had promised that the abortion would be successful. In contrast, in 2001 Kim Nicholls of Staffordshire who was told by practitioners that an abortion of twins had been successful received compensation of £25 000 when one of the unborn children survived the abortion (www.archive.lifenews.com/nat2576.html.

Conclusions

The changes effected in the Abortion Act 1967 by the Human Fertilisation and Embryology Act 1990 have enabled terminations of pregnancies to take place at a much later date than the previous laws, since the time limit of 24 weeks only applies to the first condition for termination under Section 1(1)(a). However, in practice there are very few terminations after 24 weeks. In practice too, the method of ending a late gestation usually ensures the death of the fetus in the womb so that a living child is not the result of the termination. There will always be continual pressure for legislative change in this emotive area since pro-life groups will continue to press for the criminalising of termination of pregnancy. There are also likely to be concerns over the availability of terminations within the NHS, and guidance may be issued by the National Institute for Health and Clinical Excellence over the provision and availability of termination services.

Questions and exercises

1. A mother with four children (the last one only 12 months old) tells you that she is pregnant and probably over 24 weeks. She is anxious to obtain an abortion. What is the legal position?
2. You have been asked to assist in the gynaecology ward in the termination of pregnancies. You are not happy taking part in this work, since you wished to work only as a midwife. What is your legal position and what assistance does the law and the NMC Code of professional conduct give you?
3. A client tells you that her 14-year-old daughter is pregnant but wants to have an abortion. The client wishes to bring up the child herself and prevent the daughter having a termination. What is the legal position? (See *Chapter 6.*)
4. Access the website of the Department of Health and find the most recent statistics on termination of pregnancy (www.wp.dh.gov.uk/transparency/files/2012).

References

Abortion (Amendment) Regulations 2008 SI 2008/735

Abortion (Amendment)(England)Regulations 2002 SI 2002/887

An NHS Trust v D; sub nom D v An NHS Trust (Medical Treatment: Consent: Termination) [2003] EWHC 2793; [2004] 1 FLR 1110; Lloyd's Rep. Med [2004] 107

C v S [1988] 1 All ER 1230

Department of Health (1993) *Changing childbirth: Report of Expert Maternity Group.* HMSO, London

Department of Health (2001) *The Royal Liverpool's Children's Inquiry Report.* HMSO, London

Department of Health (2003) *Code of practice. Families and post mortems.* HMSO, London

Department of Health (2004) *Q and A on disposal following pregnancy loss before 24 weeks gestation.* HMSO, London

Department of Health (2012) *Abortion Statistics England and Wales 2011.* HMSO, London

Doogan and Anor Re Judicial Review [2012] ScotCS CSOH 32

Doogan and another v NHS Greater Glasgow and Clyde Health Board [2013] ScotsCS CSIH 36

Gibb F (2001) High Court challenge to morning-after pill. *The Times* **3 May**

Gledhill R (2004) Congregations keep faith with women priests. *The Times* **17 May**

House of Commons May 1983 42 Parl Deb HC 238

Human Tissue Authority (2009) *Code of Practice 1 on Consent.* HTA, London

Human Tissue Authority (2010) *Code of Practice 5 on Disposal of Human Tissue.* HTA, London

Janaway v Salford [1988] 3 All ER 1051

Jones G, Dawson A (1992) *Personal communication.* University Hospital of Wales.

Kelly v Kelly [1997] SLT 896

Lister D (2005) Mother sues NHS after twin survives abortion. *The Times* **25 April**

Marsh B (2013) Hidden abortion of 'imperfect' babies. *The Sunday Times* **3 February**

Medical Protection Society (1983) *Annual Report.* MPS, London

Morrow and others v Director of Public Prosecutions High Court of Justice QBD [1993] 14 BMLR 54 (reported in Medical Law Review 1994 99)

Naughton P (2012) Mother given 8 years for aborting full-term baby. *The Times* **18 September**

NHS Trust v D [2003] EWHC 2793

NICE (2008) *Antenatal care: Routine care for the healthy pregnant woman. Clinical guidelines, CG62.* NICE, London

Nursing and Midwifery (2004) *Code of professional conduct: Standards for conduct, performance and ethics.* NMC, London

Paton v BPAS [1978] 2 All ER 987

Paton v Trustees of the British Pregnancy Advisory Service [1978] 2 All ER 987

Paton v United Kingdom [1980] 3 EHRR 408 (EcomHR)

R (On the application of Axon) v Secretary of State [2006] EWHC 37 admin

R v Price [1969] 1 QB 541

Rance v Mid-Downs HA [1991] 1 All ER 801

Re P (a minor) [1982] 80 Local Government Reports 301

Royal College of Nursing (2001) *Sensitive disposal of all fetal remains.* RCN, London

Royal College of Nursing of the UK v Department of Health and Social Security [1981]

AC 800; [1981] 1 All ER 545

St George's Healthcare NHS trust v S; R v Collins ex parte S [1998] 44 BLMR 160

Templeton A (2001) *Audit of abortion services.* Royal College of Obstetricians and Gynaecologists, London

The Abortion Regulations 1991 Statutory Instrument 1991 No 499

The Private and Voluntary Health (England) Regulations 2001 SI 2001 No 3968

The Times (2005) News item: Abortion Bill. *The Times* **23 March**

Chapter 14

Legal issues relating to fertilisation, embryology and genetics

---

Scenario 14.1. Surrogacy

Mary, a midwife of over 20 years experience, learns by chance that one of her clients is having a surrogate pregnancy and plans to hand over the baby to the child's genetic father and his wife. She seeks advice on the legal implications of this arrangement.

Scenario 14.1. is discussed on p. 276.

Introduction

Estimates are given that at least one in 10 couples are affected at some stage in their lives by infertility problems. The midwife is therefore quite likely to have clients who, as a result of problems in conception and fertility, may be involved with *in vitro* fertilisation (IVF) and/or surrogacy. This chapter considers the legal issues that arise and the framework that has been established by statute. It also considers recent developments in genetics and the legal implications.

Human embryos and *in vitro* fertilisation

The present law dates from the Warnock report which was published by the Department of Health in 1984. Many of its recommendations were subsequently incorporated into the Human Fertilisation and Embryology Act 1990 which was substantially amended by the Human Fertilisation and Embryology Act 2008 in the light of scientific and other developments. The Act covers the topics shown in *Box 14.1*.

Human Fertilisation and Embryology Authority (HFEA)

This Authority is appointed by the Secretary of State as a statutory non-crown body. The Secretary of State also appoints the chairman and deputy chairman. Registered medical practitioners, those concerned with the keeping or using

---

Box 14.1. The Human Fertilisation and Embryology Act 1990 as amended

- Establishes a statutory authority.
- Prohibits specific activities in connection with embryos and gametes.
- Enables licences to be issued by the authority.
- Defines mother and father.
- Regulates disclosure of information and confidentiality.
- Amends the Surrogacy Arrangements Act 1985.
- Amends the Abortion Act 1967 (see *Chapter 13*).
- Provides a defence of a conscientious objection.
- Gives powers of enforcement and creates offences.
- Makes provision in relation to the giving and withdrawal of consent.

---

of gametes or embryos outside the body and any person concerned with commissioning or funding research are ineligible to be appointed as chairman or deputy chairman.

The functions of the HFEA are shown in *Box 14.2.*

Unauthorised activities

The Act regulates activities in respect of embryos (i.e. a live human embryo where fertilisation is complete, and an egg in the process of fertilisation) outside the human body, and gametes (eggs or sperm). Some activities are completely prohibited, others can be undertaken but only under a licence.

The court has held that the criminal liability for offences in relation to an embryo otherwise than in accordance with a licence contrary to Section 3(1) and 41(2)(a) of the 1990 Act did not extend to the person responsible for the supervision of the activities at the clinic where the alleged offences had taken place (*Re Attorney General's Reference*).

Granting of licences

The Authority can grant licences:

- Authorising activities in the course of providing treatment services.
- Authorising the storage of gametes and embryos.
- Authorising activities for the purpose of a project of research.

Box 14.2. Functions of HFEA

1. Keep under review information about embryos and advise the Secretary of State.
2. Publicise the services provided to the public by the Authority.
3. Provide advice and information for person to whom licences apply or who are receiving treatment.
4. Grant, vary, suspend and revoke licences through licence committees.
5. Issue directions either generally or specifically.
6. Maintain a code of practice giving guidance about the conduct of activities and treatment services.
7. Maintain a register containing specified information.

These functions were amended by the 2008 Act to include:
(ca) Maintain a statement of the general principles which it considers should be followed:
    (i) in the carrying on of activities governed by this Act, and
    (ii) in the carrying out of its functions in relation to such activities.
(cb) Promote, in relation to activities governed by this Act, compliance with:
    (i) requirements imposed by or under this Act, and
    (ii) the code of practice under Section 25 of this Act.

The HFEA is also required under the 2008 Act to
(1) ...carry out its functions effectively, efficiently and economically.
(2) In carrying out its functions, the Authority must, so far as relevant, have regard to the principles of best regulatory practice (including the principles under which regulatory activities should be transparent, accountable, proportionate, consistent and targeted only at cases in which action is needed).

Conditions for the giving of licences are laid down in Sections 12, 13, 14 and 15, and Schedule 2 as amended by the 2008 Act. Sections 16–22 cover the granting, revocation and suspension of licences.

Definition of mother and father

The definition of mother for the purposes of the Act is shown in *Box 14.3* and the definition of father in *Box 14.4*.

Box 14.3. Definition of mother (Section 33 of the 2008 Act)

(1) The woman who is carrying or has carried a child as a result of the placing in her of an embryo or of sperm and eggs, and no other woman, is to be treated as the mother of the child.

(2) Subsection (1) does not apply to any child to the extent that the child is treated by virtue of adoption as not being the woman's child.

(3) Subsection (1) applies whether the woman was in the United Kingdom or elsewhere at the time of the placing in her of the embryo or the sperm and eggs.

Box 14.4 Definition of father (as amended by 2008 Act)

Section 35. Woman married at time of treatment

(1) If

    (a) at the time of the placing in her of the embryo or of the sperm and eggs or of her artificial insemination, W was a party to a marriage, and

    (b) the creation of the embryo carried by her was not brought about with the sperm of the other party to the marriage,

then, subject to Section 38(2) to (4), the other party to the marriage is to be treated as the father of the child unless it is shown that he did not consent to the placing in her of the embryo or the sperm and eggs or to her artificial insemination (as the case may be).

(2) This section applies whether W was in the United Kingdom or elsewhere at the time mentioned in Subsection (1)(a).

Section 36. Treatment provided to woman where agreed fatherhood conditions apply

If no man is treated by virtue of Section 35 as the father of the child and no woman is treated by virtue of Section 42 as a parent of the child but:

    (a) the embryo or the sperm and eggs were placed in W, or W was artificially inseminated, in the course of treatment services provided in the United Kingdom by a person to whom a licence applies,

    (b) at the time when the embryo or the sperm and eggs were placed in W, or W was artificially inseminated, the agreed fatherhood conditions (as set out in Section 37) were satisfied in relation to a man, in relation to treatment provided to W under the licence,

    (c) the man remained alive at that time, and

Box 14.4. contl

(d) the creation of the embryo carried by W was not brought about with the man's sperm,

then, subject to Section 38(2) to (4), the man is to be treated as the father of the child.

Section 37. The agreed fatherhood conditions

(1) The agreed fatherhood conditions referred to in Section 36(b) are met in relation to a man ("M") in relation to treatment provided to W under a licence if, but only if,

(a) M has given the person responsible a notice stating that he consents to being treated as the father of any child resulting from treatment provided to W under the licence,

(b) W has given the person responsible a notice stating that she consents to M being so treated,

(c) neither M nor W has, since giving notice under Paragraph (a) or (b), given the person responsible notice of the withdrawal of M's or W's consent to M being so treated,

(d) W has not, since the giving of the notice under Paragraph (b), given the person responsible:

(i) a further notice under that Paragraph stating that she consents to another man being treated as the father of any resulting child, or

(ii) a notice under Section 44(1)(b) stating that she consents to a woman being treated as a parent of any resulting child, and

(e) W and M are not within prohibited degrees of relationship in relation to each other.

(2) A notice under Subsection (1)(a), (b) or (c) must be in writing and must be signed by the person giving it.

(3) A notice under Subsection (1)(a), (b) or (c) by a person ("S") who is unable to sign because of illness, injury or physical disability is to be taken to comply with the requirement of Subsection (2) as to signature if it is signed at the direction of S, in the presence of S and in the presence of at least one witness who attests the signature.

Sperm donors

Under the 2008 Act, same sex couples are the legal parents of children conceived through donated sperm, eggs and embryos. The 2008 Act extended the law governing the rights of sperm donors to cover same sex couples. In one of the earliest cases to come before the court on the impact of the new provisions of the 2008 Act, it was held in a family court ruling on 31 January 2013, on an application under Section 8 of the Children Act 1989, that a sperm donor has the right to contact with his children. The ruling was that a sperm donor did not need to have a sexual relationship with a mother in order to influence the child's upbringing (*S and D and E and in the matter of Z [a minor] T and X and Y*). See also the Court of Appeal case of *A v B and another (Lesbian mother and role of biological donor father)*, where the Court of Appeal ordered a rehearing on the amount of contact the biological donor father should have with the lesbian parents who were bringing up the child. The Court of Appeal did not accept the concept of primary and secondary parent.

Disclosure of information and confidentiality

The 2008 Act replaces Section 33 of the 1990 Act with a new Section 33A. It prohibits any member or employee of a licensing authority disclosing information that is contained in the register so that an individual can be identified. However, the consent of the person(s) protected by these confidentiality provisions can release the person from the prohibition. The Human Fertilisation and Embryology (Disclosure of Information) Act 1992 was passed to enable additional exceptions to the duty of confidentiality to be recognised since the original restrictions were seen as being too tight. The 1992 Act was repealed by the Human Fertilisation and Embryology Act 2008 and its provisions incorporated by the 2008 Act in a revised Section 33A.

The following sections in the 1990 Act, as amended by the 2008 Act, cover the keeping and disclosing of information.

- 31. Register of information.
- 31ZA. Request for information as to genetic parentage etc.
- 31ZB. Request for information as to intended spouse etc.
- 31ZC. Power of authority to inform donor of request for information.
- 31ZD. Provision to donor of information about resulting children.
- 31ZE. Provision of information about donor-conceived genetic siblings.
- 31ZF. Power of authority to keep voluntary contact register.
- 31ZG. Financial assistance for person setting up or keeping voluntary contact register
- 31A. The Authority's register of licences.
- 31B. The Authority's register of serious adverse events and serious adverse reactions.

- 32. Information to be provided to Registrar General.
- 33A. Disclosure of information.
- 33B. Power to provide for additional exceptions from Section 33A(1).
- 33C. Disclosure for the purposes of medical or other research.
- 34. Disclosure in interests of justice.
- 35. Disclosure in interests of justice: congenital disabilities, etc.

Section 33A prevents the disclosure of information specified in Section 31(2) (identifiable treatment services, gametes, embryos, etc.) unless it comes under one of the exceptions set out in Sections 31ZA–E. The legislation can be downloaded from the legislation website (legislation.gov.uk).

A person of 18 or over has had, since 2005, the right to obtain information from the HFEA if that person was born in consequence of treatment services, but an opportunity for proper counselling must be provided before disclosure. Section 31ZA inserted by the 2008 Act enables those over 16 years to obtain non-identifying information from the HFEA.

Disclosure in the interests of justice can be made under Section 34 in proceedings before a court when the question of whether a person is or is not the parent of the child by virtue of the Act falls to be determined.

Under the Congenital Disabilities (Civil Liability) Act 1976, the court can make an application to the Authority authorising it to disclose information kept in the register and relevant to the issue of parentage (see *Chapter 7* on the 1976 Act).

Mistake in fertilising eggs

During IVF treatment in Leeds, there was a mix up in the creation of embryos, and sperm from one man was wrongly injected into the eggs of the woman of another couple receiving IVF treatment. The error came to light at the birth of the children since one couple were both white and gave birth to twins of mixed race. In the subsequent court hearing to determine who should be treated as parents of the children, the judge held that the mistake in the mixing of Mr B's sperm with Mrs A's egg went to the root of the whole process and vitiated the whole concept of treatment together. Mr A had not given a consent to this fertilisation. Mr B was the biological and the legal father of the twins. An adoption order could safeguard the rights of the twins (*The Leeds Teaching Hospitals NHS Trust v. Mr A; Mrs A; YA and ZA; The Human Fertility And Embryology Authority, Mr B and Mrs B Lloyds Rep Med*).

Conscientious objection

Section 38 provides a similar provision to that contained in the Abortion Act 1967 to protect any person who has a conscientious objection to working in the field. Its provision is shown in *Box 14.5*. There is no statutory definition of what constitutes a conscientious objection and an interpretation similar to that used for the Section in the Abortion Act 1967 can be expected. This did not protect a secretary who refused to type correspondence relating to abortions (see *Chapter 13*). Unlike the conscientious objection in a termination of pregnancy there is no exception for emergencies.

Box 14.5. Conscientious objection: Section 38

(1) No person who has a conscientious objection to participating in any activity governed by this Act shall be under any duty, however arising, to do so.
(2) In any legal proceedings the burden of proof of conscientious objection shall rest on the person claiming to rely on it.

Enforcement provisions and offences

Any member or employee of the authority, on entering and inspecting premises, has the right to:

- Take possession of anything that he has reasonable grounds to believe may be required.
- Take steps to preserve anything or prevent interference with anything.
- Obtain from a Justice of the Peace, if there are reasonable grounds for suspecting that an offence under this Act is being (or has been) committed, a warrant to enter premises, using such force as is necessary and to search premises.

Offences include:

- Undertaking activities prohibited by Section 3(2) or 4(1)(c) without a licence or doing anything that cannot be authorised by a licence.
- Providing false or misleading information for the purposes of a licence.
- Disclosing information in contravention of the Act.

The consent of the Director of Public Prosecutions is required before proceedings can be commenced.

Consent to treatment

The principles of law relating to the giving of consent are covered in *Chapter 3*. The 1990 Act makes very detailed provisions relating to the giving and use of gametes and embryos and the Act requires counselling to be given before consent is obtained. Schedule 3 of the 2008 Act amending the 1990 Act covers the consent to the use and storage of gametes, embryos or human admixed embryos, etc. Consent has to be given in writing and effective consent means consent that has not been withdrawn.

The provisions of the Schedule 3 of the 2008 Act are set out in *Box 14.6* and can be accessed on the legislation website (www.legislation.gov.uk).

Box 14.6 Consent provisions under Schedule 3 of the 2008 Act

Cover: general requirements as to consent
- Terms of consent.
- Information to be given to a person giving consent.
- Variation and withdrawal of consent.
- Withdrawal of consent to storage: notification of interested persons.
- Application of consent provisions to non-medical fertility services.
- *In vitro* fertilisation and subsequent use of embryo.

Use of embryos obtained by lavage, etc.
- Consents in relation to storage.
- Cases where consent not required for storage.
- Creation, use and storage of human admixed embryos.

Cases where human cells, etc. can be used without consent of person providing them:
- Adults lacking capacity: Exemption relating to use of human cells etc.; consulting carers; effect of acquiring capacity.

The case of Diane Blood (*R v Human Fertilisation and Embryology Authority, ex parte Blood*) illustrated how tight the rules on consent to the use of gametes were. Mr and Mrs Blood had been married for three years and were hoping to start a family when Mr Blood contracted meningitis and went into a coma. Mrs Blood asked for sperm to be taken from him and he died shortly after. Both the High Court and Court of Appeal refused her application for her to be impregnated with the sperm, since the husband had not given written consent required under Section 4(i) and Schedule 3 of the 1990 Act. However the Court of Appeal said that she would be able to seek treatment abroad.

In a more recent case, a couple wished to have children but the husband had had a vasectomy. They agreed to surgical retrieval of the husband's sperm and consent forms regarding the storage and disposal of the sperm were signed. The sperm was retrieved and stored. Subsequently, the husband agreed to sign an amendment to the form which allowed the embryos and sperm to perish after death or incapacitation. There was one attempt at pregnancy which failed and then the husband died unexpectedly. The Centre sought a ruling on the storage and use of the stored sperm and the High Court held that Mr U gave a valid consent to the destruction of his sperm after his death and so the sperm could be destroyed (*Centre for Reproductive Medicine v Mrs U*). Mrs U's appeal against this decision was dismissed by the Court of Appeal (*Mrs U v Centre for Reproductive Medicine*), which held that Mr U's amendment to the initial consent was not obtained by undue influence and there was no effective consent for the Centre to continue to store or use the sperm following his death.

Following the Blood case, the government set up a review of the law under the Chairmanship of Professor Sheila McLean and a report was published in 1998 (McLean, 1998). The report recommended that, in exceptional circumstances, the removal of gametes from an unconscious person should be permitted, if that were in the best interests of that person. It also suggested that the 1990 Act should be amended to remove the need for written consent from the donor for storage. In August 2000, the government published its response to the McLean Report (Department of Health, 2000a). It accepted all the recommendations of the report and went further, suggesting a retrospective effect:

- The father's name should be allowed to appear on birth certificates where his sperm has been used after his death.
- The legal position on consent and removal of gametes should remain unchanged: gametes can be taken from an incapacitated person who is likely to recover, if the removal of gametes is in their best interests.
- The HFEA should have the power to permit the storage of gametes where consent has not been given, so long as the gametes have been lawfully removed. This will also benefit children who are about to undergo treatment which will affect their future fertility.

- Families will be able to make these birth certificate changes retrospectively.
- The best practice is for written consent to be obtained, since this most clearly constitutes effective consent. Where there is doubt over whether an effective consent has been obtained, this should be a matter for the courts.

Subsequently, Diane Blood won her claim to have her late husband legally recognised as the father of her two sons, when the Department of Health dropped its opposition (Rumbelow, 2003). The judge accepted that her inability to name her deceased husband as the father of her children was contrary to her human rights and he ordered the Department of Health to pay Mrs Blood's £20000 legal costs.

The immediate legislative change implemented following the McLean report was the Human Fertilisation and Embryology (Deceased Fathers) Act 2003 which came into force on 1 December 2003 and specified the circumstances in which a deceased father can be recorded on the birth certificate. Further provisions relating to deceased fathers and also covering women in civil partnerships were included in the 2008 Act.

Code of Practice

The HFEA has published and amended a Code of Practice that licensed centres must follow. This covers such topics as the decisions over which persons can obtain IVF treatment.

Access to fertility services

There is no legislation that gives a statutory right to access fertility services within the NHS. There is no enforceable statutory right for an individual to be given IVF treatment and the Code of Practice gives advice to the Licensed Centres on which persons to treat.

No woman can be provided with treatment services unless account has been taken of the welfare of any child who may be born as a result of the treatment, including the need of that child for a father (amended by the 2008 Act) to the need for supportive parenting, and of any other child who may be affected by the birth (1990 Act Section 13(5) as amended).

In one case, this Section was applied to a woman who had a criminal record including offences for prostitution – *R v Ethical Committee of St Mary's Hospital (Manchester) ex parte H*. In the case in *Box 14.7*, the woman, aged 37 years, brought an action because she had been turned down by the Health Authority when she sought IVF treatment.

Box 14.7 Refusal to provide IVF treatment
(R v Sheffield Health Authority, ex parte Seale)

The applicant, aged 37, and was refused IVF treatment by the Health Authority since 35 had been set as the upper limit for such treatment. The judge held that her application for judicial review of this decision must be refused. There was no law to prevent the Health Authority setting limits for its financial expenditure.

Since 2 October 2000, and the coming into force of the Human Rights Act 1998, an application could be made under Article 8 of the European Convention (see *Chapter 2*), which gives a right to respect for private and family life. However, this argument failed when a prisoner sought the right of access to artificial insemination facilities for the purpose of inseminating his wife while he was in prison (*R v Secretary of State ex parte Mellor* 2000). The Court of Appeal dismissed the prisoner's appeal saying that the refusal to agree to the request was not a breach of the Convention, nor unlawful nor irrational (*R v Secretary of State ex parte Mellor* 2001). However, in 2007, a prisoner won his case before the European Court of Human Rights (*Dickson v United Kingdom*) (see *Chapter 2*).

In 2000 the Department of Health (2000b) announced its intention of ending the postcode lottery of infertility treatment following a survey showing considerable variation in access to treatments across England. It asked the National Institute for Health and Clinical Excellence (NICE) to produce guidelines on access to fertility treatment. In February 2004 it published guidelines on access to fertility services within the NHS (NICE, 2004) (see *Chapter 8* for further discussion of NICE). NICE recommended that couples in which the woman is aged 23 to 39 years at the time of treatment and who have an identified cause for their infertility problems or who have infertility of at least three years' duration should be offered up to three stimulated cycles of IVF treatment. The guidelines are considered by Ashcroft (2003). In its response to the recommendations, the Department of Health (2004) stated it would look to primary care trusts to offer all women aged 23–39 who meet the NICE clinical criteria, a minimum of one full cycle of IVF from April 2005.

In February 2013 NICE issued new guidelines recommending a change in entitlement to IVF services and suggesting that the age limit should be raised so that women up to 42 years should receive at least one IVF treatment on the NHS. Critics have pointed out that the earlier guidance had not been universally implemented for financial reasons and there is even less chance of the new guidance being implemented.

Surrogacy

Surrogacy is the use of another person for the production of a child. The surrogate mother might have no genetic link with the child she carries, if an embryo is implanted in her. Or she may herself provide the egg and be inseminated with donor sperm or the sperm of the husband of the couple wishing to have the child. Until the passing of the Surrogacy Arrangements Act 1985 the only law which related to a surrogacy situation was Section 50 of the Adoption Act 1958, which prohibits any payment in connection with adoption. The application of this Section to a surrogacy situation arose in the case *Re A (an adoption)(surrogacy)* (see *Box 14.8*).

Box 14.8. Re A (1987)

In this case, Mr and Mrs A were unable to have children and, because of their age, had been refused as adoptive parents. They entered into surrogacy arrangements with Mrs B. It was agreed that she would be paid £10000 to give up her job and have the child. Eventually she accepted £5000 which did not cover her financial losses. The couple applied to adopt the baby. The judge held that a payment to a mother in a surrogacy arrangement did not contravene the Adoption Act if payments made by those others to the natural mother did not include an element of profit or financial reward. Even if they were made for reward, the court had a discretion under the Act to authorise the payments retrospectively. The court granted the adoption order.

The public disquiet over the actions of commercial companies led to the passing of the 1985 Act.

Surrogacy Arrangements Act 1985 as amended by S 59 of 2008 Act

This Act defines "surrogate mother" as:

> ...*a woman who carries a child in pursuance of an arrangement*
> (a) *made before she began to carry the child, and*
> (b) *made with a view to any child carried in pursuance of it being handed over to, and the parental rights being exercised (so far as is practicable) by, another person or other persons.*

Section 36 of the Human Fertilisation and Embryology Act 1990 added a new Section 1A to the 1985 Act as follows:

No surrogacy arrangement is enforceable by or against any of the persons making it.

The effect of this Section is that if the surrogate mother were to refuse to hand over the baby following the birth, the couple who made the arrangements could not enforce the agreement in court.

If a midwife is told that one of her clients has entered into a surrogacy agreement and is pregnant as a result of this, she should ensure that her duty to the mother and the child comes before the interests of any person on whose account the mother is bearing the child. She should ensure that she is aware of the legal position and that her supervisor is informed of the situation.

The Brazier report (Department of Health, 1998) recommended that the Surrogacy Arrangements Act 1985 and Section 30 of the 1990 Act should be replaced by new legislation and its provisions were incorporated in Sections 54, 55 and Schedule 6 (see below – parental orders and surrogacy). It recommended that a Code of Practice on surrogacy should be drawn up by the Department of Health.

The Court of Appeal has held that a woman is not entitled to the costs of making a surrogacy arrangement when she had been negligently deprived of the prospect of conceiving and bearing a child naturally – *Briody v St Helens and Knowsley AHA (Claim for damages and costs) sub nom Briody v St Helens and Knowsley AHA.*

Not-for-profit bodies are permitted to receive payment for carrying out activities in initiating negotiations with a view to the making of a surrogacy arrangement and in compiling information about surrogacy. However, only reasonable payment can be made (i.e. it does not exceed the costs reasonably attributed to the activity). Not-for-profit bodies will not be permitted to receive payment for offering to negotiate a surrogacy arrangement or for taking part in negotiations about a surrogacy arrangement. These activities are not unlawful if there is no charge. Section 59 also makes changes in relation to advertising by non-profit-making bodies. Under the 1985 Act, it is an offence to publish or distribute an advertisement that someone may be willing to enter into a surrogacy arrangement, or that anyone is looking for a surrogate mother, or that anyone is willing to facilitate or negotiate such an arrangement. This is amended to enable a non-profit-making body to advertise about activities that may legally be undertaken on a commercial basis, for example, that it keeps a list of people seeking surrogate mothers.

Parental orders and surrogacy

Section 54 of the 2008 Act replaces Section 30 of the 1990 Act and maintains the same criteria for a parental order as in the 1990 Act, with the exception of the eligibility criteria that now permits civil partners and couples in an enduring family relationship to apply for a parental order, in addition to married couples.

Under Section 55 of the 2008 Act, regulations have been drawn up which enable specified adoption legislation to be applied, with modifications, to parental orders. These regulations came into force on 6 April 2010. For England, Schedule 1 of the Regulations applies, with modifications, the Adoption and Children Act 2002 to a parental order. Thus, principles such as the welfare of the child is the paramount consideration and a checklist for determining the welfare of the child will apply to a parental order.

In the case of *Re L (a minor)*, the judge granted a parental order even though more than the reasonable expenses had been given to the American natural mother. This illustrates the discretion on the judge towards the paying of expenses.

The HFEA issued a guidance note in 2009 on legal parenthood which is available on its website.

The law relating to surrogacy is as follows:

- The surrogate has the legal right to keep the child, even if s/he is not genetically related to her.
- Surrogacy arrangements are not legally enforceable, even if a contract has been signed and the expenses of the surrogate have been paid.
- The surrogate will be the legal mother of the child unless or until parenthood is transferred to the intended mother through a parental order or adoption after the birth of the child.
- The surrogate has the legal right to change her mind and keep the child, even when the baby she gave birth to is not genetically related to her.
- The child's legal father or second parent is the surrogate's husband, civil partner (unless it is shown that husband/civil partner did not consent to the treatment) or partner (if the partner consented to being the father/second parent).
- If treatment was performed in a licensed clinic and the surrogate mother has no partner, the child will have no legal father or second parent.

- If the intended parents wish to become the legal parents of the child, they may either apply to adopt the child or apply for a parental order. A parental order transfers the rights and obligations of parentage to the intended parents, providing certain conditions are met (Section 54 of the 2008 Act).
- Applications for a parental order must generally be made to the court within six months of the birth of the child.
- To obtain a parental order, at least one of the commissioning couple must be genetically related to the baby, i.e. be the egg or sperm provider. Couples must be husband and wife, civil partners or two persons who are living as partners.
- If the commissioning couple cannot apply for a parental order because neither of them is genetically related to the baby (i.e. donor egg and donor sperm or donor embryos were used), then adoption of the baby is the only option available to them.
- A registered adoption agency must be involved in the surrogacy process if adoption is required.

The HFEA does not regulate surrogacy itself (although any IVF used would come under the Authority's licences and regulations) but its website does provide information about the process and the law (www.hfea.gov. uk/1424.html). Section 14 of the 8th Code of Practice of the Authority covers surrogacy and sets out the mandatory requirements (www.hfea.gov.uk/ docs/8th_Code_of_Practice.pdf).

Scenario 14.1. Surrogacy: Discussion

Mary should ensure that all the basic principles in antenatal care are followed in relation to her client. She must remember that although the client might have agreed to undertake the pregnancy on a basis of surrogacy and of handing over the child, the contract is unenforceable and she has the right to change her mind. Since the man is the genetic father of the baby, he can apply for a parenthood order under the provisions of the 2008 Act.

Preimplantation genetic diagnosis

Preimplantation genetic diagnosis is a technique that is used to detect whether an embryo created *in vitro* is carrying a genetic defect that will give rise to a serious inherited genetic disorder. The HFEA and the Advisory Committee on

Genetic Testing (now absorbed into the Human Genetics Commission) issued a consultation paper at the end of 1999. Licences were issued in 2002 by the HFEA for genetic screening and IVF treatment to take place to ensure that an embryo was a compatible donor for a sibling who suffered from a genetic disorder. In one case the sibling suffered from a rare blood disorder which could be treated by a suitable bone marrow transplant (Hawkes, 2002).

The HFEA originally took the view that where the embryo does not benefit from preimplantation genetic diagnosis then a licence will not be granted. It turned down the application from the Witakers to use IVF techniques to select a baby who would be a perfect tissue match for Charlie aged three who had a rare blood disorder and required a bone marrow transplant. The Authority refused the application because embryos may be screened only if they might carry a serious genetic risk (Peek, 2002). However, the Authority changed its views and held that where there is a benefit to the embryo (as well as to an existing sibling) then preimplantation genetic diagnosis would be allowed.

In one case, Raj and Shahana Hashmi (*Regina [Quintavalle] v Human Fertilisation and Embryology Authority* 2003) wished to bear a child who would be free of the genetic blood disorder, beta thalassaemia major, and whose tissue type would match that of their young son Zain, who suffered from the life-threatening disorder. They were successful in their application for a licence, which was challenged by Josephine Quintavalle on behalf of Comment on Reproductive Ethics. The Court of Appeal held that the HFEA had the power to grant a licence to permit simultaneous tests to be carried out on an embryo for the purpose, not only of identifying genetic defects in the embryo, but also of ascertaining whether or not the tissue type of the embryo would match that of an existing child. The House of Lords confirmed this ruling in *Regina (Quintavalle) v Human Fertilisation and Embryology Authority* (2005) holding that the 1990 Act defined in broad terms the HFEA power to grant licences.

In January 2005 the Authority announced a new process to speed up applications for preimplantation genetic diagnosis.

Further information on preimplantation genetic diagnosis together with the list of genetic diseases for which it is available is on the Authority's website (www.hfea.gov.uk). Section 9 of the 8th Code of Practice covers preimplantation genetic diagnosis. Developments in prenatal genetic diagnosis that are non-invasive (and which are discussed by Kerry Oxenford and others, 2013) may remove many of the legal and ethical issues relating to this form of genetic selection.

Gender selection

There has been publicity given to a business that claimed to be able to assist parents in having a child of a specified gender. It used methods which were not covered by the HFEA or the provisions relating to genetic screening. There are at present no laws to prevent the commercialisation of this. Only where the child is born through IVF or where embryos are involved would the activities come under the licensing authorities. The HFEA has licensed centres to carry out preimplantation genetic diagnosis (see above) which can be used to determine the sex of an embryo where a family is at risk of passing on a serious sex-linked disorder, such as Duchenne's muscular dystrophy. However, the guidelines of the HFEA do not allow couples to select the sex of their embryos for non-medical reasons. Section 10 of the 8th Code of Practice covers embryo testing and sex selection.

Gene therapy

Concern relating to experimentation with genes which would not be covered by the Human Fertilisation and Embryology Act 1990 (except insofar as it prevented research taking place on embryos after the appearance of the primitive streak or 14th day after mixing) led the government to establish a non-statutory body, the Committee on the Ethics of Gene Therapy, chaired by Sir Cecil Clothier, in November 1989. Its terms of reference were to draw up ethical guidance for the medical profession on treatment of genetic disorders in adults and children by genetic modification of human body cells, to invite and consider proposals from doctors wishing to use such treatment on individual patients, and to provide advice to UK Health Ministers on scientific and medical developments which bear on the safety and efficacy of human gene modification. The Committee reported in January 1992 and made significant recommendations. These included the view that research should continue, but a distinction should be drawn between germ line gene therapy, which affects future generations (gene modification of the human gene line should not be done) and somatic cell gene therapy, which is concerned only with that person and should be subject to the requirements for other human research and should initially be for life-threatening diseases or those that cause serious handicap and for which treatment is at present unavailable or unsatisfactory, and should not yet be used for non-disease situations. Early proposals to be approved by the Clothier Committee included research into adenosine deaminase deficiency, cystic fibrosis and skin cancer.

The Clothier Committee also recommended that there should be a new expert/ supervisory body to provide scientific and medical advice on matters germane to the safety and efficacy of human gene modification and its use and, as a consequence, the Gene Therapy Advisory Committee was set up to review all proposals for gene therapy in the UK. New arrangements for ethics applications came into force in December 2012 when the Gene Therapy Advisory Committee was closed (www.nres.nhs.uk/).

Genetic screening

A project was proposed by Robert Sinsheimer in California in 1984 to identify the protein building blocks that shape human life. Known as the Human Genome Project, it was completed in 2000. The fact of identification of genetic predispositions raise huge ethical and legal dilemmas which are only just being confronted. One of the issues is the right to screen genetically persons for insurance or employment purposes. On the one hand it could be argued that the employer or the insurance company is entitled to receive all relevant information that would affect the decision to take a person on as an employee or for the purposes of insurance cover. On the other hand, it can be seen that without statutory protection against unfair discrimination, the person who presents a risk could be subjected to extremely unjust treatment when there is only a probability rather than a certainty that the particular genetic predisposition will materialise.

Association of British Insurers' Code of Practice

The Association of British Insurers published a Code of Practice in 1997, subsequently updated. It has agreed a concordat and moratorium on genetic testing with the Department of Health and the present agreement is valid until 2017, being reviewed in 2014. It can be found on the Association of British Insurers website (www.abi.org.uk). Under this voluntary code, insurers should not require a person to take a genetic test in order to obtain insurance cover. The only approved test is for Huntingdon's chorea but the results of such a test will only be taken into account for life insurance of over £500000. Any one refused insurance cover or who wishes to complain can contact the Association of British Insurers.

The Nuffield Council on Bioethics was established in 1991 to consider the ethical issues presented by advances in biomedical and biological research. The subject of its first report, produced in December 1993, was genetic screening. Its main conclusions were that:

- Adequately informed consent should be a requirement for all genetic screening programmes.
- Counselling should be readily available for those being genetically screened, as well as for those being tested on account of a family history of a genetic disorder.
- Health professionals should seek to persuade individuals, if persuasion should be necessary, to allow the disclosure of relevant genetic information to other family members
- Appropriate professional bodies should prepare guidelines to help with the difficult decisions over confidentiality and the passing on of information within the family.

It also made recommendations in relation to the roles of the Department of Health, the Department of Employment and the British Insurers.

In April 1999 a Genetics and Insurance Committee was established by the Department of Health (www.doh.gov.uk/genetics/gaic) to develop and publish criteria for the evaluation of specific genetic tests, their application to particular conditions and their reliability and relevance to particular types of insurance. In October 2000 the Genetics and Insurance Committee recommended new guidelines and suggested that while insurers could not require tests for Huntingdon's chorea to be taken, they could inquire whether the person had been tested and take this into account (Department of Health, 2000c). The agreement takes into account the concerns of the House of Commons Science and Technology Committee Report on Genetics (2001).

The Genetics and Insurance Committee was wound up on 1 July 2009 and absorbed into the Human Genetics Commission. The Commission conducted many consultations on genetic testing, paternity testing and reproductive decision making. It published its final report in July 2012. It has now been abolished and reconstituted as a departmental expert committee, the Emerging Science and Bioethics Advisory Committee, which has a wider remit than human genetics. Information on the work and constitution of the Committee is available on the Department of Health website.

Genetic disorders and the midwife

The opportunity for genetic screening to take place raises major concerns for the midwife who may be involved in the decision as to whether or not screening should go ahead. The midwife requires training in this area so that she has the skills to give the appropriate advice to a mother who is contemplating being screened. The midwife should ensure that she is familiar with the ways in which the mother can receive counselling in relation to the disease and the risks in relation to any future pregnancy. She should ensure that:

- The confidentiality of the information received from the mother is protected.
- The mother has full information.
- The mother knows that she has the right to refuse any genetic testing.
- The mother should be protected against any zealous researchers anxious to explore the genetics of the mother and child.

In addition, it is foreseeable that a mother might seek advice and comfort from a midwife when told that her child is suffering from a genetic disorder. The midwife should ensure that the mother receives all the appropriate information in relation to that disorder and that the child receives the correct treatment and care. The midwife should protect the rights of the mother and child at a time when the mother is likely to be extremely vulnerable and also protect the mother from any attempt to compel her to allow disclosure of this genetic information to other members of the extended family until such time as the mother is able to make a clear reasoned decision on her own account.

Conclusions

The area of fertilisation and genetics is one where the law usually lags behind the scientific developments and is always trying to catch up. The 1990 Act has been significantly amended by the 2008 Act but changes are still being proposed, including those relating to the implantation of a modified embryo where diseased mitochondria is replaced by healthy mitochondria from another egg. This was the subject of consultation initiated by the Human Fertilisation and Embryology Authority in September 2012 the results of which were announced in March of 2013 (www.hfea.gov.uk/6896.htlm). Legislation to legalise the procedure is awaited. The Nuffield Council on Bioethics also carried out a consultation in 2012 which can be accessed on its website (www.nuffieldbioethic.org/mitochondrial-dna-disorders). The announcement that the first deposit of stem cells (made without animal products) which can be used to treat humans has been made at the UK Stem Cell Bank opens up the possibility of treatments being available without risks of infections and immune reactions (Lighton, 2012).

Questions and exercises

1. A client tells you that she has agreed to bear a child for her sister. How would this affect your work as a midwife?
2. Obtain a copy of the latest Code issued by the Human Fertilisation and Embryology Authority and discuss the implications for midwifery (www. hfea.gov.uk/code.html).
3. A pilot study is being launched for screening for a genetic disposition for coronary heart disease. A client has asked for your advice on whether she should take part with her children. What advice would you give?
4. In what circumstances do you consider that a child should have the right to refuse consent to a genetic screening test?
5. Access the website of the Human Fertilisation and Embryology Authority (www.hfea.go.uk) and analyse the relevance of their information on IVF to your practice as a midwife.
6. Access Schedule 4 to the Human Fertilisation and Embryology Act 2008 (www.legislation.gov.uk) which inserts a new Schedule 3ZA into the 1990 Act setting out the circumstances in which an offer of counselling is required as a condition of licence for treatment. To what extent to you consider it relevant to a practising midwife?

References

A v B and another (Lesbian mother and role of biological donor father) [2012] EWCA Civ 285; The Times 13 June 2012

Ashcroft RE (2003) *In vitro* fertilisation for all? *British Medical Journal* **327**(7414): 511–12

Briody v St Helens and Knowsley AHA (Claim for damages and costs) sub nom Briody v St Helens and Knowsley AHA [2001] EWCA Civ 1010 [2001] 2 FCR 481 CA

Centre for Reproductive Medicine v Mrs U [2002] Lloyds Rep Med 93

Department of Health (1998) *Surrogacy: Review for Health Ministers of Current Arrangements for Payments and Regulation. CM 4068.* Department of Health, London

Department of Health (2000a) *Press announcement.* Department of Health, London

Department of Health (2000b) *Working towards the ending of postcode lottery of infertility treatment.* Department of Health, London

Department of Health (2000c) *Committee on Genetics and Insurance Report.* Department of Health, London

Department of Health (2004) *Health Secretary welcomes new fertility guidance*

2004/0069. Department of Health, London

Dickson v United Kingdom [2007] ECHR 1050

Hawkes N (2002) Couple win right to create life-saving baby. *The Times* **23 February**

House of Commons Science and Technology Committee (2001) *Genetics and insurance*. Available from: www.publications.parliament.uk.pa/1d200001/1dsclect/1dsctte ch/57/5701.htm

Human Fertilisation and Embryology Authority (2009) *Guidance note 6. Legal parenthood*. HFEA, London

McLean S (1998) *Review of Common Law Provisions Relating to the Removal of Gametes and of the Consent Provisions in the Human Fertilisation and Embryology Act 1990*. HMSO, London

Mrs U v Centre for Reproductive Medicine Lloyd's Rep Med [2002] 259

NICE (2004) *Fertility: Assessment and treatment for people with fertility problems*. NICE, London

Oxenford K, Karunaratna M et al (2013) Progress in prenatal genetic diagnosis: Using cell-free fetal DNA in maternal blood. *British Journal of Midwifery* **21**(2): 84–90

Peek L (2002) Couple lose fight for designer baby. *The Times* **2 August**

R v Ethical Committee of St Mary's Hospital (Manchester) ex parte H [1988] 1 FLR 512

R v Human Fertilisation and Embryology Authority, ex parte Blood [1997] 2 All ER 687 CA

R v Secretary of State ex parte Mellor Times Law Report 1 May 2001

R v Secretary of State ex parte Mellor Times Law Report 5 September 2000

R v Sheffield Health Authority, ex parte Seale [1994] 25 BMLR 1 QBD

Re A (an adoption)(surrogacy) [1987] 2 All ER 826

Re Attorney General's Reference (No 2 of 2003) [2004] EWCA Crim 785 The Times April 21 2004

Regina (Quintavalle) v Human Fertilisation and Embryology Authority Times Law Report 20 May 2003 C A; Lloyd's Rep Med 6 [2003] 294

Regina (Quintavalle) v Human Fertilisation and Embryology Authority Times Law Report 29 April 2005 HL

Re L (a minor) [2010] EWHC 3146

Rumbelow H (2003) Victory for Mrs Blood changes law of paternity. *The Times* 1 March:12

S and D and E and in the matter of Z (a minor) T and X and Y [2013] EWHC 14 Fam.

The Human Fertilisation and Embryology (Parental Orders) Regulations 2010 SI 2010/985

The Leeds Teaching Hospitals NHS Trust v Mr A; Mrs A; YA and ZA; The Human Fertility And Embryology Authority, Mr B and Mrs B Lloyds Rep Med [2003] 151

Chapter 15

Compensation for vaccine and other damage

Scenario 15.1. Vaccine damage

Amil decided to allow her daughter to receive all the recommended vaccinations in spite of the considerable controversy at the time. A few days after being vaccinated her daughter became ill and subsequently it is found that she has severe brain damage. What action can she take and is anyone to blame?

Scenario 15.1. is discussed on p. 292.

Introduction

Our system of compensation by means of civil action for negligence involves establishing fault, i.e. a breach of the duty of care owed to the person injured. (For further details on the tort of negligence see *Chapter 8*.) This can be difficult to establish and may mean that many claims are either not brought or are abandoned at an early stage. Critics have demanded a system of no-fault liability such as pertains in New Zealand, Finland and Sweden where compensation is paid for untoward medical accidents without the need to establish that one or more persons is at fault. The Department of Health in 2001 indicated that it was prepared to consider the introduction of major changes to our system for compensation including a no-fault system of compensation for certain kinds of harm. A consultation paper, *Making amends,* was published by the Department of Health in 2003 and resulted in the NHS Redress Act which has not yet been fully implemented and which did not introduce non-fault liability.

Compensation schemes

We do, however, have examples of compensation paid on a no-fault liability basis. One such is the payment for vaccine damage. Another statutory scheme for compensation is the criminal injury compensation scheme (see *Chapter 12*). A scheme for compensation and a trust fund for those who have suffered from variant Creutzfeldt-Jakob (vCJD) disease or bovine spongiform encephalopathy (BSE) and their families has been set up. The vCJD Trust advises on applications for compensation from the fund and can be accessed on its website (www.vcjdtrust.co.uk/scheme). The manufacturers of thalidomide, Distillers, established a fund to pay those who were its victims and this fund was subsequently topped up by Diageo who took over Distillers. It has contributed £160 million to the fund over the past 16 years. On 21 December 2012 it was announced that the government was paying £80 million in compensation to thalidomide victims to help with their increasing needs over the next 10 years. Victims in Scotland would share £14 million and an announcement was awaited about Wales and Northern Ireland.

In August 2003 the Secretary of State for health announced that the government intended providing compensation to those people who were infected with hepatitis C from contaminated blood products and a fund of £100 million was set up for compensation, with the intention that sufferers would obtain between £20000 and £40000. The details of the scheme and payments were announced by the Department of Health in January 2004.

Under the scheme an *ex gratia* payment of up to £45000 was to be payable to those who were alive on 29 August 2003 and whose hepatitis C infection is found attributable to NHS treatment with blood or blood products before September 1991. Those people infected were to receive an initial lump sum payment of £20000 and those developing a more advanced stage of the illness, such as cirrhosis or liver cancer, were to get a further £25000. In addition, people who contracted hepatitis C through someone infected with the disease would also qualify for payment. The scheme was criticised by some because it excluded widows and those who had already died from the disease (Lister, 2004). The Archer Inquiry was set up to investigate NHS contaminated blood and blood products and reported in 2009. It can be accessed on the internet (www.archercbbp.com). The Government's response was published in February 2010 and is available on the Department of Health website. A private members' bill was introduced into the House of Lords in October 2010 to provide compensation for those who have been infected by contaminated blood – Contaminated Blood (Support for Infected and Bereaved Persons) Bill 2010–11 – but it failed to progress. The government has increased the amounts paid to the MacFarlane and Eileen Trusts which compensate individuals infected with human immunodeficiency virus (HIV) via blood and blood products. The Skipton Fund provides lump sum payments to people infected with hepatitis C from infected blood and blood products and is to be reviewed in 2014.

Compensation for vaccine damage

It is in the public interest for as many children as possible to be vaccinated against infectious diseases. However, it is recognised that on very rare occasions there can be side effects of a very crippling kind from vaccines. The Royal Commission on Civil Liability and Compensation for Personal Injuries (The Pearson Report) (1978) recommended that where vaccine damage could be proved to have followed from medical procedures recommended by the government, then those who suffered serious damage should be entitled to bring an action in tort against the government on the basis of strict liability. It did not recommend the abandonment of fault liability in other cases of personal injury arising from medical accident. In the light of the Pearson recommendations the government introduced the Vaccine Damage Payments Act 1979 to provide for payments to be made out of public funds in cases where severe disablement occurs as a result of vaccination against certain diseases or of contact with a person who has been vaccinated against any of those diseases. The sum payable was originally £10000 but this has been increased over the years and at the time of writing stands at £120000 (Vaccine Damages Payments Statutory Instrument 2007 SI 1931). Further information is available from the government website (www.direct.gov.uk/disability-vdp). Payments can be claimed via the vaccine damage website (www.gov.uk/vaccine-damage-payment/) and forms can be downloaded from that site. The Department of Health publishes the Green Book giving information on vaccines and preventable infectious diseases which is updated on a regular basis and available on the Department of Health website.

The diseases to which the Act applies are shown in *Box 15.1*.

Box 15.1 Diseases covered by the Vaccine Damage Payments Act 1979

- Diphtheria
- Tetanus
- Whooping cough
- Poliomyelitis
- Smallpox (up to 1 August 1971)
- Measles
- Mumps
- Rubella
- Tuberculosis
- Swine flu (to 31 August 2010)
- Any other disease specified by the Secretary of State by statutory instrument
- Haemophilus Type B infection (hib) was added to the list in 1995 (SI 1995)
- Meningococcal Group C was added in 2001 (SI 1652)
- Pneumococcal infection (SI 2066)

> **Box 15.2. Definition of severe disability for the purposes of the Vaccine Damage Payments Act**
>
> S.1(4) For the purposes of this Act, a person is severely disabled if he suffers disablement to the extent of 60% (decreased from 80%) assessed as for the purposes of Social Security legislation. (Total loss of sight or hearing would count as 100%.)

Severe disability must be established and this is defined in the Act as shown in *Box 15.2*.

Section 1(3) of the Act also covers the situation where a person is severely disabled as the result of a vaccination given to his mother before he was born.

The conditions for obtaining the payment are set out in *Box 15.3*.

> **Box 15.3 Conditions to obtain payment under Vaccine Damage Payments Act 1979**
>
> 1 (a) Vaccination was carried out in the UK or Isle of Man,
>   (b) on or after 5th July 1948,
>   (c) in the case of smallpox, before 1 August 1971.
> 2 (a) (Except for poliomyelitis and rubella; meningococcal group C; human papillomavirus and swine flu) the vaccination was given while the person was under 18 years or during an outbreak of that disease in the UK or Isle of Man.
> 3.   The disabled person was over the age of two on the date when the claim was made or, if he died before that date, he died after 9 May 1978 and was over the age of two when he died.

Children up to the age of 18 years are now able to bring a claim, but where a claim is made in respect of a vaccination for meningococcal group C, the conditions that a person should be under 18 years at the date of the vaccination and that there should be an outbreak of the disease in the UK or Isle of Man do not apply.

Causation

It must be shown that the disablement is the result of the vaccine. Where such causation is in dispute, the Act provides that:

...the question whether the severe disablement results from vaccination against any of the diseases shall be determined for the purposes of the Act on the balance of probability.

Time limits

A claim for payment must be made within six years beginning on the latest of the following dates (Regulatory Reform [Vaccine Damage Payments Act 1979] Order 2002 SI 1592):

- Date of the vaccination.
- Date on which the disabled person attained the age of two.
- 9 May 1978.
- The 21st birthday or, if the person has died, the date they would have reached 25 years if later than 6 years from the date of the vaccination.

Referral to medical tribunal

The Secretary of State can refer to a tribunal:

- The question of the extent of the disablement suffered by the disabled person.
- The question whether he is, or, as the case may be, was immediately before his death, disabled as a result of the vaccination to which the claim relates.
- The question whether, if he is or was so disabled, the extent of his disability is, or was, such as to amount to severe disablement.

The Act also provides for the payments to or for the benefit of the disabled person and the holding of money by trustees where appropriate.

In August 2010 £90000 was paid out to a man who had suffered severe brain damage following a measles, mumps and rubella (MMR) vaccination. He was initially refused compensation but his mother appealed. Robert Fletcher, 18, at the time of the award was unable to talk, to stand unaided or feed himself, had epileptic fits and needed 24-hour care (Delgado, 2010). Figures released in 2005 from a Freedom of Information request revealed that tribunals had paid out £3.5 million in the previous 8 years.

Offences under the Act

A person who, for the purpose of obtaining a payment under the Act, whether for himself or for another person, knowingly makes any false statement or representation or produces or furnishes or causes or knowingly allows to be produced or furnished any document or information that he knows to be false in a material particular, is liable to prosecution under Section 9(1).

Civil claims

In comparison with the statutory fixed sum for severe disablement, the awards which are payable by civil action for negligence are much larger. However, as is shown in *Chapter 8*, all elements necessary to establish liability must be shown or accepted by the defendant. The person seeking compensation must therefore show that:

- A duty of care was owed.
- This duty has been broken by a failure to follow the accepted standard of care, and
- As a reasonably foreseeable consequence of this breach,
- Harm has occurred.

Severe disablement does not have to be shown to recover compensation in the civil courts.

What happens if payment has already been paid out under the Vaccine Damage Payment Act 1979? Does this prevent a civil action taking place? The answer is no. Section 6(4) states that the making of a claim for, or the receipt of, a payment under the Act does not prejudice the right of any person to institute or carry on proceedings in respect of disablement suffered as a result of vaccination against any disease to which the Act applies. However, the fact that a payment has been made under the Act must be taken into account by the court in any civil proceedings where compensation in respect of such disablement is awarded. The case of *Loveday v Renton* illustrates the difficulties of succeeding in a civil claim.

Mrs Loveday claimed damages on behalf of her daughter Susan, then aged 17 years, for permanent brain damage after a whooping cough vaccine given in 1970 and 1971. The claim was brought against the Wellcome Foundation, who made the vaccine, and against the doctor who had administered it. The claim was dismissed because she had failed to show on a balance of probabilities that pertussis vaccine could cause permanent brain damage in young children. It thus failed on the issue of causation. The judge stated that if the case had not failed on the issue of causation,

any plaintiff would face insuperable difficulties in establishing negligence on the part of the doctor or nurse who had administered the vaccine.

Such a claim would have to be based on the ground that the vaccination had been given in spite of the presence of certain contraindications, including the possibility that the vaccine was defective.

In contrast to the Loveday case, a claim against the Wellcome Foundation succeeded in an Irish case in 1992 (*Best v Wellcome Foundation*). The High Court had dismissed the plaintiff's claim because of the lack of proof of causation. However, the Irish Supreme Court held that the Wellcome Foundation was liable for the negligent manufacture and release of a particular batch of triple vaccine and that the brain damage was caused as a result. It referred the case back to the High Court on the amount of compensation. On 11 May 1993 the High Court approved an award of £2.75 million as compensation for the brain damage sustained in September 1969.

It must be stressed that in the Best case, there was evidence that the particular batch of vaccine was below standard and should not have been released onto the market. However, the contrast between the sums available if fault and causation can be established in the civil courts is clear.

Consumer Protection Act 1987

If it can be established that a person has been injured as a result of a defect in a product, then there may be a claim under the Consumer Protection Act 1987. In this case it is not necessary to establish fault, merely that there was a defect (see *Chapter 10*). It has been held that a claim can be brought under the Consumer Protection Act 1987 where the claimant was infected with hepatitis through contaminated blood transfusions (*A v National Blood Authority sub nom Hepatitis C Litigation*). This could be used as a precedent for claims in relation to defective vaccines.

Disputes over the safety of the triple vaccine

There was considerable media concern about the triple vaccine for mumps, measles and rubella (MMR). A report published in the *Lancet* by Dr Wakefield (subsequently withdrawn by *The Lancet*) suggested that the measles vaccine was linked with autism. The result was evidence of a growing number of parents choosing not to allow their babies to have the triple vaccine. The Committee on the Safety of Medicines (2002) issued a statement to show that new research showed no link between MMR and autism or bowel disease. Research from Japan in March 2005 (Hawkes, 2005) gave further support to the view that there is no scientific link between autism and MMR. The independence of Dr Wakefield's research was subsequently criticised and the safety of MMR reaffirmed. Following three years of investigations, the General Medical Council found Dr Wakefield guilty of serious professional misconduct and he was struck off the register (Rose, 2010). Since 2007 (and particularly in Swansea) an increase in measles was held to be directly linked with the failure in uptake of the MMR vaccine as a result of the controversy, and figures published in January 2010 show that there were 1348 cases of measles in 2008 compared with 56 in 1998 (Deer, 2010). The MMR controversy is explored in a book by Boyce (2007). In January 2012 Wakefield filed a lawsuit in Texas for defamation against the *British Medical Journal* and its editor and Brian Deer, a freelance writer for *The Sunday Times*. The case is ongoing.

In spite of the attempted reassurance, figures for cases of mumps are reported to be soaring (Lister, 2005).

Another scare relating to the possibility that autism has arisen from mercury being used in vaccines has been highlighted in the press (Waterhouse, 2001).

Midwives are likely to be consulted by mothers over what is best practice for their children and they must ensure that they fulfil their duty of care in providing such information. They should ensure that they have the latest Department of Health and Committee for the Safety of Medicines evidence.

Scenario 15.1. Vaccine damage: Discussion

Several avenues can be explored by Amil, depending upon the circumstances. If there is any evidence that the vaccine batch was defective she could consider civil action or action under the Consumer Protection Act. If a health professional has been negligent in administering the vaccine there may also be the possibility of a civil action. More likely, however, is the right to make a claim under the Act. Payments can be claimed via the vaccine damage website (www.gov.uk/vaccine-damage-payment/).

Conclusions

There is on-going research into the safety of vaccines, and since midwives are likely to be consulted by mothers, they need to ensure that they are up to date. The possibilities of the government introducing a new scheme for clinical compensation comparable to the present Vaccine Damages Payment Act are still remote.

Questions and exercises

1. A client asks for your advice on whether she should ensure that her children receive the triple vaccine. What advice do you give?
2. What differences are there between a claim for compensation under the Vaccine Damage Payments Act, a claim for compensation under the laws of negligence, and a claim under the Consumer Protection Act 1987?
3. Are there any other injuries or disabilities that you consider should be covered by a statutory right to compensation comparable to the Vaccine Damage Payments Act?
4. Visit the direct government website covering vaccine damage payments (www.direct.gov.uk/disability-vdp or www.gov.uk/vaccine-damage-payment/). Is the advice which you give to mothers up to date?

References

A v National Blood Authority sub nom Hepatitis C Litigation. The Times, 4 April 2001; [2001] 3 All ER 289

Best v Wellcome Foundation, Dr O'Keefe, the Southern Health Board, the Minister for Health of Ireland and the Attorney General [1994] 5 Med LR (Also discussed in *Medico Legal Journal* **61**(3): 178)

Boyce T (2007) *Health, risk and news: The MMR vaccine and the media*. Peter Lang Publ Inc, New York

Committee of Safety of Medicines (2002) *Press release*. 13 February. CSM, London

Deer B (2010) Callous, unethical and dishonest. *The Times* **31 January**

Delgado M (2010) Family win 18 year fight over MMR damage to son. *Mail on line* **28 August**

Department of Health (2001) *Press release 2001/0313. New clinical compensation scheme for the NHS*. HMSO, London

Department of Health (2003) *Making amends. A consultation paper setting out proposals for reforming the approach to clinical negligence in the NHS.* HMSO, London

Department of Health (2004) *Details of Hepatitis C ex-gratia payment scheme announced. Press release 2004/0025.* Department of Health, London

Hawkes N (2005) Study that debunks MMR autism link hailed by doctors. *The Times* **4 March**: 30

Lister S (2004) NHS hepatitis victims to get up to £45,000. *The Times* **24 January**

Lister S (2005) Mumps soars for teens who missed MMR jab. *The Times* **4 February**

Loveday v Renton The Times 31 March 1988 QBD

Regulatory Reform (Vaccine Damage Payments Act 1979) Order 2002 SI 1592

Rose D (2010) Doctor in MMR scare to challenge striking-off order. *The Times* **25 May**

Royal Commission on Civil Liability and Compensation for Personal Injuries (1978) The Pearson Report. Cmnd. 7054. HMSO, London

Vaccine Damage Payment (Specified Disease) Order 2006 SI 2066

Vaccine Damage Payment (Specified Disease) Order 2008 SI 2103

Vaccine Damages Payment (Specified Disease) Order 2001 SI 1652

Vaccine Damages Payments Statutory Instrument 2007 SI 193183

Waterhouse R (2001) New autism doubt on mercury in vaccines. *The Sunday Times* **22 July**

Chapter 16

Public health

Scenario 16.1. Hepatitis C

Sarah was expecting her first child and became ill after the birth. She was found to be suffering from hepatitis C and it was suspected that she had contracted it from the midwife who attended her. What are the implications for the midwife?

Scenario 16.1. is discussed on p. 308.

Introduction

The midwife has both a duty to ensure that she does not pass on infections to her clients and also a duty to ensure that she notifies the appropriate authorities in accordance with her duties under public health legislation. This chapter deals with both these areas and legal issues arising from AIDS/HIV and cross-infection. Reference should also be made to *Chapter 10* on health and safety and to the book by Jane Bott entitled *HIV and Midwifery Practice* (2005).

The midwife's health

There was a requirement under the former Midwives Rules that the midwife be medically examined:

> *A practising midwife shall, if the Local Supervising Authority deems it necessary for preventing the spread of infection, undergo medical examination by a registered medical practitioner. (Former Rule 39 1998)*

However, this requirement has not been included in the revised Midwives Rules which came into force in August 2004 (Nursing and Midwifery Council, 2012).

This may not be so significant however since the requirement to submit to health checks may possibly be implied in a contract of employment of a midwife (or other health professional). There may be an implied duty that she submits herself to an independent medical examination if it is feared that she is not capable, physically or mentally, of being at work.

Under the statutory duties relating to health and safety, and also under her common law duty of care to her patients, the midwife would have a wider duty in relation to the prevention of cross infection between patients and she should therefore follow a procedure that would ensure the highest standards of hygiene and infection control.

Notifiable diseases

Certain diseases are defined as notifiable and if the midwife is aware that one of her clients, or their relatives, is infected with such a disease she would have a duty to report it. Legislation on notification, formerly enacted in Part 2 of the Public Heath (Control of Disease) Act 1984, is replaced by Part 2A, enacted in the Health and Social Care Act 2008 and the three sets of Regulations (2010/657; 2010/658 and 2010/659) set out below. Information on diseases which must be notified is available on the Health Protection Agency website (www.hpa.org.uk/ Topics/InfectiousDiseases). The Health Protection Agency is now absorbed into Public Health England (see below).

The Health Protection (Notification) Regulations 2010 (SI 2010/659) can be accessed on the legislation website (www.legislation.gov.uk) and are shown together with the other two sets of Regulations in *Boxes 16.1, 16.2,* and *16.3.*

Box 16.1. Local authority powers (SI 2010/657)

The powers include:

- The requirement to keep a child away from school.
- The requirement to provide details of children attending school.
- Disinfection or decontamination of things on the request of the owner.
- On the request of person with custody or control; on premises on request of tenant.
- Requests for cooperation for health protection purposes.
- Restriction of contact with dead bodies.
- Restriction of access to dead bodies.
- Relocation of dead bodies.

Schedule 1 lists the notifiable diseases, and Schedule 2 the causative agents.

As envisaged in the Public Health White Paper, *Healthy Lives, healthy people: Our strategy for public health in England* (Department of Health, 2010), the

---

Box 16.2 Part 2A orders (i.e. Application to Justice of the Peace) (SI 2010/658)

- Duty of local authorities to give notice of Part 2A applications.
- Evidence required for a Part 2A application.
- Period for which Part 2A order in relation to persons may be in force.
- Affected persons in relation to Part 2A orders in relation to persons and dead bodies or human remains.
- Discretionary power for local authorities to charge in connection with Part 2A order in relation to things and premises.
- Duty on local authorities to provide information in relation to Part 2A order in relation to persons.
- Duty on local authorities to have regard to welfare following a Part 2A order in relation to persons.
- Duty on local authorities to report Part 2A applications to the Health Protection Agency.
- Duty on local authorities to report variations or revocations of Part 2A orders to the Health Protection Agency (now Public Health England).

Box 16.3. Notification provisions (SI 2010/659)

- Duty to notify suspected disease, infection or contamination in patients.
- Duty to notify suspected disease, infection or contamination in dead persons.
- Duty of notify causative agents found in human samples.
- Duty to provide information to the Health Protection Agency (now Public Health England).
- Duty on the relevant local authority to disclose notification to others.

Health Protection Agency was abolished by the Health and Social Care Act 2012. Its functions have been transferred to the Secretary of State and Public Health England which is an executive agency of the Department of Health and came into being in April 2013. At local level, local authorities now have responsibility for improving the health of their local populations and must employ a director of public health and publish annual reports. Local authorities will coordinate the work done by the NHS, social care, housing, environmental health, and leisure and transport services.

Diseases that are notifiable are shown in *Box 16.4*. Schedule 1 (*Box 16.4*) covers those notifiable diseases that come under the notification procedure set out in Regulation 2 (*Box 16.6*). Schedule 2 lists causative agents (See *Box 16.5*) which must be reported by diagnostic laboratories to the Health Protection Authority under Regulation 4 of the Health Protection (Notification) Regulations 2010.

Box 16.4. Diseases notifiable under Schedule 1 of the 2010 Regulations

- Acute encephalitis
- Acute meningitis
- Acute poliomyelitis
- Acute infectious hepatitis
- Anthrax
- Botulism
- Brucellosis
- Cholera
- Diphtheria
- Enteric fever (typhoid or paratyphoid fever)
- Food poisoning
- Haemolytic uraemic syndrome
- Infectious bloody diarrhoea
- Invasive group A streptococcal disease and scarlet fever
- Legionnaires' disease
- Leprosy
- Malaria
- Measles
- Meningococcal septicaemia
- Mumps
- Plague
- Rabies
- Rubella
- Severe acute respiratory syndrome (SARS)
- Smallpox
- Tetanus
- Tuberculosis
- Typhus
- Viral haemorrhagic fever
- Whooping cough
- Yellow fever

Box 16.5. Schedule 2 Causative agents

- *Bacillus anthracis*
- *Bacillus cereus* (only if associated with food poisoning)
- *Bordetella pertussis*
- *Borrelia* spp
- *Brucella* spp
- *Burkholderia mallei*
- *Burkholderia pseudomallei*
- *Campylobacter* spp
- *Chikungunya virus*
- *Chlamydophila psittaci*
- *Clostridium botulinum*
- *Clostridium perfringens* (only if associated with food poisoning)
- *Clostridium tetani*
- *Corynebacterium diphtheriae*
- *Corynebacterium ulcerans*
- *Coxiella burnetii*

Box 16.5/cont

- Crimean-Congo haemorrhagic fever virus
- *Cryptosporidium* spp
- Dengue virus
- Ebola virus
- *Entamoeba histolytica*
- *Francisella tularensis*
- *Giardia lamblia*
- *Guanarito virus*
- *Haemophilus influenzae* (invasive)
- Hanta virus
- Hepatitis A, B, C, delta, and E viruses
- Influenza virus
- Junin virus
- Kyasanur Forest disease virus
- Lassa virus
- *Legionella* spp
- *Leptospira interrogans*
- *Listeria monocytogenes*
- Machupo virus
- Marburg virus
- Measles virus
- Mumps virus
- *Mycobacterium tuberculosis* complex
- *Neisseria meningitidis*
- Omsk haemorrhagic fever virus
- *Plasmodium falciparum, vivax, ovale, malariae, knowlesi*
- Polio virus (wild or vaccine types)
- Rabies virus (classical rabies and rabies-related lyssaviruses)
- *Rickettsia* spp
- Rift Valley fever virus
- Rubella virus
- Sabia virus
- *Salmonella* spp
- SARS coronavirus
- *Shigella* spp
- *Streptococcus pneumoniae* (invasive)
- *Streptococcus pyogenes* (invasive)
- Varicella zoster virus
- Variola virus
- *Verocytotoxigenic Escherichia coli* (including E.coli O157)
- *Vibrio cholerae*
- West Nile virus
- Yellow fever virus
- *Yersinia pestis*

Box 16.6 Notification procedure (SI 2010/659 Regulation 2)

2(1) A registered medical practitioner (R) must notify the proper officer of the relevant local authority where R has reasonable grounds for suspecting that a patient (P) whom R is attending:

(a) has a notifiable disease;

(b) has an infection which, in the view of R, presents or could present significant harm to human health; or

(c) is contaminated in a manner which, in the view of R, presents or could present significant harm to human health.

What information must be notified?

Box 16.7 shows the information that must be notified.

Box 16.7. Information that must be given

2(2) The notification must include the following information insofar as it is known to R:
  (a) P's name, date of birth and sex;
  (b) P's home address including postcode;
  (c) P's current residence (if not home address);
  (d) P's telephone number;
  (e) P's NHS number;
  (f) P's occupation (if R considers it relevant);
  (g) the name, address and postcode of P's place of work or education (if R considers it relevant);
  (h) P's relevant overseas travel history;
  (i) P's ethnicity;
  (j) contact details for a parent of P (where P is a child);
  (k) the disease or infection that P has or is suspected of having or the nature of P's contamination or suspected contamination;
  (l) the date of onset of P's symptoms;
  (m) the date of R's diagnosis; and
  (n) R's name, address and telephone number.
2(3) The notification must be provided in writing within 3 days beginning with the day on which R forms a suspicion under Paragraph (1).
  (4) Without prejudice to Paragraph (3), if R considers that the case is urgent, notification must be provided orally as soon as reasonably practicable.
  (5) In determining whether the case is urgent, R must have regard to
  (a) the nature of the suspected disease, infection or contamination;
  (b) the ease of spread of that disease, infection or contamination;
  (c) the ways in which the spread of the disease, infection or contamination can be prevented or controlled; and Regulation 3 extends the obligation set out in *Boxes 16.4* and *16.5* to cover notification of a suspected disease, infection or contamination in a dead body.
  (d) P's circumstances (including age, sex and occupation).

Powers of the Justice of the Peace

The Justice of the Peace has considerable powers in relation to the protection of public health. The powers were set out in the Public Health (Control of Disease) Act 1984 which has been substantially amended by the Health and Social Care Act 2008 by the insertion of a new Part 2A to the 1984 Act. The powers of the Justice of the Peace to order health measures in relation to persons are set out in Section 45G; in relation to things in Section 45H; in relation to premises in Section 45I; and in relation to groups of people, things or premises in Section 45J.

Under Section 18 of the 2012 Health and Social Care Act, regulations may require a local authority to exercise any of the public health functions of the Secretary of State (so far as relating to the health of the public in the authority's area) by taking such steps as may be prescribed.

Tuberculosis

A National Knowledge Service has been set up to provide information directly relevant to the treatment, prevention and management of tuberculosis. It is accessible on the Health Protection Agency (HPA) website. The HPA, in cooperation with the Department of Health, is aiming to eliminate tuberculosis within England in accordance with the action plan published by the Chief Medical Officer of Health in 2004. In May 2005 more than 700 patients who had been treated at the Lister Hospital Stevenage were sent letters urging them to be alert to the symptoms of tuberculosis since an unnamed health worker has been diagnosed with the disease.

Figures from the HPA in November 2010 showed that the incidence of tuberculosis has doubled over the past decade and has reached a 30-year high. Further information on the HPA's strategy and local and national surveillance can be obtained from its website (www.hpa.org.uk/infections/topics_az/tb/). In March 2010 the website stated that:

> *Around 9000 cases of tuberculosis are currently reported each year in the United Kingdom. Most cases occur in major cities, particularly in London. The Health Protection Agency aims to contribute to the elimination of tuberculosis in England through support to the NHS and the Department of Health in the key areas identified for controlling tuberculosis in the National Action Plan, Stopping Tuberculosis in England, published by the Chief Medical Officer in October 2004. Through its Tuberculosis Programme, the HPA coordinates its tuberculosis*

control activities, which are carried out by different parts of the organisation:
the Centre for Infections, Local and Regional Services, the Regional Microbiology
Network and the Centre for Emergency Preparedness and Response. The
activities include local and national surveillance, laboratory diagnostic and
reference services, disease control in the population, international partnership
and leading edge research.

Hepatitis and HIV

The British Medical Association called for all children in Britain to be immunised
against hepatitis B since transmission rates were rising and it was 50 to 100 times
more infectious than the AIDS virus (*The Times*, 2005). In 2004 the Department
of Health issued revised guidance on prevention and testing in children for HIV,
which also covers advice about hepatitis B and C (Department of Health, 2004a).
The British HIV Association has published guidelines for the management of HIV
infection in pregnant women (British HIV Association, 2008). Sharon Wilson
describes the challenges for midwives in facing an HIV positive pregnant woman
(Wilson, 2011).

Practical advice for midwives in suggesting tests for sexually transmitted
infections in pregnancy is given by Julie Williams (2011).

Role of the midwife

If a midwife knows or suspects that one of her clients may be suffering from
an infectious disease or food poisoning she should ensure that the patient's GP
is notified. Alternatively, she could herself notify the local authority.

Midwife and protection from infection

As an employee, the midwife is entitled to all reasonable care being taken
for her safety against reasonably foreseeable risks and dangers (see *Chapter
10*). The risk of HIV/AIDS or other infections is one that could be regarded
as reasonably foreseeable. This means her employer must take all reasonable
care in terms of ensuring that a safe system of work is followed, that staff are
trained and competent, and that equipment, facilities, buildings and the working
environment are safe. The employer's duty derives both from the contract of
employment and from the criminal law and the laws relating to health and safety
at work.

Any guidance offered by professional groups on what equipment the midwife should use to be reasonably safe should be followed. If the appropriate facilities are not available, the midwife should draw the manager's attention to the deficiencies and ensure that the appropriate steps are taken. If necessary the midwife could use whistleblowing procedures (see *Chapter 10*).

What are the remedies if no action is taken?

The criminal law

A breach of the Health and Safety at Work laws could result in the prosecution of the employer. The Health and Safety Inspectorate has the duty of enforcing the provisions of these laws and making regular inspections of health service premises to ensure that the duties are being observed. If the equipment provided to midwives for home deliveries is inadequate this could also be brought to the attention of the Inspectorate. Obviously all steps should be taken to ensure that management is made aware of the problems and that it has the opportunity to remedy them before external assistance is sought.

There have been prosecutions for those who, knowing themselves to be HIV positive, have deliberately inflicted the infection onto others. The Criminal Injury Compensation Scheme recognises that a criminal offence leading to infection with HIV/AIDS should be compensated. In October 2003, Mohammed Dica was found guilty of inflicting biological bodily harm upon two lovers whom he had callously infected with HIV (*R v Dica*). He was sentenced to eight years imprisonment but won a retrial on the grounds that the trial judge should not have withdrawn from the jury the issue of whether the women consented to intercourse knowing that he was HIV positive. In the case of *R v Konzani*, the Court of Appeal set out the basic provisions that apply to this criminal offence.

The civil law

Since it is an implied term of the contract of employment that the employer should take all reasonable care for the safety of the employee, failure by the employer to provide reasonable standards of safety would be a breach of the contract of employment. In serious cases, breach of contract gives the innocent party the right to see the contract as at an end. Thus, if the midwife was guilty of gross misconduct she could be dismissed instantly without notice. Similarly, where the employer is in breach by failing to take reasonable steps to ensure the midwife's safety, the midwife could see the contract as terminated by his conduct, and if she has worked for two years or more continuously, she could bring an action for unfair dismissal in the employment tribunal. She would be alleging that there has been a constructive dismissal by virtue of the employer's failures towards her. If she is to take this latter step she must be sure that she has good legal advice and the stages are well documented in writing. (In a whistleblowing case there is no requirement of continuous service.)

Because it is unknown which mothers are likely to be a danger to the midwife it is important that every pregnant woman is treated as a potential source of infection and the same high standards are followed for every case. (For further information on health and safety law see *Chapter 10*.)

Duty to the HIV/AIDS client

If the midwife knows that one of her clients is actually suffering from AIDS or is HIV positive, what action should she take? Hopefully, her standards of care and safety are such that she would not have to take any additional precautions. However, she should ensure that she has the knowledge to answer the client's questions and advise her on breastfeeding and the problems of infecting the baby with infected milk, if the baby has not already been infected during gestation. The fact that the mother is an HIV carrier or sufferer from AIDS in no way reduces the duty of care that the midwife owes to her. Indeed in some ways it is higher because of the additional information that the midwife should be passing on.

The HIV positive child

Where a baby is thought to have contracted AIDS then the fundamental principle is that "the welfare of the child is the paramount consideration" (see *Chapter 17*). This was at the heart of a judge's decision when he ruled that a baby could be tested for HIV despite the opposition of her parents (Rumbelow, 1999). The facts of the case are shown in *Box 16.8*.

The case in *Box 16.8* came to light when a GP, carrying out a routine check-up, read in the mother's notes that she was HIV positive and raised the issue with Camden Borough Council which brought the case under the Children Act 1989. The British Medical Association and the Terence Higgins Trust supported the ruling because of the advances made in the treatment of HIV. The National Aids Trust said it was extremely regrettable that court intervention was thought necessary. Midwives need to have appropriate

---

Box 16.8. Facts of case of *Re C (HIV Test)* on baby

The mother was HIV positive but refused to allow her four-month-old baby to be tested for HIV. Both parents believed that HIV does not cause AIDS and that the conventional medical treatment of the virus did more harm than good. Judge Wilson noted that both parents were devoted to the baby and that they were knowledgeable and concerned about HIV. However, the judge accepted the current medical view that HIV could lead to AIDS and that drug therapy could be given to minimise the effect of the virus. The mother had refused to accept medical advice to have her baby delivered via a Caesarean and not to breastfeed the baby. Instead she arranged for a home delivery and was breastfeeding the baby.

---

training to advise women on HIV testing, to ensure that they are given the necessary counselling prior to having the test. The Department of Health (2003a) has set standards to support the UK antenatal screening programme. Information on screening of the newborn can be accessed on the UK Newborn Screening Programme Centre website (www.newbornbloodspot.screening. nhs.uk/).

The Department of Health (2004b) has issued guidance on HIV and infant feeding. This guidance aims to help healthcare professionals provide the necessary information, advice and support to women who are infected with HIV to help them make personal, well-informed decisions about infant feeding.

The case illustrates one of the most difficult dilemmas facing midwives, i.e. when should they seek to intervene against the wishes of the parents, in particular the mother, in order to protect the child. In the case itself, the judge ruled that an HIV test could be carried out, yet he did not rule that the mother should stop breastfeeding the child. Breastfeeding the baby by an HIV-positive mother is considered to double the chance of the baby contracting the disease.

The midwife as the carrier of an infectious disease

Liability of the midwife

The midwife has a professional duty to notify the Registration body and also her employer that she is suffering from an infectious disease or is HIV positive. The Court of Appeal ordered a former dentist who was suffering from AIDS to hand over his records so that his patients could be contacted. However, it barred the publication of his name and the name of the health authority for whom he worked (Horsnall, 2002).

There would probably be civil liability if the midwife gave blood, failing to disclose that she was a carrier of HIV/AIDS or had another infectious disease. If she gave blood deliberately knowing that she could infect others, then as well as being a civil wrong under a principle established in a 19th century case (*Wilkinson v Downton*), she could also be guilty of a criminal offence.

Protection of the midwife

A midwife who reported that she was suffering from an infectious disease or was HIV positive may have protection under the Equality Act re-enacting the provisions of the Disability Discrimination Act 1995, but the employer would be entitled to take reasonable measures to ensure that her clients and patients were protected from the risk of cross-infection. She could claim statutory protection from unfair dismissal legislation and cite breach of her human rights under the Human Rights Act 1998 should she be treated unjustly. A case in 1988 protected the confidentiality of the names of the health professionals who were found to be HIV/AIDS positive against public disclosure (*X v Y and others*).

The guidance issued by the Department of Health (2005) on the management of infected healthcare workers and patient notification is based on a new policy (announced in November 2001) on patient notification when a healthcare worker is found to be infected with HIV. It was no longer necessary to notify every patient who has undergone an exposure-prone procedure by an infected healthcare worker because of the low risk of transmission and the anxiety caused to patients and the wider public. The Department of Health recommended that the decision on whether a patient notification exercise should be undertaken should be assessed on a case-by-case basis using a criteria-based framework. Directors of Public Health are responsible for deciding whether patient notification is necessary, and the United Kingdom Advisory Panel for Health Care Workers infected with Blood-borne Viruses is available to provide advice.

The Court of Appeal has held that the identity of the healthcare worker in *H (a healthcare worker) v Associated Newspapers Ltd* who developed HIV, and also the identity of his NHS employer should not be published in the newspaper to prevent his being identified. His speciality could however be disclosed.

The third annual report 2007–2010 of the United Kingdom Advisory Panel is available online (www.hpa.org.uk/Topics/InfectiousDiseases/

BoodborneVirusesAndOccupationalExposure/UKAP). Advice can be sought from the United Kingdom Advisory Panel on its enquiry pro forma available online. Other Department of Health guidance on HIV, hepatitis B and C can be downloaded from the HPA website (www.hpa.org.uk).

A consultation on a review of Department of Health guidance on HIV infected healthcare workers closed in March 2012 and at the time of writing recommendations on new guidance are awaited.

It has been suggested that one of the main reason for the increase in HIV positive people is refugee immigrants and in consequence the Department of Health has strengthened its guidelines on the health clearance for serious communicable diseases for new healthcare workers (Department of Health, 2003b). This was updated by the Department of Health in 2007. The House of Lords has held that expulsion of a failed immigrant to a country which could not provide medical treatment equivalent to that which she had received in the UK was not a breach of Article 3 of the European Convention (the right not to be subjected to torture or inhuman and degrading treatment or punishment) (*N v Secretary of State for the Home Department*).

The National strategy for sexual health and HIV services is considered in *Chapter 6*.

Cross-infection and hospital-acquired infections

The implications for the midwife of hospital-acquired infections are clear: she is personally and professionally responsible for ensuring that her patients are safe and that she works in an environment where high standards of cleanliness and hygiene are maintained.

The last 15 years have seen a vast campaign by the government to control the level of hospital-acquired infections, and in particular the high level of infections and deaths from meticillin-resistant *Staphylococcus aureus* (MRSA) and more recently *Clostridium difficile*. At one point these infections were thought to be irradicable. However, there are now signs that, as a result of much clearer and enforced standards of cross-infection control, there is a fall in the infection rates. The remit of the Care Quality Commission includes inspection of cross-infection controls in hospitals. A Risk and Regulatory Advisory Council was set up to review regulations on health and safety. Its first project was to look at the government initiatives in relation to MRSA to assess their effectiveness (Bennett, 2008). Further information can be found on the Department of Health website.

Scenario 16.1. Hepatitis C: Discussion

The midwife, if she was aware of her health status and failed to notify her employer of her condition, faces the four arenas of accountability: dismissal from her job; herself and/or her employer being sued by the mother in the civil courts; being reported to the Nursing and Midwifery Council for fitness to practise proceedings; and being prosecuted for causing grievous bodily harm. (See the case of *R v Dica* above:) Here an offence could have been committed by the midwife who, knowing that she presented a risk to the mother, failed to take reasonable precautions to prevent that risk occurring (Griffith, 2007). Not all these scenarios will necessarily result in the same outcome. The criminal prosecution may fail, but the civil action by the mother against the employer might succeed. The midwife might lose her job, but not her registration before the Nursing and Midwifery Council, in which case she could not practise as a registered midwife.

The midwife and public health

The significant of the role of the midwife in the promotion of public health was recognised in *Midwifery 2020: Delivering expectations* (www.midwifery2020. org) which recognised public health and the role of the midwife as one of five work streams. The report emphasised the important contribution that maternity services can make in addressing health inequalities. It provides key recommendations on the role of the community midwife in knowing the health needs of the local community, the importance of her being networked into a local health and social care system, being proactive in identifying women at risk, etc.

Conclusions

Responsibilities for public health have changed as a result of recent legislation, and local authorities have taken back the duties they once had. The Health Protection Agency's responsibilities have transferred to a new organisation, Public Health England. It remains to be seen how effective and efficient these new management arrangements will be in ensuring high standards of public health control. Standards of public health and risks of cross-infections, both nationally and internationally, are still on the priority agenda for the NHS. High standards of infection control, implementation of the laws relating to notification of infectious diseases, the guidance on AIDS/HIV-infected healthcare professionals, and laws relating to the control of infections are all central to the safety of the mother and child. The midwife has a personal and professional role to play in the maintenance of high standards of infection control for which she can be held accountable. She should also be aware of the rules relating to confidentiality which are considered in *Chapter 4*. Changes in public health organisations including Health Watch and Health and Wellbeing Boards are considered in *Chapter 19*.

Questions and exercises

1. You visit a client and discover that she has been suffering from food poisoning since visiting a restaurant the night before. What action do you take?
2. A client tells you that her husband has just been diagnosed as HIV positive. In what ways, if any, will this affect your practice as a midwife in relation to the client?
3. In the case cited in Question 2, which persons, if any, would you inform of the situation?
4. How can standards of cross-infection control be improved in your own department and in the community?
5. Access the website of the Public Health England (or your own equivalent) and look at its guidelines for the diagnosis, treatment and management of sexually transmitted diseases and HIV.

References

Bennett R (2008) Risk assessment watchdog set up to halt march of the nanny state. *The Times* **16 January**

Bott J (2005) *HIV and midwifery practice*. Quay Books, London

British HIV Association (2008) *Guidelines for the management of HIV infection in pregnant women*. BHIVA, London

Chief Medical Officer of Health (2004) *Stopping tuberculosis in England*. Department of Health, London

Department of Health (2003a) *Screening for infectious diseases in pregnancy: Standards to support the UK antenatal screening programme*. HMSO, London

Department of Health (2003b) *Health clearance for serious communicable diseases. New health care workers draft guidance*. HMSO, London

Department of Health (2004a) *Children in need and bloodborne viruses: HIV and hepatitis*. HMSO, London

Department of Health (2004b) *HIV and infant feeding: Guidance from the UK Chief Medical Officers' Expert Advisory Group on AIDS*. HMSO, London

Department of Health (2005) *AIDS/HIV infected health care workers: Guidance on the management of infected health care workers and patient notification.* HMSO, London

Department of Health (2007) *Clearance for tuberculosis, hepatitis B, hepatitis C and HIV for new healthcare workers.* HMSO, London

Griffith R (2007) Criminal liability for spreading sexually transmitted diseases. *British Journal of Midwifery* **15**(7): 444

H (a healthcare worker) v Associated Newspapers Ltd and H (a healthcare worker) v N (a health authority) [2002] EWCA Civ 195 Lloyd's Rep Med [2002] 210

Horsnall M (2002) Patients to be told of HIV dentist. *The Times* **28 February**

N v Secretary of State for the Home Department The Times 9 May 2005 HL

Nursing and Midwifery Council (2004) *Midwives rules and standards.* NMC, London

Nursing and Midwifery Council (2012) *Midwives rules and standards.* NMC, London

Nursing and Midwifery Council (Midwives) Rules Order of Council 2004 Statutory Instrument 2004/1764

R v Dica [2004] EWCA Crim 1103

R v Konzani [2005] EWCA Crim 706

Re C (HIV Test) [1999] 2 FLR 1004

Rumbelow H (1999) Judge orders mother to test baby for HIV. *The Times* **4 September**

The Health Protection (Notification) Regulations 2010 No. 659

The Times (2005) News item: Doctors issue hepatitis alert. *The Times* **10 May**

UKCC (1998) *Midwives Rules and code of practice.* UKCC, London

Wilkinson v Downton [1987] 2 QB 57

Williams J (2011) Testing for sexually transmitted infections in pregnancy. *Practising Midwife* **14**(2): 36–41

Wilson S (2011) HIV and pregnancy: Challenges in practice. *Practising Midwife* **14**(3): 16–18

X v Y and others [1988] 2 All ER 648

Section E

Specialist areas

Child protection

Introduction

Midwives may become involved in issues relating to child protection. It may be, for example, that other children of the pregnant woman have to be taken into care, or the midwife might be concerned about the health or safety of the unborn child immediately following delivery. It is essential that the midwife has an understanding of the relevant laws and knows the action that she must take. This was emphasised in a publication by the Chief Nursing Officer in 2004 (Department of Health, 2004). This publication reviewed the nursing, midwifery and health visiting contribution to supporting vulnerable children and young people. In the light of the Green Paper *Every child matters* (see below), it set a clear strategy for achieving improvements in all services for children and young people. (See *Chapter 3* for the law relating to consent by a child or young person under 18 years, *Chapter 6* for the legal issues arising with teenage pregnancies, and *Chapter 12* on disputes over letting die.) More detailed information on child protection and the midwife can be found in Fraser and Nolan (2004) and Chapman (2002, 2003).

The history of child protection legislation is the account of tragic cases of child neglect and murder leading to legislative changes and new procedures. The Children Act 1948 resulted from the death of Dennis O'Neil in foster care and the Curtis Report and the death of Maria Colwell in 1973 led to the establishment of area child protection committees and ultimately the Children Act 1989. This latter Act brought into place a new framework for the law relating to children and, while not repealing all previous legislation on children, it introduced significant new provisions. Subsequently, the death of Victoria Climbié was followed by the Laming Inquiry which led to the Green Paper *Every child matters* and the

Children Act 2004. Further developments following the death of Baby P in 2007 are still being implemented or are under consideration. All these reports and changes can be accessed by a search of the internet.

The main areas covered by the Children Act 1989 are shown in *Box 17.1.*

Box 17.1. Provisions of the Children Act 1989

- General principles.
- Orders with respect to children in family proceedings.
- Local authority support for children and families.
- Care and supervision.
- Protection of children.
- Community homes.
- Voluntary homes and voluntary organisations.
- Registered children's homes.
- Private arrangements for fostering children.
- Child minding and day care for young children.
- Secretary of State's supervisory functions and responsibilities.
- Miscellaneous and general.

In this chapter we shall consider the principles established by the Children Act 1989 and the law relating to child protection. The status of the fetus is considered in *Chapter 7*. The basic principle is that an unborn child lacks a legal personality and cannot be taken into care, nor made a ward of court. See the case of *Re F (in utero)*.

The Children Act 1989

Part 1 of the Act sets out the basic principles which are to apply in the law relating to children. They are shown in *Box 17.2*. Of significance is the fact that the Act places the emphasis upon the duties and responsibilities of the parent rather than the rights of the parent. Even where the child is not living with the parent, this does not remove from the parent his/her responsibilities to the child.

- Where a child's father and mother were married to each other at the time of his birth, they shall each have parental responsibility for the child.

Box 17.2. Principles in Part 1 of the Children Act 1989

Part 1. Welfare of the child:

i. When a court determines any question in relation to the upbringing of a child or the administration of a child's property and the income from it, the child's welfare shall be the court's paramount consideration.

ii. In any proceedings relating to the upbringing of the child, the court must have regard to the general principle that any delay in determining the question is likely to prejudice the welfare of the child.

iii. The court shall have regard in particular to:

   a. the ascertainable wishes and feelings of the child concerned (considered in the light of his age and understanding),

   b. his physical, emotional and educational needs,

   c. the likely effect on him of any change in his circumstances,

   d. his age, sex, background and any characteristics of his which the court considers relevant,

   e. any harm which he has suffered or is at risk of suffering,

   f. how capable each of his parents, and any other person in relation to whom the court considers the question to be relevant, is of meeting his needs,

   g. the range of powers available to the court under this Act in the proceedings in question.

- Where they were not married at the time of his birth, the mother shall have responsibility for the child; the father shall not have parental responsibility for the child unless he acquires it in accordance with the Act and subsequent amendments.

(Provisions as to how parental responsibility can be acquired are laid down in the Act and have subsequently been amended to enable an unmarried father and step-parents to be given parental responsibility.)

- More than one person may have parental responsibility for the same child at the same time.
- Where more than one person has parental responsibility for a child, each of them may act alone and without the other (or others) in meeting that responsibility.

Parental responsibility is defined as:

...all rights, duties, powers and responsibilities and authority which by law a parent of a child has in relation to the child and his property.

Parents who fail to take reasonable care for the health and welfare of their children could be guilty of a criminal offence (see *Chapter 12*).

The court has the power to provide for the father to have parental responsibility where the couple were not married at the time of the child's birth.

The Children Act 1989 gives power to a person who does not have parental responsibility to make decisions on behalf of the child. The Children Act 1989 Section 3(5) provides that a person who (a) does not have parental responsibility for a particular child, but (b) has care of the child, may (subject to the provision of this Act) do what is reasonable in all the circumstances of the case for the purpose of safeguarding or promoting the child's welfare. This would probably include giving consent to necessary emergency treatment in the absence of the parents. In addition, professional staff would have a duty of care to take action to save life in such circumstances.

Parental rights and responsibilities

As seen above, the Children Act 1989 places the emphasis on parental responsibilities rather than parental rights. Such responsibilities remain after divorce and care orders, and will only cease with the death of the parent or the death or adoption of the child.

Where the parents are unmarried, only the mother has parental responsibilities unless the father has taken steps to ensure that he is legally recognised as having parental responsibilities. From December 2003 it has been possible for the unmarried couple to register the birth of the child together and thereby the unmarried father acquires parental responsibilities. A parental responsibility agreement can be drawn up in other cases (access www.youandyourrights.co.uk/32.asp for further details and the relevant forms). The court can also make an order conferring parental responsibilities.

Sperm donors

In a family court ruling on 31 January 2013 on an application under Section 8 of the Children Act 1989 it was held that a sperm donor has the right to contact with his children. The ruling was that a sperm donor did not need to have a sexual

relationship with a mother in order to influence the child's upbringing – *S and D and E and in the matter of Z (a minor) T and X and Y.*

Child protection

Where the midwife has reasonable cause to suspect that a child in the family of a client is being abused she must take the appropriate action. To make a diagnosis of suspected child abuse is a weighty matter.

Following the Inquiry conducted by Lord Laming into the death of Victoria Climbié (www.victoria-climbie-inquiry.org.uk/) the Department of Health (2003a) published a detailed response, *Keeping children safe,* and this was followed by a single source document for safeguarding children (Department of Health, 2003b). This document aimed to provide a single set of advice for all those involved in the care of children, and it should replace local guidance. It was followed by a Green paper, *Every child matters,* published in September 2003 (Department of Health, 2003c). The Green Paper focused on four main areas:

- Supporting parents and carers.
- Early intervention and effective protection.
- Accountability and integration – locally, regionally and nationally.
- Workforce reform.

The Green Paper was followed by the Children Act 2004 (see below). *Working together to safeguard children* (Department of Health, 1999) is a guide to inter-agency working to safeguard and promote the welfare of children. The 2010 edition of the guide replaces the earlier publication, *Working Together under the Children Act 1989,* published in 1991 and revised in 1999 and 2006. It sets out how individuals and organisations should work together to safeguard and promote the welfare of children. The guidance provides a national framework within which agencies and professionals at local level (individually and jointly) draw up and agree on their own ways of working together to safeguard and promote the welfare of children. Part 1 provides statutory guidance and Part 2 provides non-statutory guidance. The coverage of both parts are shown in *Box 17.3.* The document can be downloaded from the website (www.education.gov.uk/publications). In June 2012 three consultation documents were issued to update the guidance (www. workingtogetheronline.co.uk/).

Box 17.3. Parts 1 and 2 of *Working together to safeguard children*

Part 1 Statutory guidance
- Working together to safeguard and promote the welfare of children and families.
- Roles and responsibilities.
- Local safeguarding children boards.
- Training, development and supervision for inter-agency working.
- Managing individual cases.
- Supplementary guidance on safeguarding and promoting the welfare of children.
- Child death review processes and serious case reviews.

Part 2 Non-statutory guidance
- Lessons from research.
- Implementing the principles on working with children and their families.
- Safeguarding and promoting the welfare of children who may be particularly vulnerable.
- Managing individuals who pose a risk to children.

Children Act 2004

Under the Children Act 2004, many of the recommendations of the Green Paper *Every child matters* were implemented.

A Children's Commissioner for England (one was already appointed in Wales and another in Scotland) was established with the function of promoting awareness of the views and interests of children. In particular he was to be concerned with the views and interests of children so far as relating to various aspects of their well-being including:

- Physical and mental health and emotional well-being.
- Protection from harm and neglect.
- Education, training and recreation.
- The contribution made by them to society.
- Social and economic well-being.

The Commissioner can, under Section 3, conduct an inquiry into a case involving a child if he is satisfied that the case raises issues of public policy, with a view to making recommendations about those issues.

The Children's Commissioners for Scotland and Wales have slightly different functions. Each has a duty to submit an annual report.

Part 2 of the Act is concerned with improving the accountability for children's services within each local authority area. The local authority is required to make arrangements to promote cooperation between the various agencies which are involved in child protection, including the police authority, the local probation board, a youth offending team, a strategic health authority and primary care trust, and persons providing services under the Learning and Skills Act 2000.

Many specified agencies, including primary care trusts (now clinical commissioning groups), NHS trusts, and NHS foundation trusts are required to make arrangements together to safeguard and promote the welfare of children. Under Section 12 the Secretary of State can, by regulations, require children's services authorities to establish and operate databases containing information about children at risk.

Local Safeguarding Children's Board

Each children's services authority must establish a Local Safeguarding Children's Board whose membership derives from the agencies specified as partners of the local authority in child protection. These Boards replace the non-statutory Area Child Protection Committees.

The functions of the Board are:

- To coordinate what is done by each person or body represented on the Board for the purpose of safeguarding and promoting the welfare of children in the area of the authority, and
- To ensure the effectiveness of what is done by each such person or body for those purposes.

The Secretary of State may prescribe further functions of the Local Safeguarding Children's Board by regulation. In addition, regulations can require each children's services authority to prepare and publish a plan setting out the authority's strategy for discharging their functions in relation to children and relevant young persons.

Director of children's services

Each Children's Services Authority is required to appoint a director of children's services covering both educational and social services functions. In addition, a lead member for children's services is to be designated by each children's services authority. This would be a political appointment. Under Section 20, joint area reviews of children's services can be carried out by the persons specified in the section. These include the Chief Inspector of Schools, the Commission for Social Care Inspection and the Care Quality Commission (replacing the Commission for Healthcare Audit and Inspection).

Among the many other provisions of the Act, Section 58 restricts the grounds on which the battery of a child may be justified as reasonable punishment (see below).

A Minister for Children, Young People and Families has been created in the Department for Education and Skills.

Baby P

Baby P died in Haringey as a result of appalling abuse, despite being seen on over 60 occasions by health professionals, social services staff, police and others. He was known to be at risk. The Director of Children's Services was dismissed. (She subsequently succeeded in a claim for unfair dismissal.) The GP who saw Baby P eight days before his death was found guilty by the General Medical Council of a serious breach of a professional duty for not acting upon the visible signs of child abuse. Lord Laming was invited to report on the failings which had led to Baby P's death. Lord Laming's report published on 12 March 2009 put forward 52 recommendations for improving child protection services. Some of these are shown in *Box 17.4*.

The Baby P case shows that coordination between the various services involved meant no-one took control and that there were serious failures by doctors and health visitors to detect evidence of non-accidental injuries. There were also poor links between health and social services. As a consequence of Government action, £60 million was to be made available to bring about changes in child protection. These changes included: all children's services directors to be sent for compulsory training in the realities of frontline social work under plans to drive up standards in child protection (Bennett, 2009). A course was to be created at the National College for School Leadership.

Box 17.4. Recommendations from Lord Laming's Report in March 2009

- National agency to oversee reform implementation. Cabinet minister responsible for success.
- Social work students must get child protection training and work experience before starting their job.
- Increased quality of degrees; introduction of a children's social worker postgraduate qualification.
- Court fees for applying to take children into care should be scrapped if they affect decisions.
- Ofsted inspectors examining children's social services to have child protection experience.
- A national strategy to address recruitment problems.
- Guidelines on caseloads.
- Directors with no child protection experience should appoint an experienced social work manager to support them.

The Government's initial response to Laming was published in 2009 and a year later it published a progress report in March 2010 (Department of Health, 2010a). It looked at national leadership in the form of a Cabinet forum on which four key Secretaries of State sat; the appointment of a Chief Adviser on the Safety of Children; the establishment of a National Safeguarding Delivery Unit; the setting up of Safeguarding National Indicators and Targets; and revisions to *Working together to safeguard children*. It also reviewed the system for regulation and inspection and the role of the Care Quality Commission. It considered the revised guidance for Area Child Protection Officers on investigating child abuse and safeguarding children and the comprehensive toolkit for forces to incorporate into practice. A table sets out a comparison of Laming recommendation in 2009, the Government's response in May 2009, and progress in March 2010. An annexe provides a template for serious case review executive summaries. *Working together to safeguard children* was updated in the light of the recommendations (Department of Health, 2010b).

The Royal College of Nursing (2003) published guidance on child protection and the nurse, and emphasised the need for each trust to have a designated or named nurse for child protection, have child protection procedures in place and to have a defined policy on raising concerns about colleagues.

Procedure for the management of child abuse

There should be in existence an agreed procedure for the management of child abuse cases developed on the lines indicated in the single source document for safeguarding children (Department of Health, 2003b). An interactive web-based version of *Working together to safeguard children* was set up in March 2010 (www.workingtogetheronline. co.uk/index.htm). The website is a useful source for materials. The local child protection procedure should specifically refer to the role of the midwifery department if child abuse is suspected. This would require any professional staff working in the department who suspect that there is a possibility of ill-treatment, serious neglect, or sexual or emotional abuse of a child, to inform the senior midwife or consultant in charge of the department who should contact a consultant paediatrician. If the consultant paediatrician confirms this possibility, then she or he should inform the social services department immediately, according to the agreed procedure.

Where a woman is known to be a potential danger to her unborn child it is essential that a court order should be obtained before the child is removed from her at birth. In the case of *R (on the application of G) v Nottingham City Council* where the birth took place at 2.00 a.m. and the baby was immediately handed over to social services without a court order, the court held that there was a breach of the Children Act 1989 and also a breach of Article 8 (see also *Chapter 7*). In the case of *Coventry City Council and C,B, CA, CH* the court gave guidance on the application of Section 20 of the Children Act 1989 under which the mother had agreed to the removal of her baby after birth. She had claimed that the local authority was in breach of her human rights. The local authority accepted that it should not have sought consent under Section 20 and that the removal of the baby was not a proportionate response to the risks that then existed and that there was a breach of Article 8 rights of both mother and child.

Dangerous colleagues

Any midwife must also be alert to the possibility of a colleague causing harm to a patient. The lessons from the case of Beverly Allitt should be taken on board by midwives. Beverly Allitt, a state enrolled nurse, was convicted of murdering four children, of attempting to murder three others and of causing grievous bodily harm to six more. She was sentenced to life imprisonment on every count. An independent inquiry, chaired by Sir Cecil Clothier (1994), made significant and substantial recommendations. (See also the Clifford Ayling and Rodney Ledward Inquiries, *Chapter 5*.)

What about the midwife's duty of confidentiality?

The Nursing and Midwifery Council (NMC) *Code of professional conduct: Standards for conduct, performance and ethics* (Nursing and Midwifery Council, 2008) recognises the duty of registrants to respect people's confidentiality but also requires registrants to:

> ...disclose information if you believe someone may be at risk of harm, in line with the law of the country in which you are practising.

A breach of confidentiality may be justified in the public interest. This would include any reasonable suspicion of child abuse or of colleagues. Such information could be passed on to the appropriate agencies without fear of a successful action for breach of confidentiality by the parents (*Chapter 4*).

If a suspected case is reported to the police, social services, or the NSPCC and it turns out that the suspicions are unfounded, the parents have no right to be given the name of the informant. The House of Lords has held that it is not in the public interest for such information to be disclosed to the parents (*D v NSPCC*).

What if suspected child abuse is confirmed by the consultant paediatrician?

The agreed arrangements laid down by the Local Safeguarding Children Board should be followed immediately. The provisions of the Children Act 1989 enable the orders set out in *Box 17.5* to be made.

Further details of the Sections shown in *Box 17.5* and the other provisions of the Children Act 1989 can be found in the Department of Health guides to the Children Act 1989 (Department of Health, 1990) and subsequent guidance. The amended Act can be accessed on the legislation website (www.legislation.gov.uk/ukpga/1989/).

The extent of the local authority's duty of care to children under Section 1 of the Children Act was considered in the case of *Pierce v Doncaster Metropolitan BC* where a boy, who suffered abuse by his parents, won his case against the local authority.

Unfounded allegation of child abuse

In some situations the allegation of child abuse is found to be unjustified and a reason for the child's apparent injuries or disabilities discovered. For example,

---

Box 17.5. Orders under Part 5 of the Children Act 1989

- Child assessment order (Section 43).
- Emergency protection order (EPO) (Section 44).
- Powers to include exclusion requirements in EPO (Section 44A).
- Undertakings in EPOs (Section 44B).
- Duration of EPOs (Section 45).
- Removal and accommodation of children by police in cases of emergency (Section 46).
- Local authority duty to investigate (Section 47).
- Powers to assist in discovery of children who may be in need of emergency protection (Section 48).
- Abduction of children in care (Section 49).

---

in one case (*RK and MK v Oldham NHS Trust*), following a case conference, a baby was taken into care on the basis of medical evidence which suggested that a spiral fracture of her femur was evidence of non-accidental injury. Subsequently it was discovered that the baby suffered from brittle bone disease and the child was returned to the parents nine months after the hospital admission. The parents sued and action was also brought in the name of the child arguing a breach of negligence and breach of Article 8 of the European Convention of Human Rights. The claims failed on the grounds that the child had suffered no injury for which the law recognised a remedy; a duty of care was not owed by the defendants to the parents (the doctor owed a duty of care to the child and his obligations within the multi-disciplinary process militated against the doctor owing any additional duty to the parents in relation to the diagnosis which commenced such a process) and to hold the doctor liable to the parents would cut across the statutory scheme set up for the protection of the child. The Human Rights Act, which came into force on 2 October 2000, was not retrospective and the cause of action arose in September 1998 and June 1999.

This case, together with other similar cases, was heard by the House of Lords in April 2005 and it was held that healthcare and other child care professionals did not owe a common law duty of care to parents against whom they had made unfounded allegations of child abuse and who, as a result, suffered psychiatric injury (*D v East Berkshire Community Health NHS Trust and Another; MAK and Another v Dewsbury Healthcare NHS Trust and Another; RK and Another v Oldham NHS Trust and Another*).

However, in 2010 this was overruled in an appeal to the European Court of Human Rights which held that there were breaches of the European Convention on Human Rights (*MAK and RK v United Kingdom*). The parents, who had failed in their applications before the House of Lords, succeeded in their claim for compensation.

On 28 September 2012 *The Times* reported that Lorraine Moss, a mother who had spent 10 years trying to prove that her child was seriously ill was vindicated. She had been suspected of Munchausen by proxy and child proceedings were begun by child protection officers but dropped in 2010. Subsequently, the child was diagnosed with rheumatic fever, autoimmune thyroiditis, lupus, degenerative disc disease, postural orthostatic tachycardia syndrome, adrenal dysfunction and suspected Addison's disease.

In one case, Chana al-Alas and Rohan Wray were acquitted of killing their child Jayden of 18 weeks when it was discovered that multiple fractures found after his death in 2009 were caused by congenital rickets and not by abuse. A second child who had been removed from the couple at birth was returned to them in April 2012 (*The Guardian*, 2012). The Family Court judge, Mrs Justice Thais, stated that baby Jayden received sub-optimal care from University College Hospital, London and Great Ormond Street Hospital, London.

Duty of local authority

Recent cases have held local authorities liable in respect of failures to take action to prevent abuse and in making negligent adoption and fostering arrangements. Thus two people who had been abused as children by their step-father succeeded in their claim that the local authority had failed to provide an appropriate means of obtaining a determination of their allegations that the local authority had failed to protect them from serious ill-treatment (*DP and JC v United Kingdom*) and therefore were in breach of Article 13.

(Article 13 is not included in Schedule 1 of the Human Rights Act 1998 but states that everyone whose rights and freedoms as set forth in this Convention are violated, shall have an effective remedy before a national authority notwithstanding that the violation has been committed by persons acting in an official capacity.)

On the facts of the case there was no breach of Article 3.

In contrast, in another case (*E and others v United Kingdom*), the European Court of Human Rights held that where the local authority failed to protect children from sexual abuse by the step-father, the local authority was in violation of Article 3 and Article 13 and was held liable to pay damages. In the case of *Z v*

UK the Commission found a violation of Article 3 and Article 13 arising from the failure of the local authority to take action in respect of serious ill-treatment and neglect caused to four siblings by the parents over a period of more than four and a half years. In the case of *TP and KM v the UK*, an emergency place of safety, based in large part on video evidence from a child suspected of being abused, was misinterpreted as to the abuser by the local authority and not disclosed to the mother despite her requests. Mother and child complained that the local authority took the child into care on the basis of a careless assumption of fact in violation of Article 8. They also argued violation of Article 6 in that they were denied access by decision of the domestic courts to sue the local authority and were denied their rights to seek a remedy under Article 13. They succeeded in their claims under Article 3 and 13 but not under Article 6.

In another case against a local authority (*A and Another v Essex County Council*), this time by a couple who adopted a violent child, the couple won their case that they should have been notified by the local authority of the boy's serious and emotional behavioural difficulties. The court held that the local authority could be held vicariously liable for negligence by its employees in failing to fulfil their duty of care owed to those who might foreseeably be injured if the duty was carelessly exercised.

Protection of vulnerable adults and children

Various measures have been taken in law to prevent those who are likely to abuse children from having contact with them. The Protection of Children Act 1999, the Sexual Offenders Act 1997, and the Care Standards Act 2000 enable employers to establish if there are grounds for not employing prospective employees.

The Protection of Children Act 1999

The Protection of Children Act 1999 made statutory the Department of Health's Consultancy Service Index list and it required childcare organisations to refer the names of individuals considered unsuitable to work with children for inclusion on the list. Subsequently, the Criminal Records Bureau acted as a one-stop shop in the carrying out of checks. On 1 December 2012 the Criminal Records Bureau and the Independent Safeguarding Authority merged to become the Disclosure and Barring Service (Sections 87 and 88 of the Protection of Freedoms Act 2012). Its primary aim is to help employers make safer recruitment decisions and prevent unsuitable people from working with vulnerable groups, including children.

Further information can be obtained from the Disclosure and Barring Service website (www.homeoffice.gov.uk/dbs).

The Sexual Offenders Act 1997

The Sexual Offenders Act 1997 was passed in order to ensure that once a sex offender had served his/her sentence and was about to be released, he/she would still be subject to some form of supervision to protect persons against the risk of his re-offending. Part 1 of the Act requires the notification of information to the police by persons who have committed certain sexual offences.

Sexual Offences (Amendment) Act 2000

Under this Act the age at which certain sexual acts (for example, homosexual acts in private) are lawful is reduced to 16 years and a new defence is available so that when one party to homosexual activity is below the age of 16 and the other over 16, the younger one does not commit any offence. However, a new offence is introduced for a person "A" over 18 years to have sexual intercourse with a person or engage in any other sexual activity with another person "B" if A is in a position of trust in relation to B. "Position of trust" is defined in Section 4, where B is detained in an institution or resident in a home, or cared for in a hospital, residential care home or nursing home, where A is looking after such persons, or A looks after persons under 18 who are receiving full-time education at an educational institution and B is receiving such education.

Sexual Offences Act 2003

This Act follows the White Paper on protecting the public from sex offenders (Home Office, 2002). Part 1 makes new provision about sexual offences, covers non-consensual offences of rape, assault by penetration, sexual assault and causing a person to engage in sexual activity without consent. It is an offence for a person intentionally to penetrate with his penis (Section 5) or with any other body part or object (Section 6) the vagina, anus or mouth of a child under 13 years. Whether or not the child consented to this penetration is irrelevant. Under Section 7, sexual assault of a child under 13 is an offence and, under Section 8, causing or inciting a child under 13 to engage in sexual activity is an offence. The Act also covers child sex offences and offences involving an abuse of a position of trust towards a child. New offences give protection to persons with a mental disorder.

The age of child in the Protection of Children Act 1978 has been amended to 18 and defences are provided for in limited cases where the child is 16 or over and the defendant is the child's partner. Further safeguards for children and vulnerable adults are given by Part 5 of the Protection of Freedoms Act 2012.

New guidance has been issued by the Department of Health on the Carers and Disabled Children Act 2000 and the Carers (Equal Opportunities) Act 2004 for carers and people with parental responsibility for disabled children (Department of Health, 2005).

Disputes with parents

Parents may not always take the best course for their children and the question arises at what stage would a midwife be justified in intervening. For example, in *Chapter 16* a case is discussed when the judge ordered an HIV test to be carried out on a baby, contrary to the wishes of the mother. The situation in relation to triple vaccine gives rise to similar issues. The ultimate criteria for action to be taken is that the paramount consideration is the welfare of the child. The midwives' documentation will be extremely important in any dispute with parents. In December 2013 new government proposals were published to ensure that all children attending accident and emergency departments because of injuries should be on a national database shared between clinicians so that a reasonable judgement could be made on whether the injury results from abuse (Smyth, 2012) This national database is to come into being by 2015.

Failure to take approved medical advice

In some circumstances, the failure of a parent to take approved medical advice for their child can result in criminal proceedings (see *Chapter 12*).

Approved medical opinion

As in the HIV case, in almost all cases where parents have disputed medical recommendations about treatment for their children, the courts have supported the doctors' views. One significant case where this did not happen, *Re C (a minor)(medical treatment – refusal of parental consent)*, was where parents refused to permit a liver transplant to take place on their toddler. The Court of Appeal held that in the very specific circumstances of the case (the parents lived abroad and as health professionals they believed the transplant not to be in the best interests of the child) the transplant would not be ordered against their wishes. In contrast, there are several cases where the courts have ordered blood transfusions to be given to children of Jehovah's Witnesses. For example, *Re E(a minor)(wardship: medical treatment) Family Division* (see *Chapters 3* and *12* on letting die).

Corporal punishment

A decision of the European Court of Human Rights ruled that for a parent to use corporal punishment on a child could be a breach of Article 3 (see *Chapter 2*) (*A v The United Kingdom*). A step-father had on several occasions beaten a 9-year-old boy with a garden cane. The step-father had been prosecuted for assault occasioning actual bodily harm, but had been acquitted by the jury who accepted his defence that the caning had been necessary and reasonable to discipline the boy. The European Court of Human Rights held that ill-treatment must attain a minimum level of severity if it is to fall within the scope of Article 3. It depended on all the circumstances of the case, such as the nature and context of the treatment, its duration, its physical and mental effects and in some instances, the sex, age, and state of health of the victim. In finding that there had been a breach of Article 3 the court awarded the boy £10000 against the UK government, and costs. The UK government acknowledged that UK law failed to provide adequate protection to children and should be amended. Subsequently, guidance was issued by the government on the use of corporal punishment against children and the law was changed. A defence of reasonable punishment cannot be used where a person is charged with criminal offences of causing actual bodily harm to a child or faces civil action (Children Act 2004 Section 58).

What is meant by actual bodily harm? The authoritative textbook, *Archbold*, on criminal procedure and evidence (Richardson, 2012) states that actual bodily harm has its ordinary meaning and includes any hurt or injury calculated to interfere with the health or comfort of the victim: such hurt or injury need not be permanent, but must be more than merely transient or trifling. It may include a momentary loss of consciousness, where there is injurious impairment to the victim's sensory functions. It is also capable of including psychiatric injury, but it does not include mere emotions, such as fear, distress or panic.

The Children are Unbeatable! Alliance campaigns for the UK law to be modified to provide children with the same protection that adults enjoy (www.childrenareunbeatable.org.uk/).

Access to the midwife's and other professionals' records

Rights of access to manual and computerised records are considered in *Chapter 4.*

Children, Young People and Maternity Services National Service Framework

In September 2004 the National Service Framework for Children, Young People and Maternity Services was published (www.doh.gov.uk/nsf/children). It is considered in *Chapter 6.*

A report prepared by Sir Ian Kennedy in 2010 on cultural barriers to improving services for children led to an independent forum being established. The Forum, which reported in 2012 (Department of Health, 2012), identified eight themes that are crucial in making improvements in children's and young people's health:

* Putting children and young people and their families at the heart of what happens.
* Acting early and intervening at the right time.
* Integration and partnership.
* Safe and sustainable services.
* Workforce education and training.
* Knowledge and evidence.
* Leadership, accountability and assurance.
* Incentives for driving service improvement.

The reports are available on the Department of Health website (www.dh.gov.uk).

Scenario 17.1. Suspected child abuse: Discussion

Mavis has a duty of care to the pregnant girl. This includes the responsibility of ensuring that she is protected from abuse. She should make her concerns known to the person identified in the department's policy on safeguarding the welfare of children and follow through any action specified.

Conclusions

Midwives have a significant role to play in child protection and may become involved in giving evidence. They should take advice from senior management or from lawyers to the trust. They should ensure that they have the requisite training in child protection. Their documentation is likely to come under close scrutiny in any conflict (see *Chapter 9*). A new strategy was implemented by the Chief Nursing Officer to ensure that Nursing and Midwifery Council registered practitioners played a major role in the protection of these vulnerable persons. A children's health and maternity services E-bulletin was set up by the Department of Health to enable healthcare practitioners to have regular updates on activities supporting the *Every child matters: Change for children* agenda (Department of Health E-bulletin: MB-Childrens-NSF@dh.gsi.gov.uk). The case of Baby P has shown that there can be no complacency in child protection.

Questions and exercises

1. A 15-year-old is expecting a child and an internal examination is necessary. The client is considered too young to give a valid consent. Could consent be given by an aunt who is accompanying her?
2. There is concern about the possibility of a client abusing her two-year-old child, and about the future safety of the unborn child. What action should the midwife take?
3. A 13-year-old girl who is expecting a baby is considered to be in need of care. What should the midwife do?
4. Access the revised document, *Working together to safeguard children*, on the internet (http://www.workingtogetheronline.co.uk/) and consider the extent to which your internal procedures comply with its recommendations.
5. You suspect that a colleague may be abusing children in her care. What action do you take? What guidance is available to assist you?

References

A and Another v Essex County Council Times Law Report 24 January 2003

A v The United Kingdom [1998] ECHR 85

Bennett R (2009) Child services chiefs to be retrained in family risks. *The Times* **12 March**

Boseley S, Butler P (2012) Baby Jayden case renews concerns over rickets and 'child abuse' allegations. *The Guardian* **20 April**

Chapman T (2002) Safeguarding the welfare of children. Part one. *British Journal of Midwifery* **10**(9): 569–72

Chapman T (2003) Safeguarding the welfare of children. Part two. *British Journal of Midwifery* **11**(2): 116–9

Chief Nursing Officer (2004) *Department of Health review of the nursing, midwifery and health visiting contribution to vulnerable children and young people.* Department of Health, London

Clothier Report (1994) *The Allitt Inquiry: An independent inquiry relating to deaths and injuries on the children's ward at Grantham and Kesteven General Hospital during the period February to April 1991.* HMSO, London

Coventry City Council and C,B, CA, CH [2012] EWHC 2190

D v East Berkshire Community Health NHS Trust and Another; MAK and Another v Dewsbury Healthcare NHS Trust and Another; RK and Another v Oldham NHS Trust and Another Times Law Report 22 April 2005 HL

D v East Berkshire Community Health NHS Trust; MAK v Dewsbury Healthcare NHS Trust; RK v Oldham NHS Trust [2005] 2 AC 373

D v NSPCC [1977] 1 All ER 589

Department of Health (1990) *An introductory guide to the Children Act for the NHS.* HMSO, London

Department of Health (1999) *Working together to safeguard children.* Revised 2010. Joint statement: Department of Health, Home Office, Department for Education and Employment, the National Assembly for Wales

Department of Health (2003a) *Keeping children safe.* HMSO, London

Department of Health (2003b) *What to do if you're worried a child is being abused.* Available from: www.doh.gov.uk/safeguardingchildren/index.htm

Department of Health (2003c) *Every child matters.* Green Paper. HMSO, London

Department of Health (2005) *Carers and Disabled Children Act 2000 and the Carers (Equal Opportunities) Act 2004 for carers and people with parental responsibility for disabled children. Combined draft policy guidance.* HMSO, London

Department of Health (2009) *Interim response to Lord Laming.* HMSO, London

Department of Health (2010a) *The Government's response to Lord Laming.* HMSO, London

Department of Health (2010b) *Working together to safeguard children.* HMSO, London

Department of Health (2012) *Report of the children and young people's health outcomes forum.* HMSO, London

Department of Health E-bulletin; MB-Childrens-NSF@dh.gsi.gov.uk

DP and JC v United Kingdom (Application No 38719/97) Times Law Report 23 October 2002 European Court of Human Rights

E and others v United Kingdom (Application No 33218/96) Times Law Report 4 December 2002 ECHR

Fraser J, Nolan M (2004) *Child protection: A guide for midwives.* Elsevier, Oxford

Home Office (2002) *White Paper. Protecting the public: Strengthening protection against sex offenders and reforming the law on sexual offences.* CM 5668. HMSO, London

Kennedy I (2010) *Getting it right for children and young people: Overcoming cultural barriers in the NHS so as to meet their needs.* Department of Health, London

Lord Laming (2009) *The Protection of Children in England. A progress report.* HMSO, London

MAK and RK v United Kingdom Application Nos 45901/05 and 40146/06 Times Law Report 19 April 2010 ECHR

Nursing and Midwifery Council (2008) *Code of professional conduct: Standards for conduct, performance and ethics.* NMC, London

Pierce v Doncaster Metropolitan BC [2007] EWHC 2968

R (on the application of G) v Nottingham City Council [2008] EWHC 400

Re C (a minor)(medical treatment – refusal of parental consent) [1997] 8 Med LR 166 CA

Re E (a minor)(wardship: medical treatment) Family Division [1993] 1 FLR 386

Re F (in utero) [1988] 2 All ER 193

Richardson PJ (ed) (2012) *Archbold: Criminal pleading, evidence and sentencing* (61st edition). Sweet and Maxwell, London

RK and MK v Oldham NHS Trust [2003] Lloyd's Rep Med 11

Royal College of Nursing (2003) *Child protection: Every nurses' responsibility.* Available from: www.rcn.org.uk

S and D and E and in the matter of Z (a minor) T and X and Y [2013] EWHC 14 Fam.

Smyth C (2012) Child A & E visits logged in crackdown on abuse. *The Times* **27 December**

The Times (2012) Vindication for mother accused of making up child's illness. *The Times* **28 September**

TP and KM v the UK No 28945/95 10.9.99

Z UK [1999] 28 EHRR CD 65

Chapter 18

Mental disorder

> **Scenario 18.1. Postnatal depression**
>
> Following the birth of her first child, Martha became very depressed and neglected her baby. Her midwife was concerned for her but had great difficulty since Martha denied that there was any problem.
>
> *Scenario 18.1. is discussed on p. 349.*

Introduction

Suicide is the leading cause of maternal death in the UK (Cantwell and Cox, 2003) and there are clear implications for the role of the midwife and her records and for information sharing (Robinson, 2002). The midwife may encounter women who suffer from a mental disorder and/or those who lack mental capacity to make specific decisions. Because of the dangers of postnatal depression and puerperal fever to the mother and child it is essential that the midwife has a good understanding of the help that is to hand, the legal powers that exist if intervention is necessary and what action she should take.

A report published by *The Times* in March 2013 suggested that as many as one in seven mothers may suffer from postnatal depression and that new mothers should be interviewed: first, during the pregnancy to ascertain if there are any difficulties, and second, postnatally to assess the quality of interaction between mother and baby.

This chapter aims to raise awareness of the issue of mental disorder and to assist the midwife in seeking further information. There is evidence that midwives neglect the needs of women with mental illness (Hamilton, 2004) and developments in Northern Ireland (Murray and Hamilton, 2005) to provide an awareness of maternal mental illness and service provision may be relevant to the work of many midwives in the UK. Research using two studies to evaluate a programme to encourage midwives to detect and refer women with mental health problems is reported by Elliott and others (2007). It emphasised the need to ensure that serious mental disorder is identified before questioning mothers on lesser mental health problems.

Useful websites include that of MIND (www.mind.org.uk/help/right_and_legislation), MENCAP (www.mencap.org.uk/), the Ministry of Justice (www.justice.gov.uk), and the Care Quality Commission, which has taken over from the Mental Health Act Commission the statutory duties relating to mental health (www.cqc.org.uk/organisations-we-regulate/mental-health-services/).

Mentally incapacitated adults

The vacuum that existed in law in relation to decision-making on behalf of the mentally incapacitated adult (and which had been temporarily filled by the principles set by the House of Lords in the case of *F v West Berkshire Health Authority)* was filled by the Mental Capacity Act 2005 which came into force in 2007.

Where a midwife is aware that one of her clients suffers from learning disabilities, she would need to determine the capacity of the woman to make decisions, bringing in, if necessary, expert assistance to determine capacity. The principles set out in the Mental Capacity Act 2005 must be followed. There is a presumption that an adult (i.e. a person over 16 years) has the mental capacity to make a decision, but this can be rebutted on a balance of probabilities (see *Chapter 3*). The vast majority of those with learning disabilities are unlikely to come within the definition of mental disorder for the purposes of the Mental Health Act 1983 as amended by the 2007 Act (see *Box 18.1*) and are therefore unlikely to be compulsorily admitted to hospital for treatment. Under the Mental Capacity Act 2005 the Court of Protection has the role of making decisions in relation to care

---

Box 18.1. Definition of mental disorder

- A mental disorder is any disorder or disability of the mind.
- The previous classifications of mental illness, mental impairment and psychopathic disorder are no longer used in the statutory definition. Learning disability (which is defined as "a state of arrested or incomplete development of the mind which includes significant impairment of intelligence and social functioning") is not considered to be mental disorder unless the disability is associated with abnormally aggressive or seriously irresponsible conduct on the person's part.
- Dependence on alcohol or drugs is not considered to be a disorder or disability of the mind for the purposes of the definition of mental disorder. This means that if a woman is pregnant and abusing drugs she cannot be detained under the Mental Health Act 1983 unless she is shown to be suffering from mental disorder apart from the drug abuse.

---

and treatment, and can appoint deputies with specified powers to act on behalf of a person who lacks the requisite capacity. In addition, individuals can appoint persons to have lasting powers of attorney under which they can make decisions on their behalf. A new office of Public Guardian has been created to establish and maintain a register of lasting powers of attorney and of orders appointing deputies and supervising deputies as set out in Section 58 of the 2005 Act.

In addition, under the Sexual Offences Act 2003 (see *Chapter 17*), new offences are created in relation to sexual activity with persons with a mental disorder impeding choice, causing a person with a mental disorder to engage in sexual activity and with care workers inciting persons with a mental disorder to have sexual activity. These provisions are designed to provide more protection for vulnerable persons. Further information on the Mental Capacity Act can be found in *Chapter 3*.

Mentally disordered: An introduction

The law relating to compulsory admission of mentally disordered patients is laid down in the Mental Health Act 1983 as amended by the Mental Health Act 2007.

The philosophy behind the Mental Health Act 1983 is that, where possible, patients suffering from mental disorder should be treated without admission to psychiatric hospital. If admission is required then it should be on the basis of informal admission. Only where there is no alternative to detention should the powers of compulsory admission in the Act be used. Under the amended 1983 Act, a community treatment order has been introduced.

Most patients would therefore be cared for in the community with assistance from the community psychiatric nurse with overall responsibility taken by the GP assisted by outpatient referrals to a consultant psychiatrist and the community mental health team. Mothers may require specialist help and advice if they are taking antipsychotic or antidepressant medication when they become pregnant. The midwife should ensure that she is aware of any possible contraindications for medication at all times during and after the pregnancy. If admission to hospital becomes necessary, most patients would agree to informal (i.e. voluntary) admission. The midwife should discuss with the patient and the hospital staff the antenatal care required by the mother, and the arrangements to be made when labour commences, trying to ensure that the mother's wishes are obtained and respected.

Unfortunately, one of the characteristics of some forms of mental disorder is an absence of insight and therefore it is necessary in certain exceptional circumstances to arrange for the admission of a person compulsorily to hospital for inpatient treatment. This may be necessary following confinement if it is suspected that the mother is suffering from puerperal disorder or severe postnatal depression. Most districts now have a mother and baby unit and the midwife should ensure that she is aware of the location of these, since it may be that, with assurance, the mother might be prepared to accept informal admission to such a unit if she knows that she can take the baby with her. If the midwife is aware that no such provision has been made, she could take up the issue with her supervisor and the NHS trust or clinical commissioning body. It may be possible for admission to such a unit to be provided on the basis of an out of the catchment area referral. A national audit has been carried out of joint mother and baby admissions to UK psychiatric hospitals since 1996 (Salmon et al, 2004). The National Institute for Health and Clinical Excellence (NICE) estimated that around 140 women per year (40 per 1000 deliveries) will require referral to a specialist perinatal mental health service and of these 15 will require admission to a mother and baby unit (NICE, 2012). The NICE guidance recommended the development of managed clinical perinatal networks to ensure that local needs were met. The value of the midwife contributing to the commissioning and implementation of a multi-disciplinary service for the mental health needs of women is clear.

Definition of mental disorder

No person can be compulsorily detained under the Mental Health Act 1983 unless he/she is suffering from mental disorder as defined in the amended Act. The definition is set out in *Box 18.1*.

Compulsory admission

There are three main sections for the compulsory admission of the mentally disordered person (other than through the courts). These are shown in *Box 18.2*.

Section 4

This is an emergency admission section and enables a person to be detained for up to 72 hours on the basis of one medical recommendation. It must be established that it is of urgent necessity for the admission for assessment, and that compliance with the provisions for two medical recommendations would involve undesirable delay. The patient can be detained under Section 4 for up to 72 hours. The medical requirements for Sections 2 and 4 are shown in *Box 18.3*.

Box 18.2. Compulsory admission for mental disorder

- Section 4 emergency admission for assessment for up to 72 hours.
- Section 2 admission for assessment for up to 28 days.
- Section 3 admission for treatment for up to 6 months.

Box 18.3. Medical requirements for Sections 2 and 4

(a) The patient is suffering from mental disorder of a nature or degree which warrants the detention of the patient in a hospital for assessment (or for assessment followed by medical treatment) for at least a limited period; and

(b) he ought to be so detained in the interests of his own health or safety or with a view to the protection of other persons.

The applicant is usually an approved mental health professional (replacing the approved social worker) although, as with the other two Sections, it could be the "nearest relative". The approved mental health professional is "approved" because she/he has undergone a special training in mental health. In applying for a Section 4 admission the approved mental health professional has to explain why a second medical recommendation for admission could not be obtained. The application is made to the managers of the appropriate hospital and the application gives authority to ambulance men or police to transfer the patient to the hospital.

Section 2

This is an application for assessment, and under this the person can be detained for up to 28 days. There must be two medical recommendations, one of them from a doctor who is recognised as having the required expertise in psychiatric medicine, i.e. he or she is approved under Section 12 of the Act and is colloquially called a "Section 12 doctor". One of the two doctors should have had previous acquaintance with the patient and if this is not possible the approved mental health professional must explain the reasons why on the application form. (Recently it was discovered that strategic health authorities had failed to delegate appropriately the powers of approval of Section 12 doctors to NHS mental health trusts which meant that retrospective legislation was required to validate the detention of over 2000 patients who had been illegally detained because the approval processes were invalid. The

Mental Health (Approval Functions) Bill was rushed through Parliament to remedy the situation. The medical requirements shown in *Box 18.3* must be present.

Section 3

This is an admission for treatment and can last up to six months. Two medical recommendations are required. The medical requirements shown in *Box 18.4* must be present. Again one of the medical recommendations must be by a Section 12 approved doctor and preferably at least one of the doctors should have had previous acquaintance with the patient. The nearest relative should be consulted over the application by the approved mental health professional and has the right to object to the application being made.

Box 18.4. Medical requirements for Section 3 admission

(a) He is suffering from mental disorder that is of a nature or degree which makes it appropriate for him to receive medical treatment in a hospital; and
(b) Deleted by 2007 Act.
(c) It is necessary for the health or safety of the patient or for the protection of other persons that he should receive such treatment and it cannot be provided unless he is detained under this Section.

Definition of nearest relative

The relative who is "nearest" is defined by statute (Section 26 of the Mental Health Act 1983). Where the patient is married it would be the spouse or civil partner. A cohabitee would count as the nearest relative where the couple had been living together for a period of not less than six months. A person other than a relative could be classified as a relative if he/she had been ordinarily living with the patient for at least five years.

Treatment for mental disorder

Compulsory treatment for mental disorder can be given under the Act to the patient detained under either Section 2 or Section 3, but not to the patient who is detained under Section 4. This is so even though Section 2 is described as admission for assessment.

Box 18.5. Treatment for mental disorder

- Section 57. Surgery destroying brain tissue, hormonal implants to control sexual urge and other treatments specified by the Secretary of State. The patient must consent and the understanding of the patient to consent should be certified by three persons appointed by the Care Quality Commission, one of whom must be a registered medical practitioner. The latter must certify that the treatment should be given.
- Section 58. Medication after three months and electroconvulsive therapy (ECT). The patient must either consent or a second opinion must be obtained from an independent doctor appointed by the Care Quality Commission. The 2007 Act introduced new provisions relating to electroconvulsive therapy (ECT) and compulsory treatment, preventing a patient who refuses to give consent to ECT or has drawn up an advance decision refusing the treatment, being compelled to have ECT. If a patient lacks the capacity to give consent, ECT cannot be given if there is a valid advance decision against it.
- Section 63. Any treatment not covered by Sections 57 and 58 which is given for mental disorder under the direction of the responsible medical officer.
- Section 62. This Section enables the provisions of the above Sections to be dispensed with in an emergency situation.

Box 18.5 shows the treatments that can be given and the conditions required. It should be noted that if medication is required after three months and the mother is either unable or unwilling to give consent, a second opinion doctor must be called in to decide if the treatment should be given. She has a duty to examine the patient, determine whether the patient is incapable of giving consent or is refusing consent, talk to the responsible medical officer about the proposed treatment, and decide whether the treatment should be given against the patient's will. Before she decides she must consult with two persons: one a nurse who is professionally concerned with the treatment of the patient, the other who is neither doctor nor nurse, who is also professionally concerned with the patient. This latter person could be a midwife if she is sufficiently involved with the patient. The second opinion advisory doctor merely has to record on the statutory form (Form 39) the names of the nurse and the other professional whom he has consulted. He does not have to record what the advice was. If the midwife were to be the second professional to be consulted it would be advisable for her to ensure that she records in her patient records the content of her advice to the second opinion advisory doctor.

The midwife must of course take particular precautions to ensure that any treatment being given for mental disorder will not be harmful to the pregnancy or breastfeeding.

In one case (*Tameside and Glossop Acute Services Trust v CH*, which is discussed in *Chapter 3*) the judge decided that the woman, who was suffering from paranoid schizophrenia, who was detained in a psychiatric hospital under Section 3 and who was refusing to have a Caesarean operation, could be given a Caesarean operation under Section 63 of the Mental Health Act 1983 as being treatment for mental disorder. This decision was highly disputed, and following the decisions in *Re MB* and in *St George's Hospital v S,* would not be followed (see *Chapter 3*).

After-care services. Section 117 Mental Health Act 1983 as amended by the 2007 Act

It is a statutory duty for the health service and local social service authorities, in cooperation with relevant voluntary agencies, to provide after-care services for patients who have been detained under specific Sections including Section 3 and Section 37. The duty continues until they are satisfied that the person concerned is no longer in need of such services, but they shall not be so satisfied in the case of a community patient (i.e. a patient under a community treatment order, see below) while he remains such a patient. Charges cannot be made for these services.

Community treatment order

The Mental Health (Patients in the Community) Act 1995 saw the introduction of after-care under supervision, or supervised discharge as it became known. This Act was however repealed by the Mental Health Act 2007, which introduced a community treatment order under Section 32, which added new Sections 17A–G into the Mental Health Act 1983. These cover the following subjects:

- 17A Requirements for a community treatment order.
- 17B Conditions for a community treatment order.
- 17C Duration of a community treatment order.
- 17D Effect of a community treatment order.
- 17E Power to recall to hospital.
- 17F Powers in respect of recalled patients.
- 17G Effect of revoking a community treatment order.

See the legislation website for full details (www.legislation.gov.uk/ukpga/2007/12).

Treatment provisions for those on a community treatment order

The Mental Health Act 2007 inserts into the Mental Health Act 1983 a new Part 4A which sets out the provisions for the treatment of community patients who are not recalled to hospital. Sections 64A–K set out the conditions on which treatment can be given in the community. Section 64D enables treatment to be given to an adult who lacks the requisite capacity, if specified conditions are met, but force may not be used. Section 64G enables emergency treatment to be given to patients lacking the capacity or competence to give consent and, under this Section, force can be used provided certain conditions are met and the treatment is to prevent harm to the patient, and the force must be a proportionate response to the likelihood of the patient suffering harm and to the seriousness of that harm.

The full details can be accessed on the legislation website (www.legislation. gov.uk/ukpga/2007/12).

Common law powers

These are powers recognised by the courts which were relied upon prior to the implementation of the Mental Capacity Act 2005 when life-saving treatment was required for a patient incapable of giving consent. Again, any treatment had to take into account the pregnancy or if the mother was feeding the baby. Common law powers are now replaced by the Mental Capacity Act 2005 (see *Chapter 3*).

The informal inpatient

If the mother is already in hospital as an informal patient and wishes to take her own discharge and it would be dangerous to her health or safety or to other people for her to do so, she could be detained under the provisions of the Mental Health Act 1983 as amended. See *Boxes 18.6* and *18.7*.

Renewal

Sections 4, 2, 5(4) and 5(2) are not renewable. A patient on Section 2 who needs to be detained for longer can be further detained on Section 3. Section 3 can be renewed for a further six months and then for one year at a time. The procedure for

---

Box 18.6. Section 5(4): Holding power of the nurse

This enables a nurse qualified in mental disorder to prevent an informal patient who is being treated for mental disorder from leaving the hospital. The detention can exist for up to six hours but it will end as soon as the responsible medical practitioner or clinician (or his nominee) arrives to see the patient. He or she may then, following an examination of the patient, decide to detain the patient further.

Box 18.7. Section 5(2): Power of doctor to detain an in-patient

This enables the patient's doctor or his/her nominee to detain the patient for up to 72 hours to enable an application to be considered for admission under the Mental Health Act 1983. It may be that after the doctor has examined the patient it is decided that compulsory admission is not necessary and the Section will then end and the patient will become informal. Alternatively, following examination by the patient's own doctor and by another doctor and the approved mental health professional, an application is made under Section 2 or Section 3. For Section 5(2) to be used, the in-patient need not have been admitted for the treatment of mental disorder. Section 5(2) could therefore be used on non-psychiatric wards.

---

the renewal is that the responsible clinician in charge of the patient's care examines the patient, within the period of two months ending with the date the Section is due to end and, if it appears to him that the specific condition of mental disorder is present and the other conditions required by Section 20 are present, he must furnish to the managers a report to that effect and the patient's detention is then renewed. The managers in their review can decide that the patient should be discharged.

Appeals against detention

The patient can appeal to a Mental Health Review Tribunal for discharge or to the managers of the hospital. There are set times for applying to the Tribunal but not to the managers. The nearest relative also has the right to apply to a Mental Health Review Tribunal if his/her attempt to discharge the patient under Section 23 has been barred by the responsible medical officer under Section 25.

Where a patient has not himself applied for a Mental Health Review Tribunal hearing during the first six months and after that at least once every three years, the managers of the hospital have a duty to refer the patient to the Tribunal. (In the case of those under 18 years, the time limit is every year.)

The nearest relative has the right to request the discharge of the patient but must give 72 hours notice to the hospital managers of the intention to remove the patient and during this time the responsible clinician can prevent the discharge by reporting to the hospital managers that the patient would act in a manner dangerous to her or to others. The nearest relative can apply to the Tribunal on behalf of the patient within 28 days of the responsible clinician's report to the hospital managers.

It may be that, if the midwife has remained in close contact with the patient during a period of detention, a report and/or oral evidence might be required from the midwife at a Tribunal or manager's hearing giving her views upon the discharge. Article 5 of the European Convention of Human Rights recognises that:

> Everyone has the right to liberty and security of person. No one shall be deprived of his liberty save in the following cases and in accordance with a procedure prescribed by law. One of the cases listed is...
>
> (e) The lawful detention of persons for the prevention of the spreading of infectious diseases, of persons of unsound mind, alcoholics or drug addicts or vagrants.

This exception covers those suffering from mental disorder, providing they are detained in accordance with a procedure established by law. There have been several successful appeals to the European Court of Human Rights by patients detained under the Mental Health Act 1983 because their human rights have not been respected. In the case of *Osman v United Kingdom*, the European Court of Human Rights held that Article 2 placed upon authorities a positive duty to prevent suicide attempts through risk assessments and appropriate policies and staffing levels. Placing a detained patient under seclusion was challenged by judicial review as being contrary to Article 3 of the European Convention of Human Rights i.e. "inhuman and degrading treatment or punishment" (*S v Airedale National Health Service Trust*). The High Court held that while seclusion is capable of infringing a patient's rights under Article 3, it did not *per se* amount to a breach of those rights. In the case of *Munjaz v UK* the European Convention of Human Rights held that there was no breach of Article 8 in relation to the seclusion of a detained patient at Ashworth. There was sufficient indication of the scope of the discretion that Ashworth enjoyed and the manner this discretion was exercised with sufficient clarity to protect the applicant against arbitrary interference with his Article 8 rights. See also the case of *MS v UK* which is considered in *Chapter 2*.

Information to the patient

One of the duties on the managers introduced by the 1983 Act is to ensure that the patient receives, both in writing and orally, information relating to her Section, the right to apply to the managers and the Mental Health Review Tribunal, and the rules relating to consent to treatment. This duty is usually delegated by the managers to the nursing staff or the medical records staff. Leaflets are available giving the information for each of the different Sections and these are available in a wide variety of languages. A midwife who has a client detained in hospital should ask to see the leaflet so that she herself understands the implications of the Section the patient is under.

Information to the nearest relative

The information that is given to the patient must also be given in writing to the nearest relative. However, the patient has a statutory right to object to this information being given to the nearest relative.

Mental health managers

In respect of an NHS trust these are the non-executive board members and only they, with their co-opted members, can carry out the function of hearing appeals to the managers by the patient against detention, or renewing the patient's detention following a report from the responsible medical officer. Other functions in respect of the Mental Health Act can be delegated to officers.

The Mental Health Act Commission and the Care Quality Commission

In 1983 a watchdog for detained patients was established, known as the Mental Health Act Commission. It consisted of about 90 different professionals and lay people whose jurisdiction was to visit the detained patients and to take up any complaints from them where they were not satisfied by the response from the managers, or any other complaint relating to the exercise of powers and duties under the Mental Health Act. It also had statutory duties in relation to the withholding of mail in the special hospitals (i.e. Broadmoor, Rampton and Ashworth). It also had a duty every other year to provide a report to the Secretary of State which he must place before each House of Parliament. In April 2009 the Mental Health Act Commission was merged into the Care Quality Commission which became responsible for carrying out the statutory duties of the Mental Health Act Commission. Its annual report on the Mental Health Act for 2011/2012 can be found on its website (Care Quality Commission, 2013; www.cqc.org.uk).

Independent mental capacity and independent mental health advocates

Both the Mental Capacity Act 2005 and the Mental Health Act 1983 (as amended) enable the appointment of independent advocates to support those in need of such services. The midwife caring for a pregnant woman who lacks the requisite mental capacity or who suffers from a mental disorder should ascertain if such appointments have been made and, if not, consider whether they should.

Code of practice

The Secretary of State has a duty under mental health legislation to prepare and revise as appropriate a Code of Practice. Midwives who are involved in the care of mothers with a mental disorder would find this a useful tool of reference. Codes of Practice have also been prepared under the Mental Capacity Act 2005 which can be accessed from the Ministry of Justice website (www.justice.gov.uk/).

Caesareans and mental disorder

There have been examples where pregnant women being treated for mental disorder under the Mental Health Act 1983 have been compelled to undergo a Caesarean section. These are considered in *Chapter 3* where the guidance from the Court of Appeal is discussed.

Protection of vulnerable adults

Legislation establishing lists of those who are a potential danger to children and vulnerable adults, and statutory requirements to consult these lists, are considered in *Chapter 17*. Midwives caring for women with learning disabilities have a responsibility as part of their duty of care to take into account their level of capacity to make decisions and should ensure that their standards of information giving and communication with the women take into account the disabilities. In November 2001 an Oxford midwife who shouted at a mother and her partner, (both of whom had a learning disability), and told them that their newborn twins would be taken away from them by social services, was removed from the Register following a hearing before the UKCC Professional Conduct Committee (UKCC, 2001).

National Service Frameworks

The government has published National Service Frameworks for different specialties to ensure that there is a minimum standard of provision across the country. The National Service Frameworks for Mental Health were published in 1999 and set standards in five areas:

- Standard 1: Mental health promotion.
- Standards 2 and 3: Primary care and access to services.
- Standards 4 and 5: Effective services for people with severe mental illness.
- Standards 6: Caring about carers.
- Standard 7: Preventing suicide.

The implementation of these standards is overseen by the Care Quality Commission, formerly the Healthcare Commission (Commission for Healthcare Audit and Inspection which replaced the Commission for Health Improvement).

National Institute for Health and Clinical Excellence (NICE) and Department of Health guidance

NICE published guidelines on antenatal and postnatal mental health in 2007 which require the midwife to enquire about past or present severe mental illness and encourage the development of managed clinical perinatal networks (see above). However, it was disappointing that a survey reported in 2011 showed that many health practitioners lacked the required knowledge or skills to identify and manage mental disorders effectively (Rothera and Oates, 2011). This suggests that the NICE guidance of 2007 has not been fully implemented.

In August 2012 the Department of Health published a maternal mental health pathway, which, in the words of the Department of Health:

- Sets out the benefits and principles for health visitors, midwives, specialist mental health services and GPs working together in pregnancy and the first postnatal year, as the basis for the detailed local pathway to meet the physical and mental health and wellbeing needs of parents, babies and families.
- Builds on good practice and evidence drawn from the professions.
- Outlines the challenges and potential opportunities.
- Endorses the practice of joint working and encourages an integrated approach to service delivery.

Scenario 18.1. Postnatal depression: Discussion

The midwife must not assume that Martha is suffering from a mental disorder justifying compulsory admission under the Mental Health Act. She must obtain for Martha an assessment of her condition, obtaining the assistance of the health visitor, the GP and the community mental health team. It may be that with support and counselling Martha will be able to look after her baby and recover. Close supervision of Martha is required. If it is clear that she needs more support, every effort should be made to secure her voluntary admission to a mother and baby unit. The midwife should have information about local support services for Martha.

Conclusion

A panel of experts in June 2012 stated that the NHS was failing to deal with a big rise in mental illness: nearly half of all illness in people under the age of 65 years is mental illness and accounts for nearly half of all people on incapacity benefit (Layard, 2012). There is an attempt to change attitudes in relation to mental health. The Mental Health (Discrimination) Act 2013 changes the law in relation to the disqualification to be a member of Parliament, serve on a jury or remain as a company director by reason of mental health. It is essential that the rights of the mentally disordered pregnant woman and those lacking the requisite mental capacity to make their own decisions are safeguarded, and appropriate provision made for the care of the mother and baby. Midwives have an important role to play in ensuring that high standards are set and implemented and, in order to secure this, a good understanding of the mental health laws is essential. Midwives also need to ensure that the rights of these client groups are protected in relation to their pregnancy and the after-care of mother and baby, particularly in relation to the law of consent and compulsory Caesareans. This is considered in *Chapter 3* (which also looks at the law relating to mental capacity).

Questions and exercises

1. You are concerned that a patient of yours who is extremely depressed and is 36 weeks' pregnant might be in need of assistance. You have discussed this with her but she refuses to see her GP or seek other help. What action do you take?
2. You visit a mother who gave birth two days ago, and she seems very disturbed and irrational. You are worried about her mental health. She has made it clear that she would refuse to see her GP and would not be prepared to consider informal admission for treatment. What action do you take and what is your legal liability?
3. Access the report on Maternal Mental Health Pathway published in August 2012 by the Department of Health (www.dh.gov.uk/health/2012/08/ maternalmentalhealthpathway) and consider its relevance to your own unit.
4. A 17-year-old woman with severe learning disabilities is about 10 weeks' pregnant and her mother wishes her to have a termination of pregnancy and be sterilised. What is the law and what action would you take? (See also *Chapters 3* and *6*.) Would your answer be different if she were aged 21?

References

Cantwell R, Cox JL (2003) Psychiatric disorders in pregnancy and the puerperium. *Current Obstetrics and Gynaecology* **13**(1): 7–13

Care Quality Commission (2013) *Mental Health Act annual report*. Care Quality Commission, London. Available from: www.cqc.org.uk

Department of Health (2012) *Maternal mental health pathway*. HMSO, London

Elliott S, Ross-Davis M, Sarkar A, Green L (2007) Detection and initial assessment of mental disorder. The midwife's role. *British Journal of Midwifery* **15**(12): 759–64

F v West Berkshire Health Authority [1989] 2 All ER 545

Hamilton S (2004) Mind … the gap! Maternal mental illness. In Wickham S (ed) *Midwifery: Best practice* (pp 92–4). Books for Midwives, Edinburgh

Layard Lord (2012) *How mental illness loses out in the NHS*. London School of Economics, London

MS v UK [2012] ECHR 804

Munjaz v UK [2012] ECHR 1704

Murray K, Hamilton S (2005) Perinatal mental health: A Northern Ireland experience. *MIDIRS Midwifery Digest* **15**(1): 121–4

NICE (2012) *Commissioning antenatal and postnatal mental health services*. NICE, London. Available from: www.nice.org.uk/using guidance/commissioning

Osman v United Kingdom [2000] 29 EHRR 245

Re MB (an adult: medical treatment) [1997] 2 FLR 426

Robinson J (2002) The perils of psychiatric records. *British Journal of Midwifery* **10**(3): 173

Rothera I, Oates M (2011) Managing perinatal mental health: A survey of practitioners' views. *British Journal of Midwifery* **19**(5): 304–13

S v Airedale National Health Service Trust Times Law Report 25 July 2003; Lloyd's Rep Med [2003] 21

Salmon MP, Abel K, Webb R et al (2004) A national audit of joint mother and baby admissions to UK psychiatric hospitals: An overview of findings. *Archives of Women's Mental Health* **7**(1): 65–70

St George's Healthcare NHS Trust v S; R v Collins ex parte S [1998]; 44 BMLR 160 CA

Tameside and Glossop Acute Services Trust v CH [1996] 31 BMLR 93

The Times (2013) News item. *The Times* **21 March**

Chapter 19

The future

Introduction

The NHS is in the throws of another major reorganisation. The Health and Social Care Act 2012 heralds significant changes to the organisation of the NHS bringing in considerable modifications, many of which will not have been implemented before this book is published. The Francis Report on Mid-Staffs NHS Foundation Trust will also have an as yet unknown but hopefully significant impact upon the culture of the NHS. An updated NHS Constitution, based on a consultation on strengthening the guiding principles was published in March 2013. Significant strategies for maternity services have been published over recent years. This final chapter seeks to identify the most important changes and their implications for midwives.

Health and Social Care Act 2012

The main provisions of the Act are set out in *Box 19.1*. The full Act can be accessed on the legislation website (www.legislation.gov.uk).

Box 19.1. Main provisions of the Heath and Social Care Act 2012

Parts 1 and 2: Overview and provision of health services
   Sections 1–8: Duties of Secretary of States in relation to: promoting comprehensive health service; improving the quality of services; the NHS Constitution; reducing inequalities; promoting autonomy; research; education and training; reporting on and reviewing treatment of providers.
   Section 52: Duty to keep health service functions under review.
   Section 53: Secretary of State's annual report.
   Sections 9, 23: The NHS Commissioning Board.
   Sections 10, 25, 26: Clinical commissioning groups.
   Sections 11–19, 46–50: Protection of public health (see *Chapter 16* of this book).
   Section 29: Health service functions of local authorities.
   Section 33: Abolition of Strategic Health Authorities.
   Section 34: Abolition of Primary Care Trusts.
   Section 35: Fluoridation of water supplies.

Box 19.1/cont

Sections 38–45: Mental Health matters: Approval functions, discharge and after-care of patients.

Sections 46–47: Role of the Board and clinical commissioning groups in respect of Emergencies; powers of Secretary of State.

Section 54: Certification of death.

Part 3: Regulation of health and social services

Sections 61–71: Monitor: duties, powers and functions.

Sections 72–80: Competition.

Sections 81–114: Licensing.

Sections 115–127: Pricing sections.

Part 4

Sections 151–180: NHS Foundation and NHS Trusts.

Part 5

Sections 181–200: Public involvement and local government; Healthwatch England; Activities relating to local care services; Local authority arrangements; Independent advocacy services; Requests, rights of entry and referrals; Joint strategic needs assessments and Joint health and wellbeing strategies.

Sections 194–200: Establishment of Health and Wellbeing Boards: duty, other functions, participation of NHS Commissioning Board; Care trusts.

Section 201: Disclosure of reports etc. by the Health Service Commissioner.

Part 6

Sections 202–208: Primary Care Services.

Part 7

Sections 209–231: Regulation of health and social care workers.

Part 8

Sections 232–243: NICE.

Part 9

Sections 250–251: Health and Adult Social Care Services Information.

Section 250: Powers to publish information standards.

Sections 252–277: Health and social care information centre.

Part 10

Sections 278–283: Abolition of certain bodies.

Part 11

Sections 287–302: Miscellaneous.

Part 12

Sections 303–304: Final Provisions.

23 Schedules.

It will be noted that the 2012 Act only applies to England; the devolved assemblies of Northern Ireland, Scotland and Wales have the opportunity to organise their NHS services to meet local needs and concerns. Further information can be obtained on the websites of their assemblies.

Key features of the 2012 Act

NHS Commissioning Board now known as NHS England (www.england.nhs.uk)

This was established as an arm's length independent body. Its initial function was to authorise clinical commissioning groups and it took up its full functions on 1 April 2013. From this date the Commissioning Board has taken on many of the current functions of primary care trusts with regard to the commissioning of primary care health services, as well as some nationally based functions previously undertaken by the Department of Health.

NHS England aims to:

- End unjustifiable variations in services and a reduction of health inequalities.
- Secure better outcomes for patients, as primary care clinicians are empowered to focus on delivering high quality, clinically-effective, evidence-based services.
- Achieve greater efficiencies in the delivery of primary care health services through the introduction of standardised frameworks and operating procedures.

The functions of NHS England include those specified in the 2012 Act which are shown in *Box 19.2*.

Box 19.2. Specified functions of NHS England

13C Duty to promote NHS Constitution
(a) act with a view to securing that health services are provided in a way which promotes the NHS Constitution, and
(b) promote awareness of the NHS Constitution among patients, staff and members of the public.

Box 19.2/cont

13D The Board must exercise its functions effectively, efficiently and economically.

13E The Board must exercise its functions with a view to securing continuous improvement in the quality of services provided to individuals for or in connection with

(a) the prevention, diagnosis or treatment of illness, or

(b) the protection or improvement of public health.

In particular, the Board must act with a view to securing continuous improvement in the outcomes that are achieved from the provision of the services; in particular

(a) the effectiveness of the services,

(b) the safety of the services, and

(c) the quality of the experience undergone by patients.

It must have regard to

(a) any document published by the Secretary of State relating to this duty, and

(b) the quality standards prepared by NICE under Section 234 of the Health and Social Care Act 2012.

13F Duty as to promoting autonomy.

13G Duty as to reducing inequalities.

13H Duty to promote involvement of each patient.

13I Duty as to patient choice.

13J Duty to obtain appropriate advice.

13K Duty to promote innovation.

13L Duty in respect of research.

13M Duty as to promoting education and training.

13N Duty as to promoting integration of those services.

13O Duty to have regard to impact on services in certain areas.

13P Duty as respects variation in provision of health services.

13Q Public involvement and consultation by the Board.

13R Information on safety of services provided by the health service.

13S Guidance in relation to processing of information.

13T Business plan.

13U Annual report.

13V Establishment of pooled funds.

13W Board's power to generate income, etc.

13X Power to make grants, etc.

13Y Incidental powers.

13Z–13Z4 Exercise of functions and interpretation.

Clinical commissioning groups

Clinical commissioning groups have been established as corporate bodies with the function of arranging for the provision of services for the purposes of the health service in England in accordance with the 2012 Act (amendment of Secretary of State's duties under Section 3 of the NHS Act 2006). Each clinical commissioning group must arrange for the provision of the following to such extent as it considers necessary to meet the reasonable requirements of the persons for whom it has responsibility:

(a) Hospital accommodation.
(b) Other accommodation for the purpose of any service provided under this Act.
(c) Medical, dental, ophthalmic, nursing and ambulance services.
(d) Such other services or facilities for the care of pregnant women, women who are breastfeeding and young children as he considers are appropriate as part of the health service.
(e) Such other services or facilities for the prevention of illness, the care of persons suffering from illness and the after-care of persons who have suffered from illness as he considers are appropriate as part of the health service.
(f) Such other services or facilities as are required for the diagnosis and treatment of illness.

In exercising its functions a clinical commissioning group is required to act consistently with:

(a) The discharge by the Secretary of State and the Board of their duty under Section 1(1) (duty to promote a comprehensive health service), and
(b) The objectives and requirements for the time being specified in the mandate published under Section 13A (see below).

Each clinical commissioning group has the power to commission such health services or facilities as it considers appropriate for the purposes of the health service that relate to securing improvement:

(a) In the physical and mental health of the persons for whom it has responsibility, or
(b) In the prevention, diagnosis and treatment of illness in those persons.

A clinical commissioning group may not arrange for the provision of a service or facility if NHS England has a duty to arrange for its provision by virtue of Section 3B or 4.

Discussion

Clinical commissioning groups are GP-led and present a challenge to midwives to improve communications between GPs and midwifery services. (In recent years it seems that GPs have become more remote from maternity services.) Suzanne Tyler (2013) analyses the opportunities and challenges for midwives in the new commissioning arrangements. She points out the advantages of greater collaboration between maternity services, mental health services and primary care and notes that the Royal College of Midwives has developed a set of prompt questions for clinical commissioning groups so that they ask intelligent questions of their local maternity services. She identifies five key areas for clinical commissioning group analysis and also points out the local issues to be addressed.

Lord Darzi expressed concerns that the groups will struggle to reshape services given the power of the large hospitals (Illman, 2013).

A reminder of the importance of following minutely the rules on public consultation for hospital reorganisations was provided by the victory in Leeds (High Court ruling on 7 March 2013) where local people succeeded in challenging the closure of heart surgery for children in Leeds in a High Court action on the grounds that the consultation was flawed. This may pave the way for further challenges to significant reorganisation of services.

The Mandate

Under Section 13A of the amended NHS Act 2006, before the start of each financial year, the Secretary of State must publish and lay before Parliament a document to be known as "The Mandate". In this the Secretary of State must specify:

(a) The objectives that the Secretary of State considers NHS England should seek to achieve in the exercise of its functions during that financial year and such subsequent financial years as the Secretary of State considers appropriate, and

(b) Any requirements that the Secretary of State considers it necessary to impose on the Board for the purpose of ensuring that it achieves those objectives.

The Secretary of State must also specify in the Mandate the amounts that the Secretary of State has decided to specify in relation to the limits on capital and revenue resource use. Also specified may be the ways in which the Secretary of State proposes to assess the Board's performance in relation to the first financial year to which the Mandate relates.

NHS England has the responsibility of seeking to achieve the objectives specified in the Mandate, and complying with any specified requirements.

In preparing the Mandate, the Secretary of State must consult NHS England, the Healthwatch England committee of the Care Quality Commission and any other appropriate persons.

Monitor

Monitor (www.monitor-nhsft.gov.uk) has an ongoing role in assessing NHS trusts for foundation trust status and for ensuring that foundation trusts are financially viable and well-led in terms of both quality and finances. The functions of Monitor include licensing providers of NHS services in England; setting prices; enabling integrated care; preventing anti-competitive behaviour and supporting commissioners to maintain service continuity. New enforcement guidance was published on 28 March 2013 and can be found online (www.monitor-nhsft.gov.uk).

Healthwatch England and Local Healthwatch

Healthwatch England

Under Section 181 of the 2012 Act, the Care Quality Commission must establish a committee known as Healthwatch England. The purpose of the Healthwatch England committee is to provide the Commission or other persons with advice, information or other assistance in accordance with provision made by or under this or any other Act. The majority of members of the committee must not be members of the Care Quality Commission. The Care Quality Commission must arrange for the Healthwatch England committee to exercise specified functions on its behalf, including providing local Healthwatch organisations with general advice and assistance in relation to the making of arrangements and the carrying on of activities for local involvement networks – Sections 221(1), 222(2B) and 221(2) of the Local Government and Public Involvement in Health Act 2007. Healthwatch England can also make recommendations of a general nature to English local authorities about the local involvement networks

Where the Healthwatch England committee is of the opinion that the activities specified in Section 221(2) of that Act are not being carried on properly in an English local authority's area, it should give the authority concerned written notice of its opinion.

Healthwatch England must also provide (a) the Secretary of State, (b) NHS England, (c) Monitor, and (d) English local authorities with information and advice on:

(a) The views of people who use health or social care services and of other members of the public on their needs for and experiences of health and social care services, and
(b) The views of Local Healthwatch organisations and of other persons on the standard of provision of health and social care services and on whether or how the standard could or should be improved.

A person provided with advice must inform the Healthwatch England committee in writing of his response or proposed response to the advice.

The Healthwatch England committee may provide the Care Quality Commission with information and advice on the matters mentioned above and the Commission must inform the committee in writing of its response or proposed response to the advice.

In performing functions under this Section, the Healthwatch England committee must have regard to such aspects of government policy as the Secretary of State may direct.

Local Healthwatch

From April 2013, local Healthwatch organisations have taken over functions from local involvement networks (see *Chapter 5*) and, funded by local authorities, exist as independent organisations able to employ their own staff and involve volunteers so they can become the influential and effective voice of the public. They have to keep annual accounts and produce annual reports. They are accountable to the local authority for their ability to operate effectively and to be value for money. The 2012 Act requires a local authority to provide advocacy services to people who wish to complain about local NHS services from April 2013. Local authorities have the responsibility of commissioning the advocacy services from any provider, which could include the local Healthwatch.

Health and Wellbeing Boards

Local authorities are required under Section 194 of the 2012 Act to set up Health and Wellbeing Boards for their areas. The composition is shown in *Box 19.3*.

Box 19.3. Composition of Health and Wellbeing Board

(a) At least one councillor of the local authority.
(b) The director of adult social services for the local authority.
(c) The director of children's services for the local authority.
(d) The director of public health for the local authority.
(e) A representative of the local Healthwatch organisation for the area of the local authority.
(f) A representative of each relevant clinical commissioning group.
(g) Such other persons, or representatives of such other persons, as the local authority thinks appropriate.

Functions of the Health and Wellbeing Board

The Health and Wellbeing Board has a duty under Section 195 to encourage integrated working. It:

- Must, for the purpose of advancing the health and wellbeing of the people in its area, encourage persons who arrange for the provision of any health or social care services in that area to work in an integrated manner.
- Must, in particular, provide such advice, assistance or other support as it thinks appropriate for the purpose of encouraging the making of arrangements under Section 75 of the National Health Service Act 2006 (arrangements between NHS bodies and local authorities) in connection with the provision of such services.
- May encourage persons who arrange for the provision of any health-related services in its area to work closely with the Health and Wellbeing Board.
- May encourage persons who arrange for the provision of any health or social care services in its area and persons who arrange for the provision of any health-related services in its area to work closely together.

NHS England is required to appoint a representative to the Health and Wellbeing Board in the preparation of the assessment of need and/or the strategy under Sections 116/116A of the Local Government and Public Involvement in Health Act 2007.

The Joint Strategic Needs Assessment prepared by the Health and Wellbeing Boards will be supported by a joint strategy on how these needs are to be met, including the commissioning and integration of services. This will involve a consideration not just of health and care needs, but also housing, children and environmental services.

A significant provision of the 2012 Act is the transfer of public health responsibilities to local authorities. This is considered in *Chapter 16*.

Privatisation

One of the main disputes during the progress of the Bill through Parliament was the extent to which the Act would facilitate the increase of privatisation of health services. Concerns about the extent of privatisation of the NHS led to draft Regulations (under Section 75 of the Act: requirements as to procurement, patient choice and competition) for the clinical commissioning groups being withdrawn in March 2013 amidst criticisms that the exemptions from competitive tendering were too narrow and were designed to encourage the use of non-NHS services.

Impact of 2012 Act changes on midwifery

Midwives cannot ignore the new organisational arrangements for the provision of health and social care. It is essential that, early on, they ensure that they have a strong input into the thinking behind the Mandate, and that they can influence the local assessment of needs and strategy for their area. It is possible that, as a result of the new commissioning arrangements, maternity services will be more competitively priced with greater clarity over the costs of care. Midwives should ensure that they have an input into these figures. There is hope for more patient involvement through the actions of local Healthwatch organisations; again maternity provision should feature in the thinking. The main determinants of quality standards will be NHS England, Monitor, the Care Quality Commission, Healthwatch England and the Health Service Commissioner, and in relation to the standards of registered practitioners will be the Professional Standards Authority for Health and Social Care (being the renamed Council for Healthcare Regulatory Excellence) and the registration bodies.

Mid-Staffordshire NHS Foundation Trust Public Inquiry

The Report of this Public Inquiry, which was chaired by Robert Francis QC, was published on 6 February 2013. It made 290 recommendations to change the culture of the NHS to avoid a repeat of the tragedy. The report can be downloaded from the public inquiry website (www.midstaffspublicinquiry.com).

Robert Francis, in a letter to the Secretary of State for Health published with the executive summary of the report, described the essential aims of the report and these are shown in *Box 19.4*.

Box 19.4. Essential aims of the Francis Report on Mid-Staffordshire NHS Foundation Trust

- Foster a common culture shared by all in the service of putting the patient first.
- Develop a set of fundamental standards, easily understood and accepted by patients, the public and healthcare staff, the breach of which should not be tolerated.
- Provide professionally endorsed and evidence-based means of compliance with these fundamental standards, which can be understood and adopted by the staff who have to provide the service.
- Ensure openness, transparency and candour throughout the system about matters of concern.
- Ensure that the relentless focus of the healthcare regulator is on policing compliance with these standards.
- Make all those who provide care for patients – individuals and organisations – properly accountable for what they do to ensure that the public is protected from those not fit to provide such a service.
- Provide for a proper degree of accountability for senior managers and leaders to place all with responsibility for protecting the interests of patients on a level playing field.
- Enhance the recruitment, education, training and support of all the key contributors to the provision of healthcare, but in particular those in nursing and leadership positions, to integrate the essential shared values of the common culture into everything they do.
- Develop and share ever-improving means of measuring and understanding the performance of individual professionals, teams, units and provider organisations for patients, the public and all other stakeholders in the system.

Some of the key recommendations to secure the achievement of the aims shown in *Box 19.4* included:

- Changing the culture of the NHS, for which three characteristics are required: openness, transparency and candour.
- A statutory obligation should be imposed on healthcare providers, registered medical and nursing practitioners to observe the duty of candour.
- There should be a statutory obligation on directors of healthcare organisations to be truthful in any information given to a regulator or commissioner.
- There should be a criminal offence for any registered doctor, nurse or allied health professional or director of a registered or authorised organisation to obstruct the performance of these duties or dishonestly or recklessly make an untruthful statement to a regulator.
- Enforcement of the statutory duties should be by the Care Quality Commission.
- Increased focus on a culture of compassion and caring in nurse recruitment, training and education.
- Registration system to be introduced for healthcare support workers.
- NHS Constitution should be the first reference point for all NHS patients and staff and the common values of the service should be enshrined and effectively communicated by the NHS Constitution which should set out the system's values and the rights, obligations and expectations of patients.
- A simpler system of regulation.
- Non-compliance with a fundamental standard leading to death or serious harm of a patient should be capable of being prosecuted as a criminal offence, unless the provider or individual concerned can show that it was not reasonably practical to avoid this.
- Complaints relating to possible breaches of fundamental standards and serious complaints, should be accessible to the Care Quality Commission, relevant commissioners, health scrutiny committees, communities and local Healthwatch. Recommendations of the Patient's Association on complaints handling should be implemented. Any expression of concern by a patient should be treated as a complaint unless the patient's permission is refused.

Discussion of the Francis Report

Perhaps the main concern is that the recommendations of the Francis Report may be ignored. Unfortunately, the NHS has a history of ground-breaking reports which hit the headlines but then gather dust (Normansfield, 1978; Bristol Inquiry, 2001). The Bristol Inquiry recommended a duty of candour which it was hoped would be incorporated into the NHS Redress Act but this did not happen and the Act has never been fully brought into force. Possibly the way forward has been indicated in a letter to *The Times* sent in advance of the publication of the report by Dr Kim Holt, Founder and Chair of Patients First (who wrote to the managers at Great Ormond Street Hospital raising concerns about Baby P and who was removed from her post), and Professor Sir Brian Jarman at Imperial College (Holt and Jarman, 2013). They recommended changes to the NHS culture towards whistleblowers.

They urged three changes:

- The Government accepts that the NHS needs to be more open and accountable.
- The Health Select Committee should set up hearings into the treatment of whistleblowers and address the culture that seems to find the suppression of truth acceptable.
- Ongoing unresolved disputes involving NHS whistleblowers should be subject to fully independent and expert scrutiny.

Phil Hammond (2013), in a leader in *The Times*, warned that real action in the form of ensuring that whistleblowers retain or regain their jobs is required to make certain that whistleblowing is effective, and that gagging clauses do not operate secretly.

In order to secure significant change, there must be a willingness to hold senior management accountable for serious failings. Sir David Nicholson, the Chief Executive of the NHS, told the Public Accounts Committee of the House of Commons on 19 March 2013 (Smythe, 2013a) that all NHS staff are free to speak out irrespective of any gagging clauses. He stated that, so far in 2013, 44 staff had been paid a total of £1.3 million to settle disputes with bosses. He did not know how many of the agreements contained gagging clauses.

There has been no use of the Corporate Manslaughter and Homicide Act in relation to deaths within the NHS.

Following the Francis Report, the NHS Alliance (which represents GPs and other primary care staff) called for a radical change in attitude to hospital care, recommending that only the most serious cases should be treated in hospital. Tens of thousands of vulnerable and elderly patients should be treated in the community because hospitals can be dangerous places (Barrow, 2013).

Nick Timmins (2013) suggested that prevention of another Mid-Staffs lies with those inside the service and what they will tolerate. Similarly, Fiona Ross emphasises the importance of registered practitioners (and students) having the courage to care and to speak out against unacceptable practices. Nurse lecturers should have a more visible presence in practice so that they can see what is happening for themselves and be available to support mentors and students (Ross, 2013).

Implications for midwives

It is the responsibility of every individual registered practitioner to ensure that the recommendations of the Francis Report are implemented. The attitude of basic grade midwives is important in ensuring that sound standards of practice are followed.

Bullying in midwifery is not uncommon and steps need to be taken to ensure that managers protect whistleblowers and respond constructively to suggestions for improvement to services (see *Chapter 10*).

NHS Constitution

The seven key principles of the NHS Constitution are shown in *Box 19.5*.

The NHS Future Forum recommendations on the NHS Constitution in November 2012 led to a consultation on the guiding principles of the NHS Constitution. This should result in an amended NHS Constitution being published in March 2013.

The NHS Forum suggested three essential steps:

- To raise awareness of the public, patients and staff about the meaning of the NHS Constitution.
- The Constitution must be clearer about what happens when the NHS falls short of people's rights and expectations.
- The content needs updating and reinforcing in the following areas: involving patients in the decision making about their care, supporting staff, encouraging feedback and a more open culture, how information is used and protected, and making every contact between health professional and patient count.

The new NHS England has a statutory responsibility to promote the NHS Constitution and awareness of it. Each midwife should have easy access to a

---

Box 19.5. Seven key principles of the NHS Constitution

1. The NHS provides a comprehensive service, available to all irrespective of gender, race, disability, age, sexual orientation, religion, belief, gender reassignment, pregnancy and maternity or marital or civil partnership status.
2. Access to NHS services is based on clinical need, not an individual's ability to pay.
3. The NHS aspires to the highest standards of excellence and professionalism – in the provision of high quality care that is safe, effective and focused on patient experience.
4. The NHS aspires to put patients at the heart of everything it does.
5. The NHS works across organisational boundaries and in partnership with other organisations in the interest of patients, local communities and the wider population.
6. The NHS is committed to providing best value for taxpayers' money and the most effective, fair and sustainable use of finite resources.
7. The NHS is accountable to the public, communities and patients that it serves.

---

copy and understand its significance for her professional responsibilities. It is accessible on the NHS website (www.nhs.uk/choiceintheNHS/Rightsandledges/NHSConstitution).

Strategies for maternity services

Midwifery 2020 Final Report was launched in 2010 and covers the UK (Chief Nursing Officers of England, Northern Ireland, Scotland and Wales, 2010). It was commissioned by the Chief Nursing Officers of the four constituent countries of the UK with the aim of ensuring that women have a safe and emotionally satisfying experience during their pregnancy, childbirth and postnatal period. The final document drew on the reports of five workstreams. They are:

- The core role of the midwife.
- Workforce and workload.
- Education and career progression.
- Measuring quality.
- Public health and the role of the midwife (see *Chapter 16*).

Midwifery 2020 has been preceded by a plethora of reports, recommendations and strategies for midwifery over recent years. They include:

- The Department of Health (2008a) published *Delivering high quality midwifery care* in 2008. This outlines the priorities, opportunities and challenges for midwives arising from the Next Stage Review (Department of Health, 2008b) and Maternity Matters (Department of Health 2007).
- The Healthcare Commission published (for England only) *Towards better births* in 2008.
- The Prime Minister Commission on the future of nursing and midwifery was published in 2010 (HM Government, 2010).
- In Wales there is a *Strategic vision for maternity services* (Welsh Government, 2012).

It is hoped that Midwifery 2020, endorsed as it is by the four Chief Nursing Officers, will not gather dust on the shelves but provide a framework for NHS England and clinical commissioning groups in the commissioning of maternity services.

High stillbirth rate

There are, however, still many fundamental problems to resolve, including a high stillbirth rate. It was reported in November 2012 that 1:200 babies is born dead and yet it is estimated that 25% of these deaths could be prevented if systematic monitoring of the growth of the baby was implemented (Smyth, 2012).

In the dispute over the funding of the West Midlands Perinatal Institute, leading midwives and obstetricians claim it had achieved a 38% reduction of stillbirths with fetal growth restriction in Birmingham (Smyth, 2013b). Fears were expressed about the ending of central funding in April 2013 as the shift to GP-led commissioning takes over.

Shortage of midwives

On 22 January 2013 a report by the Royal College of Midwives presented to Parliament warned that maternity wards were at a tipping point as an extra 5000 midwives were required in England. These shortages will, unless they can be rectified, have a huge impact on practice, including choices for home births, and may undermine the morale of midwives generally. The shortage of midwives coincides with a large increase in the birth rate.

Financial constraints

The chair of the Public Accounts Committee of the House of Commons stated on 21 March 2013 that "the finances of some trusts are fragile and there is a risk they may resort to cost-cutting rather than efficiency savings". The NHS has to save £20 billion in the four years to 2014–5 to keep pace with growing demand. Midwives are finding that they are working in an increasingly pressurised and demoralised environment.

Practical issues for the individual midwife

Even for midwives practising outside England, the implications of the above developments cannot be ignored, since in due course the devolved assemblies will be learning the lessons from England and be making appropriate changes to their own NHS organisations. Midwifery 2020 is, of course, a strategy for midwives across the four nations and the implications of the Mid-Staffs Inquiry are of value to all registered health practitioners wherever they work. The following are a few suggestions for the individual midwife to make the most of these developments:

- Be conversant with the new organisations. Understand their features, their powers and functions, and their relationship with maternity services.
- Identify local groups. Get to know those who are on the local Healthwatch organisations or their equivalent elsewhere across the UK. Be prepared to have an input and to interact with them to share concerns and ideas about maternity services
- Identify the needs of clients, any deficiencies in the service and any possible developments and raise these with senior management. Be aware of the wider public health responsibilities of the midwife (see *Chapter 16*).
- If there are any concerns, raise these with the appropriate persons. Clarify in writing any worries and what action should be taken.
- If there is no or minimal response, be prepared to take concerns further, seeking advice and guidance from other bodies, such as the Nursing and Midwifery Council and the Royal College of Midwives.
- If necessary follow closely the whistleblowing procedures drawn up by your employer.
- Keep squeaky clean, i.e. do not give grounds for complaint against yourself.
- Advocate a policy of openness in relation to clients and colleagues, but ensure that confidentiality is respected where appropriate.

- Respect complainants and their complaints and follow the procedure for handling complaints (see *Chapter 5*).
- Use the NHS Constitution as a learning experience for both you and clients.
- Be conversant with NICE guidelines and other standards of professional practice and identify changes in the practice of midwifery care.
- Embrace developments in technology and acquire the necessary training.
- Make use of internet resources and embed these into your professional practice.

Conclusion

Midwives and midwifery face significant challenges: the implementation of the 2012 Act, taking on board the recommendation of the Francis Inquiry, and achieving the targets set in Midwifery 2020. At the same time, they are dealing with a soaring birth rate and a reducing midwifery force with many midwives coming up to retirement. There will be strong pressures to make greater use of maternity support workers. Financial constraints are requiring trusts to adopt new technologies without which they will not be able to make the essential quality, innovation, productivity and prevention savings. The announcement of the setting up of another independent inquiry (Templeton, 2013), this time into the situation at the University Hospital of Morecambe Bay NHS Foundation Trust following the deaths of 16 babies and two mothers, suggests that the situation in Staffordshire is not unique and many more trusts may have to take significant steps to protect patients. The greatest protection of the client is the willingness of the individual midwife to stand up and be counted in ensuring that professional standards and the human rights of the client are respected. It is hoped that this book can go a small way in assisting in this responsibility.

References

Barrow M (2013) Keep out of dangerous hospitals, GPs warn. *The Times* **13 March**

Department of Health (2008a) *Delivering high quality midwifery care.* HMSO, London

Hammond P (2013) The NHS is not safe for whistleblowers. *The Times* **15 March**

Healthcare Commission (2008) *Towards better births.* Healthcare Commission, London

HM Government (2010) *Report by the Prime Minister's Commission on the Future of Nursing and Midwifery in England.* HMSO, London

Holt K, Jarman B (2013) Letter to the editor. *The Times* **4 February**

Illman J (2013) Ex minister warns GP groups could struggle. *Local Government*

Chronicle **1 March**

Ross F (2013) Having the courage to care – lessons learnt after Mid-Staffordshire. *British Journal of Nursing* **22**(5): 296

Royal College of Midwives (2013) *Second annual report: State of maternity services.* Royal College of Midwives, London

Smyth C (2012) Chaotic NHS fails to prevent hundreds of still births. *The Times* **27 November**

Smyth C (2013a) NHS boss tells gagged staff they are now free to speak out. *The Times* **19 March**

Smyth C (2013b) Closure of baby research centre will put lives at risk, say midwives. *The Times* **5 February**

Templeton SK (2013) Independent inquiry ordered. *The Sunday Times* **10 March**

Timmins N (2013) After Francis: Has the shock been big enough? *British Journal of Healthcare Management* **19**(3): 150

Tyler S (2013) Brand new commission. *Midwives* **1**: 48–50

Welsh Government (2012) *Strategic vision for maternity services.* Welsh Government, Cardiff

Further reading

Allen R, Crasnow R, Beale A (2007) *Employment law and human rights* (2nd edn). Oxford University Press, Oxford

Appelbe GE, Wingfield J (eds) (2009) *Dale and Appelbe's pharmacy: Law and ethics* (89th edn). Pharmaceutical Press, London

Atkinson J (2007) *Advance directives in mental health – Theory, practice and ethics.* Jessica Kingsley Publications, London

Barrett B, Howells R (2000) *Occupational health and safety law: Text and materials.* Cavendish, London

Beale HG (ed) (2006) *Chitty on contracts.* (3rd cumulative supplement to 29th edn). Sweet & Maxwell, London

Beauchamp TL, Childress JF (2001) *Principles of biomedical ethics* (5th edn). Oxford University Press, Oxford

Beddard R (1994) *Human rights and Europe* (3rd edn). Grotius Publications Ltd, Cambridge

Benny R, Sargeant M, Jefferson M (2006) *Employment law. Questions and answers* (2nd edn). Oxford University Press, Oxford

Blom-Cooper L et al (1996) *The case of Jason Mitchell: Report of the Independent Panel of Inquiry.* Duckworth, London

Blom-Cooper L, Hally H, Murphy E (1996) *The falling shadow. One patient's mental health care 1978–1993* (Report of an Inquiry into the Death of an Occupational Therapist at Edith Morgan Unit, Torbay 1993), Duckworth, London

Brazier M (2011) *Medicine, patients and the law* (45th edn). Penguin, London

British Medical Association (1998) *Medical ethics today.* BMJ Publishing, London

British Medical Association (2001) *Consent, rights and choices in health care for children and young people.* BMJ Books, London

Britton A (2004) *Health care law and ethics.* W. Green, London

Carey P (2009) *Data protection – a practical guide to UK and EU law* (3rd edn). Oxford University Press, Oxford

Clarkson CMV, Keating HM (2010) *Criminal law. Text and materials* (7th edn). Sweet and Maxwell, London

Clements L (2004) *Community care and the law* (3rd edn). Legal Action Group, London

Clerk JF (2010) *Clerk and Lindsell on torts* (19th edn). Sweet & Maxwell, London

Committee of Experts Advisory Group on AIDS (1994) *Guidance for health care workers' protection against infection with HIV and hepatitis.* HMSO, London

Connolly M (2006) *Discrimination law.* Thomson, Sweet & Maxwell, London

Cooper J (ed) (2000) *Law, rights and disability.* Jessica Kingsley, London

Deakin S, Johnston A, Markensinis B (2007) *Markensinis and Deakin's tort law* (6th edn) Clarendon Press, London

Denis IH (2007) *The law of evidence* (4th edn). Sweet & Maxwell, London, London

Department of Health (1993) *AIDS/HIV infected health care workers.* HMSO, London

Dimond BC (1992) *Accountability and the nurse.* Distance learning pack, South Bank University, London

Dimond BC (1996) *Legal aspects of child health care.* Mosby, Maryland Heights, MI

Dimond BC (1997) *Legal aspects of care in the community.* Macmillan, London

Dimond BC (1997) *Legal aspects of occupational therapy.* Blackwell Scientific, Oxford

Dimond BC (1997) *Mental Health (Patients in the Community) Act 1995: An introductory text.* Mark Allen, London

Dimond BC (1998) *Legal aspects of complementary therapy practice.* Churchill Livingstone, Edinburgh

Dimond BC (1999) *Legal aspects of physiotherapy.* Blackwell Science, Oxford

Dimond BC (1999) *Patients' rights responsibilities and the nurse* (2nd edn). Central Health Studies Quay Publications, London

Dimond BC (2005) *Legal aspects of midwifery* (3rd edn). Books for Midwives Press, London

Dimond BC (2008) *Legal aspects of death.* Quay Publications/Mark Allen, London

Dimond BC (2008) *Legal aspects of mental capacity.* Blackwell Publishing, Oxford

Dimond BC (2009) *Legal aspects of consent* (2nd edn). Quay Publications/Mark Allen, London

Dimond BC (2011) *Legal aspects of nursing* (6th edn) Hemel Hempstead: Pearson Education, London

Dimond BC (2012) *Legal aspects of pain management* (2nd edn). Quay Publications/Mark Allen, London

Dimond BC (2012) *Legal aspects of patient confidentiality* (2nd edn). Quay Publications/ Mark Allen, London

Dimond BC, Barker F (1996) *Mental health law for nurses.* Blackwell Science, Oxford

Eliot C, Quinn F (2007) *The English legal system* (118th edn). Pearson Education, London

Fraser J with Nolan M (2004) *Child protection: A guide for midwives* (2nd edn). Books for Midwives, London

Glynn J, Gomez D (2012) *Regulation of healthcare professionals fitness to practise: healthcare regulatory law.* Principles and process. Sweet & Maxwell, London

Grainger I, Fealy M with Spencer M (2000) *Civil procedure rules in action* (2nd edn). Cavendish, London

Griffith R, Tengah C, Patel C (2010) *Law and professional issues in midwifery.* Learning Matters, Exeter

Grubb A, Laing J, McHale JV (2010) *Principles of medical law* (3rd edn). OUP, London

Harris DJ (2005) *Cases and materials on the European Convention on Human Rights* (2nd rev edn). Butterworth, London

Harris P (2007) *An Introduction to law* (7th edn). Butterworth, London

Health and Safety Commission (1992) *Guidelines on manual handling in the health services*. HMSO, London

Health and Safety Commission (1992) *Manual handling regulations: Approved code of practice*. HMSO, London

Health and Safety Commission (1999) *Management of Health and Safety at Work Regulations: Approved Code of Practice*. HMSO, London

Hendrick J (1010) *Law and ethics in children's nursing* Wiley Blackwell, Oxford

Hendrick J (2006) *Law and ethics in nursing and healthcare* (2nd edn). Nelson Thornes Publishers, London

Herring J (1012) *Medical law and ethics* (4th edn). Oxford University Press, Oxford

Heywood-Jones I (ed) (1999) *The UKCC Code of Conduct: A critical guide*. Nursing Times Books(4th edn).

Hockton A (2002) *The law on consent to treatment*. Sweet & Maxwell, London

Hoggett B (2005) *Mental health law* (5th edn). Sweet & Maxwell, London

Holland J, Burnett S (2006) *Employment law*. Oxford University Press, Oxford

Howarth DR, O'Sullivan JA (2000) *Hepple Howarth and Matthews tort: Cases and materials* (5th edn). Butterworth, London

Howells G, Weatherill S (2005) *Consumer protection law* (2nd edn). Ashgate, Dartmouth

Humphreys N (2005) *Trade union law and collective employment rights* (2nd edn). Jordans Employment Law, Bristol

Hunt G, Wainwright P (eds) (1994) *Expanding the role of the nurse*. Blackwell Scientific, Oxford

Hurwitz B (1998) *Clinical guidelines and the law*. Oxford Radcliffe Medical Press, Oxford

Hurwitz B, Paquita Z (2006) *Everyday ethics in primary care*. British Medical Association, London

Ingman T (2006) *The English legal process* (11th edn). Blackstone Press, Vancouver, BC,

Jay R (1012) *Data protection law and practice* (3rd rev edn). Sweet & Maxwell, London

Jones MA (2007) *Textbook on torts* (9th edn). Oxford University Press, Oxford

Jones MA (2010) *Medical negligence* (5th edn). Sweet & Maxwell, London

Jones MA, Morris AE (2005) *Blackstone's Statutes on Medical Law* (4th edn). Oxford University Press, Oxford

Jones R (2012) *Mental Capacity Act manual* (4th edn). Sweet & Maxwell, London

Jones R (2012) *Mental Health Act manual* (150th edn). Sweet & Maxwell, London

Keenan D (2004) *Smith and Keenan's English law* (14th edn). Longman, Harlow

Kennedy I, Grubb A (2000) *Medical law* (3rd edn). Butterworth, London

Kennedy T (1998) *Learning European law*. Sweet & Maxwell, London

Kidner R (2003) *Blackstone's Statutes on employment law* (13th edn). Oxford University Press, Oxford

Kloss D (2005) *Occupational health law* (4th edn). Blackwell Scientific, Oxford

Leach P (2005) *Taking a case to the European Court of Human Rights* (2nd edn). Blackstone Press, Vancouver, BC

Lee RG, Morgan D (2001) *Human fertilisation and embryology*. Blackstone Press, Vancouver, BC

Lewis T (2005) *Employment law* (6th edn). Legal Action Group, London

Lockton D (2007) *Employment law 2007–8* (5th edn). Routledge-Cavendish, London

Lynch J (2009) *Health records in court*. Radcliffe Publishing Ltd, Abingdon

Macdonald S, Magill-Cuerden J (eds) (2011) *Mayes' midwifery* (15th edn). Balliere Tindall, London

Mahindra Raj (2008) *Medical law handbook*. Radcliffe Publisers Ltd, Abingdon

Mandelstam M (1998) *An A–Z of Community care law*. Jessica Kingsley, London

Mandelstam M (2005) *Community care practice and the law* (3rd edn). Jessica Kingsley, London

Mason D, Edwards P (1993) *Litigation: A risk management guide for midwives*. Royal College of Midwives, London

Mason JK, McCall-Smith RA, Laurie GT (2012) *Law and medical ethics* (86th edn). Butterworth, London

Matthews M, O'Cinneide M, Hepple J (2912) *Howarth and Matthews tort: Cases and materials* (6th edn). Butterworth, London

McHale J, Fox M (2007) *Health care law* (2nd edn). Sweet & Maxwell, London

McHale J, Tingle J (2007) *Law and nursing* (32nd edn). Butterworth Heinemann/Elsevier Health Sciences, London

McLean S (2007) *Impairment and disability: Law and ethics at the beginning and end of life*. Routledge-Cavendish, London

Metzer A, Weinberg J (1999) *Criminal litigation*. Legal Action Group, London

Miers D, Page A (1990) *Legislation* (2nd edn). Sweet & Maxwell, London

Miles A, Hampton J, Hurwitz B (2000) *NICE, CHI and the NHS reforms – enabling excellence or imposing control?* Aesculapius, Phoenix, Arizona

Montague A (1996) *Legal problems in emergency medicine*. Oxford University Press, Oxford

Montgomery J (2003) *Health care law* (2nd edn). Oxford University Press, Oxford

Murphy J, Witting C (2012) *Street on torts* (123th edn). Butterworth, London

Nairns J (2006) *Discrimination law: Text cases and materials*. Oxford University Press, Oxford

National Association of Theatre Nurses (1993) *The role of the nurse as first assistant in the operating department.* NATN, London

National Association of Theatre Nurses (1998) *Principles of safe practice in the perioperative environment.* NATN, London

National Association of Theatre Nurses (1998) *Safeguards for invasive procedures.* NATN, London

Painter RW, Holmes AEM (2006) *Cases and materials on employment law* (6th edn). Oxford University Press, Oxford

Pitt G (2007) *Employment law* (6th edn). Sweet & Maxwell, London

Pyne RH (1998) *Professional discipline in nursing midwifery and health visiting* (3rd edn). Blackwell Scientific, Oxfod

Richardson PJ (ed) (2012) *Archbold criminal pleadings evidence and practice* (55th rev edn). Sweet & Maxwell, London

Rogers WVH (2010) *Winfield and Jolowicz on tort* (187th edn). Thomson Sweet & Maxwell, London

RoseKay M, Sime S, French DW (eds) (2012) *Blackstone's civil practice.* Oxford University Press, Oxford

Rowson R (1990) *An introduction to ethics for nurses.* Scutari Press, London

Rowson R (2006) *Working ethics – how to be fair in a culturally complex world.* Jessica Kingsley, London

Royal College of Midwives (1993) *Examples of effective midwifery management.* RCM, London

Royal College of Midwives (1993) *The midwife: Her legal status and accountability.* RCM, London

Royal College of Nursing (1992) *Focus on restraint* (2nd edn). RCN, London

Rubenstein M (2002) *Discrimination – guide to relevant case law* (15th edn). Eclipse Group, London

Rumbold G (1999) *Ethics in nursing practice* (3rd edn). Baillière Tindall, London

Salvage J (1998) *Nurses at risk: Guide to health and safety at work* (2nd edn). Heinemann, London

Sellars C (2011) *Risk assessment with people with learning disabilities.* Blackwell, Oxford

Selwyn N (2006) *Selwyn's law of employment* (14th edn). Butterworth, London

Silverton L (1998) *The art and science of midwifery.* Pearson Education, London

Sime S (2012) *Practical approach to civil procedure* (159th edn). Blackstone Press, Vancouver, BC

Skegg PDG (1998) *Law ethics and medicine* (2nd edn). Oxford University Press, Oxfod

Slapper G, Kelly D (2013) *The English legal system 2013–14* (148th edn). Routledge-Cavendish, London

Social Security Inspectorate, Department of Health (1993) *No longer afraid: Safeguard of older people in domestic settings.* HMSO, London

Stauch M, Wheat K (2011) *Text and materials on medical law and ethics* (4th edn). Cavendish, London

Steiner J, Woods L (2009) *Textbook on EUC law* (109th edn). Oxford University Press, Oxford

Stevenson K, Davies A, Gunn M (2003) *Blackstone's guide to Sexual Offences Act 2003.* Oxford University Press, Oxford

Stone J, Matthews J (1996) *Complementary medicine and the law.* Oxford University Press, Oxford

Storch J (2004) *Towards a moral horizon: Nursing ethics for leadership and practice.* Pearson Education, Toronto

Symon A (2001) *Obstetric litigation from A to Z.* Mark Allen Publishing, Wiltshire

Taylor S, Emir A (2006) *Employment law: An introduction.* Oxford University Press, Oxford

Tilley S, Watson R (eds) (2004) *Accountability in nursing and midwifery* (2nd edn). Blackwell Publishing, Oxford

Tingle J, Cribb A (2013) *Nursing law and ethics* (4th edn). Blackwell Publishers, Oxford

Tingle J, Foster C (2006) *Clinical guidelines: Law policy and practice* (2nd edn). Cavendish, London

Tolley's (2012) *Health and safety at work handbook* (24th edn). Tolley, London

Tschudin V (2003) *Ethics in nursing: The caring relationship* (3rd edn). Butterworth-Heinemann, London

Vincent C (ed) (2001) *Clinical risk management* (2nd edn). BMJ Publishing, London

Wheeler J (2006) *The English legal system* (2nd edn). Pearson Education, Toronto

White R, Carr P, Lowe NA (2002) *Guide to the Children Act 1989* (3rd edn). Butterworth, London

Wild C, Weinstein S (2010) *Smith and Keenan's English law* (16th edn). Longman, Harlow

Wilkinson R, Caulfield H (2000) *The Human Rights Act: A practical guide for nurses.* Whurr Publishers, London

Wyndham-Kay J (Chairman) (1991) *Report of Royal College of Midwives' Commission on legislation relating to midwives.* RCM, London

Young AP (1989) *Legal problems in nursing practice.* Harper & Row, New York

Young AP (1991) *Law and professional conduct in nursing* (2nd edn). Scutari Press, London

Zander M (2005) *Police and Criminal Evidence Act* (1st supplement to 5th edn). Sweet & Maxwell, London

Reference should also be made to the many articles on different legal aspects of midwifery practice which can be found in *The Practising Midwife*, *The British Journal of Midwifery*, the *Midwives Chronicle*, *Midwifery Matters*, *Midwife*, and similar journals for registered practitioners.

The Midwives Information and Resource Service (MIDIRS) provides an extremely useful guide to articles relevant to midwifery published in other journals.

There is also an internet service for midwifery publications: www.intermid.co.uk

Websites

Abortion Rights	www.abortionrights.org.uk
Action for Advocacy	www.actionforadvocacy.org
Advocacy support	www.seap.org.uk
Association of British Insurers	www.abi.org.uk
Audit Commission	www.audit-commission.gov.uk
British and Irish Legal Information Institute (case law and statute resource)	www.bailii.org
British National Formulary	www.bnf.org.uk
BUPA	www.bupa.co.uk
Care Quality Commission	www.cqc.org.uk
Carers Federtion	www.carersfederation.co.uk
Children are Unbeatable!	www.childrenareunbeatable.org.uk
Citizens' Advice Bureau	www.citizensadvice.org.uk
Civil Procedure Rules	www.justice.gov.uk/courts/procedure rules
Clinical Negligence Scheme for Trusts	www.nhsla.com/Claims/Schemes/ CNST/
Commission for Racial Equality	www.cre.gov.uk/
Consumer rights	www.youandyourrights.co.uk
Contaminated blood and blood products	www.archercbbp.com
Counsel and Care	www.counselandcare.org.uk
Council for Healthcare Regulatory Excellence	www.nhsjusticegroup.co.uk
Council of Europe	www.echr.coe.int
Crown Prosecution Service	www.cps.gov.uk
Data Protection and Freedom of Information	www.ico.gov.uk
Department for Education	www.education.gov.uk
Department for Children, Schools and Families	www.dfes.gov.uk
Department for Work and Pensions	www.dwp.gov.uk
Department of Health	www.dh.gov.uk
Digital Journal	www.digitaljournal.com
Domestic violence	www.domesticviolence.gov.uk

Drugs and Alcohol Information	www.knowthescore.info
Equality and Human Rights Commission	www.equalityhumanrights.com
European Union Law	www.eur-lex.europa.eu
Foundation for People with Learning Disabilities	www.learningdisabilities.org.uk
Frank – Drugs advice	www.talktofrank.com
General Medical Council	www.gmc-uk.org
Health and Safety Executive	www.hse.gov.uk
Health and Social Care Information Centre	www.hscic.gov.uk
Health Professions Council	www.hpc-uk.org
Health Protection Agency	www.hpa.org.uk
Health Service Ombudsman	www.ombudsman.org.uk
HM Courts Service	www.hmcourts-service.gov.uk
Home Office	www.homeoffice.gov.uk
Human Fertilisation and Embryology Authority	www.hfea.gov.uk/
Human Genetics Commission	www.hgc.gov.uk
Human Rights	www.humanrights.gov.uk
Human Tissue Authority	www.hta.gov.uk
Independent Complaints Advocacy Service	www.icas
Independent Mental Capacity Advocate	www.dh.gov.uk.imca
Information Commissioner's Office	www.ico.gov.uk
International Confederation of Midwives	www.internationalmidwives.org
Law Centres Federation	www.lawcentres.org.uk
Legal cases (England and Wales)	www.bailli.org/ew/cases
Legislation	www.legislation.gov.uk
Marie Stopes	www.mariestopes.org.uk
Maternity Action	www.maternityaction.org.uk
Maternity Alliance	www.maternityalliance.org.uk
Medicines and Healthcare Products Regulatory Agency	www.mhra.gov.uk
Mencap	www.mencap.org.uk
Mental Health Foundation	www.mentalhealth.org.uk
Mental Health Matters	www.mentalhealthmatters.com/
Mid-Staffs Inquiry	www.midstaffspublicinquiry.com
Midwifery 2020	www.midwifery2020.org

Mind	www.mind.org.uk
Ministry of Justice	www.justice.gov.uk
Monitor	www.monitor-nhsft.gov.uk
National Audit Office	www.nao.gov.uk
National Clinical Assessment Service	www.ncas.nhs.uk
National Health Service Litigation Authority	www.nhsla.com
National Information and Governance Board for Health and Social Care (now replaced by the HSCIC)	www.nigb.nhs.uk
National Institute for Health and Clinical Excellence (NICE)	www.nice.org.uk
National Patient Safety Agency	www.npsa.gov.uk
National Perinatal Epidemiology Unit	www.npeu.ox.ac.uk/
National Research Ethics Service	www.nres.nhs.uk
National Treatment Agency	www.nta.nhs.uk
Newborn Bloodspot Screening Service	www.newbornbloodspot.screening.
NHS	www.nhs.uk
NHS Business Services Authority	www.nhsbsa.nhs.uk
NHS Connecting for Health	www.connectingforhealth.nhs.uk
NHS Direct	www.nhsdirect.nhs.uk
NHS Employers	www.nhsemployers.org
NHS England	www.england.nhs.uk
NHS Institute for Innovation and Improvement (From April 2013 to be hosted by the NHS Commissioning Board)	www.institute.nhs.uk
NHS Professionals	www.nhsprofessionals.nhs.uk
NHS Wales	www.wales.nhs.uk
NICE	www.nice.org.uk
Northern Ireland Government	www.nidirect.gov.uk, www.northernireland.gov.uk
Nursing and Midwifery Council	www.nmc-org.uk
Office of Public Guardian	www.publicguardian.gov.uk
Office of Public Sector Information	www.opsi.gov.uk
Official documents	www.official-documents.gov.uk
Official Solicitor	www.officialsolicitor.gov.uk
Open Government	www.open.gov.uk

Parliamentary publications	www.publications.parliament.uk
Patient Concern	www.patientconcern.org.uk
Patient Safety	www.patientsafetyfirst
Patients' Association	www.patients-association.org.uk
People First	www.peoplefirst.org.uk
POhWER	www.pohwer.net
Pro-life news source	www.lifenews.com
Public Concern at Work	www.pcaw.org.uk
RIDDOR	www.riddor.gov.uk
Resuscitation Council	www.resus.org.uk
Royal College of Midwives	www.rcm.org.uk
Royal College of Nursing	www.rcn.org.uk
Royal College of Obstetricians and Gynaecologists	www.rcog.org.uk
Royal College of Paediatrics and Child Health	www.rcpch.ac.uk
Royal College of Psychiatrists	www.rcpsych.ac.uk
Royal College of Surgeons	www.rcseng.ac.uk
Royal Pharmaceutical Society	www.rpharms.com
Scottish Government	www.scotland.gov.uk
	www.scottish.parliament.uk
Self-help from Citizens Advice Bureau	www.adviceguide.org.uk
Shipman Inquiry	www.the-shipman-inquiry.org.uk/ reports.asp
Skipton Fund	www.skiptonfund.org/Eng
Society for the Protection of the Unborn Child	www.spuc.org.uk
Stillbirth and Neonatal Death Society	www.uk-sands.org
UK Legislation	www.legislation.gov.uk
UK Parliament	www.parliament.uk
Variant Creutzfeldt-Jakob Disease Trust	www.vcjdtrust.co.uk
Victoria Climbie Inquiry	www.victoria-climbie-inquiry.org.uk
VOICE UK	www.voiceuk.clara.net
Wales Drug and Alcohol Helpline	www.dan247.org.uk
Welsh Assembly Government	www.wales.gov.uk/topics/health
WHO Europe	www.euro.who.int
Working Together to Safeguard Children	www.workingtogetheronline.co.uk
World Health Organization	www.who.int

Glossary

acceptance an agreement to the terms of an offer which leads to a binding legal
   obligation, i.e. a *contract*

accusatorial a system of court proceedings where the two sides contest the issue (contrast
   with *inquisitorial*)

Act of Parliament statute

action legal proceedings

actionable per se a court action where the claimant does not have to show loss, damage
   or harm to obtain compensation, e.g. an action for trespass to the person

actus reus essential element of a crime that must be proved to secure a conviction, as
   opposed to the mental state of the accused (*mens rea*)

adversarial approach adopted in an *accusatorial system*

advocate a person who pleads for another: it could be paid and professional, such as a
   barrister or *solicitor*, or it could be a lay advocate either paid or unpaid; a witness
   is not an advocate

affidavit a statement given under oath

alternative dispute resolution methods to resolve a dispute without going to court, such as
   mediation

approved mental health professional a person recognised under the Mental Health Act
   1983 (as amended by the Mental Health Act 2007) as having responsibilities in
   relation to the admission and detention of persons under the Mental Health Act
   (replaces the *approved social worker*)

approved social worker a social worker qualified for the purposes of the Mental Health
   Act (whose former role is now undertaken by an *approved mental health
   professional*)

arrestable offence an offence defined in Section 24 of the Police and Criminal Evidence
   Act 1984 that gives to the citizen the power of arrest in certain circumstances
   without a warrant

assault a threat of unlawful contact (*trespass* to the person)

balance of probabilities standard of proof in *civil* proceedings

barrister (sometimes known as counsel) a lawyer qualified to take a case in court

battery an unlawful touching (see *trespass to the person*)

bench magistrates, *justices of the peace*

Bolam Test test laid down by Judge McNair in the case of *Bolam v Friern HMC* on the
   standard of care expected of a professional in cases of alleged *negligence*

burden of proof duty of a party to litigation to establish the facts or, in criminal
   proceedings, the duty of the prosecution to establish both *actus reus* and *mens rea*

by-laws a form of delegated legislation, usually made by local authorities

case law judge-made law, or the *common law*

cause of action facts that entitle a person to sue

certiorari an action taken to challenge an administrative or judicial decision (literally: to
   make more certain)

citation each case is reported in an official series of cases according to the following symbols: *Re F* (i.e. in the matter of F) or *F v West Berkshire Health Authority* 1989 2 All ER 545 which means the year 1989 volume 2 of the All England Law Reports page 545. Each case can be cited by means of this reference system. In the case of *Whitehouse v Jordan* (*Whitehouse v Jordan* [1981] 1 All ER 267), Whitehouse is the claimant, Jordan the defendant and "v" stands for versus, i.e. against. Other law reports include: AC Appeals Court; EWCA England and Wales Court of Appeal; EWHC England and Wales High Court; EWHL England and Wales House of Lords; QB Queens Bench Division and WLR Weekly Law Reports

civil action proceedings brought in the civil courts

civil wrong an act or omission which can be pursued in the civil courts by the person who has suffered the wrong (see *tort*)

claimant person bringing a *civil action* (originally *plaintiff*)

committal proceedings hearings before the magistrates to decide if a person should be sent for trial in the Crown Court

common law law derived from the decisions of judges, *case law*, judge-made law

conditional fee system a system whereby client and lawyer can agree that payment of fees is dependent on the outcome of the court action; also known as "no win, no fee"

conditions terms of a contract (see *warranties*)

constructive knowledge knowledge that can be obtained from the circumstances

continuous service length of service an employee must have served to be entitled to receive certain statutory or contractual rights

contract an agreement enforceable in law

contract for services an agreement enforceable in law whereby one party provides services, not being employment, in return for payment or other consideration from the other

contract of service a contract for employment

coroner a person appointed to hold an inquiry (inquest) into a death that occurred in unexpected or unusual circumstances

counsel see *barrister*

counter-offer a response to an offer that suggests different terms and is therefore counted as an offer, not an acceptance

criminal wrong an act or omission which can be pursued in the criminal courts

cross-examination questions asked of a witness by the lawyer for the opposing side: leading questions may be asked

damages a sum of money awarded by a court as compensation for a *tort* or breach of contract

decided cases cases that establish a principle and may become a *precedent*

declaration a ruling by the court setting out the legal situation

disclosure documents made available to the other party

dissenting judge a judge who disagrees with the decision of the majority of judges

distinguished (of cases) rules of *precedent* require judges to follow decisions of judges in previous cases, where these are binding on them. However, in some circumstances, it is possible to come to a different decision, because the facts of the earlier case are not comparable to the case now being heard and therefore the earlier decision can be "distinguished"

ex gratia as a matter of favour, e.g. without admission of *liability*, of payment offered to a *claimant*

ex parte on the part of one side only (an *ex parte* injunction may be made after hearing the application of only one party)

examination in chief witness is asked questions in court by the lawyer of the party that has asked the witness to attend. Leading questions may not be asked

expert witness evidence given by a person whose general opinion, based on training or experience, is relevant to some of the issues in dispute (contrast with *witness of fact*)

frustration (of *contracts*) ending of a contract by operation of law, because of the existence of an event not contemplated by the parties when they made the contract, e.g. imprisonment, death, blindness

guardian ad litem a person with a social work and childcare background who is appointed to ensure that the court is fully informed of the relevant facts which relate to a child and that the wishes and feelings of the child are clearly established. The appointment is made from a panel set up by the local authority

guilty a finding in a criminal court of responsibility for a criminal offence

hearsay evidence that has been learnt from another person

hierarchy recognised status of courts that results in lower courts following the decisions of higher courts (see *precedent*). Thus decisions of the House of Lords must be followed by all lower courts unless they can be *distinguished*

indictment a written accusation against a person, charging him with a serious crime, triable by jury

informal of a patient who has entered hospital without any statutory requirements

injunction an order of the court restraining a person

inquisitorial a system of justice whereby the truth is revealed by an inquiry into the facts conducted by the judge, e.g. coroner's court

invitation to treat early stages in negotiating a contract, e.g. an advertisement or letter expressing interest. An invitation to treat will often precede an offer that, when accepted, leads to the formation of an agreement that, if there is consideration and an intention to create legal relations, will be binding

judicial review an application to the High Court for a judicial or administrative decision to be reviewed and an appropriate order made, e.g. *declaration*

justice of the peace (JP) a lay magistrate, i.e. not legally qualified, who hears *summary (minor) offences* and sometimes *indictable (serious) offences* in the magistrates' court in a group of three (see *bench*)

legislation laws enacted by Parliament or other law-making body such as the European Parliament

liable/liability responsible for the wrongdoing or harm in civil proceedings

litigation civil proceedings

locus standi (a place to stand) the right to bring an action or challenge some decision

magistrate a person (see *justice of the peace* and *stipendiary magistrate*) who hears *summary (minor) offences* or *indictable offences* that can be heard in the magistrates' court

mandamus (we command) an order of the court requiring the defendant to take specified action

mens rea mental element in a crime (contrast with *actus reus*)

negligence a *civil action* for compensation, also a failure to follow a reasonable standard of care

next friend a person who brings a court action on behalf of a minor

obiter dicta something said by a judge which is not central to a case and does not form part of the *ratio decidendi*

offer a proposal made by a party that, if accepted, can lead to a contract. It often follows an *invitation to treat*

ombudsman a commissioner (e.g. health, local government) appointed by the government to hear complaints

payment into court an offer to settle a dispute at a particular sum, which is paid into court. The *claimant*'s failure to accept the offer means that the claimant is liable to pay costs, if the final award is the same or less than the payment made

pedagogic of the science of teaching

plaintiff term formerly used to describe one who brings an action in the *civil* courts. Now the term *claimant* is used

plea in mitigation a formal statement to the court aimed at reducing the sentence to be pronounced by the judge

pleading the documents that pass between the parties in the run-up to the hearing

practice direction guidance issued by the head of the court to which they relate on the procedure to be followed

pre-action protocol rules of the Supreme Court that provide guidance on action to be taken before legal proceedings commence

precedent a decision that may have to be followed in a subsequent court hearing (see *hierarchy*)

prima facie at first sight; sufficient evidence brought by one party to require the other party to provide a defence

privilege in relation to evidence, being able to refuse to disclose it to the court

privity relationship that exists between parties as the result of a legal agreement

professional misconduct conduct of a registered health practitioner that could lead to conduct and competence proceedings by the registration body

proof evidence that secures the establishment of a claimant's, prosecution's or defendant's case

prosecution pursuing of criminal offences in court

quantum amount of compensation, or the monetary value of a claim

Queen's Counsel (QC) a senior *barrister*, also known as a "silk"

ratio decidendi (the reason for deciding) the principle established by the case which can become a *precedent*. Contrast with *obiter dicta*

Re F ruling a professional who acts in the best interests of an incompetent person who is incapable of giving consent does not act unlawfully if he follows the accepted standard of care according to the Bolam Test. Now largely replaced by the Mental Capacity Act 2005

reasonable doubt to secure a conviction in criminal proceedings the prosecution must establish "beyond reasonable doubt" the guilt of the accused

rebut to refute

res ipsa loquitur the thing speaks for itself

rescission where a contract is ended by the order of a court or by the cancellation of the contract by one party entitled in law to do so

solicitor a lawyer who is qualified on the register held by the Law Society

specialist community public health nurse replaces the health visitor as a registered practitioner under the Nursing and Midwifery Council

statute law (statutory) law made by Acts of Parliament

stipendiary magistrate a legally qualified *magistrate* who is paid (i.e. has a stipend)

strict liability liability for a criminal act where the mental element does not have to be proved; in civil proceedings liability without establishing negligence

subpoena an order of the court requiring a person to appear as a witness (*subpoena ad testificandum*) or to bring records/documents (*subpoena duces tecum*)

summary judgment a procedure whereby the *claimant* can obtain judgment without the defendant being permitted to defend the action

summary offence a lesser offence that may only be heard by *magistrates*

tort a *civil wrong* excluding breach of contract. It includes: *negligence*, *trespass* (to the person, goods or land), nuisance, breach of statutory duty and defamation

trespass to the person a wrongful direct interference with another person. Harm does not have to be proved

trial a court hearing before a judge

ultra vires outside the powers given by law (e.g. of a statutory body or company)

vicarious liability liability of an employer for the wrongful acts of an employee committed while in the course of employment

volenti non fit injuria to the willing there is no wrong; voluntary assumption of risk

ward of court a minor placed under the protection of the High Court, which assumes responsibility for him or her and all decisions relating to his or her care must be made in accordance with the directions of the court

warranties terms of a contract that are considered to be less important than the terms described as conditions: breach of a condition entitles the innocent party to see the contract as ended, i.e. repudiated by the other party (breach of warranties entitles the innocent party to claim damages)

Wednesbury principle court will intervene to prevent or remedy abuses of power by public authorities if there is evidence of unreasonableness or perversity. Principle laid down by the Court of Appeal in the case of *Associated Provincial Picture House Ltd v Wednesbury Corporation* [1948] 1 KB 233

without prejudice without detracting from or without disadvantage to. The use of the phrase prevents the other party using the information to the prejudice of the one providing it

witness of fact a person who gives evidence of what they saw, heard, did or failed to do (contrast with *expert witness*)

writ a form of written command, e.g. the document that used to commence civil proceedings. Now a claim form is served

Table of cases

Table of statutes

Index